"SCOTLAND AND S

IN

THE EIGHTEENTH CENTURY

FROM THE MSS. OF

JOHN RAMSAY, ESQ. OF OCHTERTYRE

EDITED BY

ALEXANDER ALLARDYCE

AUTHOR OF 'LIFE OF ADMIRAL LORD KEITH,' ETC. ETC.

IN TWO VOLUMES

VOL. II.

WILLIAM BLACKWOOD AND SONS
EDINBURGH AND LONDON
MDCCCLXXXVIII

CONTENTS OF THE SECOND VOLUME.

SCOTLAND AND SCOTSMEN IN THE EIGHTEENTH CENTURY.

———◆———

CHAPTER VII.

THE CHURCH AND THE SECESSION.

THE members of the Established Church did not bear their good fortune after the Revolution with becoming thankfulness and moderation. The disputes between the two great parties about the claims of the Christian people continued as fierce as ever, and with various success. As the Act 1690 had been repealed to make way for patronage, the popular men contended that no regard was due to it in cases where no presentation appeared. So to clear that matter, an Act of Assembly was passed in the year 1732, which gave the power of election to heritors and elders when patrons forbore to exercise their right. It was perhaps carried through with too much heat and precipitation ; but nothing could justify the audacity with which it was attacked by Mr Ebenezer Erskine, minister of Stirling.   In a Synod at Perth he preached a sermon wherein he told his audience " that by this Act the corner-stone is receded from ; He (Christ) is rejected in His poor members, and the rich of this world put in their room.   If Christ were personally present, when I am, by the Synod's appointment, in His stead, He would say in reference to that Act, ' Inasmuch as ye have done it to the least of those little ones, ye did it to me.' "

Mean as this sermon may seem in point of matter and style, its author was well qualified to head the multitude.   He had a boldness and firmness which he exerted on all occasions in supporting its favourite prejudices.   Though no orator in Church courts, his pulpit eloquence was copious and keen, familiar and unpolished, perfectly suited to the taste and calibre of his admirers, who loved to hear him hunt a metaphor through all its mazes, or inveigh against the *defections* of the times.   The loudness and harshness of his tones, joined to his gestures, accorded well with his inflammatory topics, and made a deep impression upon the lower classes of people, who regarded him as the champion of their rights and privileges.   Neither did his blunt rustic manners hurt him in their esteem, as they were by that time much prepossessed against polished ministers.   Perhaps silent contempt would have been the best answer to this fanatical ebullition, but passion seldom failed to beget passion. The sermon was censured by the Synod ; Mr Erskine would not yield one step. The affair was carried before the General Assembly, where, in place of submitting to a rebuke, he insulted his judges and spurned every concession. A little more temper might have prevented the schism at that time, but the patience of Job could hardly have borne his insolence. The matter hung over for several years, when Mr Ebenezer Erskine and his associates were finally deposed by the General Assembly, 1739, very much to their own satisfaction.

To show how ineffectual all concessions on the part of the Establishment would be, they had some years before formed themselves into what they called the Associated Presbytery, which ordained ministers and exercised spiritual jurisdiction in a very exalted sham. They likewise published their judicial testimony and other pamphlets, which were bitter libels on the late General Assemblies, and defiances of the power of future ones. Even the repeal of the Act 1732, which had been the cause of the breach, made no impression on them, whom, it would seem, nothing would content but the bringing things back to the precise state in which they stood in the year 1650.

Numerous as the party had been in the Church courts, only seven members gave up their charges to join them. To say nothing of better motives, perhaps the dread of depending on a capricious people for bread deterred many of the high-flying clergy. It might, however, have been foreseen that the temporal interest of the deposed brethren would be promoted by the sacrifice they had made. Although few of their adherents were persons of figure or education, numbers of them were substantial burghers or farmers, who thought they were promoting their best interests when they provided for their pastors, whom they looked on as confessors for the faith. And a little from each of those zealous men, joined to occasional presents, amounted to a greater sum than could have been expected.

Nothing could exceed the perverse industry with which the seceding ministers sowed their tares. To their former congregations they seemed to have some claim; and had they confined their attempts to the flocks of the unpopular clergy, none needed to have been surprised. But they were at equal pains to make divisions in parishes where there was not the smallest reason to find fault with the incumbents, who were precise, orthodox, useful men.

At Logie a tent was set up, from which Ebenezer and two of his colleagues held forth for days, to a great audience composed of all sects and parties. Mr Duchel [the minister] was confessedly the ablest man in the Presbytery of Dunblane in those days. The soundness of his doctrine could only be equalled by his love for the people; whilst the scholar, the gentleman, and the Christian were conspicuous in his actions and language.

As soon as their presbytery became numerous

enough to form a congregation and endow a church, it was not difficult to find labourers for their new vineyard. What had taken place from mere necessity at the Revolution was repeated on this occasion, and seemed to accord with their designs and wishes. Some of the ministers whom they ordained at an early period were mean men, who had a mean education. Furious zeal for their peculiar crotchets stood in place of a clerical spirit and clerical endowments. Indeed their very cant and rusticity seemed to endear them to their people, who by that time regarded erudition and urbanity as indications of unsoundness in the faith. Yet strange to tell, the prayers and sermons of those half-educated men proved more acceptable to the depraved tastes of their audience, than the discourses of a Barrow and a Tillotson had been to learned, pious, intelligent hearers. Such, however, were the genuine fruits of spiritual pride, grafted on half-knowledge. Now that the first set of seceding ministers are gone, it is almost impossible to give the rising generation an adequate idea of the tones and gestures of some of them, who were greatly admired in their day. Yet in all probability they were not more faulty in these regards than some of the Established clergy, whose sentiments of Church government and divinity did not accord with theirs.

One would almost imagine that very vulgar broad Scotch had the same effect as Low Dutch, which is supposed to humble, and sometimes to degrade, the most dignified subjects. The pulpit performances of some of the fathers of that sect would appear as ridiculous at present to serious persons as the spiritual interludes of the middle ages, which, spite of their absurdities and indecency, delighted the multitude beyond measure. One thing is certain, the former would be reprobated nowadays by nineteen out of twenty Seceders, who have no longer any taste for a drawling unnatural manner in praying and preaching, though they adhere to their congenial principles. Tones and gestures are in their nature more fluctuating and fugitive than the opinions of sectaries. But we are entitled to form a decisive estimate of the talents and designs of the seceding clergy from their own publications. Making every allowance for them that charity could desire, the promoters of that schism appear to have been harsh, narrow-minded men, incapable of submitting to any regular government. Their abilities were in general below par, and their learning inconsiderable. They had an unhappy talent at splitting hairs, and of taking offence at persons and things without a cause.

The grievances of which they complained so tragically were either unfounded or exceedingly exaggerated. And could they have accomplished their favourite purposes, religion would hardly have been a gainer by it, there being a degree of gloom and austerity and ostentation in their manners and language which genuine Christianity does not warrant. Nothing, indeed, is more severely condemned by the great Author of that religion than a sour pharisaical spirit, which spends its zeal on little matters, very questionable or nowise enjoined. And as violence was the instrument by which they wished to effect their plans of reform, they appealed on all occasions to the people. With this view, they contended with as much fierceness for certain superinductions upon Presbytery which had done so much mischief in the Covenanting times, as if these had been the sum and substance of the Gospel, to which the present Protestant Churches, at home and abroad, had given their full assent. Though Separatists themselves, monuments of the mildness of government, yet, in imitation of their prototypes the Remonstrants, they railed at the toleration of any sect but themselves. In short, in the first stages of that schism, they displayed an arrogance and conceit that would have rendered truth itself unamiable.

There is, however, no reason to question their sincerity or good intentions; we would therefore fain believe they knew not what they did while intoxicated with passion and prejudices of long standing. If their notions of Church government were extravagant and mischievous, their theological notions were no less reprehensible. They professed themselves the champions of the Antinomian doctrines which had been disclaimed by the General Assemblies 1720 and 1722, and by all sober Protestants. Upon these, however, they put a construction of their own, in which it is admitted that in one sense their propositions may be all of them truly affirmed, and in another sense they may all of them be truly denied. Supposing, what may be true, that these paradoxical positions, in their sense, could do no harm, it must be confessed that they sounded ill, and might be grossly abused by a half-taught enthusiastic, whose interest and passions stood in direct opposition to his duty. Without concerning himself deeply with metaphysical distinctions, he would, in the hour of temptation, flatter himself that the purity of his faith would compensate for a few deviations from the paths of virtue.

But whilst we disapprove of their maintaining those fanatical tenets, let us do the seceding clergy the justice to say, that in their practice none were more disposed than they to make their hearers virtuous and honest. Their discipline for breaches of morality and decency, if anything, were too severe. To judge from their lives and converse, one would have thought they trusted much to their good works, and little to faith. Whatever may be said in their justification upon that head, there are other points of view in which it is impossible to vindicate them. Nothing but an overheated imagination and want of sound judgment could have made them think of setting up the Assemblies of 1648 and 1649 as patterns of imitation for any Church at a time when every sober Presbyterian condemned the conduct of those conventions as savouring of frenzy and delusion. Why then rend without necessity their National Church at a period when it was in a flourishing condition, just what its best friends in former times had wished in vain to see? Why vilify, and, as far as in them lay, render useless a learned, conscientious, affectionate clergy, who at that time would have done honour to any Church, because they would not adopt their peculiar crotchets about Church government? Were they themselves zealous for the doctrine of Calvin? So were nineteen out of twenty of their brethren of the Establishment, though they did not think it incumbent on them to adopt certain opinions which that great reformer would have reprobated with severity. Did they avow themselves the champions of the Christian people, inimical to every invasion on their rights and privileges? Their opponents were, in the truest sense of the word, the friends of the lower classes of men.

It is true, they did not make it matter of conscience to humour them when they were evidently wrong, the slaves of their own or other men's passions and whims. But those that led the Church judicatures had long laid it down as a maxim to resent violent settlements, and not to cross a well-meaning, affectionate commonalty in a matter which it regarded as its highest luxury and cordial. The petulance, injustice, and rancour with which some of them opposed unexceptionable candidates, chiefly because they had the good wishes of the gentry, did more to hurt the popular cause, in the opinion of all indifferent men, than the arguments and machinations of those that laboured to introduce patronage, or at least to set aside that intrinsical power of exception which, till then, all parties in the Church concurred in giving to the bulk of a congregation.

It is impossible, at this distance of time, to assign the causes which actuated people on that occasion; but doubtless some of them were influenced by levity or fashion, as much as by conscientious motives. However chimerical their divine right to choose their own pastors by a plurality of votes might be, all the power of wit and eloquence could not eradicate it from their imagination.

The more effectually to widen the breach, and to make the deeper impression on the minds of the people at large, they renewed with great solemnity the Covenants of the last century, which had all along been their idols. But as they did not wish to tread in the steps of the Cameronians, they took care to add explanations of them, abundantly perplexed and metaphysical, but suited as they said to the times. In short, their minds were in such a feverish wayward state, that a little indiscretion on the part of Government might have driven them to madness. Having already bid defiance to ecclesiastic superiors, to whom their founders had solemnly promised obedience, it was but one step more to insult and resist the civil powers. Had our statesmen been as hot-headed and intolerant as those of former times, they wanted not pretexts to interfere and chastise their arrogance. But adhering to the policy which had been laid down at the

Revolution, they looked on with seeming indifference, resolving all the while to support the Established Church in its just rights. They thought the best way to stop a popular contagion was to let it alone till its bad humour should evaporate or become nauseous. It was well known the Seceders were zealous Whigs, and however much they might dislike some things in the present administration, there was not the smallest reason to apprehend a coalition between them and the Jacobites.

The first ecclesiastic matter that attracted the attention of the public after the Rebellion, was a violent quarrel among the Seceders, maintained on both sides with the same rancorous inflexible spirit which they had displayed at their first outset. In every point of view it was a ruinous, humiliating thing for themselves. Had they been wise enough to have lived at peace with one another, whilst they fostered and inflamed the prejudices of the multitude, no rising sect had ever a better game to play. Every falseness on the part of the Church courts, every imprudence on the part of patrons or heritors, bade fair to have increased their revenues and influence; and as their tenets accorded entirely with the taste and inclination of their hearers, there was little risk of their ever returning to their parish churches. It was, however, nothing extraordinary that the same arts which had given rise to their schism, should impede its progress and throw discredit upon it.

Among other steps towards *reformation*, their Synod, in the plentitude of its power, declared the oaths of abjuration and allegiance *sinful*, because these did not accord with the obligations of the Covenants in Charles I.'s time. Emboldened by the neglect of Government, some of their rising young men, seconded or prompted by Mr Mair, a man who seemed to have had the happiest talents for strife, thought it would raise their fame if they should fly at lower game, in which, too, there was little danger. In the burgess oaths of a few royal burghs, there was a clause by which intrants became bound " to maintain the true religion as presently professed within this realm, and authorised by the laws thereof." To a sober Presbyterian no proposition seemed more self-evident. Yet by means of perverse ingenuity in torturing words, did these wrong-headed men insist that it was inconsistent with their principles and professions. Here, however, they were mortified to meet with violent opposition from some of their brethren, who had had an active hand in breaking off from the Church. The two Erskines and a number of ministers took the other side, with their usual heat and obstinacy. It would be beneath the dignity even of an historian of private life to state the arguments of both parties, which were expressed in perplexed uncouth language. We believe both sides meant well, and were both right, taking their sense of the words. This unmeaning yet angry controversy which subsists to this day, reminds one of the question about the oath to be taken by persons passing over a certain bridge, which was decided by Sancho Panza. One could hardly have believed that it would have convulsed a synod of Protestant divines towards the middle of the eighteenth century. It is, however, connected with our purpose to mark the consequences of this breach upon the Seceders and their neighbours. So keen were both sides, that they did not intermit their debates during the time that a civil war was raging in the kingdom. At last, after much ill blood, things came to an open rupture in the month of April 1747, which was attended with great violence; nor was it easy for an impartial bystander to say which of them was most culpable and implacable. From this time forth the Burghers and Anti-Burghers, as they were called, formed distinct and independent synods, which hated each other worse than the Jesuits did the Jansenists.

The latter, which seem to have been the more fanatical and intolerant, proceeded, in defiance of decency and common-sense, to fulminate a sentence of excommunication against their refractory brethren, with whom they no longer lived in communion. It was a miserable spectacle to see professing Christians delivering one another over to Satan, not for gross heresy or scandalous reprobate lives, but for captious quiddities for which both parties had something plausible to say. And in ninety-nine out of a hundred points they were perfectly at one, their virtues and

their faults and foibles being nearly akin. Both of
them, it is believed, wished to promote the best
interests of their people, though they might mistake
the means. And they both lived unblemished lives.
But their good qualities were miserably obscured by
spiritual pride, overweening conceit, and a sour un-
charitable spirit, which even good intentions could
not justify. In most cases the people adhered to
their own ministers with implicit faith, after this
rupture made it necessary for them to take a side ;
though in some places, owing to particular circumstances, they were much divided, which gave occasion
to new churches. In this country,[1] where the fame
of Mr Ebenezer was high, the Burghers therefore had
the superiority.

The Anti-Burgher Synod, wishing to make itself
considerable, condemned afterwards other oaths, about
which few entertained any scruples but themselves.
In their acts for that purpose they displayed a rugged
captious spirit, which vented itself in coarse embarrassed language. They seemed to set at naught all civil
authority that did not rest on their beloved Covenants,
of which, like the Remonstrants of old, they themselves were to be the expounders. One would have
thought these men had sat down to contrive how
they might puzzle and distress their followers in the
ordinary business of life. They surely succeeded in
setting their conscience and their temporal interests
at variance, a situation in which no faithful pastor

[1 Stirling, Fife, and the West]

would wish to see his people unnecessarily placed.
Here, however, not even fanaticism itself could long
sustain them. There must be burgesses and constables under the conditions prescribed by law; and
there was neither honour nor profit to be got by fine
or imprisonment. In order to reconcile these jarring
interests, they connived at their people taking the
exceptionable oaths, provided they acknowledged their
sin and submitted to a rebuke. What was this but
playing fast and loose with things sacred?—first
condemning things that were in their own nature
innocent and even expedient, and afterwards reserv-
ing to themselves something like a power of dis-
pensing with the breach of their own laws. Instead,
therefore, of making men better by their rigour and
extravagant zeal about questionable matters, it had a
tendency to give their minds a wrong direction.

The conduct of both classes of Seceders in the
course of this quarrel exposed them to much ridicule
and contempt, confirming the members of the Established Church in their attachment to it. And had
the two great parties in the Church courts been wise
and temperate, there can be little doubt that, in the
course of a few years, the secession would have
dwindled to nothing, so low had it fallen in the
opinion of the public.

Yet with all the advantages which the Established
clergy had over their rivals, their quarrels among themselves obscured their virtues, and did more mischief
to the Church than the assaults of its worst enemies.

No sooner was public tranquillity restored than the popular clergy seemed keener than ever to fight the battles of the Christian people, and to flatter them in their least laudable conceits. In the heat of their zeal and resentment they sometimes maltreated candidates of irreproachable lives, forgetting that candour and benignity which became ministers of the Gospel. In that party's notions of ecclesiastic polity there was a considerable difference, some of them, and these not the least respectable, being rather Independents than Presbyterians. Be that as it may, most of them were much too hot, and desperate to carry matters to extremity. Whenever, then, they had a decided majority in the General Assembly, they laid it down as a principle to pay no regard to presentations. In some cases they directed a popular man to be settled. But though their decision was final as to the cure of souls, it could give the minister no right to the temporalities. These were adjudged by the courts of law to belong to the patron, so long as his right should be invaded. When the popular men were outnumbered in the Assembly, they strove to protract the settlement, even when it was apparent that the objections to the candidates were false or frivolous, dictated by spite or systematic prejudice.

On the other hand, the Moderate party, as it affected to be called, was not always superior to passion and interested considerations. From the death of Professor Hamilton to the present times, almost every leader has carried matters with a higher hand than his predecessor. Dr Cumin (who at this period was looked on as the Duke of Argyll's confidential man in that department) ventured, from the commencement of his political career, upon measures which Carstairs or Hamilton would have considered too strong, and likely to be attended with mischievous consequences. But friendly as that gentleman was to the best interests of the people, he did not think he should serve them by giving way to their wayward humours. Though his own language and manners were smooth and conciliatory, a number of his friends were less delicate, treating parties before the Assembly, and their champions, the popular clergy, more cavalierly than in former times. Yet even then it was with great difficulty that the Church courts would settle a presentee without the concurrence of the gentry and a number of heads of families. Indeed, so rooted and insuperable was the aversion to patronage, that for some years after the last rebellion nine settlements out of ten were conducted in the spirit of the Act 1690, even when the presentation was secured. But when patrons were resolved to enforce their right in the face of a strong opposition, it was sometimes necessary to do things that were accounted harsh. Knowing the dislike most presbyteries had to take an active hand in such settlements, the Assembly or Commission sometimes appointed a committee to carry the sentence into execution. These riding committees saved the credit of their refractory brethren who had gone too far to recede with a good grace.

The committees, however, could not proceed sometimes without being protected by the military. Those strong measures exasperated the multitude, creating much odium against the clergy, who had a share in advising or carrying them into execution. It was not uncommon to see clergymen who had been settled in that ungracious manner conciliating the afflicted of their flock by their piety and exemplary conduct.

Whilst the broils about patronage divided and inflamed the clergy of the Established Church, the two kinds of Methodists were exceedingly busy in making proselytes in Scotland. The celebrated Wesley directed his attention particularly to a country where a plentiful harvest might be expected. With a few exceptions, however, his followers were low people, principally in the great towns. Besides being an Arminian on some doctrinal points, it was an unsurmountable obstacle to his progress that he had no connection with the parochial ministers.

His rival Whitfield had many advantages on these points over him. Though much of his time and attention were bestowed on America, he made repeated visits to Scotland, to confirm and add to the number of his disciples. But though on intimate terms with some worthy ministers of the popular party, he never took any share in our Church politics, considering himself only as an occasional resident in the country. As his stay was seldom long, his admirers all along were more actuated by impulse and

affection than by system. Of course they were at
little pains to scan his doctrine and peculiarities, or
to inquire whether their own ministers did not enforce
the same truths in a less animated manner. Indeed,
with the exception of his favourites, he branded them
by the lump as *velvet-mouthed* preachers.

About the year 1766 or 1767, some persons of
rank and fortune embraced with great keenness the
opinions of Whitfield ; and they afterwards formed
strong connections with his successors, who, if inferior to him in eloquence, were at least equally fervent and industrious in making proselytes. Some
of them who officiated at the Tabernacle paid visits
to their friends in Scotland, where they met with a
gracious reception from a number of the Established
clergy. The whole weight of the patrons of this new
party was thrown into the scale of that motley opposition that was raised against Robertson. In some
particulars the Methodist teachers differed widely
from every other denomination of Seceders, for they
laid little stress on forms of worship or Church government. On the contrary, they professed their readi-
ness to join with the members of every sect that
agreed with them in the articles of faith.

Although Whitfield, Townsend, and De Courcy
were clergymen of the Church of England, the two
last having benefices, they were exceedingly welcome
to the most rigid Presbyterians, nor did they make
any scruple of using extempore prayers, dealing likewise in extempore sermons once or twice a-day.

Spite of this show of liberality, those itinerant preachers breathed a narrow intolerant spirit. They accounted every man unsound in the faith who differed from them in one single particle. Indeed they talked as if they alone understood the Scriptures, not considering that all sects and parties found their belief on them, and that there are certain knotty points on which the most eminent Protestant divines are not agreed. This will, in all probability, be ever the case, as long as the right of private judgment is not fettered in despotism. Nor were they more friendly to learning, or those pursuits that delight and ennoble the soul. They declaimed against all reading that had not their peculiar system for its object. The admired performances which either enforce the moral duties in a most persuasive strain, or which by a chain of deep reasoning illustrate the great truths of revealed and natural religion, were deemed useless. if not dangerous, by those new - fashioned ghostly fathers. Whilst they condemned with open mouth the works of the most celebrated English divines, nothing could be nearer, in point of matter and composition, than some of their favourite authors. They proscribed cheerfulness and innocent gaiety, as if these were not compatible with, and indeed consequential of, true religion. They entered warmly into the highest notions of the Puritans of the last century, and not only condemned theatrical entertainments (which were doubtless often exceedingly reprehensible), but also balls and assemblies, where inno-

cence and strict decorum were preserved; and they
recommended a plainness in dress and an inattention
to exteriors, which, being enjoined by no positive pre-
cept, were altogether unsuitable to the age and station
of many of their proselytes. Indeed, one would have
imagined that elegance and polished manners were in
their eyes deadly sins. The faces of many of them
were indexes of bigotry and gloom and spiritual
pride. To see them assembled, one would have
thought that their tenets led them "to hang the
head like a bulrush," and render religion cumbersome
and unlovely.

Allowing, then, the merit of excellent intentions,
they cannot be vindicated for encroaching on the province of the Established clergy. Nothing less than
such a general depravity among that order of men as
prevailed in the times of darkness before the Reformation, could have warranted those extraordinary courses.
Their want of charity, too, towards ministers who
were their equals in piety and usefulness, and in
every other respect their superiors, was inconsistent
with the real spirit of the Gospel. The least apology
that can be made for the new teachers is their being
under the influence of an enthusiasm which spurned
the dictates of sober reason. They, indeed, taught
their disciples to expect supernatural impulses and
illuminations. Yet, while we admit the possibility
of a special divine interposition in behalf of sinners,
it is no breach of charity to say that in many instances these pretensions are only the illusions of fancy.

They likewise endeavoured to persuade their disciples that it was incumbent on them to hear long
prayers and sermons every day, and that the greatest
part of their time should be spent in spiritual exercises. Parade and ostentation are, however, exceedingly suspicious in matters of religion. Evangelical
devotion shuns the applause of men, being contented
with having the Almighty for its witness and judge.
Nor is anything condemned with more severity by
the great Author of Christianity than the long prayers
and starched appearances of the Pharisees.

But in a few years these new-fangled spiritual
guides were discarded by their patrons, who doubtless meant excellently well. Some of them were at
last convinced that their zeal had carried them too
far. A few of the well-meaning persons, who had
joined them in their cruise after religious novelty,
did not stop short when they did. From vilifying
and rejecting one species of clergy without just cause,
they were led, in no unnatural progression, to think
a standing ministry entirely useless. Indeed, when
men once abandon the received standards of faith
and government, there is no saying to what length
they may not go.

Among the other religious excrescences of this
period may be reckoned the Bereans, who are high-
flying Antinomians. In point of government they
are Independents, their ministers being mostly tradesmen, generally illiterate. They are mostly of the
very dregs of the people, who, after having lived

loosely, took at last a serious turn. For their tenets
we refer to the printed books of Barclay their founder,
performances the wildest and most extravagant that
ever disgraced the sacred name of religion. This sect
had no connection either with the Church or the
sectaries. Nor were they even very dangerous or
numerous.

Though few of the popular clergy went all the
length of the Methodists, they were supposed to
lean to their favourite tenets. Their zeal for high
Calvinism went even beyond that of the former generation, who reprobated Antinomianism in every form.
Whatever might be the subject of their sermons, they
contrived to introduce their peculiar doctrines in
season and out of season, not without a fling at those
who differed from them. They were disposed to lay
too much stress on things that were immaterial in
themselves, and apt, when carried far, to spoil men's
tempers. In their Church politics they were violent
beyond measure, and that at a time when their party
seemed to have lost all its influence in the General
Assembly. Their being humbled there, made them
redouble their diligence elsewhere. In presbyteries
and synods they missed no opportunity of mortifying
and thwarting their adversaries, of many of whom
they thought much worse than they deserved.
When outnumbered there, they did all in their
power to gain the affections of the people at large,
encouraging them in their crotchets and prepossess-
sions, and indifferent as to the consequences. Had

they confined their attention to their own congregations, it would have been less culpable ; but some of
them, whose zeal surpassed all bounds, were accused
of widening the breach between ministers and their
flocks, when the former had talents and piety to have
made them eminently useful, could they have had a
kind reception and a patient hearing. In encouraging the people to abandon a worthy minister because
in some things he was not to their taste, these men
seemed to take a wayward pleasure, as if the Church's
loss had been their gain.

And now of some of the lesser consequences which
resulted from these clerical feuds. One of them was
a remarkable alteration in the manner of administer-
ing the Communion. In former times eight or ten
parishes used to join together, so that from the beginning of June to the middle of August that sacrament
was given in one of them every second Sunday. It
was dispensed only once in the two years in many
country places ; but that made little odds, as the two
next parishes gave it alternately. Nor could it be
had annually without infringing the plan. By this
means the whole clergy of a district were closely connected together in the most solemn exercise of religion. Whatever were their sentiments in other
matters, here nothing was to be seen but unity and
love. The popular men supported the unpopular,
whilst the former were somewhat restrained by the
presence of their brethren, whose parts and learning
were commonly superior. When there was no sermon

at home, the young folks followed their minister, whilst the aged stayed behind.

The Scottish Presbyterians have always had a wonderful liking to preaching in the field. It seems to have originated from the vast crowds which, towards the middle of the last century, usually resorted to celebrate Communions. And hence, when the popular men were ejected after the Restoration, recourse was had to field-conventicles, in which it was imagined a double portion of the Holy Spirit was conferred on all concerned. And therefore, after Presbytery was established by law, tent-sermons were retained by general consent. Indeed, the multitudes assembled upon these occasions could not have been accommodated in any other way.

Much may surely be said in behalf of this practice. The sight of a vast congregation assembled in the open air, in the finest season of the year, greatly contributed to expand the mind, and to animate both the preacher and his auditors. It affords both instruction and wholesome exercise to people that had wrought hard through the week. If young people resorted thither to see and be seen, rather than from purposes of a better kind, it was, at least, the most innocent entertainment they could have. Nor could they be a whit the worse for having two or three sermons from ministers whom everybody revered.

The service was in general of an unmeasurable length, so that the most tenacious memory could not retain the tenth part of it. Diffuse discourses, and

the same topic set in different lights, were, however,
far from being unsuitable to heavy illiterate men,
whose ideas are neither clear nor many.   Some
indecencies doubtless took place upon these occasions,
as a few coarse people intermixed themselves with the
crowd.   If it was not the very best mode of celebrating the Communion, the relinquishing it has been
attended with no good consequences. Of all the popular attachments, it was perhaps the most harmless.

The exclusion of ministers whose settlements had
been violent was an unhappy, ill-advised measure.   It
was the first thing that broke the chain which had
for many years connected the clergy together by the
closest ties, operating likewise as a severe stigma on
the persons that were neglected.   And it established
a precedent of which the new-fashioned popular men
failed not to avail themselves.   For they made a
further discrimination, and left out some of their
neighbours, to whom there could be no other objection save their being of an opposite party in Church
politics.   In their room some flaming zealots were
brought from a distance, who set the people's heads
agog, and confirmed them in all their prejudices.
Neither would the popular clergy assist their obnox-
ious brethren ; or if, immediately on the admission of
the latter, they condescended to display their pulpit
talents, it was confined to the week-days.   But as
these gave no invitation in return, the correspondence
soon ceased.

Their opponents were therefore obliged, in self-

defence, to solicit the assistance of their friends from
other quarters. And hence, while some Sacraments
were amazingly crowded, there was hardly the face of
a congregation in other places. Nor did it prevent
people from wandering. For when a tent-preaching
could not be had in their own or some neighbouring
parish, they went without scruple to the Seceders,
Cameronians, or Bereans.

Zealous as the Seceders had ever been for the
Protestant succession, they seemed now fully sensible of the blessings they enjoyed in common with
their fellow-subjects. Neither bigotry nor scrupulosity
could impute to the present king [1] any of the ecclesiastic grievances, of which they had complained so
loudly. Soon after his accession, a motion was made
in the Anti-Burgher Synod to address him ; but, nega-
tived for reasons peculiarly their own, there was no
want of loyalty and respect in their resolutions. This
was the more pleasing, that in the end of the former
reign, a time when nobody complained of grievances,
some of their ministers were desirous of approaching
the throne with an address of a very different kind.

Having for a number of years been separated from
the Established Church, they now regarded it with less
wrath and rancour than formerly when contending for
mastery. They wanted not sagacity to see that the
two great parties in the General Assembly were, in
fact, playing their game, perhaps without intending
it. And therefore, in talking of the Church, they

[1] George III.

contented themselves with a few commonplace de-
clamations with regard to the defections and corruptions of its judicatures, which made very little
impression on those who heard them. Their spleen
and scrupulosity and resentment found, however,
vent in keeping up the controversies that subsisted
either between the two rival synods, or with the
Presbytery of Relief, which last was much more hurtful and formidable than the Establishment. Some of
the pamphlets published on this subject savour strongly
of the sour fermented leaven which was so conspicuous
in the early publications of the Seceders. But these
things were no longer read with the same avidity as
between twenty and thirty years before; for by this
time almost every man had taken a decided part, from
which neither eloquence nor reasoning of the most
persuasive kind could make him swerve. Their chief
effect, therefore, was to rankle and exasperate the
hearts of well-meaning bigoted men against brethren
who agreed with them in essentials. But the most
interesting thing in this part of their history is the
great but gradual change which took place in their
manners and pulpit exhibitions. The first generation
of their ministers were by that time quitting the
stage, one after another. Their successors were, in
general, young men, who had no access to see the
broils and animosities which had convulsed or deformed
their societies at a more early period. They had
discernment to see, amidst all their peculiar prejudices,
that the harshness and vulgar cant, so disgusting in

some of their eminent men, were totally unconnected
with their principles and professions, being, in truth,
rather to be rejected than imitated. Most of them
were more learned and better educated than the persons whom the Associate Presbytery thought proper
to ordain after breaking with the Church. A few
of them cultivated some branches of polite literature. Though zealous for the policy and doctrines
for which their fathers had earnestly contended, they
thought it incumbent on them to make use of smooth
language, and of tones and questions less ungracious.
Nor did they continue to hunt metaphors to the same
extravagant pitch as their predecessors had done.
Still, however, their matter made ample amends for the
change of their manner, which last gave no offence to
their hearers, whose tastes had likewise undergone
some alteration. In these circumstances, the Anti-
Burgher Synod thought proper to interpose by an
Act, cautioning " those who may be pointing towards
public work in the Church against an affected pedantry
of style and pronunciation and politeness of expression." They were apprehensive that the affectation
of accommodating the Gospel in point of style would
at length lead to accommodation likewise in point of
matter to the corrupted taste of a carnal generation.
On the other hand, whilst they recommended to ministers to manifest the truth in plainness and gravity,
they cautioned them against all such meanness and
impropriety of language as hath a tendency to bring
discredit on the Gospel, and also against using tech-

nical, philosophical, and learned terms, that are not commonly understood. Though some part of this Act was abundantly rational, the cautioning young men against politeness of style was like striving against the stream. The younger sort thought that their peculiar tenets would not be the less relished for being clothed in a decent, agreeable dress. Nor were they mistaken in their opinion; for the old-fashioned men were rather esteemed than admired and run after. Yet, spite of all their improvements, the genius and peculiarities of their sect were conspicuous to the most superficial observer. If they had no longer the drawling sing-song of Mr Ralph Erskine, their language and manner betrayed strong traces of the vulgarity and meanness inseparable from the low company with whom they conversed. In all probability they resembled the high-flying clergy of the Established Church between the Union and the year 1730, and that in their virtues as well as in their faults and foibles. It is no more than justice to the seceding ministers of both sorts to say that their morals were unimpeached, and their fidelity in discharging the duties of their function highly meritorious. Such as thought the least favourably of them could not refuse them the praise of sincerity and usefulness. And they deserved much commendation for the strictness and attention with which their students of divinity were bred up, some of their professors having been men of considerable parts.

It is curious, however, that the *divine right* of the

Christian people, which was long the shibboleth and support of their sect, should at last have produced such heart-burnings and even convulsions as almost baffled their Synod to compose. Some congregations were kept vacant for years, it not being possible to fix the people by chopping and changing the candidate, an expedient which used to prove effectual, and which, in fact, threw the choice into the hands of the clergy.

This took place in the case of Mr Campbell of Stirling, who was a man superior to most of his brethren. Though he had a very great majority upon their own principles, his opponents would not yield a single iota. After spinning out matters to a great length, a scrutiny into the moral character of the electors was demanded. This being granted somewhat inconsiderately, produced both unpleasant and laughable consequences, which found employment for the Commissary Court. After all, the minority would not submit to the decision of the Synod; but, after an ineffectual attempt to form a new sect, a junction took place between them and the Cameronians. Some of the most sensible Seceders scrupled not to say that they would have been much the better for a good patron. Having happened whilst the schism overture was under consideration, it did not make any party in the Assembly more in love with popular elections or clerical cabals; for great part of the mischief was owing to some pragmatical ministers who had purposes of their own to serve.

For a while the Presbytery of Relief seemed to carry

all before it.   The Secession being somewhat out of
fashion, every violent settlement or breach between
a minister and his congregation produced one of their
meeting-houses, to which, from various motives, persons from the neighbouring parishes resorted.   It
would seem, however, that the parts and wisdom of
its leaders bore no proportion to the popularity of its
constitution and tenets.   There seemed to be something of a radical defect in their policy, which, unless
corrected, threatened to shake its stability and prevent
its increase.   They appear to have carried their system
much too far.   From a desire to avoid those rocks and
quicksands on which their rivals the Seceders had
wellnigh split, they reduced the jurisdiction of their
Church courts almost to nothing, lest it should hamper
or trench upon the *divine right* of the people to choose
their pastors.   If there was a spice of independent
principles in lessening the power of the clergy, it
served not only to please their flocks, but also to
prevent quarrels among the brethren.   It deprived,
however, their presbytery of that wholesome control
over candidates and electors which might have prevented the latter from sometimes fixing upon the
weakest man that was in their offer.

There appears to have been something wrong in
the way in which they trained up students of divinity
and licensed probationers.   In their important articles
the Seceders have evidently the advantage over them.
But as the founders of the Relief were never above
mediocrity, young men desirous of entering their

society had no standard of excellence to form themselves upon. No wonder, then, that some of their ministers should have been persons of mean parts and little learning, who obtained a high character by the wildness of their doctrine, and by inveighing in season and out of season against patrons and intruders. It was likewise much against them that the partiality which some worthy Established ministers showed for their sect ceased upon the death of Gillespie, Bain, and Boston. They have not had much reason to plume themselves of some preachers that came over to them from the Church, for most of them were poor wrong - headed creatures who had little chance of getting a settlement anywhere. By flattering the people, and humouring them in all their prejudices and prepossessions, they were sometimes preferred to better men. But their after-conduct was not calculated to raise their fame or to ensure the love and esteem of their congregations, there being some palpable flaw in their parts or morals. Nothing is more contemptible and useless than a Dissenting minister in that predicament. But whilst the weakness, the violence, or the narrowness of some Relief ministers were highly censurable, the bulk of them deserved much praise for the unwearied pains they took to instruct their hearers both in public and in private. If a few of them had fallen into gross scandals, none of their sect was ever charged with infidelity.

Engaged, as we are, in a ruinous unsuccessful war,[1]

---

[1] [The war in the Peninsula.]

it is impossible to say what shall be the issue. But if for the sins of a guilty ungrateful people, surfeited with blessings, our enemies, foreign and domestic, shall finally prevail, it may be worth while to guess at the consequences that would probably result from the abolition of religious establishments. Next to the pulling down of monarchy, that is the great point which both fanatics and infidels seem to have most at heart.

The possibility of men being good Christians in a country where the clergy are neither paid nor patronised by the State, needs not be disputed, any more than the possibility of their being useful and respectable members of society by obeying the dictates of natural religion.[1] But to rest on *possibilities* is no wise course in the ordinary business of life. America is perhaps the only great empire since the days of Constantine the Great where a national Church has not been closely interwoven with the civil constitution. Whether the interests of society or the State have gained or lost in that country by the want of a

---

[1] No two countries differ more in that respect than Britain and America. Indeed the latter had, properly speaking, no regular Church government before its revolt in 1776. If a few colonies made legal provision for the ministers of religion, special care was taken to exclude them from any jurisdiction in matters ecclesiastic. And hence religion was somewhat in a state of nature, unless so far as the clergy and people were regularly the divines of the mother country, Episcopalian, Presbyterian, or Independent. Though under no obligation to submit to the decision of their British brethren in points of faith, they generally adopted them without reserve. In framing their new constitution, Congress copied the British constitution in everything but monarchy and Church government. Until some memorable revolution shall take place on either side the Atlantic, the Americans will probably continue to look to us in matters of theology.

national Church, is a question which can only be solved by persons intimately acquainted with it, both before and since the revolution.

There is, however, a wide difference between pulling down venerable fabrics and leaving things precisely in the same state in which they had all along been. Supposing religious establishments to be laid aside without any violent convulsion, it would probably be attended with some mischievous effects. The creeds and confessions which, after being canvassed by learned men, had received the sanction of synods and parliaments, would be exploded as incompatible with liberality of sentiment and the natural rights of man. Of course, articles of belief would be as various and ill-according as their complexions or political whimsies. In that temper of mind there is a strange propensity to abuse liberty. What absurdities would this produce in a country where ingenuity was more regarded than truth or usefulness, novelty being the great criterion of genius and spirit! If by means of brilliant talents or charming eloquence, combined with superior sanctity, any clergyman should gain a decided sway over his countrymen of high or low degree, he must consult the genius of the times, and strike boldly into some unbeaten track. With this view he must either outdo the Unitarians in what they are pleased to call *liberality*, or the Antinomians in cant and enthusiasm. Yet whether his new system was calculated to catch the base or the rigid, it would want that polish and proof which are best obtained by

collision of sentiment. If the decisions of national
synods have not always carried conviction with them,
they have often checked the pride and presumption of
theologists over fond of peculiar crotchets. In consequence of full and fair discussion, they found it
necessary to make some concessions to their brethren,
who were as learned and pious as themselves. Nay,
the interference of kings and ministers of State in
conventions of that kind has sometimes moderated
the spleen and petulance of rival Churchmen. Supposing, however, these people sound in the faith, how
could ministers whose bread depended on the favour
of the rich, or the caprices of the multitude, reprehend
those vices and follies which must ever subsist more
or less in the world under the best governments?
Instead of speaking with boldness, tempered with
discretion and kindness, they would be tempted to
curry favour with the one, and to encourage the other
in their prejudices and weaknesses. At present a
clergyman whose income does not depend on his congregation can discharge the more unpleasant path of
his duty with laudable firmness, knowing that he will
be supported by the civil magistrate.

Such are a few of the disadvantages likely to result
from the want of a national Church, supposing it to be
abolished quietly and by men thoroughly convinced
of the great truths of Christianity, though not at one
as to its appendages. It can never take place in
Britain but in consequence of a revolution similar to
that in France. In that case, however, the plot would

be laid and conducted by a set of men as hostile to
revealed religion in every form as to monarchy itself.
They might doubtless have the address to carry a
number of wrong-headed fanatics along with them.
Being the ablest and most versatile, they would probably continue to steer the helm, in which station
they would, with all the bigotry of modern philosophers, look upon their serious coadjutors with ineffable contempt. But be the religious professions of
the leading men what they would, the bloodshed and
plunder unavoidable on occasions of that kind, must
harden the hearts and sear the consciences of those
that had risen to wealth and eminence by such guilty
means. In their new-created stations they would be
too busy and too much intoxicated to let spiritual
considerations break their rest. Amidst those horrid
scenes the cause of virtue and piety must decline
apace. If the reigning demagogues had been previously initiated in the mysteries of infidel philosophy,
they would now cherish them as opiates admirably
calculated to stifle troublesome reflections. Even they
who had once some serious impressions would be disposed to lay aside what accorded so ill with their
present views and actions. If a sense of their mis-
deeds did not hurry them into speculative or practical
atheism, they would land either in deism or the
modes of Christianity that come nearest it. Be that
as it may, they would have a striking resemblance to
the Sadducees among the Jews, who confined their
views and wishes to this world, not daring to look

beyond it. As they that confine themselves to natural
religion have hardly any places of worship, so the
Unitarians are much belied [1] if they be not grossly
negligent in their attendance upon public worship
and the more solemn ordinances of religion. Yet,
admitting the disciples of Priestley and Lindsey to
be exemplary and pious, according to their own sense
of duty, the chance is that, in times like those in
question, their sons or proselytes would sink as much
below their standards as theirs are under those of the
Church. There is a strong propensity in the human
heart never to stop short in search of paradoxical
novelties. Whilst men of licentious principles and
hands imbrued in blood bore sway, what protection or
encouragement could the ministers of religion or devout Christians expect? It must either be want of
power or prudential considerations that could prevent
their maltreating or persecuting them.

We have already had some experience of the baneful
effects of irreligion upon persons of rank and fortune,
whom it has not made wiser or more respectable than

---

[1] Some years ago Mr Sommerville of Stirling was in company with a Dissenting clergyman in a great manufacturing town of Yorkshire, for whom he
preached. After sermon there was a Communion, attended only by the two
ministers and ten or a dozen of women. The Elements being blessed, the
clergyman harangued upon charity and social love, without speaking of our
Saviour and His sufferings. On Mr Sommerville's wondering at that omission,
the other said it was sometimes introduced, but they did not think it indispensable. "What, then, do you teach your people?" "Morals and politics,"
answered the other. An eminent merchant in that town being asked why
there were so few communicants, answered that their old ministers made
such ado about it that people were afraid, and the present ones made so light
of it, that their hearers cared less about it than they should.

their fathers.   In them, however, it was in some measure counteracted by their living in a country where the laws of the land and of the Church were both in full force.   A sense of honour and desire to stand well in the opinion of the world served to hide their other deficiencies.   The number of persons in the vale of life who have openly disclaimed religious principles is very inconsiderable.   Yet small as it is, the dread of the severest punishments cannot deter them from the commission of crimes of the deepest dye.   A change of government effected by the multitude, set on by domestic incendiaries or foreign enemies, would for a while throw all power and authority into the hands of mean men who had imbibed the spirit and principles of their prototypes, the French philosophers.   A farmer, a shopkeeper, or a pettifogger, vested with uncontrolled power, would not be one whit more amiable and gentle in office that he had renounced the faith of his fathers.   An upstart, flushed with the spoils of his betters, would stick at nothing that promised to improve his fortune or strengthen his political interest.   Nor would his disposition or manners be much sweetened by the fears that continually haunted him of some fatal reverse which might expose him to be degraded, perhaps butchered, by some of his late confederates in anarchy; for the quarrels of democrats are more rancorous than even those of theologists.

Numerous and successful as these apostates might be, neither rebellion nor foreign conquest would be

sufficient to make a great majority of the middling
and lower classes of Scots exchange Christianity for
the meagre comforts of infidel philosophy. Not even
the most sanguinary measures could make them *all at
once* submit to that sacrifice. If, therefore, their new
rulers had one spark of common-sense, they would see
the expediency of indulging their subjects in that
favourite article.[1] Indeed, no bait would be more
flattering to the populace than the turning out, in a
tumultuary way, all the Established clergy that had
incurred their indignation. In this, however, they
would probably act with their wonted caprice and
injustice. Not contented with wreaking their vengeance upon ministers whose laxity of doctrine, and
levity if not looseness of life, merited little sympathy, they would extend it to men whose learning,
sanctity, and zeal would have done honour to the
purest times. Nay, some worthy pastors who had
once stood high in their esteem, would fall martyrs
to that constitution which they had sworn to maintain. And the imposition of new tests or oaths of
opinion by the Legislature might be regarded as
preludes to persecution for conscience' sake.

In choosing their ministers, the people would probably show little more wisdom or judgment than they
do at present, when the power is entirely in their own
hands. They would continue to run after every furi-

[1] Such appears to have been the conduct of the French in Holland; for,
though there is no longer a national Church, all sects are freely tolerated.
How long that may continue depends entirely on the chapter of accidents, and
the progress of infidelity in that distracted country.

ous half-educated man who should stoop to flatter their passions and their prejudices, which last would be regarded as first principles. Where, indeed, should they look for learned conscientious pastors to preach to them the words of soberness and truth? In all likelihood the universities would either be suppressed, or converted into schools for teaching the new philosophy. Should divinity be still taught in those seminaries by Unitarian or Antinomian professors, the interests of genuine Christianity would be little advanced by the change. Without a total revolution in the principles and views of our common people, neither eloquence nor purity of life will ever reconcile them to Socinianism in any form. On the other hand, Calvinistic notions, carried to an extravagant pitch, and engrafted on levelling principles, would neither improve faith nor morals.

But though a vast majority of the Scots would not be *constrained* to give up religion on the requisition of their new rulers, means might be fallen on to blunt its force and subvert its foundations by degrees. Rapid changes from poverty to fulness and ease, from a very humble station to power and eminence, are at all times temptations too great for human virtue to withstand. Nor would their strength be diminished by the violent breaking down of ancient landmarks, which would bring back things nearly to a state of nature, or, in other words, to a state of anarchy. As the democrats have it much at heart to make a new partition of property, the first-fruits of the revolution would be the proscription of nine-tenths of the property of the kingdom, which would be divided among persons of their own kidney. It cannot be expected that the farmer or mechanic who should obtain a slice of his landlord's estate in the scramble would be a better Christian or a better neighbour for his acquisitions, supposing them not to be the price of blood or rapine. Whether he had been a leader or a tool in the late commotions, success would give an entire new cast to his character and language. To complete what he had begun, he must be engaged in perpetual cabals against the dominant party, faction being inseparable from a popular government. Filled with high ideas of his own dignity, and buoyed up by extravagant hopes, he would soon lose all relish for the ordinances of religion, and for the books which, in the times of his innocence and obscurity, had taught him how to live and how to die.

Nor is that all. The overthrow of the constitution in Church and State having been accomplished by unjustifiable means, must be maintained by a steady perseverance in the same flagitious courses with which the democrats had set out. Meanwhile, the indignation of the persons who, in the late scramble for wealth or power, had either got nothing or much less than they thought their due, would give occasion to bickerings or attempts to turn out the ruling men. To prevent their own ruin, the latter would be disposed to treat their refractory brethren as cruelly and imperiously as if they had been aristocrats.

If ever the stately cathedrals and colleges of England, and the humble parish churches of Scotland, shall be pulled down or converted to ignoble purposes, it will be well for those persons of rank and fashion who can then look back with self-approbation upon their past lives.   If in times of peace and prosperity religion served to heighten their joys and soothe their cares, it would not fail them when overtaken with calamity.   Whether they should be stripped of their honours and estates, or allowed to enjoy a pittance in obscurity, Christianity, once their favourite luxury, would prove a balsam to their wounded spirits, and enable them to bear poverty and degradation with fortitude and serenity.   By this means, losses and sufferings from which they would once have shrunk with horror, might, by the intervention of pious resignation, be endured with the spirit of martyrs; and thus things in themselves little desirable would be converted into blessings, and be matter of triumph, if not for time, at least for eternity.   Meanwhile they would not exchange situations with the mean or flagitious men who had grown great and purse-proud upon the ruins of Church and State.

Although there should be no persecution for conscience' sake, serious rational Christians, who in the late times had endeavoured to keep to the golden mean betwixt the opposite sects, must lay their account with many mortifications.   Where should they look for faithful pastors when no provision was made for their education, or for that wholesome discipline

which had once been the safeguard of their national
Church ? From their republican rulers they could
expect no favour. Such of them as openly ridiculed
all that their great Master did, and taught, and suffered, would regard them with hatred mingled with
contempt. Neither were they to look for kinder
treatment from those that professed to take the Bible
for their guide. Whilst the Unitarian despised them
for believing too much, the bigoted, narrow-minded
Antinomian, who wanted nothing but power to be a
persecutor, would reproach them with arrogance for
not holding a set of opinions which had been all along
reprobated by every sober Presbyterian. In vain
would they plead that the sum and substance of their
belief had been preached in the same terms by the
brightest luminaries of the Reformed Churches at home
and abroad. It would be a sorry consolation to see the
infidels and Unitarians quarrelling with their late
confederates the fanatics, in consequence of which
the latter would reap the bitter fruits of their folly
and perverseness. All that remained in such calamitous scenes would be to beseech the Almighty—who
had been pleased, for causes only known to Himself,
to try their Church and nation in the furnace of
affliction—that He would set bounds to the madness
of the people, and restore, in His own good way and
time, the blessings of truth and peace.

In times like these how deplorable the condition
of the infidels ! and some infidels deprived at one blow
of rank and fortune and all that they held dear. Ac-

customed to a life of frivolity and dissipation, their effeminate minds and pampered bodies would be ill prepared to meet the dreadful shock. Penury and degradation would not be sweetened by the consideration that they had long looked on their present rulers as greatly their inferiors. They would then stand in need of that divine philosophy which the Holy Scriptures hold forth to all sorts and conditions of men. Had they been allowed to retain a pittance of their fortunes upon the most humiliating conditions, it would have contributed to reconcile them to their hard fate, and have enabled them to act their part with dignity and resignation, which smile in the midst of sorrows. Whereas, when wandering wretched exiles in foreign countries, or dragged before tribunals where innocence had no justice or mercy to expect, how would the recollection of an ill-spent unprofitable life embitter their sufferings! They could hardly dare to approach the Father of mercies, whose laws they had repeatedly broken. When human help had fled, and their souls were distracted with guilt and terror, how would they execrate that impious false philosophy which had contributed to ruin them and their country!

CHAPTER VIII.

THE SCOTTISH GENTRY.

We now proceed to take a view of the principles, manners, and way of living of our gentry of the last age. When no particular place is mentioned, our observations relate to the spot of country with which we are connected—viz., the Stewartry of Menteith, and the adjacent parts of Stirling and Clackmannan shires. The bulk of it has for near two hundred years been in the hands of gentlemen having from £500 to £800 a-year, there being at the Union few commoners of larger fortune. It is true some of the nobility had more considerable estates; but they either wanted houses, or did not reside within the last threescore years. There were upwards of forty gentlemen's families in the district of Menteith, or on its borders, that lived on a friendly footing together.

A great proportion of them held their lands of subjects superior, and even such as were freeholders found it wise policy to attach themselves to some great family. It will hardly be possible for the rising generation to form a just notion of the love and affection which subsisted between a powerful nobleman and his vassals and clients before the two last rebellions. Compared with it, modern patronage is cold and unavailing. He was their oracle and champion on all occasions, and his espousing their interest with warmth served as a safeguard against the violence and injustice of private men. When his interest at Court was low, he rewarded their faithful services by giving them feus or beneficial leases.[1] And their vanity was flattered by the kind reception they found at his house and table,[2] where, in his social hour, distinctions of rank were laid aside, personal merit being in more estimation than fortune or fashion.

On the other hand, they were not deficient in gratitude. Their veneration being boundless, they entered with violence into all their patron's friendships and resentments. This was, however, a most dangerous line of conduct, as it sometimes led them to venture

---

[1] This was the case on the borders of the Highlands. The families of Montrose, Moray, and Perth gave great bargains of land to the gentry of small estate, who had the commons at their beck. Military service was the return principally expected, at least it was so originally. They were, in truth, *kindly* tenants, the rent being confessedly trifling. Some tenants of the two first families continued upon that footing little more than twenty years ago.

[2] An aged gentleman, a connection of the family, having come to pay his respects to the last Duke of Montrose, his Grace said to him after dinner, "You are now one of the few alive that used to be with my grandfather at Mugdock. Pray tell me, whether did he or I keep the best house?" The old man tried to evade the question; but at last, upon its being repeated, he said, "My lord, your Grace lives nobly, and so did your grandfather. There are, however, differences. In his days there were fewer glasses, but every man had his own bottle. Whereas at your Grace's table there is a variety of glasses and few bottles set down. And at his table the liverymen did not wait till the strong ale was called for, but were every now and then *jogging* people to drink."

their lives and fortunes in quarrels that little concerned them. And, indeed, in those matters they made to him the same transfer of principles and conscience which soldiers of fortune do to the prince whose bread they eat and whose battles they fight, without considering the justice of the war, or its consequences to themselves or their country.[1]

Of old, when a great man was malcontent, he did not show his resentment by caballing in elections and soliciting his neighbours to accept of fictitious votes. He waited till an opportunity should offer of shaking the throne, and then he summoned his friends and dependants to rise in arms. They knew well that the most acceptable service they could render him was with their sword. In the beginning of this century our low-country gentlemen were regularly trained to arms,[2] and valued according to their following and military prowess. And hence, at funerals and other

[1] The late Gartmore told me an anecdote he had from his father in law, the Earl of Glencairn, who was present. M'Farlane of Glentartan, a gentleman in the head of Menteith, brought four handsome lads of sons to wait on the last Earl of Mar, who was then at the goat whey in that neighbourhood. "My lord," said he, "I and mine have been warmly attached for ages to the family of Mar. Now I am old and infirm, unable to serve your lordship any longer. But here are my four sons, hale of lith and limb, whom I present in my stead. If they do not serve you by day and by night, in a good cause and in a bad cause, God's curse and mine light upon them!"

[2] Mrs Robertson of Myreton, who died in 1756, aged upwards of eighty, told me that before the Revolution, whilst she lived with her grandfather, Mr John Cameron, minister of Kincardine, she came into the room where he and a number of gentlemen were drinking. All of them had dirks stuck into the table, except one, Graham of the Gartur family, who had a pistol before him. Colonel Edmondstoune says that his uncle carried to Lord Dundee's army thirty five stout fellows from his own estate, most of them from the town of Newton, which was then more populous than at present.

public occasions, they were accustomed to wear swords or pistols, which sometimes was productive of unpleasant consequences.[1]

If, however, their patron was lucky enough to take part with Government, his friends and adherents were amply rewarded for their attachment. Thus, whilst the families of Mar and Perth were great at Court, the gentry of this country received many favours. And since the Revolution, the Campbells, and other connections of the Argyll family, have got more from Ministry than perhaps any set of men in the three kingdoms.

But in this country a great majority of our gentry were upon the losing side. Though most of them were warmly attached to the house of Stuart, yet their affection to the families of Mar and Perth induced a number of them to rise in the Rebellion of 1715.

However blamable the last Earl of Mar might be as a statesman and general,[2] he falls to be considered as a pattern for a great man who wishes to establish a family interest founded on the goodwill and affection of his neighbours. He was always ready to serve them, in small as well as in great matters, without

[1] The Master of Rollo having been killed in an affray by Graham of Inchbraikie, James Edmondstoune of Newton was banished for lending the latter his sword. The quarrel began about a cow. And the slaughter of Lord Strathmore by Carnegy of Phinhaven, at a burial, is well known to those who are versed in our criminal law.

[2] At the battle of Sherriffmuir, an old Highlander who had been at Killiecrankie [Gordon of Glenbucket], spying a favourable opportunity of attacking the Duke of Argyll before his line was formed, told Lord Mar of it ; but seeing his advice slighted, and the critical moment lost, he cried out with indignation, " Oh for one hour of Dundee ! "

seeming to expect anything in return, and his manners were uniformly gracious and easy at home and abroad.

The family of Perth had, however, the greatest number of vassals and followers in this country; and, indeed, for many generations it had been generally beloved for its mild, beneficent, upright conduct towards all around it.[1] The lords of that family prided themselves the longest in maintaining the state and importance of our old Scottish barons. The Chancellor, in the zenith of his power, is said to have sold a valuable estate in this parish, that he might purchase the lands of Strathgairtney, which, in case of any insurrection, would give him an additional number of Highlanders at his command. And his own and his successor's political views and disappointments after the Revolution made them anxious to secure by every means the affections of the neighbouring gentry.

Though in general they retained their political principles, the fatal issue of the Rebellion of 1715 damped, and in process of time almost extinguished, the military ardour of that set of men in this country. Even the last Lord Perth's enthusiasm and engaging manners had little influence in the year 1745. That

[1] It is a tradition among our commons that gentle James, father of the Lord Chancellor Perth, who lived sometimes at Burnbank, was so humble and courteous as to ask the herd-boys in his walks if they had a knife, an awl, stocking needles, horn and ivory combs. And when they had not, he gave them money to buy those necessary articles. How cheaply and easily may a great man make himself beloved by a little kindness and condescension towards his inferiors!

young nobleman, who by all accounts deserved a better fate, fell a martyr to ambition, and to that religion which his grandfather had embraced from mere worldly motives.[1]

The gentry were much confirmed in their political notions by the Episcopal clergy. However faulty the bishops and Court clergy might be while intoxicated with power and fretted by opposition, yet if we may trust the accounts of those that know them best, the parochial ministers were in general venerable exemplary men.[2] There were perhaps some exceptions in the western shires, where people of character were afraid to venture themselves among the Covenanters, who were bigoted and rendered furious

[1] When the Chancellor solicited George Drummond of Blair to turn Roman Catholic, he promised him honours and preferment. Blair waived the discourse; but on its being again pressed, he smiled and said, "My lord, I see my religion is better than yours." "Why so?" said his lordship. "Because you offer boot in exchange." Drummond of Pitkillony changed his religion in compliment to that ill-fated statesman. But his children always fled when the priest came to the house. One day that he was expounding the articles of faith to his convert, he told him all heretics would be damned. "Are such and such people heretics?" naming his neighbours and companions. "Yes," said the priest, "unless they return to the bosom of the Church." "Then," replied the other, "turn over another leaf; I don't believe one word of that." And in the last Lord Perth's time, his priest tried to convert David Stewart of Ballochallan; but having one day taken a pinch of snuff out of the priest's box, he said, "Mr Sanders, I fancy you have put some extreme unction among your snuff." After that profane speech, he met with no more trouble.

[2] I just remember Mr Robert Douglas, son of the Bishop of Dunblane, who had been minister of Bothwell before the Revolution. He was a pious, primitive, peaceable man, almost as ascetic as Bishop Leighton. He preached many years to a small congregation at Dunblane, from whom he would take no stipend; nor had he even a weekly collection till the year 1740, that the necessities of the poor were great. He was library-keeper. Died, aged upwards of fourscore, in 1746.

by persecution. Their principles and sufferings made
them adhere to the exiled family. No rational Presbyterian nowadays can justify the cruel tumultuary
manner in which the Episcopal clergy were ejected
at the Revolution.[1]

It is therefore little wonderful that a very great
proportion of the gentry should adhere to those good
men in their adversity. The ministers of that persuasion in this country, within my own remembrance,
were sincere, rational, valuable men, equally free
from fanatical notions and the opposite extreme.[2] In
point of breeding they were perhaps superior to the
Established clergy. It must, however, be confessed,
that in matters of Church and civil government they
were somewhat narrow-minded and violent. But that
spirit is almost inseparable from a state of suffering
and abasement.

The gentry of the last generation were not only
attached to their pastors from personal and political
considerations, but also firm believers in the doctrines
they taught. They did not imagine that religion was

[1] On that occasion the rabble broke into the house of Mr Shaw, Episcopal
minister at Logie ; and finding him in bed, the spokeswoman, after tearing off
the blankets, said, " Get up, sirrah ! are you lying on a feather bed, when my
dog Spottie lies on straw ?" She went by the name of *Spottie* Bryce ever
after.

[2] Bishop Alexander of Alloa would have been an ornament to any Church.
His learning and sanctity could only be equalled by his candour and meekness.
All parties reverenced him. Mr Blair of Ihoune was not remarkable for bril
liancy of talents : but he had the sweetness and innocence of a child, combined
with fervent piety and the desire of doing good. Though steady to his prin
ciples, not even the dregs of a civil war could make him forget the language of
charity and peace.

chiefly intended for the vulgar, and therefore they made conscience of impressing its hopes and fears upon the minds of their children. Bad company and the follies of youth might sometimes make people forget the good lessons they had learned. Yet in general the effects of a religious education evidenced themselves sooner or later. The gentlemen of this country, from the highest to the lowest, were regular attendants upon worship of one kind or other, till the meeting-houses were shut up in 1747.[1]

Some good consequences, among many bad, resulted from the firm adherence of the Jacobites to an unfortunate cause. Having no hope of Court preferment, or other resources, it constrained most of them to a rigid economy in their families. And it made them educate their children hardily and frugally, and instil into their tender minds invaluable lessons of sobriety and steadiness.[2] These virtues are almost incompatible with flattering prospects and the early gratification of every wish.

Their disaffection to the ruling powers was a bond of union, and prevented those petty rancorous broils which have lately originated from elections and local parties. Their complaints and grievances were so

[1] The late Arnprior was the first avowed unbeliever in this country. It exposed him to much obloquy, and was probably the great cause of his being accused of crimes which he never committed.

[2] A good lady in this neighbourhood (Ballochallan), whose family affairs were then in disorder, but afterwards retrieved by her exemplary conduct, said one day to her sons, who were clamouring about her for something she had no mind to give them, "My lads, I will breed you hardy; but if you thrive in the world, you will soon learn to relish better living."

many ties of mutual endearment, and in troublesome
times a decisive judgment could be formed of every
man's firmness and worth.   A vein of their romantic
politics extended itself by a natural progression into
private life.   The man who, for conscience' sake,
spurned the allurements of wealth and power, was
unlikely to act meanly or oppressively by his neighbour.   On the other hand, the friends and adherents
of Government were in those days equally keen and
equally conscientious.   Whilst we allow its adversaries private virtue and the merit of good intentions,
the principles of the Whigs were surely more rational
and enlightened.   And as they had a noble field for
virtuous exertions, so to them we are indebted for our
best barriers against oppression of every kind.   Instead
of implicit obedience to one man, however unworthy,
they held it lawful, in cases of necessity, to resist
tyranny, and even to deviate from the ordinary rules
of succession.   They were of opinion that the Protestant religion and a limited monarchy must stand
or fall together.   And they esteemed the interest of
the king to be the same with that of his subjects,
and the likeliest means of making him great at home
and abroad.   Nor did they confine their views to this
island alone, well knowing the fatal effects of selfishness upon nations as well as individuals.   The balance
of power and the liberties of Europe were therefore objects of which they never lost sight.   Indeed the glory
and power of Britain, so long as that system was
steadily maintained, are the highest eulogiums that

can be paid to Whig Ministers and Whig counsels. But to pass from their principles to their persons and conduct in common life. Though the Whig gentry were by no means numerous in this corner, they were respectable worthy people. And if they seemed less disinterested than their opponents, the posts and places they held were the just rewards of their unshaken attachment to Government in the hour of danger.

If the reigning family suffered by the influence of the Episcopal clergy, it was perhaps a greater gainer by having the Presbyterians on its side to a man.[1] They formed a vast majority of the burgesses and commonalty, and in some shires a great proportion of the gentlemen. And hence in 1715, the last Earl of Mar, with all his popularity, could not raise three men in his own town of Alloa. The same thing happened in 1745 to all the insurgents who had low-country estates. So great were the people's love of Presbytery and hatred of a Popish king!

Indeed for a number of years after the Revolution the clergy had a prodigious sway. Till the Secession broke out, they had no rivals to steal away the hearts of the people, who regarded them not only as pastors,

---

[1] Old Anthony Murray of Dollerie was one of the few Jacobites that left the Episcopal for the Presbyterian Church. But as he hated everything English with perfect hatred, so when the Non-jurors adopted the English Liturgy in the end of Queen Anne's reign, he deserted them, and went to the Established Kirk, which differed little in forms of worship from the old Episcopal. This gentleman was liker one of the fourteenth than the eighteenth century. His first toasts after dinner were regularly "to the memory of Wallace and Bruce."

but as guides and counsellors in every momentous
concern. The dread of forfeiting the minister's good
opinion was therefore a safeguard both to loyalty
and morals. In this they were powerfully seconded
by the session, which commonly consisted of the
leading farmers in the parish.

The first clergy I knew in this country were truly
respectable men, less eminent for their parts and
literature than for unfeigned piety, usefulness, and
zeal, tempered with discretion.[1] They were both

[1] Let me here speak of Mr Smith of Kincardine, the first clergyman I
knew. He was a man of truth and peace, humble and pleasant in his deport
ment. No minister was ever more solicitous to promote the spiritual and
temporal welfare of his flock, or took greater delight in his labour of love.
In sickness and distress he showed himself kind and compassionate, both in
words and deeds. His talents were moderate, and little improved by study,
but the integrity of his heart and the benevolence of his actions, joined to
plain sense, made up every defect. Indeed I used to say his life was more
edifying than his sermons ; yet these were very acceptable to the bulk of his
audience. He seldom meddled in Kirk politics, unless to moderate the keen
ness of party, or to move the Synod for a fast or thanksgiving. It was a sufficient proof of the bad spirit of the Seceders, that a number of them deserted
this good man, who was all his life the friend of the people, and partial to
their claims. But, in their fantastic phrase, " he had homologated the defec
tions of the judicatories." In private life he was no less amiable, a vein of
humanity and cheerfulness running through his conduct. Everybody that
came to his house, of whatever degree, got meat and drink and welcome. It
was wonderful how his slender income could supply it ; for his bounty was
like the widow's cruse, that never failed. The refreshment on Sunday,
between sermons, was to me, for many years, one of the pleasantest meals
through the week. Indeed, Mrs Smith, and after her his niece, were notable
housewives, and turned everything to good account. The liquors were all
made at home, and at his table he never aimed at anything above his station
Nor was hospitality his only expense. He generally had some nieces or
nephews staying with him, to whom he gave occasionally as they wanted
And upon his wife's son, by a former marriage, getting a commission in the
army, he advanced money to equip him, when his uncle, Lord Monrie, would
not give a shilling. It was his rule to sell his stipend meal in small quan
tities, a halfpenny below the market-price, by which he lost little, whilst he

loved and feared; but though unwilling to offend their meanest parishioner, they were by no means slaves to popularity, having in most cases the address to bring over the people to their opinion—at least till the Secession took place. They were in general moderate Calvinists; yet in their practice and conversation no men could be more zealous for good works, or purer in their notions of morals. They steered a middle course between the two great parties which at present divide and distract the Church, to the great scandal of religion.[1]

And now of education. In a few instances the sons of private gentlemen were bred at home by a tutor; but the far greater part went to the neighbouring schools every morning, foul day and fair day, carrying their little dinner with them. If the school lay at a distance, they were boarded at a trifling expense in some town or village. In the beginning of the present century there was an excellent schoolmaster at Stirling, Mr Thomas Darling, who was long the Busby of this country. He not only made a figure in his own profession, but was also the oracle of the magistrates and town council. And between fifty

accommodated the poor. His appearance abroad was decent and genteel, and the good plight of his servant and horses showed their master's care and indulgence. After all his hospitality and beneficence, he died worth £150 sterling.

[1] For almost forty years there hardly ever was a vote in the Presbyteries of Dunblane or Auchterarder. This made a minister, who was a firebrand in his own Presbytery, say to one of the latter, "Such a peaceable conduct is only fitted for angels or asses—and God knows, you are not angels in any respect!"

and sixty years ago, there was a great school at
Doune, kept by a Mr Brown, who bred many excellent
scholars, and taught some who afterwards figured in
the great world.

These last were nothing the worse for being bred
with the sons of their country neighbours.   All boys
below thirteen or fourteen years of age, unmoulded by
art, have the same manners and dispositions.   And
therefore in a great school where nature is allowed full
scope, the accidental differences of rank and fortune
are little considered in comparison of personal endowments.   Spirit, generosity, and sweetness of temper
are the circumstances which knit young hearts together and give a decided superiority in those little
societies—the only ones, perhaps, where vanity and
interested views have no place.[1]

The vulgarisms and rusticity contracted at country
schools gradually wore off, while some good consequences remained.   It strengthened young people's
attachment to the place of their nativity, and to every
spot which had been the scene of their boyish pas-
times.   They learned to estimate their country neighbours with justice and liberality, not to consider them
as animals of an inferior species.   It laid a foundation
for the future exercise of humanity and forbearance

[1] The boys at Dalkeith school were one day much struck at the appearance
of a nobleman's son of ten years of age in laced clothes. He was introduced
by his father and mother and a large company of ladies and gentlemen. We
looked on him as a creature of a superior species. Next morning he came to
school in a genteel undress, and after dinner in his laced apparel ; but in two
days all reverence was gone—the fine clothes being rolled in the dirt by the
schoolboys.

towards their old schoolfellows. And intimacies were sometimes formed between superiors and inferiors which after a long separation were remembered on a proper occasion, much to the honour of the one and the advantage of the other.

In those days the daughters of gentlemen of mid-dling fortune received a very moderate share of accom-plishments. Neither the circumstances of their parents nor the manners of the times would allow of excessive indulgence. It was thought sufficient to send them to the *schools* at Edinburgh,[1] where they learned needlework and other things which might qualify them to be good housewives, to which were added dancing and a little music. But what the young women of those times wanted in polish, was fully compensated in essentials — the utmost care being taken to impress their tender minds with high notions of piety and purity. Their time was chiefly occupied in learning and practising the mysteries of family management, in the course of which they acquired excellent habits of frugality and application; and whatever leisure they had, was employed in provid-ing clothes and decorations for their persons. For these frugal habits they were indebted not only to the precepts and example of their mother, but in many cases to the straits and limited income of the family. On public occasions, however, they seldom

---

[1] Mrs Abercromby said one day to a neighbour of hers, an Ochil laird, "You must shortly send your daughters to the *schools* at Edinburgh, for they are pretty girls." "No, no, madam," answered he; "I will make a touch of a country dominie serve."

failed to appear as became their birth and station. A degree of bashfulness and sweet timidity character-ised the young women of these times. This, perhaps, might lessen them in the eyes of foplings and super-ficial observers; yet it gave time to their mental faculties to ripen, and heightened their value upon an intimate acquaintance.

It must, however, be confessed that the reading of our old-fashioned ladies was exceedingly limited—being chiefly confined to books of a religious cast, or at most to the periodical papers published by Addison and Steele, and the other wits of the last age. Few of them, indeed, pretended to much knowledge of polite literature, and in epistolary correspondence they are surely excelled by their grandchildren. Their spell-ing was proverbially bad.[1] But within the last sixty years there must have been a wonderful change upon female manners, in consequence of playhouses, assem-blies, and concerts. It is true, the Duke of York had all the fashionable entertainments of the time while he held his Court at the Abbey.[2] But his stay in Scot-

---

[1] Lady Newbigging in Fife, writing to an Edinburgh shopkeeper for two necklaces, spelt it in such a way that the man read it naked lassies, and an swered her in a pet that he dealt in no such commodities. We see from Carstairs's Letters, that in King William's time our nobility and ministers of State were very deficient in orthography. This, however, may easily be accounted for: there was no longer a Court to give our language a standard.

[2] Lady Sarah Bruce says she was told by her aunt, Lady Janet, that the Duke had plays at the Abbey in which the ladies of the Court sometimes bore a share. One night whilst the Princess Anne, who played the principal part, was lying as dead upon the stage in the most interesting scene of the play. Mumper, her father's favourite dog, jumped atop of her, which discomposed

land was too short to effect any revolution in taste or manners, and there was a strong prejudice to everything he did. In those days the Scottish ladies made their most brilliant appearance at burials[1]—it being as common to get a new gown and petticoat to a great occasion of that kind as it is nowadays to a birthday ball. The Tron Church was then called the *Maiden Market*, it being there the finest women sat, which drew hither the fine gentlemen.

But about 1719 or 1720, theatrical entertainments found their way into Scotland,[2] and we have had them ever since in one form or another. Though opposed for a number of years, both by magistrates and ministers, they all along maintained their ground, being supported and attended by people of fashion.[3] With-

her gravity and set the audience in a roar. To this, perhaps, Morison of Prestongrange alluded when Queen Anne, soon after her accession, spoke to him at the levee. Thinking it incumbent on him to make some answer, he said the last time they had met was at a play ; *mair be taiken*, her Majesty had *sticked* her part. Upon reading Bishop Burnet's account of the Duke's shipwreck, Lady Janet said it was malicious to talk of the dogs as he did ; for she was at Court upon the Duke's return to Scotland, when she heard a gentleman, by way of making a compliment, regret the loss of poor Mumper. To which the Duke answered peevishly, "How, sir, can you speak of him, when so many fine fellows went to the bottom ?"

[1] Lady Manour, who was first married to Achenames [Mr Crawford] in 1694, told Mr Abercromby that she remembered that custom in her youth. The gentlemen drew up on one side of the street and the ladies on the other. Before the procession began, the men used to step over and pay their compliments to their female acquaintance.

[2] I heard the late Manour say he was present at the first play which was acted in Scotland after the Revolution. A temporary stage was erected in the tennis-court near the Abbey, which having fallen during the representation, the audience were so impatient that they obliged the actors to go on without stage or scenery.

[3] On opening the theatre in the Canongate, no play was in more request

out entering into the question whether the stage does most good or evil, we may safely affirm that in process of time it gave a new turn to the sentiments and behaviour of the ladies.

About the same time, the first stated assemblies were held at Edinburgh, which being under excellent regulations, served to polish manners, and to promote ease and elegance of behaviour.[1]   Great care was taken to prevent the intrusion of persons of low rank.   It appears strange to us, and will hardly be believed by the next generation, that the ministers of Edinburgh were for a number of years as hostile to the assembly as the playhouse.   They probably imagined that the former was of a piece with the balls at the Abbey while the Duke of York resided in Scotland.   By all accounts, the manners of his Court were abundantly loose—a thing very offensive in a country which was then remarkable for serious-ness and decorum.[2]

than "Macbeth." The Jacobites received with loud peals of applause every word in the scene between Malcolm and Macduff, which they applied to the times.

[1] Lady Sarah Bruce told me that she was one night at the assembly, when the Countess of Panmure, one of the first and most spirited of the lady directresses, observing her nephew, the Earl of Cassillis, flustered while paying his compliments to her, rose from her chair, and taking him by the hand, said, "Nephew, you have sat too late after dinner to be proper company for ladies." She then led him to the door, and calling out, "My Lord Cassillis' chair!" wished him good-night.   At another time, a brewer's daughter having come there very well dressed, her ladyship sent her a message to come back no more, she not being entitled to attend assemblies.

[2] Lady Janet Bruce, who, being then a young woman, was often at that Court, told Mr Abercromby that the horn order, which was held in such abomination, was entirely innocent. The drinking of tea was just beginning at that time, and the Duchess gave her favourites whom she wished to attend

But whatever effects public places and the reading of plays and poetry might have on persons of rank, or upon those who lived constantly at Edinburgh, it was a number of years before they could affect the manners of the gentry of small fortune, who seldom visited the capital of Scotland, and had little taste for the *belles lettres*.[1]

Before quitting female education, it is here proper to observe that between 1720 and 1730 our young ladies began to be distinguished by the name of Miss, they being formerly called Mrs Mary, &c. Indeed, Miss was formerly a term of reproach.[2] From the 'Tatlers' and 'Spectators' we see that in Queen Anne's time the same designation took place among the English ladies.

Before, and for a while after, the Union, the bulk of our gentry lived upon their estates, few of them being bred to business, or caring to enter into the sea or land service. People of moderate estate used to send their eldest son for some time to the *lattern*[3]—

her tea-table and balls a small horn spoon twisted at the end. They wore it at their breast as a sort of ticket.

[1] A gentleman's daughter from the country being one day asked by a lady what plays she had seen, answered, 'Love for Love,' and 'The Old Bachelor.' " O fie, Mrs Betty!" said her friend, "these are smutty plays, not proper for young women." " Indeed!" replied she, with great simplicity. "They *did* nothing wrong that I saw; and as for what they *said*, it was high English, and I did not understand it."

[2] An old maid remarkable for spirit and cheerfulness, giving one day a message to her servant, said, "Go to Lady —— with my mother's compliments and mine; but do not be *Missing* me, like an idiot. It is hard," said she, turning to the company, "that when I was young I should be Mrs Tibby, and now, when I am old and wrinkled, I must forsooth be a *Miss!*"

[3] From French *lutrin*, a desk.

i.e., to a writer's chamber—to learn the forms of deeds and the practice of business ; a custom which, as it gave them a smattering of law, was oftener a loss than an advantage. The more considerable families sent their heirs to some Dutch or German university to study the civil law, and afterwards to France to learn their exercises and see the world.[1]

But though the heir of the family was generally suffered to lead an idle life, a great proportion of the younger sons were sent betimes to push their fortune in the wide world. In the last century, they commonly entered into foreign service, there being few countries in Europe where the Scots have not distinguished themselves in one shape or other. The Union, however, produced many changes in people's views. Henceforth a number of these young adventurers found their way to North America, or to the East or West Indies. They generally began with small stocks and few advantages ; yet some of them were exceedingly successful. Some who did not take the oaths to Government, went into the Scotch-Dutch Brigades. And the thriving state of Glasgow made many people breed their second sons to trade or manufactures, in preference to the army or the learned professions.

[1] When George Drummond of Blair was complimented on the accomplishments of his son James, the old gentleman answered he knew nothing he had learned in his travels but to eat a snack every day, and to sup his kail twice. Before that time, it was the custom with the gentry, as it is still with our substantial tenants, for the whole company to eat broth out of one large plate.

The country gentlemen of last generation were in general a worthy, well-informed set of people—though perhaps somewhat unpolished, were they to be measured by the present standard. They were exceedingly hospitable, and lived together in the utmost harmony, insomuch that for many years there was not a single lawsuit between any two members of the Episcopal congregation at Doune, which, from the Revolution to 1747, included nine-tenths of the gentry of Menteith. This was no bad mark of the temper and good sense of that class of people.[1]

Having little business, and few resources against solitude, they were very much with one another, at no great expense. With a few exceptions, their houses were small, fitter for the reception of day than of night visitors. Unless at festivals, or upon ceremonious occasions, when the dining-room was used, people lived mostly in the family bedchamber, where friends and neighbours were received without scruple. Many an easy comfortable meal have I made long ago in that way through this country. By this means, however, the public rooms were the worst seasoned, and of course the least pleasant, of the whole. Even when strangers stayed all night, they were very easily accommodated, nothing being more

[1] Mr Walter Stewart, who between fifty and sixty years ago was Episcopal minister at Doune before he succeeded to an estate in Atholl, used to the last to talk with great warmth and respect of his old parishioners. "If," said he to a friend, "my age and infirmities would permit, I wish much to make a journey to Menteith, to see my old friends ; and though many of them are gone, I would stop at every empty door and let fall a tear."

common than to lay two gentlemen or two ladies that
were not acquainted in the same bed.[1]

In those days people commonly visited on chance.
If this sometimes embarrassed and distressed the lady
of the house, it surely gave occasion to meritorious
exertions on her part which flattered self-love. And
there were certain resources of which a good house-
wife availed herself with great dexterity. At the
worst, the having no previous intimation afforded her
a good apology for the plainness and moderation of
her fare. It was indeed an excellent preservative
against vanity and extravagance. But in order to
give time to prepare dinner, it was the fashion to
come early. The better to amuse the guests, they
were commonly taken out to walk about the environs
of the place. Upon no occasion, perhaps, was the
conversation of country gentlemen more rational and
agreeable. Their faculties were then cool and collected, and everybody came disposed to be courteous
and pleasant. In these perambulations every project
of improvement or embellishment, and every topic
that engaged the public attention, was discussed with
freedom and good-humour.[2] At table, people being

[1] It was a maxim with old George Drummond of Blair, that for every ...
... a country laird should have a thousand merks of yearly rent

[2] James Murray of Abercairney, and Mr David Graeme, advocate ...
... a neighbour, the latter fell behind, upon which his friend said, "Let us
ride a little faster; we will be too late to dinner." "I do it on purpose,"
answered he. "For if we go early, the laird will certainly show us ...
policy [grounds], and I had rather want my dinner." Mr Graeme had a
... contempt for the country. Getting wet with a shower he ...
tasting the pleasures of the country

restrained by the presence of their servants, seldom talk of anything but what is before them; and when the ladies withdraw, the conversation of the gentlemen becomes ere long noisy and uninstructive.

While guests came without invitation, it was the *ton* to have dinner precisely at the hour, to remove all suspicion of the family being surprised or in want of provisions. The old hours of eating differed widely from the present ones.[1] For some years after 1745, most families in this country breakfasted between eight and nine, dined precisely at one, and supped at eight. The dining at two was then regarded as a mark of fashion and figure. And I remember the same hours among the burghers of Edinburgh in 1748. By degrees, however, almost imperceptible, great changes took place in town and country.

In speaking of *minutiæ* of manners characteristic of the times, the fashion of pressing people to eat must not be omitted. As it originated in kindness, it was so far commendable; but it became at last troublesome and disgusting.[2] It was indeed no easy matter

---

[1] In 1713, Mr Abercromby lived in the north with his grandmother, the Lady Braco, who was very old, and very tenacious of the customs that prevailed in her younger years. She breakfasted at seven in the morning, dined at noon, and supped at six at night—the last was her chief meal. But in the article of hours she was singular. He was often with Lord Drummore at his country house, who in winter breakfasted at eight o'clock by candlelight; and while his mother lived, the same custom took place at Tullibody.

[2] A gentleman whose lady was beyond all measure kind, said to her one day at table, "Goodwife, if you would but press your guests to drink as much as you do to eat, you would be an excellent landlady." George Home of Argaty, though a pleasant-humoured man, used to throw down his knife and fork when importuned to eat. His neighbour Newton said he knew how

for a modest person to resist, and over-eating one's self
only provoked additional importunity. The best
security was to keep one's plate full.

Few of our gentry kept a full or regular table ; and
as their guests were for the most part upon an easy
footing, broth, a couple of fowls newly killed perhaps,[1]
or a joint of meat, was thought no bad dinner. And
the arrangement of dishes was little studied in former
times. In summer there was plenty of lamb and
chicken, and towards August excellent little mutton
from the hills. Beef was seldom fit for killing in open
pastures till October or November, and even then was
hardly to be got in the market in small pieces. Salmon, which is now a luxury, was then cheap and
plentiful, being in the summer months the chief food
of the servants.

In the beginning of this century, there being few
grass enclosures, the fat cows intended for winter provision, and bought at the fairs of Stirling, Dunblane,
and Doune, were slaughtered all together upon being
brought home.[2] It was imagined they would *slide* —

to deal with Argaty when he had a little dinner. On the other hand, g...
old Auchleshy was so accustomed to be pressed, that if left to himself he
would hardly have swallowed a morsel.

[1] An uncle of Baron Clerk, who from his many travels was nicknamed the
"Wandering Jew," used, when the family lived at Penicuik, to visit the
Tweeddale lairds in the forenoon. He stayed till he heard the hens intended
for his dinner give their last scream, after which, in spite of all they could say
he very ill naturedly went off.

[2] In these times, fat cattle being very cheap, a plentiful provision was laid
in. At Polmaise there would have been a dozen of cows killed at a time.
And Provost Chrystie said, when he first knew Stirling, it was the custom
for the more substantial burgesses of Stirling to lay in at the lawder time a
cow for every person of the family, the sucking child not excepted.

i.e., lose beef and tallow—by the change of food and the boisterous weather common at that season. The *laidner*, or slaughtering time, was therefore an occasion of much festivity, friends and neighbours being invited to partake of the good cheer. "November," said an old laird, "is a fine month; there being then plenty for man and beast. Pity, however, that Martinmas should spoil it!"

Indeed in those times people depended chiefly upon salt beef and kain hens. No fresh beef or mutton could be had for money after the middle of December till well on in summer. Towards March, which was the dearest and severest time, there were veal and pork, and sometimes capons.[1] Even within the last twenty-five years, when great changes had already taken place, there was not the tenth ox killed in the market of Stirling from February to May that is at present. And spite of the high price of fresh meat, it was no easy matter to find merchants for a few beasts fattened with turnips or greens.

Broth, or kail, was a standing dish in every family; yet of old we had no barley but what was imported from Holland. Its place, however, was supplied either by *grotts*—*i.e.*, oats stripped of husks in the

---

[1] Some of the more rigid Episcopals observed Lent with great precision, abstaining not only from animal food, but from snuff and other indulgences. Old Lanrick, who was a strong man, used to fast from the morning of Good Friday to the afternoon of Easter Sunday. But a number of serious people, of that persuasion considered the injunction of abstaining from flesh at that season as a political and not a religious duty. It being one day said that the true way to keep Lent would be to eat what was least agreeable to the palate, Commissioner Campbell said he would keep Lent on kain hens.

mill—or by *knocked* bear. Every family had therefore a knocking-stone, wherein the bear was beat
early in the morning by the kitchen-maid. The first
barley-mill was erected in Salton, in East Lothian,
upon a plan which William Adam, the architect, is
said to have made from memory. The taking of
models of the barley-mills in Holland would have been
severely punishable in a stranger. Still, however,
when there was no ceremonious company, *grotts* were
very much used in gentlemen's families in this neighbourhood less than forty years ago.

Our forefathers were also indifferently provided in
garden stuff, kail and leeks being their chief dependence.[1] The onions used of old were mostly imported
from Holland or Flanders, it being imagined they
would not grow in this country. But long after that
was found to be a prejudice, the shipmasters continued
to bring over casks of them upon a venture, which they
could afford cheaper than the gardeners.

Within the last thirty years little wheat-bread was
eaten in private gentlemen's families, unless at breakfast. Indeed at dinner and supper a few slices were
cut for strangers and laid atop of the cakes, which
last were generally preferred. But at the New Year,
great loaves full of aniseeds were always part of the
holiday cheer.

[1] In the household books of the Roxburghe family at Broxmouth are the
following articles: "January 1667—1 firkin of onions, 4*s.* 8*d.* Scots. October
1667 100 onions, 10*s.* 1st August 1668—1 peck of pease, 6*d.*, 30 artichokes,
12*s.*, 10 dozen saybe heads (i.e., young onions), 12*s.* 1670, January Given to
the gardener of the Lochend for parsley, beetroots, leeks, parsnips and Jeru-
salem roots, 4*s.*, &c."

Sugar, which now ranks among the necessaries of life, was originally considered as a cordial,[1] or at best as a luxury to be presented upon a proper occasion. By degrees, however, it was substituted in place of honey, being a much better sweetener.[2] But although the consumption of it has increased greatly upon our having a direct trade with the West Indies, yet within the last forty years the sugar-loaf in many families used to be locked up in the lady's press along with the 6d. loaf of bread.

The breakfasts of our gentry in the beginning of this century differed widely from the present ones, consisting of collops, fish, cold meat, eggs, milk-pottage, &c., to which was added water-gruel, *skink*—a species of soup peculiar to Scotland—strong ale, or a glass of wine and water.[3] The solidity of that meal was the less extraordinary, that in those days people generally rose very early in the morning, either to business or sport.[4] Tea, which now figures among the

[1] Lady Sarah Bruce says when she was young they had a tradition that a Lady Halket being taken ill in Dunfermline Church, Queen Anne of Denmark took her into her apartment in the Palace hard by, and opening a press or *ambry*, scraped a little off a sugar-loaf into a glass of wine and gave it to Lady Halket. The place has often been shown to Lady Sarah.

[2] In the Roxburghe household-books are stated : " March 1667—a pound of sugar, £1, 4s. Scots ; May—a pound of sugar, 18s.; June 1669—a sugar-loaf at 12s. per pound." In the books of old George Abercromby, ninety years ago, sugar-loaves from Holland are stated.

[3] The breakfasts of James Menzies of Culdares, within the last fourteen years, were as substantial. But he had only two meals a-day—viz., at noon and at six at night, which last was the chief one. He borrowed this custom from the more primitive Highlanders.

[4] In the end of the last century the lawyers were consulted at four and five in the morning—sometimes in the tavern, where they got *skink* and sweet wine by way of whet. Mr Abercromby was told by his father that he had

necessaries of life, was at first regarded as an expensive unpleasant drug.[1] But having taken deep root in England, it made its way northwards by degrees. Though the precise time of its introduction among us cannot now be ascertained, yet all our old people agree that it made a rapid progress after the year 1715: and before the Rebellion of 1745, it was the common breakfast in most gentlemen's families in this country. It was, however, very ill relished by old-fashioned[2] people, who either rejected it altogether, or required a little brandy to qualify it. But many of those who adopted it, continued to have cold meat or something more substantial than bread and butter to breakfast.

The drinking of tea is an important era in female manners as well as in housekeeping. It afforded a cheap and elegant repast to ceremonious company who came rather to pay their compliments than

in his youth attended Sir Walter Pringle's consultations at these hours. And Lord President Dalrymple told James Wright, the extractor, that when he was at the bar, Mr Buchanan, a Writer to the Signet, James's master, being very pressing for an early hour, four in the morning was named, when, before they parted, Mr Dalrymple was consulted in no less than fourteen causes.

[1] The tea-table was a matter of great astonishment at first to the common people. A Highlander being desired to inquire after the health of Mr Graham of Braco's family, brought back word that he fancied they were not well, as he found them drinking hot water out of flecked pigs.

[2] Among the former was old Anthony Murray of Dollerie, no admirer of anything modern. Though he despised tea himself, he offered it to his guests, and upon their choosing it, he said, "Well, get the kettle for them." John Stirling Keir played a trick to a neighbour that came to him a little rustic from the market of Keirhill. Tea being almost over, he was asked if he chose a dish. To this he assented, provided he got a little brandy with it; upon which Keir ordered the kettle to be filled with that liquor, and a teaspoonful being poured from a bottle into every cup, the poor gentleman expressed great satisfaction at the goodness of the tea, which soon set him asleep.

with a view to eating and drinking.[1] Accordingly, we see from the 'Spectator' and 'Guardian' that the tea-table was then the rendezvous of the fair and the gay, and the place where polite conversation was chiefly carried on. The same thing took place in Scotland, and contributed not a little to soften and polish manners.

Though our gentry lived plainly and frugally in common, yet upon certain occasions they wished to make a show. Christmas was always a season of great fulness with those of the Episcopal persuasion, who thought religion and innocent festivity nowise incompatible.[2] The Presbyterians, in general, had no objection to eat and drink with their friends at that season ; but if exceedingly rigid,[3] their feasts were delayed till the end of the old or the beginning of the new year.[4]

[1] My grandmother, who lived in Edinburgh the year before the Revolution, told me that it was then the fashion to give ladies that visited in the afternoon a glass of wine and a bit of cake. And Mr Abercromby says that in 1714 the same custom prevailed in his father's family at Edinburgh. By that time, however, there were a few ladies who had tea-tables. At the first introduction of tea, it was common for the young ladies of a family to have great tea-drinkings after the old folks were gone to bed. I have heard of very merry ones at Manour whilst Lady Kincardine lived there before marriage.

[2] Lanrick's Christmases being very crowded and hearty, there were two tables, the one for married people, the other for bachelors and maidens. After dinner it was a standing joke to drink a health to the latter by the name of *bairns*, without any regard to age. It was intended as a reproof to bachelors.

[3] Some people who adhered to all the crotchets of the Covenanters, affected to fast on Christmas-day—at least they would by no means partake of the goose, which they called a superstitious bird.

[4] Whilst the Episcopals called Christmas-week the *holidays*, the Presbyterians gave it no better name than the *daft days*. When very young, I was reprimanded by an old gentleman for using that expression. He told me very gravely it was a Whiggish phrase.

Yet Christmas was rather a time of mirth and plenty than of extravagance. It was at marriages, christenings, and burials, particularly the last, that country gentlemen were wont to exceed the bounds of moderation. Then, that they might give proofs of their Edinburgh education, the ladies displayed their skill in cookery and decking out a table.[1]

The expense of funerals was of old enormous, extending sometimes to a full year's rent of the estate.[2] Of these we have had some in this neighbourhood, within the last forty years, which one way or another lasted a week. The gentry for many miles round were collected, and treated with an ostentation that neither suited the occasion nor the circumstances of the family.[3]

[1] Whatever may have been the origin of our Scottish dishes, a number of them are admired by those whose ideas are chiefly English or foreign. Our old cookery probably differed little from the French of the fifteenth and sixteenth centuries, when we had a close intercourse with that people. It is, however, likely that some of them may have been invented or improved by the dignified Popish clergy, who were fond of good eating.

[2] The most pompous and expensive burial in this country of which we have any tradition, was that of the young laird of Keir, who died towards the end of the last century. He was a youth of great hopes, and much esteemed; and therefore, besides collecting company far and near, the Perthshire troop of horse, of which he was an officer, attended and paid him military honours. And cannon were brought from Stirling Castle to make these more grand. This was very different from the request which Sir George Stirling, who died in 1667, made to his cousin Lord Carden in his last will—viz., to bury him without embowelling, in the Church of Dunblane without trumpets, and without convening any but friends. But in those times the current ran too strong the other way. Sir George's request would be considered as the language of an old man satiated of the world, while the splendour of the young man's burial would be looked on as a proper expression of the sorrow of parents for a beloved son.

[3] A person staggering home from the house where a very worthy neighbour was lying a corpse, being asked by John Stirling of Keir, who met him on the road, whence he came in that condition, answered, "From the house of mourning."

But this was not all. At the interment of friends
and neighbours, it was almost the universal custom to
drink to excess.[1] Such a practice appears to us no
less unbecoming in the living than disrespectful to
the dead. But as the good people of these times
were far from being devoid of natural affection or
pity, let us see what may be said in alleviation of
this practice. The bulk of the company were common acquaintance, collected many of them from a
distance. Some refreshment was therefore necessary
before or after the interment. Relations and strangers being of course intermixed, familiar conversation
took place; and spite of the melancholy occasion,
people's hearts warmed to each other by degrees.
Meanwhile the glass went freely round, and nobody
thought of rising, till at length the whole company
insensibly forgot the rules of moderation and decency.

Neither is it surprising that a dying person, who
remembered how he himself had paid the last duty to
those he loved, should wish his friends and neighbours
to make a like plentiful libation to his memory.[2]
Men seldom think of inquiring deeply into the nature
and origin of customs expressive of veneration for the
dead.

We must also consider that hard drinking was the

[1] At the laird of Abbotshaugh's burial, the company appeared so rosy and
merry in the kirkyard, that some English dragoons quartered at Falkirk
said one to another, "Jolly dogs! a Scots burial is merrier than our
weddings."

[2] A very respectable gentleman of this country, being on his deathbed, and
giving his son directions about the burial, added, "For God's sake, John, give
them a hearty drink!"

favourite sin of our old gentry. It was indeed well suited to a rough, kind-hearted set of men, who delighted in society. This vice is said to have gained additional ground after the Restoration. Every breast was filled with joy upon the return of peace and order, and the appearances of preciseness and hypocrisy were so much avoided that people ran unheedingly into the other extreme. The Cavaliers seem to have placed no small part of their loyalty in drinking deep to the King's health.[1]

But whatever may have been its origin, it was, almost within our own memory, considered as want of kindness and respect in a landlord not to give his guests as much liquor as they could carry. Neither was it reckoned any breach of hospitality to allow them, when they could hardly mount their horses, to go away in a dark night, through execrable roads, sometimes across rivers. The fearlessness of drunk men was, in truth, their greatest danger; but it is marvellous how few accidents befell people in these circumstances.[2]

[1] Upon the Restoration, Graham of Gartur, and one or two more of Montrose's cavaliers, agreed to go to London to see the King, from whom they expected not only a gracious reception, but a bountiful reward for their sufferings. With difficulty a thousand merks apiece was raised. But at Edinburgh they fell a drinking helter skelter till all their money was spent. I had this from Shannochil.

[2] Lord Kames told me, that dining one day at a country gentleman's house with William Hamilton the poet, they drank excessively hard. When they came to take their horses it was pitch dark, but after the rest had mounted Mr Hamilton was amissing. Candles being brought, he was found lying under the horses' feet, hardly able to articulate more than "Lady Mary, sweet Lady Mary! when you are gone, you are too good!"—alluding to the legend of the man who, being unable to mount his horse, prayed to the Virgin for aid, and was so much strengthened, that at his next attempt he jumped over his horse.

By means of hard drinking and its usual consequences, more estates were impaired than by all the
other articles of expense in housekeeping put together.
And beside plentiful libations in one another's houses,
it was very much the fashion to drink to excess either
in the tavern or in country ale-houses.[1] In consequence of this fondness for the bottle, the company of
the ladies was greatly neglected by the gentlemen.
Even in Edinburgh, where softer manners might have
been expected, the men of the last generation spent
their evenings abroad, without thinking how their
wives and families were entertained at home.[2]

Yet even in this darling article our gentry were
abundantly frugal. In the beginning of the present
century ale was their common beverage when they
had no ceremonious guests.[3] I have heard Lady New-

[1] Within the last fifty years an estate in this neighbourhood is said to have
been adjudged, at the instance of a change-keeper, for (among other things)
4000 drams and 100,000 kail-plants.

[2] Mr Abercromby says that between 1730 and 1740 he and a set of married
friends agreed to sup alternately at one another's houses. They found this
more agreeable and less expensive than the tavern. But in those days the
latter was still very much in request, especially among people advanced in
life.

[3] It appears from the court-books of the Breadalbane family that great
quantities of ale were drunk in that country betwixt 1592 and 1680. The
tunsters or tasters continued till 1683. In 1620, at 12d. the pint, except
" frae strangers, at the market of Killin, on Sunday next "   malt £5, 13s. 4d.
the boll. In 1683, ale 20d. the pint—malt £8. The fondness of the females
for this liquor occasioned a most extraordinary Act : " 20th February 1617.—
It is statuted by the laird, with advice of the hail assize of court, that whatever person or persons, wives, ane or mae, shall happen to be found in Bread-
albine in ony brewster-house drinking outwith the company of their husbands, they shall pay to the laird £10 of unlaw *toties quoties*, and for every
chopin of ale they drink shall sit twenty-four hours in the *lang gald* "—i.e.,
a bar of iron to which offenders were tied. From the household-books of the
R——rgile family we learn that amazing quantities of malt-liquor were con-

ton say, that before 1715 great quantities of *cap* ale
(an intermediate kind) used to be drunk during the
Christmas holidays at Newton and Keir. It got its
name from the *cap* or dish out of which they drank it.
And Mr Abercromby remembers when it was the
practice in the north country, in gentlemen's houses,
to bring little barrels of strong ale into the room, and
to ask the company whether they chose old or new.

It appears already strange to us how, in Allan
Ramsay's days, gentlemen of figure and fashion
should have enjoyed a bicker of ale as much as a
bottle of claret.[1] But he only painted the manners of
his age. The *scourging a nine-gallon tree* was then a
common feat among lads of mettle. It consisted in
drawing the spigot of a barrel of ale, and never quitting it night or day till it was drunk out.

But so soon as the Scots had a direct trade with
the West Indies, persons of moderate fortune betook
themselves chiefly to punch. It was at first made of
French brandy, rum being long scarce and in no estimation.[2] But after 1745 it improved greatly, and
brandy could not be had. The drinking of punch

sumed about 1669 at Broxmouth sometimes forty gallons of the best and
thirty of the middling ale in a week. The quantity of wine is comparatively
inconsiderable.

[1] Even very lately the evening potations of the best burghers of Stirling consisted of a species of new ale called *black*, somewhat stronger than two pen.
Over ale of one kind or other the politics and scandal of that town have been
immemorially canvassed.

[2] Mr Abercromby was one of the first in the country that got rum,
made a rum, by means of a son of Collector Gordon. Though a good spirit, yet
being drunk with *three* waters like brandy, it tasted harsh. Major Dalrymple, who lived then at Nauchie, said Mr Abercromby had got a liquor that
would confiscate a man's intelligence in half an hour.

diminished the consumption of ale, which was henceforth confined to a glass or two at or after dinner,
unless among old-fashioned people.

But for many ages French wine was the favourite
regale of the Scots. Nor is the progression of its
price incurious. In the minority of Queen Mary,
the pint of Bordeaux wine brought in by the east
or north seas is directed to be sold at 10d., and the
Rochelle wine at 8d.; the pint of Bordeaux wine
brought in by the west seas to be sold at 8d., and the
Rochelle at 6d. Bordeaux wine is rated at £16 the
tun, and the Rochelle at £12 or £13. The cheapness
of the wine, as well as its relative value, appears from
the very next Act, where a tame goose is rated at
16d., and a hen at 8d.[1]

James Howell, who visited Scotland about the year
1639, says the chopin of French wine was then sold
at Edinburgh for 4d., and it was a heinous offence to
adulterate it.[2]

The late Mr Russell of Dunblane told me that
about 1720, when he was prentice to Clerk Nicol of
Stirling, two men used to frequent the chamber—
viz., Dominie Matson,[3] usher of the grammar-school,

---

[1] The town of Perth or St Johnston had liberty to sell their wine two pen-
nies the quart dearer than the adjacent burghs.

[2] Perhaps Howell did not know that it was once a *capital* crime in Scotland : " And gif ony sik (*i.e.*, mext or corrupt wine) happenis to be sent hame,
that na man sell or tap it frae it be declared be the baillies and gusters of
wine that it is mext or corrupt, but send it again furth of the realme, under
the pain of death. And that na person within the realme tak upon hand in
time to cum to mex wine or beere, under the pain of death."

[3] Matson was a lively entertaining old man. The late Manour, who knew
him well, told me the following anecdotes which he heard him tell : He was

and *Skart* Robertson, a town officer, both of them upwards of a hundred years of age. One day talking over old stories, the one said to the other, " Do you remember when wine was cried through Stirling for six shillings Scots the chopin?" "Well do I that," said the other; "but you surely recollect the bellman going through the town next day to give notice that in another house they would get it at the same price, and cheese and raisins to the bargain."

William Mayne Powis told Mr Abercromby that on the market-days of Alloa he used to breakfast with old George Abercromby at Tullibody upon sack and saps : but coming in one morning, the latter said to him, " William, you must now be contented with ale, sack being raised from four to eight shillings the chopin." This was probably some time after the Revolution.

The duties imposed upon wine from time to time, and the interruption of our trade with France, rendered claret too costly a liquor for gentlemen of moderate fortune to drink in their own houses.[1] But

present when Cromwell at St Ninians ordered a soldier to be instantly hanged for stealing hens from a poor woman, who pointed out the delinquent in the ranks. And at Stirling he saw another at the head of the regiment with tongue bored with a red hot iron for cursing and swearing. The latter loved to talk of the rejoicings at the Restoration. A great number of country gentlemen came into Stirling upon that occasion : and a clergyman in a gown said grace at a collation near the bonfire, who, after drinking a few glasses, was going away, being to preach next day. But one of the gentlemen (either Touch or Polmaise) clapped him on the shoulder, saying "Stay with us a while to-day, and we will take *cold kirk het again* with you to-morrow." "But I trow," said Mateson, "the Kirk of Stirling was well heated that day."

If the old claret was very cheap, it had little strength. Judge Graham of Airth told Mr Abercromby that the wine imported in his younger days kept very well from November or December that it came in, till the summer

for many years they hardly drank anything else in
the tavern,[1] where it was sold for 18d. the chopin,
till 1720, when the plague at Marseilles stopped all
intercourse with France. Upon that pretence the
wine merchants raised it to 20d.; and soon after that
bottled wine came into request, 4d. more was charged
for the bottle. But spite of these variations in the
Edinburgh prices, wine continued very cheap in the
remote countries.[2]

Formerly very little port wine was drunk in Scot-
land, unless by gouty people who were forbid claret.
In 1743 a cargo of it was imported by the late Sir
Laurence Dundas, then a wine merchant at Airth.
Grain being very cheap, he sent a cargo of bear to
Portugal, and by way of venture brought home port.
Of this Lord Erskine and Mr Abercromby took each
a pipe, rather to serve the merchant than for any
liking to the wine. But the rebellion having broken

session. Whenever it became tart and thin, it was customary to mix it with
cinnamon and sugar, which made what was then called a *tapped hen*.

[1] New wine was formerly so much in request, that decanting was unnecessary. At Sir Laurence Dundas's marriage in 1738, crystal decanters were
set down, which was then accounted a novelty. Ross's tavern was the last
in Edinburgh where one might have wine in the old style, drawn off the cask.
It was given to the company in pewter stoups, with the cream on the top.
I remember it within the last twenty-five years.

[2] The late Thomas Forrester of Denovan used to tell with much glee that
a good many years ago, being on a jaunt to the north with some friends,
they met with good small claret at Stonehaven ; and the bill being called
for after dinner, they marvelled to see it charged only a shilling a bottle.
Yet some gentlemen of the country who had dined with them abused the
landlord for charging strangers too much. The man protested he could no
longer afford it at 10d., but offered, for every six bottles they should drink,
to give one gratis. "Whereupon," said Denovan, "the horses were counter-
manded, and we sat too late, to get amends of the landlord."

out soon after, it helped to save better liquor. Port
was then thought unfit for drinking till four years
old.[1]

Before concluding the article of liquor, it is proper
to observe that in these days it was not the custom in
families of good fortune and fashion to set down wine
or punch upon the table after dinner, unless there was
company. At other times a dram or bottle of strong
ale sufficed.[2]

The dress of our gentry resembled in some particulars their domestic economy. It was in general plain
and frugal, but upon great occasions they scrupled no
expense. This is the only way of conciliating the
contradictory accounts[3] we have of the simplicity

[1] In 1746 the Prince of Isenburg, who commanded the Hessians at Stirling, invited the magistrates to a collation; and having sent for Mr Dow...wines, he pitched on port, as being, he imagined, a rare wine. But his company were ill pleased with the liquor and worse with the salt herrings ... were set down as a relisher

[2] Dr Blair told me that, being at London in 1763, he was invited to ... with Archbishop Secker, who said to him after they sat down, 'I... must call for wine in the time of dinner. It has not been the practice ... Archbishops of Canterbury since the Reformation to put down wine ... glasses after the cloth is drawn.

[3] "In Scotland, beyond Edinburgh," says Taylor the Water-poet, who ... Scotland in James VI's time, "I have been at houses like castles f... ing : the master of the house, his beaver being his blue bonnet, ... no other shirt but of the flax that grows on his own ground, and of his... daughter's, or servant's spinning; that hath his stockings, hose, ... the wool of his own sheep's backs; that never by the pride of ... caused mercer, &c, to turn bankrupt Yet this plain homespun fellow ... and maintains thirty, forty, or fifty servants, or perhaps more, every ... having three or four score poor people at his gate, and besides, ... entertainment for four or five days together to five or six earls ... sides knights, gentlemen, and their followers, if they be three ... dred men and horse of them, where they shall not only feed ... only feast but banquet This is a man that desires to know n... as his duty to God and the King; whose greatest cares are ...

and extravagance of our forefathers in this article.
Even within the last fifty years, when few country
gentlemen visited Courts or cities, something of this
spirit remained. It was the etiquette, not only when
they married, but also upon paying their addresses, to
get laced clothes and laced saddle furniture—an expense which neither suited their ordinary appearance
nor their estates. No people formerly went deeper
into that folly than the Highland gentry when they
came to the low country.[1]

In the first part of this century it was the custom
for persons of figure, whether young or old, to wear
tie-wigs in dress. By degrees, however, these were
relinquished by the young and the gay, and confined
to judges, lawyers, and other grave characters. And
though jack-boots were by that time given up as a

works of piety, charity, and hospitality. He never studies the consuming art
of fashionless fashions ; he never tries his strength to carry four or five hundred acres on his back at once. Many of those worthy housekeepers there are
in Scotland. Among some of them I was entertained, from whence I did truly
gather the aforesaid observations." This account smells strong of poetry ; yet
the groundwork may be true. Had our traveller seen these very country
gentlemen paying court to James VI. in 1617, or to Charles I. in 1633, he would
have found them as gorgeous in their apparel as they were plain and primitive
at home. Indeed the debts contracted by the nobility and gentry in consequence of these royal progresses were enormous. In the inventory of Dame
Margaret Ross, wife of Sir George Stirling of Keir, who died in March 1633,
are the following articles : " Item—a gown of Florence satin and black and
orange flowers, laid over with gold lace, price £133, 6s. 8d. Item—a gown of
orange pan velvet, laid over with silver lace, £160. Item—a petticoat of Milan
satin, £100." Sir George, who died in 1667, in bequeathing his body-clothes,
excepts his black velvet coat and his gold-and-silver belt.

[1] David Home Stewart of Argaty told me that, being in Morven before 1745
buying cattle, he spied early in the morning a person coming up laced from
top to toe. "Who is that ?" said he to his host. "It is our laird," said the
other. The gentleman came and courteously invited the stranger to his
house, which was ill suited to laced clothes, being a creel one, with timber locks

part of full dress, they continued within the last fifty years to be used in travelling.[1]

There appears to have been some analogy between the breeding and the dress of the last age. The former was stately and formal, the latter stiff and cumbrous; and thus tie-wigs, jack-boots, enormous sleeves, skirts bolstered out with buckram and buttoned to the heel, were in some measure connected with the manners of the times.

In speaking of female dress, we must confine ourselves within narrow limits—it being difficult, as well as needless, to trace the fluctuations of fashion. About the time of the Union, the attire of ladies of rank and fortune was perhaps as showy and expensive as at present. Upon occasions of great ceremony it consisted of a manteau and petticoat of silk or velvet, with a silk scarf. The cost of those gowns was no doubt out of all proportion to their other economics, but two or three of them served a lifetime. Neither was it necessary to make annual alterations or additions, for in these days finery did not wear out of fashion; and within the last forty or fifty years, when considerable changes had already taken place, the

and furniture equally primitive. Yet upon returning the visit at Balvie a some time after, he complained in the morning of having his bed ... broken pane in his bedroom.

[1] In the last century, jack-boots are said to have been an essential part high dress; even the burghers of Edinburgh appeared at the Cross This being one day spoken of in company, Graham of Kilmardinny an ... character, said, in the true spirit of hyperbole, that he remembers the time when the children were christened in jack boots and spurs. In fact bare legs being the fashion, a full bottomed periwig and jack boots were little less grotesque and ridiculous when combined.

daughters of gentlemen of four or five thousand merks a-year thought themselves well off before marriage with a single silk gown, and perhaps, by way of reserve, one of their mother's. Even the ladies of Edinburgh, who attended assemblies and other public places, were but moderately provided with fine clothes.

At home, however, or in visiting neighbours upon an easy footing, the ladies' dress was abundantly cheap and simple—stuffs of their own spinning, or what was only a few degrees more showy,[1] being the common wear of those who occasionally figured in the best company. And the making up the several articles of dress[2] and ornament was the chief occupation and amusement of gentlemen's daughters of moderate fortune when disengaged from household cares.

Yet even in the soberest times, upon a daughter's marriage every maxim of frugality was forgotten. In a variety of cases vanity or parental fondness occasioned an expense which neither suited the bride's

[1] Lady Sarah Bruce says her aunt Lady Helen used to give James Scobie, the carrier, 8s. to bring her over a Musselburgh stuff gown; and her sister, Lady Janet, was equally primitive in her home dress. Yet both these ladies had been much in the world. At the age of fourscore, Lady Janet had all the spirit and vivacity of nineteen. One day in a frolicsome company, as she and Mr Hugh Forbes were romping together like the young folks, he discovered she had on coarse worsted stockings. Upon his wondering at this, she said, "Ah, Hugh, where there is little repair there is little policy!"

[2] Upon the conclusion of the Rebellion of 1746, there was a rage of wearing tartan. The Jacobite ladies took that method of expressing their attachment to an unfortunate prince. They used tartan not only in plaids, but in gowns, riding-clothes, bed and window curtains, even in shoes and pin-cushions. The Whigs once thought of arraying the hangman in the Prince's pattern; but they did more wisely in having Whig tartan, which ere long made both parties give it over.

portion [1] nor the bridegroom's estate. In the long-
run, however, this profusion turned often to good
account. The honeymoon was no sooner over than
the family resumed its usual style. And as a lady
who lived mostly in the country had few opportunities of displaying her marriage finery, it lay almost
unsullied in her coffers till her daughters grew up.
If the family affairs were embarrassed, it helped to
rig them out and to save her husband's money.

The milliner business was hardly known in Scotland
about the beginning of this century; and though it
was introduced by degrees from London,[2] yet in 1753
there were only five or six in Edinburgh. When so
very few had an interest in changing or inflaming the
fashions, it is not surprising that the ladies' head-
dress and other decorations should be stationary. A
head-dress called *pinners* maintained its ground an
unconscionable time. It is mentioned in the 'Tatler,'
and in my younger years I remember it among the
ladies of this country. At that time, however, a few
of them that were far advanced in life wore a dress

[1] It was once humorously observed that the tocher of a country lady's
daughter turned commonly to little account: a third of it being laid out in
clothes, another third spent at the wedding, and the remainder paid fifty years
after.

[2] Lady Sarah Bruce says a Katherine Murray was the only milliner in Edinburgh when she first knew it, about 1720. Nor were female mantua-makers
very ancient in that place—Isabel Robertson, who was bred in London, having
been, about 1725, the first person eminent in that way. In the preceding age
a great part of the ladies' habiliments were made up by tailors. Nay, within
the last twenty-five years the tailors of Perth pursued the mantua-makers to
enter with them: in regard they had a real cause from William the Lion,
giving them an exclusive privilege of making all sorts of men and women's
apparel.

still more antiquated, called a *toy*, part of which hung over the shoulders. It is still worn by some very old-fashioned tenants' wives. But even then there was one article of extravagance : people thought nothing of laying out large sums of money for Brussels lace.[1] It was generally a nuptial present, being regarded as one of the appendages of wealth and fashion.

Of old, the ladies' hair cost them little trouble or expense. As it was artlessly disposed in curls or ringlets, they themselves, or their maids, could dress it—nay, their companions sometimes assisted them. Between forty and fifty years ago, Morison the barber, who had been *valet de chambre* to Lord Perth, introduced the Paris style of dressing the ladies' hair.[2]

In those days every lady in an undress wore a plaid when she went abroad. It was sometimes of one colour—scarlet, crimson, &c.—but more commonly tartan or variegated. People fond of finery had silk ones ; others wore woollen lined with silk ; whilst the lower classes were satisfied with plain worsted. We see from Allan Ramsay's poems, that in his time some attempts were made to substitute the scarf in place of the plaid, a design which he strenuously reprobates upon very plausible grounds. In 1747, when I first knew Edinburgh, nine-tenths of the ladies still wore

---

[1] Between forty and fifty years ago, an account for Brussels lace being presented to a gentleman new married, he said in a great passion, "And that it is, and that it is ! [his usual byword] ; £100 is too much for pinners." He little imagined it was sterling and not Scots money he had to pay.

[2] Mrs Drummond of Blair says she was one of the first who appeared in a public place with her head dressed by Morison in the height of the mode.

plaids, especially at church. By this time, however, silk or velvet cloaks, of one form or another, were much in request with people of fashion. And so rapidly did the plaid wear out, that when I returned to Edinburgh in 1752, one could hardly see a lady in that piece of dress. For a while they were retained by matrons attached to old modes, and by the lower classes of people; but in the course of seven or eight years the very servant-maids were ashamed of being seen in that ugly antiquated garb.

The nobility and gentry of Scotland always prided themselves upon the splendour of their appearance in public, particularly on the showiness of their servants and horses.[1] These they esteemed the surest characteristics of rank. The equipage of a man of fashion fourscore years ago differed, however, widely from the present style. Upon occasions of high ceremony, a loose was given to vanity and expense; but in common, when the gentlemen went abroad, they affected somewhat of the military character, being well mounted, and both they and their servants having pistols before them. In those days a wheel-carriage -

[1] By all accounts, the riding of the Scottish Parliament was a very magnificent show. The members rode in their robes, and were followed by their horses—i.e., in rich caparisons—led by grooms, the number of which was regulated by their rank. Every morning the Commissioner rode in state from the Abbey to the Parliament House. While the House sat, the horses were put into temporary booths erected on both sides of the Lawnmarket. Mr. William Tytler was told by his father, who added, he never saw such horses as at the Union Parliament.

[2] The morning of the Perthshire election 1761, I heard James, Duke of Athole say that in 1713, when he was chosen member of Parliament there was a great meeting, yet his father's coach was the only carriage there

was regarded chiefly as one of the appendages of greatness and fortune, not as one of the comforts of life. Indeed the roads all over Scotland were so rough and narrow that it could not be used with safety and pleasure, unless within a few miles of Edinburgh, and therefore all ranks of people travelled from choice on horseback. But persons of rank were generally preceded by a running footman or two. It is wonderful with what expedition these fellows went along, few horses being able to keep with them upon a long journey. Besides the airiness of their appearance, they were exceedingly serviceable in case of any accident upon the road.[1] The ladies sometimes rode on side-saddles, but more frequently upon a pillion behind a man.[2]

But by degrees, as our intercourse with England increased, the middling gentry got coaches or chaises.[3]

[1] Sir Archibald Stewart's running footman being asked what had kept him so long, complained of being *taigled* [detained] with a horse part of the way. So long as the Lords of Justiciary went the circuit on horseback, a running footman and a *decked* horse were part of their state. Lord Drummore was one of the last who *rode* the circuit.

[2] When Lady Braco came to see her daughter, Lady Tullibody, she made the journey on a pad. She could well have afforded a carriage, her jointure being 22,000 merks. When about to return home, Mr Abercromby says his father's tenants used, of their own accord, to accompany her as far as Auchterarder or Dunning. As she was a religious observer of old customs, this had probably been the etiquette of old.

[3] Mr Abercromby says his father got his first two-wheeled chaise from Holland. Having gone in it to the laird of Touch's burial, it occasioned much speculation, and he was greatly censured for effeminacy. The late Newton used to tell that Commissioner Campbell got a chaise when he lived at Kilbride, about 1725 ; and being one day at Newton, he requested his host to go with him to Kilbride to meet some friends. By the way, the Commissioner, who drove, expatiated on the comforts of a wheel-carriage. But as they were going very fast, one of the wheels struck against a grey stone, and they were both thrown out. Newton, being much bruised, took leave of his neighbour in very bad humour, wishing him much good of his carriage.

They were, however, not very numerous till after 1745. Few people could afford a coach-and-six; and they who might well have kept a chaise, considered it as an idle expense, and an effeminate conveyance for gentlemen. They indeed appeared to much greater advantage on horseback.

Livery servants were formerly confined to people of fortune and fashion.[1] They seem to have succeeded the armed retainers who accompanied our ancient barons in peace as well as war. In point of industry and real usefulness, both were probably on a footing; but our spruce powdered lackeys have at least the negative merit of being less ferocious and bloody-minded than the armed retainers of old. Be that as it may, in the last age people of

---

[1] In a pamphlet in answer to Bishop Burnet's charges against the S... bishops, it is asserted that only one of them, beside the Archbishop of St. Andrews, had servants in livery. Whether Bishop Leighton's men wore livery or not, they had, according to tradition, the vices of the party and fraternity. As they durst not be seen tippling in town, they persuaded their master that his horses would only drink in a burn two miles above town, where there was an alehouse. At last, teased with their irregularity, he allowed them free egress and regress, provided they neither looked home nor in. One day that he had a suit of new clothes drenched in the rain, he said not an angry word to the fellow who had neglected to bring his cloak at the hour appointed. On a gentleman's wondering at so much meekness, the Bishop smiled and said, "What? would you have me lose my own temper too?" We shall give another anecdote of this excellent man. A young woman, the widow of a minister in his diocese, to whom he had been exceedingly kind, took it into her head that the Bishop was deeply in love with her. Finding he was long of breaking his mind, she went to ... Horning, a lonely walk by the water side, where he used to meditate, and his asking her commands, "Oh, my lord," said she, "I had a revelation last night." "Indeed!" answered he, "I hardly imagined you would ever be so highly honoured; what is it?" "That your lordship and I were to be married together." "Have a little patience," replied the Bishop, in no wise abashed, "till I have a revelation too."

condition[1] could easily afford livery servants, wages being low,[2] and the expense of their maintenance, in the old style, a trifle. The liveries were, however, abundantly gaudy and costly. But within the last forty years country gentlemen of moderate fortune had no footman, contenting themselves with a maid to wait at table.[3] On going from home, they took a labouring servant, in his ordinary apparel, to ride before their cloak-bag. It is true, some persons whose vanity was excessive, used, upon ceremonious occasions, to clap a livery coat upon a ploughman or gardener. The appearance of this temporary footman at table, or on a journey, was sometimes as grotesque and laughable as that of Scrub in the play.[4]

[1] Mr Abercromby used in his youth to be frequently at Cullen House with Lord Chancellor Findlater, who lived in all the state of the preceding age. He had always ten or a dozen footmen in full liveries, fat jolly fellows, for his lordship neither liked lean men nor lean horses. After breakfasting at eight, everybody amused himself as he pleased, in riding, walking, fishing, &c., a latitude seldom allowed guests in these ceremonious times. About noon the company began to arrive, and were received in the hall by the footmen, who carried them either to the library or the garden. Dinner was served precisely at one, and his lordship sat at table conversing cheerfully till five, when he retired, and did not appear again till supper at eight.

[2] Leckie told me that one M'Culloch, who had been in his grandfather's service from eleven years of age, was not only a good gardener, but very dexterous at serving a table, and withal a notable groom and cook. He planted all the trees about the place, which are about a century old. Yet with all this versatility of genius he had only forty shillings a-year of wages. He died in 1742, aged more than fourscore.

[3] Archibald Stirling of Keir remembered when hardly any of the Glasgow merchants had footmen.

[4] Of old, eminent Edinburgh writers, in taking a progress through their clients in the country, used to make one of their apprentices ride before their cloak-bag in place of a footman. The late Sir Hugh Paterson told me that, when he was a boy, a writer came to Bannockburn attended by a genteel young man. Old Sir Hugh having spied him from the windows sauntering about,

And now of country seats. The houses in request two or three centuries ago were mostly in the castle or tower style, which was then considered as connected with birth and station. And hence, whilst feudal notions universally prevailed, even persons of moderate estate affected to copy the great barons, if not in the size, at least in the fashion, of their houses. There was no doubt much occasion for places of strength; and though towers or fortalices could not stand a regular siege, they sufficed to repel a sudden attack from freebooters or private enemies. We had them in this country of all sizes, from the royal castles, whose age is unknown, to the towers built by the feuars in the sixteenth century.

There was, however, a general resemblance in those buildings, they being commonly square or oblong, of considerable height, with very thick walls. The approaching them in a hostile manner was rendered exceedingly difficult and dangerous. A moat surrounded the tower or castle; and an iron door, consisting of massive bars, secured the entrance, which was purposely narrow. The windows near the ground were small and strongly grated; and for security against fire, the under storey was vaulted. Nor were they worse contrived for offence. From the turrets in the angles and above the door, as well as from the battlements, shot and other missile weapons could be discharged at the assailants, whilst those within were under cover.

asked who it was, and finding it a cousin of his own, Row of Invernallan ● ● n made the lad come in, and set him at dinner above his master.

In the first flat there was a spacious hall for the purposes of hospitality. As that is the darling virtue of every half-improved people, so it was intimately connected with the policy of our ancient barons. The caressing of vassals and dependants being indispensably necessary in times of anarchy and feuds, no expense was grudged to have a capacious room to receive them. And in order to have victuals dressed for such great companies, the kitchen in some of the large castles was spacious and lofty. If, however, the public rooms exceeded in size, the bedchambers were in the opposite extreme, being rather closets than rooms. It seems strange to us how, in an age of boundless hospitality, people were accommodated all night in the old castles or towers. But the family took little room, and the neighbouring gentlemen seldom thought of sleeping out of their own beds; or, upon a pinch, they made no scruple of wrapping themselves in a plaid or in blankets, and of sleeping contentedly upon the floor of the hall.

In most towers the *pit*, or thieves' hole, was beneath ground, though sometimes it was above, in the form of an oven, without a ray of light, and only a hole for the admission of prisoners. These pits were, however, a reproach to humanity, confinement in them being too great a punishment *before* conviction for almost any crime. And in the hands of men whose resentment knew no bounds, they proved engines of horrid oppression. There, in the aristocratical times, many helpless innocents were allowed to languish unheard, victims of the malice or caprice of petty tyrants. There, too, private enemies, taken with arms in their hands, were ungenerously thrown, without any regard to rank or merit. In process of time those enormities were corrected in the low country, but they subsisted in the Highlands within the memory of the last generation. And all over Scotland *pits* were accounted legal prisons for thieves and other meaner criminals till the Jurisdiction Act passed.

After the union of the crowns in the person of James VI., places of strength were no longer necessary to repel the inroads of the English, and the King would not suffer his subjects to spill one another's blood in private war. Of course a tower or castle was chiefly esteemed as a mark of dignity and consideration. In the after-part of that reign, the art of peace being generally cultivated, a set of new wants and wishes took place among our nobility and gentry. In order, therefore, to have accommodation for guests, additions were made to the towers, either behind or at a side, which gave them frequently a mean and awkward look. But in those days convenience and snugness were more considered than beauty or symmetry.

Although some of the people who, in the fifteenth and sixteenth centuries, obtained lands in feu-farm, built houses in imitation of the lesser barons, a great majority of them were contented with houses of a simpler, less expensive construction. The King's feuars were specially bound to build and maintain a hall, a chamber, and a kitchen, by which was understood a house of two storeys. It was not, however, necessary that their hall should be lofty or large enough to entertain a country. Indeed, if we may judge of the hall-houses in these times from some remaining specimens, no compliment is due to the taste or liberality of their founders, many of whom were well-born and easy in their circumstances.

The civil wars that broke out in the reign of Charles I. gave a fatal check to the useful and liberal arts. People's money and attention were, in those wretched times, engrossed by very different considerations. Indeed a very great proportion of the nobility and gentry were either ruined or reduced to straits. Nor did the restoration of the Royal family, and with it the blessings of peace, render them easy in their circumstances. Whatever was the cause, a very mean style of architecture, both in public and private buildings, prevailed in Scotland between the Restoration and the Union.[1] In many cases there was a motley compound of Gothic and modern—turrets and battlements being affected by people that never dreamt of defending their houses. Small windows and turnpike stairs were also retained, whilst the great hall, which had been the glory of the old houses, was greatly curtailed. It was indeed incompatible with an additional

---

[1] The works of Sir William Bruce are an illustrious exception—elegance, strength, and convenience being combined in them. They surely contributed to introduce a better taste. It is a tradition in the family that when his plan of Broomhall House was about to be executed, Lady Jane Bruce, who then managed the affairs of the family, clipped with her scissors the breadth of her apron off the principal rooms. She thought the plan too great for the estate.

number of bedchambers, and other conveniences unknown or despised by their forefathers.

The lowness of the roofs and the littleness of the
public rooms were probably copied from the Edinburgh houses. So soon as our country gentlemen gave
up their own fashions, they would naturally borrow
from that place. With a few exceptions, however, its
buildings did no honour to the capital of a kingdom
that once made no inconsiderable figure in the affairs
of Europe. This was at first owing to its lying exposed to the ravages of the English, who repeatedly
burnt part of it. Besides, till the year 1540, the
public offices and courts of judicature followed the
person of the King, who often resided at his other
palaces. If the accession of James VI. to the
throne of England removed all apprehension of conquest and invasion, it gave fatal check to the splendour
and prosperity of Edinburgh. It could no longer be
expected that our great men would build stately
houses in a town that was seldom or never to be
honoured with the royal presence. And as the sessions
of the Scottish Parliament were of very short duration,
the members contented themselves with such accommodation as the place afforded. They, indeed, longed
to return to their country seats, where they appeared
to the greatest advantage.

It would not be incurious to inquire how the members were lodged during the Union Parliament. We
should probably trace peers of the realm to very indifferent houses, and very respectable gentlemen to some

dirty close or alley, inhabited at present · by low tradesmen.[1]

But after the Union, when, from a combination of causes, Scotland revived apace, our country gentlemen began to show some inclination for better houses. Architecture was now studied as a science, both by private gentlemen [2] and by professional men. Though inferior in genius to Sir William Bruce, they agreed with him in reprobating the Gothic style in all its branches. If they seldom reached magnificence or elegance, absurd clumsy ornaments were exploded, nor were the rules of proportion violated, unless where economical motives interfered. For, spite of all the architect could say, the public rooms were sometimes much too small, and a foot or two of height cut off the principal storey.

It is remarkable that whilst a taste for better houses gained ground all over the country, the people of Edinburgh should hardly ever think of altering their style of building. Even within the last thirty or forty years the Lords of Session and the principal lawyers lived in houses that their clerks would now be ashamed of.[3]

[1] The Duke of Montrose at that time lived in a timber land in the head of Niddry's Wynd. It became afterwards the property of James Wright, the extractor, who said his living there was like wearing the Duke's old coat.

[2] The last Earl of Mar had a great turn for architecture, and was always ready to give his neighbours advice. Tullibody, Tillicoultry, and Blairdrummond Houses are said to have been built upon his plans. The Rebellion of 1715 broke out ere his additions to Alloa House were finished.

[3] In the end of last century our most eminent lawyers seem to have been very poorly accommodated. Lord President Dalrymple said one day to James Wright, "It was easy to make rich when I was at the bar. Though my

Upon getting good houses, a better style of finishing came into request. Though in some old-fashioned rooms there were ceilings stuccoed in an expensive manner, yet threescore years ago many private gentlemen were satisfied with having the joists smoothed, and covering them with thin deals. The walls of rooms were sometimes covered with arras, but more frequently common plaster whitened sufficed. And the windows were composed of small triangular pieces of glass, joined together with lead, like what was in church windows very lately. But by degrees great changes took place in houses lately built and in such as were modernised. People got the ceilings lathed and plastered, their rooms finished with wainscot or fir, and sashed windows hung with pulleys. But carpets being little used,[1] they were the more nice with regard to the wood and workmanship of the floors. To give them a better look, these were waxed and rubbed very hard, which made them almost as slippery as glass. In this stage of improvements, the painting and papering of rooms were very little known in the country.

If we may judge from some pieces of old furniture, the cabinetmakers of old were as fond of the Gothic and the cumbrous as the masons themselves. But though they were employed by persons of rank and fortune,

practice and office brought me in 20,000 merks a-year. I lived in a hundred pound house £5, 6s. 8d. sterling. I had only two roasts in the week viz. Sunday and Thursday."

[1] Mr Abercromby says when he was a boy at Edinburgh the first carpet he saw was in Sir Thomas Nicholson's house, who had lived much abroad.

the bulk of our country gentlemen were very easily pleased in that article—their tables, chairs, and bedsteads being commonly wainscot or plane-tree, more remarkable for strength than elegance. Indeed they seldom thought of going further than some wright in the next town. And bed and window curtains were composed of stuffs manufactured at home and made up by the ladies of the family, assisted, perhaps, by a tailor. Half a century ago, the upholsterer business was in very low repute in Edinburgh.[1] And therefore, whoever wanted silk or damask furniture of the newest fashion, or mahogany chairs, tables, and cabinetwork, found it expedient to commission them from London. But so soon as a demand for genteel furniture increased, upholsterer-shops were set up by people regularly bred in London.

In the last age the environs of country seats were abundantly plain and primitive. The smoothing of nature and concealing her lesser deformities were then little thought of. On approaching a laird's dwelling, the stable, byre, and dunghill at the very door,[2] presented themselves to view ; and all around

---

[1] John Howden, the famous fanatic, was the first excellent tradesman in that way in Scotland. He wrought much at Blairdrummond, which was elegantly furnished at an early period, John Drummond of Quarrole having sent his brother, both from London and Flanders, much rich furniture at different times. When the young ladies teased John at his work, he called them, in great wrath, "the children of Ashdod." He would have extirpated with fire and sword all that were not of his opinion, who, by the most liberal computation, never exceeded a hundred. Withal he was a Jacobite, styling George II. the *occupant*, &c.

[2] Little-houses are of no great antiquity. Within the last threescore years a member of Parliament from this county would not use one at London,

was a plentiful crop of nettles, docks, and hemlock. The unsettled state of the country, and the embarrassed circumstances of most country gentlemen, afford, however, some apology for their parsimony and slovenliness in this article.

In many cases the house was set down awkwardly on the very extremity of the estate, next the most powerful or turbulent neighbour, whichever of them was likeliest to encroach. And in old houses, which are usually very narrow, one seldom finds windows to the north, even where the prospect is pleasant and picturesque, and nothing to be seen to the south but a hill, a moor, or a morass.[1] It appears, indeed, that shelter and the kindly influence of the sun were in higher estimation with our forefathers than a fine landscape.[2] It is, however, strange, that men who defied the bitterest blasts in the open air, and in other respects piqued themselves on hardiness, should have guarded with so much anxiety against the intrusion of the northern blasts.

If we may judge from the castles of some of the

going either to the fields or some alley, which made the common Fr... think him maddish. When Lord Milton was at Dalwhinny in Strathe... the goat whey, he erected a temporary one, but no sooner was he g... carriage to go away, than the people pulled it down as an abomination

[1] Before Colonel Edmondstoune built his house, there was scarcely a gen... man on the banks of the Teith that had a full prospect of the river f... windows. Even at Lanrick, which was within fifty yards of it, the... houses entirely obstructed the view.

[2] Lord Kames used to tell of a neighbour in the Merse who having so... vista on Home Castle, asked a countrywoman if she saw you through the trees! "See what!" said she. "Home Castle," said the other. "A great distance of that! I cannot go out to make my burn without seeing H... Castle"

more considerable barons, the beauties of nature were
by no means neglected in the earlier ages. And indeed, when men are neither warped by fantastic imitation nor depressed in their circumstances, they are
seldom destitute of that taste which is intimately connected with good sense. Taking the royal castles for
their pattern, they chose romantic situations, from
whence there was a full prospect of the country
around. Even in their state of ruin and decay there
is something that commands respect. Some analogy
may be discerned between their founders' temper of
mind and the site of those castles. Both were bold
and stately, superior to minute decorations.

But the middling and smaller gentry that sprang
up in great numbers during the fifteenth and sixteenth
centuries, seem to have adopted the style of the religious houses, which were generally set down in low
sheltered situations, near some lake or river. Their
embellishments without doors were professedly copied
from the convents, where, before the Reformation,
the arts of polished life were chiefly studied. Though
it was natural for the laity to consult the monks in
whatever related to taste, the latter stuck close to
their own models, without attempting to suit their
plans to the character and circumstances of the persons for whom they were designed. High walls, and
venerable trees overshadowing the windows, were
doubtless congenial to the monastic state, which professed to exclude the world from its view. But as
the gentry were a free, open-hearted people, enemies

to gloom and constraint, their country seats should
have been rendered cheerful and airy, without giving
up altogether shelter and snugness. It requires, however, original genius, together with ease and affluence,
for men accustomed to a beaten track to strike out a
new though more natural one. And in the Popish
times, laymen were the more easily reconciled to
sombre dwellings that, notwithstanding vows of mortification, the cloister was the seat of festivity and
abundance. There the neighbouring gentry used to
be sumptuously entertained at the three great festivals of Christmas, Whitsunday, and Easter.[1]

Whatever may have been their origin, it was the
practice, within the last fourscore years, to have
courts enclosed with high walls, pillars with massive
gates and iron bolts, which seemed to bespeak dis-
trust and apprehension on the part of the proprietor.
The trees stood also so near the house that they rendered it damp and darksome. Had these either been
planted in avenues, or scattered through the fields

---

[1] It was the custom of old to lock the gates and admit no visitors at certain
times. Mr Abercromby told me that a number of years ago, walking with
the late Sir Thomas Kirkpatrick in his gallery at Closeburn which was afterwards burned by accident, he asked for whom the portrait decked with
ribbons was intended. "He was," said Sir Thomas, "a son of this family, a
merchant in London, who, coming to make a visit to his brother, happened
to arrive at dinner time, when the gates were shut, and the keys carried to
the hall. After knocking a while, the laird sent out word that in the time of
dinner he would not open the gates for the King. 'Well,' said the merchant, 'tell my brother that I will put a better dinner past his hearing that
ever stood on his board.' He went over to Drumlanrig Castle, where his
sister was lady, and dinner being over, was admitted without difficulty. It
is said the family of Queensberry is now possessed of a handsome estate that
came to it by the caprice of the merchant.

at some distance, they would have produced a fine effect.

The policy of feuing out the Crown and Church lands, which was at its height in the sixteenth century, proved exceedingly favourable to the planting of trees. Though commonly confined to a small spot hard by the house, it must ere long have altered the appearance of the country very much to the better. The frequency of the plantations compensated in some degree for their want of size. Half a century ago this part of the country was perfectly to the taste of Mr Addison, who held an open unenclosed country, interspersed with houses and clumps of trees, to be the most beautiful and picturesque of any. We are far from condemning the improvements that have taken place of late years. The poet and landscape-painters see things in a very different light from the gentleman farmer of the present times, who regards enclosing as essential to the security of his crops, and mere beauty as a very secondary consideration.

In fact a number of our best trees were undoubtedly planted by feuars of one denomination or another. Nor are we to wonder at it. The very idea of property operated in all probability with greater force than the rules and regulations prescribed to the King's feuars. A tenant is seldom any friend to the rearing of trees, his attention being confined to crops suited to his lease and abilities; nor will he willingly labour when he knows that another man is to reap the fruits of his toil and care. Whereas he who obtains a perpetuity, extends, by an easy transition, his views to future times. To him it is a matter of little consequence whether his son or grandson be to benefit from his plantations. If the profit be remote, his pleasure in making them and marking their progress is immediate as well as continued.

In many cases a shrewd guess of the age of the feu may be formed from that of the oldest trees, where these have not suffered from avarice or false taste. When there are well-grown trees of different ages, the younger ones may commonly be referred to some second founder of the family, concerning whom traditions are preserved. The want of authentic registers of the age and progress of trees is much to be regretted. Strange that naturalists should pay so great attention to shrubs and flowers, things of short duration, and yet suffer fruit and forest trees the noblest productions of the vegetable world—to pass almost unheeded! At best, we can only trace them by means of tradition, which is too uncertain a guide to warrant any conclusions.

Though within memory of man the trees of this country have suffered great havoc, some fine ones still remain—monuments of the skill and industry of our forefathers. One can hardly forbear a wish that some legal restraint was laid on the greed or caprice of landed men. A noble tree is in some measure a matter of public concern ; nor ought its proprietor to be allowed wantonly to strip his country of its fairest ornament.

The orchard, which usually lay near the house, was the chief ornament of the place without doors, whether great or small. Around it also stood the forest-trees —these having been fenced from cattle while young, and afterwards spared as a screen to the fruit-trees. Our forefathers appear to have been well acquainted with this branch of gardening—the old orchards being generally well sheltered, of a rich soil, and stored with the best native kinds. They, indeed, needed only to take a pattern from the abbey gardens,[1] which were the only thing that escaped the fury of the Reformers, and continued in perfection long after the dispersion of the monks. In the orchard our old gentry had a little cutting-grass for horses and cows, as well as the little kitchen-stuff then used.[2] The dunging and digging about the roots of the fruit-trees must have promoted their growth and fertility ; and the great size of the barren trees was probably owing to the nourishment they derived from the rich garden-mould.

Such was the style of country seats in the first part of the present century. Yet in those unadorned mansions did content and hospitality and elevation of mind dwell with pleasure. Though most of them have been transmogrified of late years, Lanrick and

---

[1] It seems odd that the monks, who were certainly good gardeners, should often plant fruit-trees without grafting. To that, however, we probably owe the Achan, Muir-fowl-egg, and other Scots pears. It was surely the likeliest way to have wretched fruit. The Abbot's Tree in Pittencrieff garden, hard by Dunfermline Abbey, is a noble one ; but its age, size, and the *badness* of the kind show it to have been ungrafted.

[2] In a pamphlet published about ninety years ago, the East Lothian farmers are advised to have yards for kail and leeks. As for *bowkail* and *sybows*—i.e., cabbage and onions—they cannot expect to raise these.

Old Newton remain in their primitive state, and show how easy it was to please the last generation. But as places that have been a while neglected present a very inadequate notion of the old inhabitants and their modes of life, he who wishes to see things that will shortly be found no more, should visit Clackmannan Castle. There he will still find the house, the furniture, and the environs in all the simplicity of former times, yet not without an air of dignity ; and what is more rare and precious, he will see in the lady a living specimen of the style and manners of the last age.

Though we seldom characterise the living, there is little danger of committing any mistake with regard to this venerable matron, who is now near the end of her course. She is a proof of what may be done by that exemplary management which seeks to save that it may have the more to bestow on worthy purposes. With a very moderate income, she has for many years —both in her husband's time and in her widowhood— seen a great deal of good company in her house, besides giving plentifully to her indigent neighbours. Her plain hearty meals, seasoned with kindness and care, are more pleasing to a sentimental guest than the studied refinements of the vain and luxurious. She never changed her fashions, but adhered strictly to the maxims and economics that prevailed in her younger days; and in her house there is no waste, nor any of those modish innovations which straiten other people without having any show. When on the borders of fourscore, she used to rise at six in the morning to see that everything was in order.[1]

We shall now mention a few circumstances relative to the first essays in embellishing and enclosing about gentlemen's houses in this country.

Though the King, as well as some of his nobles, had *parks*[2] at a very early period, these were probably of the same nature with the English ones, intended for venison and sport. The idea of enclosing land for winter crops, or for fattening domestic animals, is

---

[1] Her husband was a steady, honest, gallant man, much respected by those that differed widely from him in matters of principle. He was remarkably taciturn, seldom opening his lips till he had drunk a couple of bottles, when he became a very facetious, pleasing companion : this the lady called *loosing* the laird's tongue. A neighbouring lady wrote him that she understood he had shot one of her husband's hawks ; that though Sir John was in great wrath, yet if he would come to their house (where he never visited) and ask pardon on his knees, she would endeavour to make his peace. He returned her this laconic answer : "Supposing I had shot the hawk, rather than do what you require, I would shoot the hawk, Sir John, and your ladyship." The entertaining guests was therefore the lady's province. Dr Parker, parson of St James's, being in the neighbourhood, was carried to see the castle and its inhabitants. At taking leave, he invited them (as he did many others) to his parsonage house. To which unmeaning compliment the lady answered : "It is not likely, Doctor, we will ever be in London unless there should be a coronation of *our own*; in which case we will certainly wait on you at the parsonage house of St James's."

[2] Charter of excambion, David, King of Scots, whereby, in recompense of the two *parks* of Stirling and the lands of Strougarthrie, he grants to Robert of Erakyn, knight, his Majesty's well-beloved confederate, and Christian of Keith, his Majesty's cousin, the lands of Alloa and Gabbardston, with the isle of Clackmannan and the lands of Bornhaugh, in the forest of Clackmannan, with the hail grass of the hail forest ; the lands of Ferryton, with his Majesty's *park* of Clackmannan,—dated in the thirty-fifth year of his reign. In Sir Duncan Campbell of Glenorchy's private memoirs, it is said that in 1621 the great *park* at Finlarig was finished. And in 1622, William M'Ilroy, son of James M'Ilroy, in park of Keir, renounces, in favour of Sir Archibald Stirling of Keir, a tack of the forestership and keeping of the wood and *park* of Keir, and the 40s. land belonging thereto.

probably not very ancient. Nor did the law of Charles II. produce much immediate effect in this country.[1] And thus, at the Union, the fields were generally open, and ploughed up to the very door of a gentleman's house.

William Edmondstoune of Cambuswallace was a remarkable character in his day. Instead of spending his time in country sports, or carousing with his neighbours,[2] he delighted in rural occupations and embellishments, when these were in very low repute among his countrymen. At an early period of life[3] he planted the hill behind his house, which formed in time a beautiful amphitheatre of wood that did no discredit to his taste and skill as a planter. And he made a neat garden, and enclosed some fields below the house.[4]

---

[1] Lord Carden, or his son, made two enclosures at Keir; but even in the late James Stirling's time, these were either ploughed, or left out in... the *fattening* cattle in parks being as yet little known. His grandfather made a park soon after, which was long the only one betwixt Stirling and Dumbarton. And in Lanrick's minority, one of his enclosures was... the stones of which are said to have been carried in barrows across the T...

[2] It was not a little peculiar that he drank nothing but water... he was forty, after which he took to strong ale, which he had always in great perfection. To the last he used a cup in preference to a glass.

[3] Colonel Edmondstoune says Cambuswallace imbibed a taste for planting, &c., when he and the other gentlemen of Menteith accompanied the Marquis of Athole [in his raid] to Argyleshire. The Earl of Argyll had a little before made noble plantations at Inverary, which suffered much from the Marquis's Highland host, by whom some of the young trees were carried off.

[4] It was long believed by the country people that Cambuswallace's wraith, i.e., a spirit or phantom in his shape, was sometimes seen in the summer mornings before sunrise. This originated from his getting up before break of day to see that no cattle had got into his plantations; and having found a fellow breaking over his fences, he belaboured him soundly and then returned to his bed without being seen by the servants.

About 1725 he left Cambuswallace, which was then in great beauty,[1] having surrendered it to his son upon his marriage.   He lived afterwards in Stirling, where, while walking on the Castle hill, he used to cast many a wishful look towards his beloved plantations.   Nor did his taste for rural elegance forsake him even in a town.   He projected the back walk, as well as the plantations below it.   In spite of our late refinements on pleasure-ground, this walk must be allowed to be sweet and picturesque.   It was also one of the first in this country.   He died in 1748, aged eighty-nine.

As the rearing of forest-trees was his passion, his brother Coldoch took equal pleasure in making an excellent orchard.   But after decking up his little place, a graceless son poisoned his peace.   Twice, by his industry and parsimony, did he retrieve the estate ; and twice, by his misjudged indulgence, was it spent. He passed the latter part of his life at Cramond, where he had a salmon-fishing, which he turned to greater account than the people who succeeded him.

The last Earl of Mar proceeded upon a great scale. His gardens at Alloa were in the Dutch taste, on the model of Hampton Court, the favourite residence of King William.   They were very nicely kept, a master gardener and twelve men being constantly employed till after the forfeiture.   But though much visited and admired, they were too magnificent and expensive to

---

[1] At whatever time he began his operations, in 1723 he cut a tree of his own planting, which he intended for his coffin, but was laughed out of it.

be imitated by the country gentlemen of those times.
By their means, perhaps, the rearing and trimming
of hedges was first introduced among us. This nobleman planted great numbers of forest-trees. He
made, however, no enclosures for pasture; nor did
he attempt to meliorate or dress the fields around
the house.

Between 1720 and 1725, Sir John Erskine made very
considerable enclosures at Alva. Having been some
time in Parliament, he became a passionate admirer of
the English husbandry, though he had little partiality
to the persons or manners of that people. Though
originally a Whig, he entered warmly into Lord Mar's
resentments after the death of Queen Anne, and took
an active part in the Rebellion of 1715. He was a man
of wit and genius, but the heat and volatility of his
fancy would not be regulated by prudential considerations. His natural bent to speculation was greatly
encouraged by the discovery of a rich vein of silver,
that indeed might have intoxicated a man of more
coolness. But ere long he dissipated all that was
gotten from it in projects of mining and coal.

Though he was unfortunate in other things, his
enclosures were substantial, and in a few years turned
to great account in the hands of his creditors; and
the high rents got for them in grass induced others to
enclose lands. He had also the merit of introducing

[1] To it, however, he owed his pardon, it being imagined he was possessed
of valuable secrets about the Ochil mines.
[2] He was one of the first Scotsmen who attempted inland navigation,
having laid out largely on a canal between the Devon and his coal.

red clover into this country. Having made hay of a field of it without rag-grass, the country people, who admired none of his projects, called it *English weeds*, and would not believe that any beast would eat such black rotten-looking stuff. He made also large plantations, and projected, and in part executed, a handsome plan of policy [1] [grounds and plantations]. In short, this gentleman may be regarded as the prototype of those men of speculation who of late years have done some good and much mischief to their country, without benefiting themselves or their families.

Before purchasing the barony of Kincardine, James Drummond of Blair and his father intended to have built at the Firpark, near Blackdub. The house was founded in 1715, on a bare moorish farm, the occupiers of which were nicknamed the *grey meal* Murdochs, from the poverty of their grain. The stones, which were of bad quality, came from Craigarnal quarry. It was a bold, and in some measure a disinterested undertaking, for one to set down such a house in a situation where he could hardly expect to be sheltered by trees of his own rearing.[2] He

[1] One day, after his affairs were in confusion, walking out with a neighbour, he expatiated with much eloquence upon his policy and improvements. The other could not help saying, "Sir John, all this is very fine and very practicable, but it would require a princely fortune." To which the knight answered, "George, when I first formed my scheme of policy for this place, I was drawing such sums out of the mine that I could not help looking upon the Elector of Hanover as a small man."

[2] So bleak and unpromising did everything appear to old Boutcher, the nurseryman, who was then consulted in matters of taste, that he told Blair most insolently he would submit to be hanged on the first tree about the place that would bear his weight. And he *modestly* proposed lifting the house

therefore trusted to the industry and good fortune
of his posterity, in which his most sanguine wishes
have been gratified. The want of trees perhaps induced him to set down the house under shelter of
the hill to the north. Though he planted a great
deal, both about the house and at a distance, yet so
limited were the ideas of those times, that at his death,
in 1739, his enclosures for grass and tillage did not
exceed fifty acres, subdivided into small closes.

For some time after he succeeded to the estate, the
late George Drummond did little towards improvement of the place ; and when he began to enclose to a
considerable extent at Daira, it was chiefly with a view
to natural grass, which was then much in fashion.
In 1742 or 1743 he made a kitchen-garden upon a
more regular and extensive plan than any in this part
of the country ; the walls of it were faced with brick,
a material hitherto little used among us. And in
1750 he built a very small pine-house, the model of
which, and the plants, were brought from Logiealmond
by a young man who returned from England for
want of health. Yet in this trifling hut Daniel Stalker,
an excellent gardener, contrived to raise pine-apples
superior in size and flavour to any I have seen since.
Though Blairdrummond was then esteemed a neat
place, yet in its first stage of embellishment (to which

1000 yards north before he could give any plan of policy. The trees behind
the house were planted about 1720, in the wilderness style, except the larixes
which are eighteen years younger. These last were a present to Blair fr...
James Graham of Killearn, who got larix seed by mistake from a accidental.
They were sent over packed as warmly as greenhouse plants.

we here confine ourselves) it was very limited and in an indifferent taste.

Francis Lord Napier intended to have fixed the seat of his family at Ballinton. For which purpose, soon after marrying Lord Hopetoun's daughter, he rented Craighead House hard by, and began to make plantations, and to enclose his fields with hedges. But having imbibed a set of novel notions,[1] he could not think of living in the old house, which, though in the tower style, irregular and darksome, was roomy and substantial. It might at a very moderate expense have been fitted up for the accommodation of a large family. In an unlucky hour, therefore, he pulled it down, with a full purpose of building upon a more elegant plan—which, however, he found himself unable to do. The want of a house gave him a dislike to this country, where he had a very valuable property, of which he afterwards disposed piecemeal, at prices that were thought low at the time. He was one of the last persons of condition among us who feued out lands farm by farm. His leaving the country was a loss to it, he being a man of lively, pleasing conversation, and withal an excellent scholar. No man was more disposed to live on a sociable footing with his neighbours, and less attentive to punctilios of rank.

[1] His ideas were very much English. Whilst the affair of Norriestown Chapel was in agitation, he wrote the Presbytery signifying his disapprobation of settling a *curate* there. The brethren were exceedingly offended that their *ruling* elder should use a phrase so entirely Episcopal. Even his cousin, good Mr Archibald Napier, could not defend him.

In the year 1716 or 1717, Manour, my mother's father, began to plant trees near the house, but the hill was not planted till 1725. He got most of his tree seed from Blairlogie, which he raised in his own nursery. It was a beautiful dry situation,[1] preferable in many respects to Manour.[2] Yet there a most hospitable pleasant family lived long in much plenty and esteem. He died in 1729, on which the old house was abandoned, the last Manour living either in Stirling or at Pathfoot till 1747, that he built a small snug house at Airthrey. Conscious of his ignorance of country affairs, he contented himself while there with making a kitchen-garden, and having few acres in grass, without any corn farm, or adding to his father's small enclosures. He indeed spent the time which other men devote to rural occupations among his books. To the want of proper relish for a country life, rather than the extent of his debts, may be ascribed the rash sale of this sweet place to Captain Haldane.

[1] He exchanged Airthrey for Stonehill, a little place within pistol shot of Hopetoun House. The first Earl of Hopetoun tried every method to make his father sell it, and among the rest kindness. One day he came (as he often did) to dine with Manour, who was a genteel sensible man, and brought with him some company of the first rank. They were well received. On coming in from walking in the garden, the strangers were surprised to see the table covered with a coarse but clean tablecloth, and salt herrings set down. "Eat and welcome, my lords," said their host; "this is such fare as I can afford, and you shall have plenty of ale and brandy." The frolic took, and the company either were or appeared to be well pleased. But when dying he advised his son to sell or exchange.

[2] Manour, or Kingsnow House, had been a Roman station, some vestiges of the trenches being lately visible. It was part of the lordship of Stirling and feued by the Callenders about 1479. They held it 150 years, and are represented by Mr Callender, Depute Clerk of Session.

Let me here recall with pleasure, mingled with regret, the time I spent in my younger days at Airthrey with this good man. His candour, meekness, and benevolence, his piety and spotless morals, commanded the esteem of all that knew him; whilst his cheerful sweet disposition,[1] joined to a great fund of anecdote, rendered him an agreeable instructive companion. He unhappily dipped.too deep into polemical divinity, which, though it did not abate his charity towards those who were of a different opinion, exposed him in the decline of his faculties to the snares of Popish emissaries. He died in 1780, aged seventy-nine.

The old house of Tullibody stood nearly where the gardener's now does. It was built a few years before the Restoration by Mr Robert Meldrum, who made a figure among the Covenanters, and lived much in England. In point of shape it resembled the old house of Newton, being only larger. Mr Abercromby remembers it before his father demolished it in order to build the present house, which he set down in a

---

[1] Though a sober, almost an ascetic man, yet when he did take a glass he was generally the merriest in company. John Stirling of Keir, who had a sort of magic in his conversation, was one of the very few who could bring him into that jovial frame. When they were both young men at Edinburgh, a plot was laid to engage Manour in a riot. Accordingly, a party being formed, they went to Dalkeith, where the glass went so freely round that he soon became frolicsome, and had a démélé with Bailie Elphinston, who was going to commit him, had not Keir interposed. With great difficulty he was got back to Edinburgh, supported on his horse. Next morning Keir, with a grave face but much glee, began to recount his last night's adventures; when Manour in great confusion interrupted him, saying, "I am heartily ashamed of my behaviour; but say no more on that head. I have already asked the Almighty's pardon."

corn-ridge, there being at that time nothing enclosed about the place but an old orchard [1] to the west-ward. The old gentleman made the two kitchen-gardens on each side of the house, and enlarged the orchard [2] very considerably. Excepting the great oak near the stables, and a few more whose age is unknown, most of the trees are of his planting. He made a few small enclosures towards the Cambus : but nothing he did turned to more account than his fir woods, taken off the moor, which were enclosed and planted between 1725 and 1773. In less than fifty years they brought his family £5000 sterling.

Upon his lady's death in 1743 [3] he gave up the management of the estate to his son, and brought him and his daughter-in-law to Tullibody. From the time of their marriage they had lived at Menstry, [4] a place

[1] The lands of orchard of Tullibody are mentioned in the chartulary of Cambuskenneth in 1521. No expense had been spared in making it, there being in the heart of it a road of ground or thereby, paved two feet below the surface, which rises above the level of the other ground. Lighter moulds from another place had been laid atop of the pavement.

[2] He got an assortment of excellent plums from Holland, which are now worn out ; and the hurricanes in January 1773 blew down many large old pear and apple trees.

[3] She was dead before I remember, but by all accounts she was a kind hearted honest woman. And her husband was one of the pleasantest old men I ever knew. In an age of seriousness he was eminently pious. Whatever company was at his house, he made conscience of having family worship; morning and evening. He was weakly till past fifty, but for the last thirty years of his life he enjoyed excellent health. His only infirmity was deafness which he bore with great good-humour, never appearing jealous or curious to know what was said in conversation. He liked, however, to converse, with people that chose it, by means of a trumpet.

[4] Menstry was feued from the Argyll family by the father of the first Earl of Stirling. This nobleman had an uncommon share of taste for his time. He made a terrace-walk from Myretoun to Playgreen, which commanded a delightful prospect of the Forth and the country round. His other walks are also

of great capability, where the same money laid out in policy would have gone three times further than in the Carse. Some people, therefore, think it ought to have been the family seat.

After coming to Tullibody, his son made some capital improvements. Between 1745 and 1748 he enclosed and drained the wood ; and by grubbing out the bushes and coppice - roots, the remaining trees showed to great advantage. Upon this he laid out £500, which the crops of corn repaid, and the rent rose from £25 to £114 sterling. At different times he enclosed the sea greens and the skirts of the estate, which answered well. And by putting in a pier, he not only checked the encroachments of the tides, but also gained some excellent land from the river. The wall below the terrace was finished before 1745, and covered with the best fruits, particularly French pears, which were then rare.

Thirty years ago Tullibody was one of the neatest and best places in the country. It was, no doubt, in the very reverse of the present airy style. If, however, avenues and clipped hedges conveyed an idea of formality and constraint, they afforded shade and shelter both in heat and cold. And they were commonly disposed either to set capital objects in a striking point

---

pointed out, though the trees that shaded them have been cut down long ago. To give his fruit-trees the benefit of the reflected sun-rays, he planted them against a perpendicular rock to the north of the garden. Their roots were visible within Mr Abercromby's remembrance. In the civil wars the house with its battlements was burnt by the Covenanters. It was rebuilt by the Holburnes, one of whom, about 1700, planted an excellently assorted orchard.

of view or to hide deformities. An orchard on one side of the house contributed to warmth, and pleased the eye, both in fruit and flower, besides yielding a great rent in proportion to the ground. At the same time, Tullibody had a set of beauties which were independent of modes of taste. The river in sight of the windows, and the rich open fields of Bandeath, checkered with trees, presented a lawn more picturesque in summer than most of those that are made at a great expense by our modern artists skilled in perspective.

Perhaps I am partial to the place where I spent many of the happiest days of my youth—where I learned what no books can teach, and where I formed my earliest friendships and views of life. There is hardly a spot without or within doors that does not recall to my remembrance some pleasing incident relative to the living or the dead. I never knew a pair that enjoyed more rational felicity in a country life than Mr and Mrs Abercromby. This was owing in a great measure to the social and sober virtues being happily blended together.

About 1724, Alexander Bruce of Kennet,[1] in the

[1] I never saw the last Kennet, but his neighbours speak of him with affection and respect. In his youth he had been a soldier and a free liver, but afterwards he took an opposite turn, and became exceedingly zealous for the interests of religion. A question having occurred in the Assembly, whether a minister deposed for fornication should be repossed on giving evidence of his contrition, Kennet contended violently against it. He thought such a man could be of no use, purity being indispensable to the ministerial character. Mr Ramsay of Kelso then rose, and after reprobating the sin, said he always understood our Church admitted of repentance in that case. "Else, Moderator, how many burning and shining lights would this house want to-day?" "This is intolerable," said Kennet, in a rage. "Wait a little," said Ramsay, dryly,

lifetime of his father, the Brigadier, set about making a new place at Brucefield.[1] It was seemingly a wild undertaking to set down a house upon the top of a moor without a tree. The want of natural beauties was the more striking for its being so near a rich variegated country. His plantations, however, answered beyond expectation, having in less than half a century produced more than the value of the lands in their natural state. The reclaiming moss by burning and draining has all along been the chief means of improvement. It affords, no doubt, an immediate return, but is neither so permanent nor profitable in the long-run as forest-trees. In the garden, which lies on a warm south bank, the last Kennet used to raise the earliest and best kitchen crops in the country. And upon a gable of the house he had a peach-tree which produced plenty of well-flavoured fruit, a thing uncommon at that time in the country. It may, however, be questioned whether the family gained essentially by making Brucefield. The same money and attention bestowed upon their old seat threescore years ago, would have made a far better return, even in the article of timber. About the year 1758 or 1759, Lord Kennet sold Brucefield to the late James Abercromby, who took a strong attachment to it. But

"I am not come the length of the ruling elders, being only among my own brethren."

[1] The very name "Brucefield" was new, it being part of the barony of Hartshaw, which belonged to a family of Stewarts. David Stewart, Dominus de Hartshaw, is a witness to a deed in 1422. Their castle stood near the mill, but has long been ruinous. Their orchard was paved like that of Tullibody. The arms were the same with the Rossyth family.

his embellishments and improvements were mostly posterior to the period under review.

Henry Cunningham of Boquhan owed his preferments chiefly to his having opposed in 1713 the commitment of Sir Robert Walpole to the Tower. Upon the latter being made Prime Minister, he did not forget those who had stood by him in the time of persecution. Though a bustling political man all his life, Mr Cunningham was passionately fond of Boquhan, the place [1] where he had gathered birds' nests while a boy. And therefore, when a taste for policy and improvements became fashionable, he got plans from Boutcher, the nurseryman, for laying out and decorating his grounds. His operations were well advanced when he was called to the government of Jamaica, which, however, he enjoyed a very short time, having died there in 1736, the year after his arrival.

He was a man of pleasant manners and great address, being reputed the best boroughmonger in his time. There was no doubt sound policy, as well as an appearance of goodness of heart, in the attention that he showed to his constituents. He did not, like many of his brethren, make an evident distinction between the first and last year of a Parliament, but was uniformly courteous and kind. And hence, though a professed ministerialist, he was esteemed by a set of neighbours that were either hostile to the family of

[1] When going about his farm, he used to wear a black kilt coat and a blue bonnet like a common farmer. He also took great pleasure in binding peas and beans, and in forking corn to his stacks.

Hanover or in opposition to Sir Robert Walpole. Notwithstanding the lucrative employments conferred upon him at different times, he appears to have been no gainer by parliamenteering and a London life— the estate being sold by a judicial sale, after his death, for the payment of his debts.

About the year 1715, Dr Murray of Struan, father of the late Lady George Murray, made some enclosures at Arnhall. After her daughter's marriage, his widow did a good deal to improve and adorn the place, under the direction of Lord George, who had an active turn and a strong bent to husbandry.[1] A number of hedges were planted and kept very neat. The kitchen-garden, finished about 1740, was probably the first in this corner where wall-trees were regularly trained and dressed. The house remained without alteration, no bad specimen of the half-tower, half-monastery style. Lord George's engaging in the Rebellion of 1745 put a fatal stop to all his projects.

His lady[2] was a virtuous respectable woman, who

[1] Abercairney told me that, being at Arnhall with James Duke of Athole and some other company, Lord George proposed a walk before dinner to see his *labouring*. "What!" said a gentleman, "has your lordship a labouring here too?" "Ay," said the Duke, "he has a labouring here, another at Tullibardine, a third at Glencarse, and a fourth in Glenalmond; and for all that he does not thrive."

[2] Her grandmother and mother were successively heiresses of Arnhall. At a time when all our ladies prided themselves upon their hospitality and kindness, the former outdid them all in kindness. It was her maxim that everybody who came to her house was hungry; for which reason, whether high or low, she did all she could to cram them. Though her daughter, the last Lady Struan, fell far short of her, she outdid anything I ever met with in that way. Having, when a boy, been at Arnhall with my father, she made me eat most plentifully of her good things, and at going away crammed my pockets with fruit and sweetmeats till I was hardly able to walk.

bore the misfortunes of her family with the fortitude
and equanimity of a Roman matron.   I never saw
her till just before her son became Duke of Athole,
when she behaved with a temperance and humility
which showed what excellent use she had made of
adversity.

Forty years ago Kippenross was much admired for
neatness as well as natural beauties.   In the beginning
of the fifteenth century it was the seat of the Kinrosses—a considerable family, in whose possession it
remained till about 1630, when Pearson, Dean of Dunblane, purchased it.   The old trees, which have all
along been the glory of the place, were in all probability of their planting.   Hugh Pearson, or his eldest
brother, enclosed a good deal of ground with stone-
dikes or hedges, but the most remarkable thing done
by the former was the walk by the side of the river,
made in 1742, and probably the second artificial one
of any extent in this country.   He died in 1749;[1]
and in her son's minority great havoc was made
among the planting, particularly a row of noble trees

[1] In those days there were three things remarkable for size about Kippenross—viz. the laird, the great plane-tree, and a bottle which was occasionally
brought into the room by two men on a barrow. The laird was an honest
good humoured man, passionately fond of society. Keir having asked a gentleman whom he met near Calder how Kippenross was, the other answered,
"Very well. He got a christening t'other day at James Russell's; and if he
gets a burial or two, it will put him on to Yule." He was of enormous size.
A person told the same gentleman "he was not unlike the Duke of Cumberland, if he had Kippenross in his wame." The age of the great tree is uncertain, but in 1740 a widow Gillespie, who had lived all her life about the place
said she remembered no odds on it for more than seventy years, though she
was sensible of an alteration upon most of the other trees.

on the side of the road to Dunblane, that were cut down in 1760. The family was then in no want of money ; nor did the price of the trees compensate for the irreparable damage done to the place. There are no vestiges of the tower of the Kinrosses; for the house, burnt in the late John Pearson's time, had been built by the first of the Pearsons soon after the purchase.

There was an old house at Powis which resembled that of Newton. It formerly belonged to Stirling of Herbertshire,[1] from whom it was acquired by William Mayne in Cambus for his second son Edward. He got the money from his brother Edward, who was an eminent merchant at Lisbon.[2] This gentleman acted a sensible, generous part towards his relations in Scotland. To some of them he gave liberally in his own time ;[3] others he introduced into business; and he left

[1] I have heard Newton say Powis was liferented by a lady who had other two jointures. Having lived to a very great age, upon her death a lock was put on her coffin, and keys sent to the three fiars.

[2] Mr Abercromby says that Robert Anderson, the founder of the family, was born in a house behind the kirk of Tullibody. It seems he would not submit to sit upon the black stool for having got a girl with child ; whereupon he ran away, and went to sea. After a variety of adventures, he became a shipmaster, and afterwards settled at St Lucar, in Spain, as a merchant. He sent over for Edward Mayne, son of John Mayne in Cambus, who married his sister. The latter afterwards removed to Lisbon.

[3] Whilst William lived at Cambus, his brother used yearly to send him over from Lisbon a hogshead of white wine and a parcel of sweetmeats. The former stood near the fire and was drunk out of bickers, and the latter was given to the ploughmen for *kitchen*. One day a fellow chawing sweetmeats was heard saying, "This is excellent, but indeed my teeth *lair* in it." [It is impossible to define the Scots word "kitchen" by any English equivalent. "Relish" comes nearest to express its meaning, but it is not comprehensive enough. "Kitchen" includes anything that may make the staple articles of food, such as bread, meat, or potatoes, more palatable. To "lair" is to sink as in a bog.]

a large sum of money to be divided after his death among the rest, in shares sufficient to make them easy and independent. William was a pleasant, worthy, intelligent countryman, and lived all along in great familiarity with the neighbouring gentry. After leaving Cambus he dwelt for some time at Logie, which he purchased from one Forrester. He was four times married, and had a very numerous offspring, some of whom rose high in the great world. Died about the year 1740.

In 1746 or 1747 his son Edward built a modern house at Powis, in place of the old one. Though his policy was very limited, on account of the richness of the ground, he had the merit, at an early period, of dressing up his doors neatly and airily. He was an honourable well-intentioned man, of unbounded philanthropy. His abuse of words,[1] and ignorance of the ways of the world, joined to a *naïveté* peculiar to himself, made his friends sometimes smile, without lessening their esteem. In 1745 he commanded a company of seceders; and as he acted from principle in taking it up, so he showed good sense and humanity in laying down his commission.[2] He was an excellent magis-

---

[1] One day, at a justice of peace court, a number of people were fined, at the instance of Ireland, the stamp-master, about yarn, linseed, &c. After the business was over, Mr Mayne interceded for some of the delinquents, who, he alleged, had transgressed from ignorance. "Oh," said Ireland, very petulantly, "you are now *functus.*" "*Functus,* fellow!" answered Mr Mayne, in a rage; "do you say I stink!" and kicked him down stairs.

[2] After Culloden, General Blakeney sent for him and the other militia captains, and said it was the Duke's desire that they should continue in arms and apprehend the straggling rebels. "General," said Mr Mayne, "whilst the rebels threatened our constitution in Church and State, I opposed them at the

trate; for as he had no by-views, he feared not the face of man in doing his duty. His reasonings were sometimes lame, but his rectitude was above suspicion.[1] For a number of years he was indefatigable with regard to the statute work upon the highroads. In short, no man ever made a better use of the talents intrusted to his charge.

The House of Keir stood originally in the low grounds near the Teith. Being burnt by the express order of James III., immediately before the field of Stirling, it was afterwards removed to the present elevated situation. The new house consisted of a tower and a number of additions made at different times.[2] None of the first planted trees now remain. They lay to the south and south-west of the house, and were mostly ashes. Mr Henry Stirling remembers the

hazard of my life and fortune ; but now they are dispersed, I will retire to my farm. Let the gentlemen of the army, that are paid for it, apprehend the unhappy rebels. I might fall in with some of my neighbours, and I would not hurt a neighbour for the world."

[1] The late Lord Cathcart, having expressed a wish that the justices, after doing their business, might go home to dinner, " My lord," said Mr Mayne, before anybody else could speak, " I am against that proposition. We sometimes differ in court, and if we parted immediately, a rash word, uttered in the heat of debate, might rankle. Whereas, when we dine together and take a social glass, our hearts open to each other, and we mellow into friends." At another time the late Clackmannan and a collector of the customs being brought before the justices for triple chaise-duties, nobody cared to speak, till at last Mr Mayne said, " Collector, it is a shame to you, who have a handsome income from Government, not to pay your taxes. As for my friend Clackmannan, he and I are half-pay officers (on opposite sides). When we get our arrears, we will pay our taxes punctually. Every morning I pray I may do some good through the day ; if ever you pray, it is for a seizure." The penalties were waived.

[2] If we may judge from the expression of a notary, who in 1574 dates an instrument "ante palatium de Keir," the new house was accounted no mean building in those days.

three last of them, which were of great size; but being very much decayed, the late John Stirling of Keir ordered them to be cut down. Compared with them, the other trees now about the place appeared modern.

The old house being partly pulled down, the new one was just roofed in when James Stirling of Keir went into the Rebellion of 1715—in consequence of which the estate was forfeited, and he himself forced to live in banishment for eight or ten years. He was a man of weight and fashion, exceedingly beloved by his neighbours. Attachment to the family of Stuart was the ruling passion of his life.[1] His principles were so well known, that in 1745, at an advanced age, he was imprisoned on suspicion in the castle of Dumbarton. His lady bore him three-and-twenty sons and daughters.

The estate being purchased by the friends of the family, was committed to the charge of his son John while yet a very young man. In that delicate situation he conducted himself with so much wisdom, that though the family was no doubt obscured for a while, yet in the long-run it suffered little by the forfeiture.

[1] Keir, Touch, Carden, Kippendavie, and Newton were tried for their accession to a rising in 1708, when the French fleet was expected. It was the last trial according to the Scottish forms, a new treason-law being made soon after. On that occasion Daniel Morison, Keir's man, not knowing what might be the result of the trial, resolved not to speak one word of truth. On their acquittal (which, Sir Hugh Paterson said, was a matter concerted between Duke Hamilton and the Whig Ministry), Keir asked Daniel what he meant by for-swearing himself? "Sir," answered he, "I thought it better to put myself in the Almighty's hands, than to trust your honour to the mercy of the Whigs." Daniel died very old, multurer of the mill of Keir.

During the old gentleman's life it resided mostly at Calder, so that, with the exception of a few additional enclosures for grazing cattle, things at Keir remained in the same state as at the forfeiture. But upon his death in 1749, John Stirling sold the estate of Calder to his brother Archibald, who had lately returned from the East Indies. He then fitted up the House of Keir with great elegance. Besides enclosing upon an extensive scale, he dressed up the environs of the house in very good taste, converting at a considerable expense deformities into beauties.

In this gentleman there was an assemblage of qualities that well deserves commemoration in a work of this kind. Wit and humour, and the most joyous sociability, were in him perfectly compatible with sense and knowledge of business.[1] He could extract information or entertainment from almost any company, without descending from his dignity. To have witnessed the frolic of his convivial hour, one would not have imagined him the oracle of his neighbours, or the second founder of his family. It was a proof of superior strength of mind that, after living a number of years very privately, no sooner were his affairs upon a proper footing than all at once he changed his style, and showed a way as became his rank and fashion ;

---

[1] He was much employed in arbitrations, in which he seldom gave a decision unless both parties were satisfied. The matter was commonly canvassed over a bottle, when he had such a fund of argument suited to the parties, and what was more powerful, such bewitching pleasantry, that he compassed things impossible for other men. The confidence reposed in his understanding and integrity made the one party give more, and the other take less, than they would otherwise have done.

and that at a time of life when most other men find it impracticable to change rooted habits. His humanity equalled his understanding.[1] He died in 1757.

The house of Cardross was built about 1593, by David Erskine, Commendator of Dryburgh and Inchmahome, a natural son of the family of Mar. He either disliked living in the Isle of Menteith,[2] or being a zealous Protestant, wished to break off all connection with the monastic state. Be that as it may, in his buildings he affected the style of a considerable baron. In 1606, after his death, the benefices possessed by him were erected into a temporal lordship in favour of Lord Cardross, a younger son of Lord Treasurer Mar, who was much in the good graces of James VI.[3] It is impossible to ascertain whether

[1] He had two tenants in the Quigs, the one thriving and purse-proud, the other poor and encumbered with a large family. The former came one day and said to Keir, "My neighbour is a weirdless creature; your honour had better set me his mailing." "Content," said Keir; and his tacks being printed on stamped paper, there was nothing wanting to complete the bargain but to fill up the blanks. The fellow went home in high spirits and insulted his poor neighbour, saying he would make him his cottar. The latter went next day to his master, and with tears in his eyes begged to know what he had done to give offence. "Nothing," answered Keir. "I meant you well. Is not your neighbour's farm in better condition than yours?" "Oh yes," said the man; "he is rich, and able to do well to it." "Then," quoth the other, "take you his farm, which will do you service, and punish him sufficiently for his greed and hard-heartedness."

[2] John M'Courton, whose predecessors for four generations have been gardeners in the Isle of Menteith, says it is a tradition in their family that the first of them who came to the Earl of Menteith's service, soon after the Restoration, planted the whole trees that are now in the island, there being then only a few to the south of the priory, which have been long ago cut down.

[3] Being bred up together when boys in the Castle of Stirling, they were always friends. The King nicknamed the Earl "John of Slates," and upon his marrying Lady Mary Stewart, promised to make all their sons lairds.

the fine old trees about the place were planted by the
Commendator or by the first Lord Cardross. Perhaps
a number of very good ones are not older than the
Restoration.

The affairs of the family having gone into confusion,
the estate was sequestered about the Revolution, and
continued in the hands of the creditors till 1746, when
it was bought at a judicial sale by the late Mr John
Erskine, whose father was a son of Lord Cardross. It
turned out an excellent purchase ; yet to a person
about to fix his residence there, it surely had an
appearance somewhat unpromising at that time. The
house had been long deserted, serving principally for
a garrison in times of trouble. There was doubtless
a collection of very fine trees, but these choked up
the house and added to the general gloom. There
were no enclosures, and hardly any roads to the place.
In a few years, however, the face of things changed
wonderfully to the better. The house was fitted up,
and proved roomy and comfortable.[1] And though
many of the trees were unavoidably felled for the
sake of air and openness, a sufficient number remained
scattered up and down to give the place the air of a
park. By the help of Bowie, who was then beginning
his embellishments, the environs were smoothed and
rendered gay. A proper domain for the use of the

[1] The ceiling in the drawing-room was preserved as a piece of excellent
workmanship. It was executed by some of Cromwell's soldiers who were
quartered in the neighbourhood. There are ceilings of the same kind at Calder,
which, Keir says, were done by Cromwell's troopers that lay at the Kirkton
of Calder.

family was enclosed, and the roads gradually made good.

A better or pleasanter pair than Mr Erskine and his lady have seldom appeared in any country. His learning and judgment could only be surpassed by his modesty and rectitude. He had the happiest talent of communicating what he knew; and, exclusive of law, he knew a great deal of curious matter relative to men and things which could only be gathered from conversation. Though a sound lawyer, and of course likely to avoid those rocks and quicksands on which rash or ignorant litigants make shipwreck, no man was more averse to lawsuits or at greater pains to recommend peace and conciliation to those that sought his counsel.[1] Yet he had a warmth and keenness in conversation, which, as he never assumed, tended only to enliven it. By temperance and the unwearied attention of his family, he enjoyed, in spite of a very delicate constitution, tolerable health for a number of years. It is true he made some wonderful escapes from death. Till a few weeks before his dissolution,

[1] His father Colonel Erskine, was deeply engaged in those disputes wh. h in the last age were almost inseparable from landed property Being well convinced of the justice of his claims, he expressed a fear on his deathbed that his son John, out of *simplicity*, would make up his lawsuits a fresh to which was verified after his death In his politics he was equally keen Though a zealous Whig, he was a bitter enemy to the Union being afraid that the English would, by dint of numbers, sooner or later impose Episcopacy and the Book of Common Prayer on the Scots when some of his Jacobite neighbours alleged that he was almost as disaffected as themselves. He said with great animation, "Lads, I would sign a league with you on a drumhead to break the Union." He had always a hundred stands of arms, which were yearly cleaned with a view to a rising.

he spent daily some hours in his study revising or
enlarging his works. And when worn to a shadow,
he retained his mental faculties unimpaired, and, what
was no less gratifying to all around, that cheerfulness
and animation which flowed from piety and the remembrance of a well-spent life. At length, in a good
old age, happy in his prospects on both sides the
grave, he breathed his last with the same composure
that the wearied child lies down to sleep. This event
took place in March 1768.[1]

Mrs Erskine well deserves to be chronicled among
the female worthies of her age and country who made
a useful and respectable figure in social and domestic
life. She inherited an ample share of the worth, sense,
and humour of her father's family. If she brought
her husband little portion, he got what was infinitely
better—namely, a virtuous woman, who could compass what enormous wealth and unruffled prosperity
often miss. Her meritorious management and exertions helped Mr Erskine not only to preserve his
father's acquisitions, but also to purchase the estate
of Cardross. She brought up a number of children
soberly; but though chiefly attentive to essentials,

[1] Once when his family was assembled round his bed in expectation of his
death, he asked with a feeble voice if Mr Row of Doune was in the room. Being
told he was, the good man asked if he had his flute with him. "Oh," said
Mrs Erskine, "he is raving." "No, my dear," answered he; "but I would
fain hear once more the 'Flowers of the Forest.'" When seized with his last
illness, Dr Stirling was sent for. "Doctor," said Mr Erskine, "to-morrow is
Fasten's Even. I have been always accustomed to eat fat brose on that day.
Will a spoonful of it do me any harm?" The doctor smiled, and gave him
liberty if he chose it.

proper regard was paid to accomplishments. As a reward for her unceasing attention to their best interests, she lived to see most of them happily settled and highly thought of before she quitted the world. As her hospitality did not flow either from vanity or interested views, it accorded with the taste of every guest. She was fortunate in having a numerous and valuable set of connections, whom she received both in town and country with an ease and dignified cordiality which gave great satisfaction. Nothing could be more serene or gratifying to her feelings than the greater part of her widowhood. At last she was seized with a palsy, of which she died in May 1779 in her son David's house. She lived for some years at Keir when in that helpless state, attended by her grandchild Mary Stirling.[1]

[1] Ere long it will hardly be believed that Mr and Mrs Erskine lived for a number of years in a very indifferent darksome house at the foot of Merlin's Wynd, in which few mechanics nowadays would submit to live. There, however, they were visited by first rate people; and there, as the poet says, "Content could dwell and learned care." One may sometimes judge of families by their domestics. George Mason was one of those antique footmen who, being warmly attached to their family, think themselves entitled to free liberty of speech. He thought himself entitled to admonish guests that frequented the house. When hob or nob was first introduced, on a young gentle man calling for wine a second time during dinner, George whispered him loud enough to be heard, "Sir, you have had a glass already." When Mrs Erskine asked him the *price* of lamb in the market, he answered archly, "It is not come to *your price* yet." He died in Mr David Erskine's house in 1750

CHAPTER IX.

SOME SCOTTISH LADIES.

I SHALL be very brief as to female dress. Indeed one
may as well think of giving an account of the last
year's clouds, as of the variations in the ladies' habiliments. It is sufficient to say, that during the whole
of this period they have been equally costly and
fluctuating. That was not surprising, considering
the number of persons that had an interest in
changing and inflaming the fashions. They took
care to flatter the taste and vanity of old and young,
who were of the same mind as to these points,
and not easily diverted from their purpose by considerations of economy or expediency. However, the
younger branches of the family had no reason to complain of their being stinted in this important article,
there being no bounds set to parental indulgence. A
comparison between the bills of 1765-1766 and those
of 1805-1806 would set this matter in a striking point
of view. Between forty and fifty years ago, the business and even the name of a haberdasher were hardly
known in Edinburgh, and of milliners there were only

a few. If fewer silk gowns are at present worn, the expense of a tonish lady's dress is by no means diminished. If the wives and daughters of country gentlemen seldom take the lead in the article of dress, yet they are early apprised of what is going on in the metropolis of Scotland. And nothing can be more elegant and showy at balls and other novel conventions, some of them commissioning their dress and ornaments from London, which is considered as the mint of fashion, and the likeliest way of eclipsing rivals and companions. To a certain extent attention to dress is laudable, and in fact it may be considered as the ruling passion of the female world in every age and country, though it assumes various shapes and hues. It may, however, be carried to extravagance, and defeat the purpose it was intended to promote.

In mentioning fashions of a fugitive nature connected with the spirit of the times, the scantiness and thinness of the fashionable ladies' clothing must not be omitted, in consequence of which they make no scruple of displaying those beauties which they used either to conceal or give only a glimpse of. That, however, is by no means peculiar to the present times. The rules of Queen Anne's reign were very severe upon a similar practice. And in 1753 it was no less common at Edinburgh, it being difficult to say whether the ladies' necks or legs were most exposed to the public eye. It is, however, peculiar to the last five or six years to find the fashion of unveiling hidden beauties, accompanied with wearing very few or scanty garments, which is no less indecent than dangerous in a changeable climate conducive to consumption. It is one of the absurd or worse than absurd fashions which originated in France, and was from thence imported into Britain by travelled ladies enamoured of novel fashions.[1] They surely lost sight of nature and common-sense, for beauty is never so attractive as when half withdrawn. There are, however, certain follies so gross and ridiculous, that even the breath of fashion cannot sanction them for any length of time. One extreme often leads to another. Ere long the ladies' bosoms, or necks as they are called, may be as much concealed as in the days of Queen Elizabeth, when nothing was seen of women below their chin. To these scanty garments, ill calculated to repel cold, may succeed large hoops, *manteaux*, and petticoats of silk or velvet, such as were in high request fifty and sixty years ago.

Lady Hamilton was the daughter of James Stirling of Keir, and wife to Sir Hugh Hamilton of Rosehall, a man of large estate in Lanarkshire. If I mistake not, they were married in 1746 or 1747, when the lady was under thirty, and her husband a middle-aged man. He died soon after she had brought him a daughter, who, to her mother's great sorrow, died when eight or nine years of age. After quitting the

[1] About sixteen or seventeen years ago, a shopkeeper in Stirling that had been *swindled* out of goods and money by English adventurers who pretended to be people of family, said, " Filthy cattle ! I might have known that she was little worth from her wearing very few and very thin petticoats."

family seat, Lady Hamilton took up her residence in
East Lothian, renting the house and enclosures of
Monkrigg, within a few miles of Haddington, amidst
her friends and relations.   Thither she was accompanied by her brother James, a sensible, kind-hearted
man, somewhat rough in his speech and manners.
After remaining some years in Scotland, he found it
necessary to return to Jamaica, where he died, leaving a great property to his brother Archibald.   His
sister Magdalen lived also much with her for a number of years,[1] than whom she could not have had a
more agreeable, better informed companion.

Let us now see how Lady Hamilton comported herself during a widowhood of more than half a century.
And at the commencement it may be affirmed she
acted her part with applause, having fine talents for
society, which turned to the greater account that her
heart was generous and kind.   Hospitality in a style
somewhat primeval may be said to have been her
ruling passion.   To that, indeed, she had been ha-
bituated from her early years.   Notwithstanding her
father's attainder, he continued to be eminently hospitable and beneficent.   During the eclipse of the family,
he resided mostly at Calder, where he was much respected and beloved by his neighbours.   After her
marriage, she lived handsomely and fully, which accorded with her own disposition, and was justified
by her husband's fortune.   Of course she saw a great

---

[1] Miss Magdalen lived much for seven or eight years at Calder with her
brother William, who lost his first lady in the year 1775, and married the
second one in 1783.

deal of good company, her house being one of the
pleasantest in the country. Little change took place
as long as her daughter lived; but when bereaved of
her, and circumscribed in her income, the seeds of
the social virtues were too deeply implanted in her
nature to be eradicated by a change of circumstances,
to which she accommodated herself with great dexterity and success. For a number of years her house
at Monkrigg was the seat of mirth and good cheer,
frequented by the young and the old, the gay and
the grave, whom she received with equal grace and
kindness, and entertained with care and propriety. To
fastidiousness and forbidding pride she was an utter
stranger. She regarded love and affection among
neighbours and relations not only as the great cor-
dials of life, but as moral virtues which it is every
one's interest and duty to practise. Her appearance
was all along pleasing and prepossessing. As she had
been handsome in her youth, so when handsomeness
and beauty had fled, she continued to be amiable and
lady-looking. If not a *belles lettres* woman, her conversation bespake her sound understanding, and she
had a vein of that wit and pleasantry for which some
of her brothers and sisters were so remarkable. Meanwhile sense and benignity were conspicuous in all she
said. One must have been strangely warped with
prejudice and affectation, who should have found
fault with this good lady for speaking her native
dialect without disguise, or for her partiality to old-
fashioned maxims and manners. She might be re-

garded as a precious relic of the ladies of the feudal times, when the barons were actuated by the spirit of chivalry which served to soften and humanise the manners of warriors. It behoved in those days a baron's lady to be kind and dignified, frank and conciliating, in her language and demeanour. This was the way to increase her husband's popularity and her own. For that purpose she was courteous and beneficent to her neighbours, guests, and dependants, whom she entertained in her hall in a way that gained their hearts. In that date of society hospitality was sound policy, and the likeliest way to strengthen one's influence and power. Long after the feudal system was abased and proscribed in Scotland, feudal notions and maxims maintained their ground among the nobility and gentry. And I need hardly add, that they subsisted in Lady Hamilton's young days, having cost her father very dear.

Meanwhile this good lady well knew that there could be no hospitality without good and plentiful cheer, few being disposed to fare like hermits, let the conversation be never so good. As she was never so well pleased as when her table was full, she took care to gratify the palate of her visitants. In this she had only to tread in the steps of the revered characters whom she knew in her youth and prime. Her provisions, therefore, were always of the best kinds, and she found means to procure them on easy terms. Her meat was well dressed, and served up as became a woman of fashion, not perhaps in the newest mode.

But if the groundwork of her domestic economy was Scottish, she had too much good sense not to borrow good things from her Southern neighbours, without being a servile imitator, or undervaluing her own country. In fact, her table was less antiquated and primeval than her language and notions, to which she was the more attached, that they were in no repute among the votaries of taste and fashion. She adhered all along to the style of receiving company which prevailed in her happiest days, when friends and neighbours and relations were made welcome, upon very short intimation. In that, however, people were guided by common-sense and circumstances. No wonder, then, that she should reprobate that part of the new code of manners which teaches people, more fastidious than wise or provident, to look coldly upon connections and neighbours who had been regarded as hereditary friends, in consequence of a reciprocation of good offices. She foretold, without the gift of prophecy, that the dropping one's natural connections, and taking up with those whose greatest merit was their wealth, would, if carried very far, give a mortal stab to social intercourse, and lead to something like a new date of society. She indeed lived long enough to be sensible that the finical selection, or, to speak more properly, the curtailing the number of guests, had not contributed to make families more easy and independent than their predecessors, who would have, and have regarded it as a species of high treason against society and good-neighbourhood. Among new

modes and maxims may be enumerated a great increase in the scale of expense, which cut the deeper,
that as it was not sanctioned by precedents, none
could tell where or when it would stop.

It is therefore little surprising that for a number
of years Lady Hamilton should have been one of
the most popular characters of her time. One never
entered her house but with pleasure, or quitted it
without regret. Had her fare been plainer than it
was, her courtesy and good-humour would have given
it a relish which the banquets of lords and nabobs
often want. I am sensible it is difficult to find language and colouring to appreciate the hospitality
of coeval worthies, which is not precisely the same
in all things. Though I never visited her at Monkrigg, I have reason to think the outlines of the sketch
tolerably correct, my information being derived from
people who lived long with her upon an intimate footing, and always spoke of her social hour with a
warmth and a reverence which said much for her and
themselves.

It will naturally be inquired whether the lady had
an income that warranted her keeping what would
now be esteemed open house, in an expensive country not far from Edinburgh. The reader, if young,
and perfectly modern in her views, will be astonished
to hear that her chief reliance for a number of years
was upon her jointure, which did not exceed £300
per annum. That was much too small for her husband's great estate; but her brother John, who ad-

justed her contract of marriage, was entirely satisfied
with that sum. In the last age it was not the fashion
to make very liberal provisions for brides. Be that
as it may, Sir Hugh ought, when he found himself
declining, to have given her an additional provision :
the rather that, in case of her daughter's decease,
her estates would go to distant relations. As long
as James lived in the family with her, he made her
a handsome allowance, and she got a share of her
elder brother's executry, which exceeded £10,000
sterling. And two of her brothers in Jamaica left
her legacies; but these, owing to the embarrassment
of their affairs, she did not receive till late in life.

In fact this excellent woman owed the figure she
made in life to her grafting hospitality on rigid economy, and that exemplary management which seeks
to save, that there may be the more to spend or
give away. It is a trite observation, but a just one,
that good frequently has resulted from seeming evil.
For her skill in household management she was probably indebted to the straitened state of her father's
circumstances, and to the number of his children.
Without strict frugality, and unceasing attention to
little matters, he and his lady could not have entertained so many company at Calder as they did, while
the family was eclipsed. There she acquired at an
early period that knowledge in the mysteries of economics, which stood her in much stead, both in her
married and widowed state. "Nescis," says an ancient
sage, "quantum vectigal sit parsimonia." But so

much has been said of it in some of the preceding
sketches, that it is needless to enlarge upon that topic.
Suffice it to say, that with a very moderate income,
Lady Hamilton compassed things which opulence and
greatness frequently miss. For she was eminently
hospitable and beneficent, without forfeiting her independence. This was owing to her steady adherence
to a few plain maxims, founded on common-sense,
that require to be accommodated to time and place.
While living a rational respectable life, she used to
spend a good part of the year with her relations and
friends in the country, to whom her company was
highly acceptable. As Christmas was a season of
devotion and innocent festivity with the members of
her Church, she had always a party either at home
or at the house of some of her friends. On those
occasions she was cheerful without levity, and dignified without being dainty or supercilious. I met
with her repeatedly at these high times at Keir or
Cardross, where she appeared to great advantage. I
took the more pleasure in her company that by this
time a Scotswoman of the old school was a sight
hardly to be seen. On those occasions, when in high
glee and fond of the party, she used upon entreaty
to sing with great spirit and humour, in a way that
would have become a baron's lady of the last age.[1]

[1] In 1787-88 at Cardross, towards the end of the New Year, the good lady
was requested to give some of her favourite songs. A motion was made that
justices of peace and officers should be considered as no part of the company.
She complied, and entertained us with a set of poignant songs, some of which
I had never heard and was not very likely to hear again.

It may be well thought that by that time she had little taste for amatory songs connected with our national melodies, of which she had been once exceedingly fond in her younger years. Her songs, therefore, were mostly political, breathing much of the spirit of 1745-46, when party ran very high. If the words sometimes bordered upon treason, or lampooned characters that had deserved well of their country, the keenest Whig, at the distance of more than forty years, could not but be diverted with the squibs of wit and humour which had served to reconcile a respectable party to defeat and abasement. On such occasions recourse is had to satire, which, when seasoned with keen irony, affords entertainment. If these compositions sometimes betoken a bad spirit, they remind one of Priam's javelin, hurled with a feeble unavailing hand. It was, however, very seldom, and in companies much to her taste, that she brought forward those relics of party; for she was too well bred and discreet to introduce them in mixed companies, where they might give offence, and could make no proselytes. It is sufficient to say that she was all along warmly attached to the abdicated family, and to Episcopacy. Nothing in her declining years gave her more concern, or excited so much of her indignation, as to find the laity or clergy of her communion giving up or explaining away their principles, without having an adequate object. In not paying court to the powers *that be*, and adhering pertinaciously to the shibboleth that had cost her family or allies very dear, this

venerable matron acted a consistent part; for in
truth she had nothing to hope, and as little to fear,
from her rulers.   One cannot help respecting and
applauding a person that acts steadily and consci-
entiously.

It was a great mortification to her to be obliged
to quit Monkrigg, as she was fond of the place and
neighbourhood.   But the estate having been sold,
the purchasers found it expedient to dwell in the
house.   Not being able to get another house in the
country that would accommodate her, she resolved
to take up her abode in Edinburgh, though that was
to her a very new and untried scene.   Being a measure
rather of necessity than of choice, she submitted with
a good grace to the inconvenience and fatigue of a
removal at a late period of life.   She purchased a
good house in Buccleuch Place, and was soon reconciled to her new habitation, and to something like a
novel state of society.   In that town she had troops
of friends, who paid her much attention, wishing to
render her evening of life serene and comfortable.
That was the more practicable that when she left
Monkrigg little change took place in her manners and
maxims.   As long as she enjoyed tolerable health and
spirits, her favourite luxury was to entertain her
friends and relations in her accustomed style.   Her
parties at dinner and supper were easy and natural,
very different from the modish ones, where there were
often more splendour and fulness than mirth and
good conversation.   She certainly lived at a con-

siderable expense, as she saw much company in an uceremonious style.[1] Meanwhile her matters were well arranged, and went on like clockwork. She either sent to invite her friends to eat with her, or, if they called in a morning, asked them to dine with her that day or the next. As long as she retained her faculties, nothing could be more gratifying to a sentimental guest that wished " to catch the manners as they rose," than this lady's plain plentiful meals, given with all the heartiness and freedom of the former generation. One often met with people worth conversing with, and the manners of their hostess were calculated to banish stiffness and ceremony, and to make people think themselves at home. In short, whether in town or country, Lady Hamilton made a very respectable figure at the head of her table.

The death of her sister Magdalen was a severe blow to that good lady. The former was a woman of excellent understanding and very amiable dispositions. She had a happy intuition into character, and a strain of humour very much her own. Though the two sisters were not precisely the same, yet, like different keys in music, they served to enliven or diversify the intellectual concert. By that time, however, Lady Hamilton's feelings were much blunted by age or infirmities. Yet while gradually declining, she retained her philanthropy when she could hardly

[1] I forget whether she kept her carriage at Edinburgh or hired horses as she wanted them. At Monkrigg she all along kept one, the enclosures affording her provender for her horses.

see or hear. Nay, her speech was at last only intelligible to the female friend that lived with her. When interpreted, it commonly imported an invitation to eat or drink. For some years she was no more than a venerable wreck; but that is to be expected when people approach their eightieth year. At length, in October 1802, this excellent woman was gathered to her fathers, like ripe corn in its season, having had repeated shocks of the palsy—a disease which had proved fatal to others of her family. She survived all her brothers and sisters, amounting to twenty-three, great part of whom lived to be men and women. It was a severe tax on this good lady to see them drop off one by one before her.

To conclude : if from principle and habit she had made parsimony and beneficence go hand in hand, be it recorded to her honour that she never carried one or the other too far. While she prized independence, she scorned to hoard money. Neither old age nor infirmities could contract her heart, for in the penult year of her life she gave a grand-nephew setting out for the East Indies a present of £500 sterling. And, strange to tell, the nephew whom she made her heir got fully £1000 sterling by the succession. Her story reminds one of the widow's cruse that never failed.

Lady Sarah Bruce deserves to be commemorated in a work which professes to record the antiquities of

manners, as she lived to be one of the oldest women
of quality in the three kingdoms : she retained to the
last her faculties and sprightliness. With her, and
the persons she liked best, did I pass many happy
days. Her story is, of all the worthies whom I have
attempted to delineate, the least striking or diver-
sified. It is, however, a pleasing view of still life.
She was the daughter of Thomas, Earl of Kincardine,
who in 1699 married at London, when a second
brother, Miss Pauncefote, a lady of good family, by
whom he had a number of children.[1] If I mistake
not, Lady Sarah was born in the last year of the
seventeenth century, and remained in England till
she was sixteen or seventeen years old. After her
father became Earl she lived in family with him at
Broomhall. The late Mrs Abercromby, who met with
her soon after she arrived in Scotland, told me that
she was at that time a handsome woman, much
admired. Upon the death of her father, she and the
Countess-Dowager removed to Torryburn, where they
lived very comfortably for a number of years.[2] There,

---

[1] Lady Christina Erskine gave me a copy of her grandmother's letter on her
marriage to her mother-in-law, the lady of Sir Alexander Bruce, afterwards
Earl of Kincardine, which does honour to the head and heart of the writer.

March 9, 1699.

"MADAM,—Since the providence of God hath brought me into a near
relation to your ladyship, whose character, as it is honourable, so it is eminent
for everything that is excellent. As I claim the privilege of having the
honour of such an alliance, I presume, madam, to beg the favour of your
blessing and prayers, believing myself under the same obligation of duty to
your ladyship as to my own mother. As I esteem it my highest honour, so I
shall make it my utmost endeavour, to approve myself, madam, your obedient
daughter and most humble servant,   RACHEL BRUCE."

[2] James Spittal of Leuchal, an elegant-mannered man and a great traveller,

about 1754 or 1755, the latter died in advanced age.
I can give no account of Lady Sarah for a number
of years.   Suffice it to say, much of her time was
spent with her sister-in-law, the Countess of Kincardine, or with her sister, Lady Rachel Lundin.
It is the less necessary to enter into particulars, that
I was not acquainted with her till she approached
to sixty ; but for more than thirty years I had frequent occasion to converse with her at Edinburgh,
or in the houses of our common friends.   From the
time I first knew her till the close of her very long,
and on the whole pleasant life, she was acute, lively,
and well bred.   If her conversation was seldom brilliant or original, it was often interesting, always
dignified, and becoming her rank and years.   As she
had long consorted with people of fashion, she was
no stranger to what was going on in the gay or
literary world.   In her younger years, under her
mother's direction, she had read more than was common in those days ; but she made no parade of her
knowledge and taste.   When an octogenarian, her
memory and judgment continued unimpaired.   No
wonder, then, that she should all along retail with
great spirit and *naïveté* short interesting scraps of the
history of private life, which, as they came in naturally, pleased all that heard them.   She was, however,
no story-teller, or disposed to be eloquent in her talk,

used to say that he never admired the English language so much as when he
heard it spoken by old Lady Kincardine. His own Scotch was the language
of a scholar in the first part of the eighteenth century by first rate people.

which last she thought ill-breeding. Neither did she, like many persons past their prime, find fault with the times, or, what is considered as tantamount, give a decided preference to those that were past. On the contrary, she seemed perfectly reconciled to the modes and manners which had been introduced into Scotland within her own remembrance. She always saw things in the fairest point of life; and she had great allowances to make for youth and gaiety, and had no objection to a degree of frolic and merriment when kept within bounds. Indeed, her conversation never savoured of the old woman, her views and notions being quite modern and liberal, befitting a person in the prime of life whose affections were warm. Though steady in her religious and political opinions, she did not obtrude them in company, being aware that these topics were apt to engender strife and bad humour. If sometimes keen and ardent in her remarks,[1] few people were more free from peevishness and fretfulness, for she never allowed little things to disturb the tranquillity of her mind. In a word, this good lady was one that added a great deal to society, without taking aught from it, being a safe companion and an easy friend.

---

[1] A minister in the neighbourhood, in whose welfare she was much interested, called a meeting of friends to discuss the question whether his only son should be a clergyman or manufacturer. The father and son were of opposite sentiments. At last the former said, with some emotion, "But who will, after I am gone, take the charge of my MSS. on the fathers, which have employed so much of my time?" "Singe hens with them, Mr Thomas," said Lady Sarah, with great keenness, "and let your son follow his own inclination." The young man was gratified in that matter.

I am perfectly persuaded that the benignity and evenness of her temper, conjoined with constitutional or hereditary good-nature, contributed to prolong her life beyond the ordinary bounds. It is true she had no domestic cares and grievances to ruffle or agitate her mind, seeing she never had a house of her own. Having no part to act, no pressures to guard against, she had only to conform to the humours of the families in which she lived, and in situations abundantly delicate, she conducted herself with that discretion which good sense points out. It was her good fortune for many years to enjoy uninterrupted health. Meanwhile she ate heartily, and seemed to set old age at defiance. Nor was that the effect of regimen and care, for she exposed herself to cold. When reprehended for eating things not good for her, she said that old as she was she hardly knew she had a stomach, for she and it agreed passing well. " Indeed," added she, " were it not for the sight of my wrinkled face which I behold in the glass in the morning, I should hardly think I was old. For that reason, however, I am less fond of contemplating my sweet person in the mirror than I was fifty years ago, when I could hardly be persuaded that age and wrinkles would ever overtake me."

It would serve no purpose to write annals of this venerable lady's evening of life, which was steady and serene, unmarked by vicissitudes or alarms.

Suffice it here to say, that for more than thirty years she formed part of the Lundin or Perth family, in

whose fortune, good and bad, she took a warm concern.
And therefore, in all her peregrinations to this country, for the last ten or twelve years of her life, she
was accompanied by her niece, Lady Rachel Drummond; and as they were seldom seen separate, they
never appeared to more advantage than in each
other's company; for though great friends, nothing
could be more defameless than their manners and
style of conversation.   That, however, will appear
more clearly in a sketch of the niece, who was a
strongly marked and withal meritorious character,
such as is seldom to be seen in common life.   Tended
by her, and gratified with her discourse, did Lady
Sarah at last sleep the sleep of death at Stobhall
in the end of June 1795, in the ninety-fifth or ninety-
sixth year of her age.   She died rather of a failure of
nature than of sickness or disease—one of the few
instances of a comfortable, dignified old age.   She
was, therefore, one of those that were to be regretted
rather than lamented.

Lady Rachel Drummond was the daughter of
James Lundin of Lundin, who, upon the death of
Lords John and Edward Drummond, assumed the
title of Earl of Perth.   Though he has been dead
twenty-five years, it will be impossible to describe
his daughter without giving a slight sketch of him.
It may be said with truth that her virtues and good
qualities were her own, whilst her faiths and peculiarities were either to be referred to him, or to her

education.   He was the grandson of the first Earl
of Melfort by his first wife, Sophia Lundin, the
heiress of the family of Lundin.   Being a second
brother, without fortune, he was bred a writer at
Edinburgh, but on the death of the eldest he succeeded to a fair estate.   Being much at his ease and
a handsome man, not arrived at his prime, he lived
in a great style, and mixed with the fashionable
world, setting up a handsome equipage.   Not long
after he married Lady Rachel Bruce, who inherited
the worth and sweet dispositions of her family, with
whom he lived happily for a number of years.   After
his marriage it is agreed that Lundin lived for a brace
of years in a very extravagant style, without paying
proper attention to his affairs, or setting bounds to
luxury and pomp, which last he connected with the
dignity of his family, which was no less ancient than
considerable, little inferior, in his estimation at that
time, to the family of Perth save in rank and titles.
A man who gives free scope to show and expense
makes no bowels of running in debt, looking upon
economy and attention to probable considerations as
plebeian and below his notice.   It required, however,
a considerable while before the effects of his miscon-
duct became apparent.   Meanwhile he made a very
respectable figure as a country gentleman.   Besides
the advantage of a good person and address, he was
a man of parts and information.   If haughty and
headstrong in his conduct, he had an exuberant share
of wit and fancy, which rendered him a delightful

companion, giving an additional relish to his viands and liquors, which were of the best. And therefore at the head of his table he was much liked if not admired. There are, however, people that never say a foolish thing and yet do not act wisely. In truth, he was in every part of his life actuated by passion or caprice ; and with him prejudices, although old or rashly taken up, were cherished as principles or self-evident positions. Here it is proper to observe that, though originally a zealous Whig, he thought proper after his marriage to become a Jacobite, with all the zeal of a new convert. It is impossible at this distance of time to say what were his views and motives; but surely it did not promote the interest or grandeur of his family, which he had always much at heart. Perhaps it induced the Duke of Perth a little before the Rebellion to settle his estate on the Lundin family as his next heirs;[1] but Lundin's claim was rejected, to his great mortification.

In the meantime, his heedlessness and profusion involved him in difficulties which would have broke most other people's heart; but so lofty were his pretensions, and so exuberant his hopes, that he did not lower his tone when his fortune was declining apace. As he lived in a cheap and plentiful country, and his household matters were well conducted, he still continued to see much company upon an easy footing, whilst everything he did or said tended to

---

[1] Lord John Drummond, who managed the family affairs in the Duke's minority, used to call Lundin " the Protestant heir," by way of derision.

raise his own dignity and importance in the eyes of all that approached him. That, however, he sometimes carried too far. The lustre of ancestry is at best a borrowed light, which attracts little reverence unless it be accompanied with personal merit or much opulence. The bulk of men are therefore disposed to thwart the claims of the proud and vainglorious, when brought forward unreasonably or urged as matter of right. Nevertheless, for a number of years this gentleman kept up the part of the German prince, his house having the air of a court in miniature. Every day before dinner he appeared in full dress, expecting the same thing from his guests and inmates. To all of them he gave an audience in his turn, as if it had been a levee. If these things gave people disgust, no sooner was the ice of ceremony thawed than he gave full scope to his wit and fancy, which were exuberant and luxuriant when he liked the company. It may well be thought he was never less pleased than when he entered into politics, or fell foul of persons who he thought had injured him or his family. In those cases he set no bound to his satire and irony, which were keen and cutting; and it was not in his favour that they were often carried away and repeated as epigrammatical sallies.[1] It is

---

[1] His attachment to puns was at least venial. On being asked what he was busied with, he answered, "In doing what King George could not do, in making a Scottish peer on his estate." He called Addison a dull fellow, who, because he wanted genius to pun, condemned that species of wit by the lump. However, either a very good or a very bad pun contributes at times to put ceremonious company into good humour.

not necessary to trace his progress minutely. He
had a number of friends, warmly attached to his
family, that were willing and able to have saved him
in the first stages of his embarrassments; but he was
too high-minded and obstinate to adopt any practicable plan, for he insisted on retaining the power of
management, which put an end to those conferences,
and made his best friends leave him to himself. In
order to lighten his burdens, he sold a considerable
part of his estate, which, to his great mortification,
was purchased by people whom he did not love or
respect. Ere long he found himself more straitened
than ever. In those circumstances he did what is
too often done—namely, he attempted to involve his
best friends, which was injuring them without benefiting him. He seemed to think that in taking that
step they did what was their duty and their honour.
Things at last came to that pass, that the residue of
the estate must be sold. Had that been done in time,
he might have had a handsome reversion; but that
measure he opposed with no small ingenuity and
address to the very last, throwing every obstacle in
the way. And when it was bought at the sale by
Mr David Erskine, who wished to serve the Elgin
family, nothing could exceed the anger of this gentleman, who some years before had, contrary to the
opinion of those that wished well to his family, taken
up the title of Earl of Perth. When forced to leave
Lundin, of which he was passionately fond, the Commissioners of Annexed Estates allowed him to take up

his residence at Stobhall, the jointure-house of the Duchess-Dowager of Perth, who was lately dead. At that place he lived till his demise, which took place in summer, 1779. There, by all accounts, he did not drop his stateliness and crotchets, which he all along laboured to instil into his family. However unfortunate in his management and conduct he might have been, he had from first to last a plausibility in his talk, and powers of persuasion, which were not easily withstood by such as were much in his company. Perhaps no man ever possessed greater powers of self-delusion; and his excessive vanity could make him swallow anything, however gross.[1] What wonder,

[1] The summer before the late Lord Elgin set out on his travels, he and Lundin made a tour to the north of Scotland. At Elgin they were made burghers, and handsomely entertained by the magistrates, who were charmed with Lundin's wit and eloquence. Having sat very late, the Provost said, by way of compliment, that his lordship was most fortunate in having such an accomplished governor. At this the other fired, saying with great indignation, "Governor, sir! I would have you know that I represent two no less ancient and greater families than his lordship's, when I accompany as my ally and pupil."

At the funeral of the Countess-Dowager of Kincardine, who died at Torryburn, Lundin presided, Lord Elgin being abroad. After the interment there was a great dinner, numerously attended by the relations and connections of the family. Among them was the late Patrick Edmonstoune of Newton whose political sentiments were the same with those of his entertainers. Neither of them had any doubt of a speedy restoration, which would assuredly make Lundin a great man. Newton, whose wit and irony was abundantly coarse, told Lundin that he had a boon to request of him. "When you, sir, shall in good time be made Lord Chancellor of Scotland, I hope to have the honour of being your purse-bearer." To this a full assent was given, with an eulogium on Newton's loyalty and sufferings in the cause. A while after, when in high glee, the latter making up a table-napkin in the form of a ribbon, put it across Lundin's breast, saying he trusted it was only a prelude to the Garter. The company stared, and were afraid of a quarrel, for it was evident Newton was playing on him. Instead of being offended, the latter attended the stranger to his bedroom with great courtesy; and next

then, that he should not make that figure in the drama of life which his talents and advantages entitled him to have done! He may be regarded as a rural Lord Bristol, as that eccentric nobleman is painted by the masterly hand of Lord Clarendon, who saw into the recesses of the human heart. In a word, Lord Perth was a man with whom one would rather have drunk a bottle than done business; who was more his own enemy than anybody else's, seeing he had more wit than wisdom, more imagination than sound judgment or discretion. He is a character which it is neither easy nor pleasant to delineate as large as the life. Such as are well acquainted with his story and proceedings will confess that I have by no means magnified his faults and failings. Less, however, could not be said by way of introduction to the story of Lady Rachel, who looked up to her father as an oracle and pattern, seeing everything with his eyes. In this she carried filial duty sufficiently far, but great is the force of blood and example.

In nothing, perhaps, was Lord Perth more repre-

morning told some of the company that Newton was one of the best-bred men he had ever seen not to have been in France.

In 1763 or 1764, after returning from Germany, the late Sir Ralph Abercromby was sent by his father to visit Lundin, with whom he had been long very intimate; but by that time a coolness had taken place, owing to that gentleman's strange conduct. The young officer was most graciously received, and stayed a couple of days. How much was he astonished, in the course of their walks about the place, to hear his host call Mr Pitt, afterwards Lord Chatham, a bitter enemy to him and his family. "Why, Ralph," added he, "I discovered some years ago, when that fellow was in the zenith of his power, that he had sent money to raise mutinies among my colliers and salters. Besides being idle and unmanageable, they had good clothes and plenty of money, which they had not earned lawfully."

hensible than in the education he gave his children, and the notions he impressed on their minds, which assuredly cut very deep. His three sons got no more book-learning than a private tutor, very indifferently qualified, could give them. Though his house lay not far from St Andrews, he did not send them to college to acquire a competent knowledge of science and the *belles lettres.* Nor did he send them when big lads to Edinburgh, to learn their exercises and acquire the graces. · He had, it was said, singular notions on that head, wishing to trust more to nature than to cultivation. That, however, was at best a hazardous experiment, and he had no reason to boast of his success. As it had all the faults of a home education, so it prevented the young men from pushing their fortune betimes in the world. So lofty were his ideas, that hardly anything within their reach would have contented him, and he made it matter of conscience to ask no favours from Government, which, in his case, was not willing to obtrude them. In the meantime the sons' notions of persons and things were entirely derived from him, who often saw objects through a jaundiced medium. As years added strength to his prejudices and prepossessions. so at no period of his life was he remarkable for sound judgment, acting and speaking under the impulse of spleen and passion. The best friends of the family lamented that the young men's precious time should be so much misspent, but to those remonstrances their father lent a deaf ear.

It is now more than time to speak of the education
given to Lady Rachel Drummond, or Miss Rachel
Lundin, as she was called for a number of her happiest
years.   That was likewise contracted, and much out
of the ordinary road, being in a great measure a home
or domestic one.   In her infancy and early years she
was, from all that I have heard, greatly indebted to
her mother, who was an amiable, sensible, well-prin-
cipled woman, who inherited the prominent features
of her own family, among which benignity and
rectitude were not the least valuable.   She doubtless
gave her daughter a number of excellent lessons,
which made an indelible impression upon a young
mind lively and susceptible.   Meanwhile, the father
was taken into all their counsels.   From whatever
cause, the young lady was not sent at the usual
age to a boarding-school, when she might have had
companions of her own rank and years.   In those
little female academies, conducted by steady discreet
matrons, qualified to form the minds and manners of
young women, every prejudice and every crotchet
might either have been lopped away or greatly softened.   Instead of that, at the time when her mind
was most flexible, ready to receive any impression, she
remained at home romping with her brothers, or
listening to the discourse of her father or his guests.
What wonder, then, that her habits should acquire a
firm seat at an early period !   Be these things as they
would, when about fourteen or fifteen years of age,
Miss Lundin lived at least a winter with Lady Kames

at Edinburgh,[1] than whom a young woman could
not have had a better instructress, she being a discreet, elegant, strong-minded woman, perfectly acquainted with the polite world and its modes, both
great and small. There she no doubt attended the
proper masters and schools, and she was likely to be
an apt scholar, her apprehension being very quick.
In all likelihood Lady Kames was at due pains
to form the manners and polish the mind of this
young lady, who was very promising and pleasing,
wanting nothing but a little pruning and polish.
And the precepts and conversation of such a woman
could not but make a deep and lasting impression.
However, Lord Kames did not make her a philosopher or *belles lettres* woman. She had, in truth,
too masculine a mind for him, who was sufficiently
fond of *sentiment* and soft sensibility. Both he
and his lady were much pleased with their fair
inmate, who was lively and sensible beyond her
years, sweet - blooded and well - intentioned. Her
peculiarities they imputed to home education and
filial reverence. And as long as they lived, a great
friendship subsisted among them. In these days Miss
Lundin lived much at Edinburgh with her aunt, Lady
Kincardine, and her daughters, from whom many
excellent lessons were to be learned. With them she
took a share of the public places in vogue, and was
introduced to first-rate company. In spite of those

[1] By way of exchange, Lord Kames sent his son to live at Lundin, where
he remained till fit to go to the College of St Andrews

opportunities of improvement, it was apparent that this young lady never acquired by collision with the young and the gay that gloss of fashion and these lesser elegancies of behaviour which add grace and dignity to rank and honourable descent. The truth was, she had, from her outset in life, something of a provincial, or rather family cast, of which she could not, or cared not, to get rid. By no unnatural progression of ideas, she afterwards undervalued them too much, affecting to regard them as gewgaws of little consequence. In that, however, she by no means judged wisely; for both males and females entitled to give the law in matters of taste and politeness always have, and always will, appreciate one another rather by external accomplishments, grafted on a strict adherence to decorum and propriety, than by essentials. Being a woman of an independent spirit, superior to petty considerations, she proceeded to form her views and manners by a standard of her own. She was regardless of the censures of foplings and fashionable belles who took the lead in public places and drawing-rooms, which were, when she approached fast to womanhood, considered as schools of elegance and refinement, where the two sexes studied to be amiable and engaging in one another's eyes. In those conventions the seeds of many a virtuous passion were sown, which often ended in a happy union.

But whatever proficiency the subject of this sketch might make while in town, consorting with people of

rank and elegant demeanour, she was likely to gain
nothing on her return home, where she was caressed
and admired. In those cases people must either
advance or lose ground ; and when excellence is not
within their reach, they take up with mediocrity.
The females of her family were more remarkable for
sense and virtue than for accomplishments or knowledge. Her father's conversation and that of his companions were not always more than delicate and
guarded. And what was more, such was her spirit
and pleasantry of humour that ere long she acquired
a decided ascendancy in her father's little court, as
her sentiments were generally in unison with his.
That cut deeper than her Doric dialect, which was
still spoken by many persons of figure and fashion.
What wonder, then, that her topics and sentiments
should at times require to be refined through some
gentle strainers! It was not in favour of her and
her elder brother that they were much too fond of
fun and of practical jokes, which they sometimes
carried too far. If in these circumstances, from the
exuberance of her spirits and the openness of her
disposition, which made her lay too little stress upon
punctilios, she at times fell into what fastidious people
accounted solecisms in breeding and discourse, her
friends and companions, being well apprised of her
worth and innocence of heart, considered them as
peccadilloes when put in the balance with her better
qualities.

If I forget not, the first time I met this good lady

was at Tullibody, in the month of October 1762, for
she was much attached to that family, Mrs Abercromby being the coeval and contemporary of her
mother, Lady Rachel.   There she fell in with people
as fond of fun as herself ; and they did not fail to
exercise their talents, which occasioned much laughter
and merriment at the expense of people not disposed to retaliate, or even to be out of humour at
these frolics.   She afterwards accompanied that lady
and her daughter to a ball at Stirling, given by Colonel
Masterton and the late Mr Drummond of Blair.   The
latter, who had once been her father's intimate friend,
and was always fond of her, engaged her to dance with
Mr Mackenzie of Balmaduthy, an advocate and a
genteel young man.   Whatever might be her reason,
she took umbrage at her partner : and therefore, not
to be troubled with him, resolved to pass as a fool,
in which, to the great entertainment of her companions, she completely succeeded.   She pretended she
could not dance a minuet, and as for country-dances,
the figures of them were much too kittle for her.   They
therefore sat down when it was their turn to dance.
At supper, being seated by her partner, she entertained him with strange topics that coincided with
her wayward resolve.[1]   This was not wise or polite

[1] Sir Hugh Paterson, a fine lively old man, who outlived all the cavaliers
of this country, having made a motion for annual balls at Stirling for fifty
years, this lady observed to Mr Mackenzie, "That in much less time the
worms would be playing *backbendy* through Sir Hugh and the bulk of the
company. Is not that, sir, a melancholy consideration, or sufficient to damp
our mirth ?"

to her friend, who had engaged her to an unexceptional
young man. Nay, she could not forbear playing her
tricks on him, who was no subject for them, he being
a man of excellent sense and dignified manners. It
was not the way to increase the number of her admirers.
To that the more attention was due, that she was
then in her bloom, very agreeable and well connected.
Some time after, when resident at Broomhall, a gentleman of fortune, an inmate of the family, fell in love
with her, and was about to have paid his addresses,
but she and her brother played him so many comic
tricks that he was disgusted, and soon after married
another lady.[1] It was the more to be regretted as
she had not a spark of ill-nature and malevolence in
her disposition, her playfulness being perfectly innocent, designed to promote merriment, without hurt-
ing anybody's feelings. I suspect, however, her practical wit to have been a hereditary trait. Be that
as it may, it is not much better than punning and
other false wit. In a word, when the lady in question was in tip-top spirits, and in a frolicsome humour,
what Horace says of Glycera might be applied to
her—" Urit grata protervitas et vultus nimium lubri-

[1] They contrived to hang up the gentleman's embroidered vests as scare-
crows on the trees; and when in a violent hurry to dress for dinner, he found
his shoes filled with swans. General Bruce, then a young man, had his vest
gradually straitened every morning, which made him very apprehensive.
Nay, they did not spare the amiable Earl himself, who received a splendid
card from the Marquis of Titchfield, then in Scotland, reminding him of their
acquaintance abroad, and announcing a visit at Broomhall some days after. So
completely was he taken in, that he held a council with Lady Elgin about the
style in which they should receive and entertain their noble guest. In these
tricks there was a climax and a degree of ingenuity.

cus adspici." Had she met with a helpmate worthy
of her, she was likely to have made a respectable
figure in the married state.

For a number of years I had little occasion to meet
with Lady Rachel, who lived mostly at Lundin and
Stobhall with her father. To him, after the death of
her mother, she proved a great comfort, for as she
was a very lively interesting companion, she accommodated herself to his ways with great dexterity.
Like a dutiful daughter, she stood by him when
fallen into what he accounted dark and evil times,
seeing her fairest prospects were one after another
blasted or clouded.

The death of Lord Drummond was the severest
blow which could have befallen the father or daughter
in this life. After that young man had lost a number
of precious years at home, without any object to
occupy him, his father at last consented to send him
over to America, to look after the Melfort estate in
the province of New Jersey, which after the attainder
of that family had either been in the hands of its
creditors, or of new granted by the governor and his
council, in terms of the provincial laws. Had it not
been dilapidated, it was a princely grant; and there
could not be a doubt that the Earl of Perth was the
only person that could put in a legal claim to it, the
representatives of the original grantee being aliens,
and having their blood attainted. Although Lord
Drummond came upon what was deemed an ungracious errand, he met with a very gracious recep-

tion.   In the management of a very difficult and
complicated business, where he had many antagonists
to contend with and soothe, he discovered parts and
address which could not have been expected from his
education and opportunities.   Had not that country
been not long after the seat of convulsions and civil
war, he bid fair to have got out of the wrecks of the
fortune a fine estate, which might in time have turned
to great account.   I need not say that something like
a new state of society took place in that country, in
consequence of which royal grants were all forfeited,
or resumed by the new states.   He met with all the
encouragement that the King's governors and generals
could give him ; and it was said he was employed by
them in some nice negotiations with the provincials,
who were by that time in a state of insurrection.   But,
to the inexpressible sorrow of his family, he was cut
off by sickness soon after the commencement of hostilities.   Had his life been spared, he bid fair ere
long to have been restored to the noble estate of the
Perth family ; for by that time a great change had
taken place in the views and sentiments of Ministers
of State.   I remember, however, it was the general
wish that the restoration might not take place in the
father's time ; for old as he then was, there was no
saying how far he might have gone wrong.   But
he met with great compassion on this occasion.   In
fact, the death of Lord Drummond was a great loss
to this country, which looked to him for the resus-
citation of a noble and respectable family.   By that

time his spirits were much broken, and infirmities
had weakened him. But he did not long survive
his beloved son. At no period of life was Lady
Rachel more worthy of praise and admiration than
when attending upon her father in circumstances far
from pleasing. In paying this duty to her surviving
parent, she spent a number of her best years in a way
that virtue and religion could not but approve.

After Lord Perth's death, I had often occasion to
meet with Lady Rachel at Clackmannan Castle, Bran-
field, Cardross, Stirling Castle, or Newtoun, all of them
families very much to her taste, where she was ever welcome. It was not the less agreeable that her venerable
friend Lady Sarah was commonly one of the party.
She was by that time approaching to forty, and much
changed in her looks and humour. Her youth and
bloom were past. In features she resembled her
father, as much as a woman could a man; and the
configuration of their minds was somewhat similar;
at least she had caught much of his manner and
sentiments. If her vivacity was not extinguished,
wanting only time and opportunity to rekindle it,
it assumed a very different form from what it had
worn twenty years before in the heyday time of life.
She had no longer any relish for frolic and practical jokes, which did suit her time of life, to say
nothing of the disappointments and sorrows she had
met with in the journey of life. It was, however,
obvious that her heart was warm and generous, ever
ready to serve and oblige her friends. Indeed, simu-

lation and dissimulation had no part in her ethics, she being too much disposed to act and speak on the impulse of the moment, without regarding appearances or weighing consequences. She surely had a great deal of the Drummonds' *Ire*,[1] but that was more conspicuous in her sayings than in her deeds, which breathed a beneficent spirit, though not insensible to injuries, real or fancied. Indeed it was not expedient to contravert her opinions in matters great or small, for she had words and topics at will, which served to confound, if they did not convince gainsayers. She had a flow of eloquence peculiarly her own, which induced her friends and companions who cared not to combat her with her own weapons to grant her propositions sufficiently questionable. In matters connected with her partialities and dislikes, it was not prudent to interfere, both of them being often carried too far. If her singularities could not be entirely justified, they were, in the opinion of every candid person, compensated by her integrity and good intentions, which might be misled, but still her judgment was more to blame than her heart.

It must be confessed by such as were most partial to Lady Rachel, that her conversation resembled that of no other person of rank and fashion. Nobody ever trusted less to the tale of the day, or gave herself less concern about what was going on in the gay, the fashionable, or literary world; but if no sciolist in

[1] Culuhey prayed to be delivered from the *Ire* of the Drummonds, &c. &c.

the *belles lettres,* she had read a great deal. No one was more deeply learned in the history of *private* life, or in what may be termed the antiquities of manners. As she had an ample stock of information little known, she was not sparing or unskilful in retailing fragments of it, with equal *naïveté* and force, which were naturally introduced; for her narratives never exceeded in prolixity or embarrassment, and she did not disgust by her repetitions. She had the art of clothing them in glowing energetic language, every word of which told. In this she had advantages peculiar to herself. With the people and manners of Charles II.'s and James VII.'s time she was well acquainted. For these she was chiefly indebted to her father, who was partial to the times when the family of Perth was great at Court; and as that was his favourite theme, he had access in his youth to converse with aged persons of the same time. He had all the information that his lady's aunt, Lady Janet, could give him, who, as she lived to be very old, was a woman of sense and great spirit, quite entire to the last.[1] Nay, by means of Lundin of Drums, his cousin and competitor, he could go still further back: for when that gentleman spoke of the Court, he meant that of James V. or VI. at Falkland, of which he used to give curious interesting anecdotes. It was a pity that these had not been

[1] In 1680 and 1681, when seventeen years old, Lady Janet lived at Holyrood Abbey with the Duchess of Rothes, and was often at the Duke of York's Court, of which she gave a very lively account.

set down in writing; but in that way traditional
history, transmitted from father to son, must, sooner
or later, be lost irrecoverably. And with the provincial history of Fife and Perthshire for a century
back, and with the revolutions that had taken place
in families and manners, she was perfectly acquainted.
But had her memory been less tenacious, or her mind
less susceptible of impressions, she could not help
contracting a relish for these topics which her father
from first to last loved to discourse and comment upon.
That he or she always judged soundly of persons or
things need not be asserted, seeing their views were
strongly tinged by their prejudices in politics. Still,
however, a person must have been narrow-minded and
touchy, who had found fault with Lady Rachel for
sporting her antiquated notions with great acidity,
at a time when party spirit and its ordinary appendages appeared to be extinguished and excluded from
good company. But the abasement of this noble
family represented by her father, and the uneasiness of
her own fortune, made her be regarded as a privileged
person. If the tide of manners and principles was
taking a new direction, she was none of those who
paid much regard to the breath of fashion or the
sentiments of others. By keeping aloof from the
circles of the gay and polite, she unavoidably sometimes appeared awkward and uneasy [1] in mixed com-

[1] One afternoon at Blairdrummond, in a small party much to her liking, a
company of strangers was unexpectedly announced. It struck her into a
heap, and for two hours she hardly uttered a syllable. But after supper,
somebody having said that Mr David Erskine (whom she never forgave for

pany, when she might have been entirely at her ease, and her sense and spirit would have enabled her to shine. She certainly had little resemblance to the ladies of quality of the present day in her address or talk.

A very little must now be said of her political opinions. When her education and the company she kept in her youth are considered, it would have been exceedingly strange if she had not been zealously attached to the exiled family; and her partialities and aversions had some relation to one another. When her passions were much agitated, she spake what she thought without disguise, sometimes with an asperity which may be more easily accounted for than justified. Yet even on those topics people were diverted with the poignancy and originality of her remarks and sarcasms, which savoured strongly of the dregs of a civil war; and some allowance is due to a fallen party. By the time I was much in this good lady's company, party rancour had either evaporated or was much softened, Whigs and Jacobites being disposed to live in charity, if not in love and unity. It was therefore regarded as bad breeding to speak of politics in mixed company. If she sometimes transgressed that rule, her wit and irony made some amends.[1] Even after she found it expedient to

buying her father's estate) could not get evergreens to grow on his garden wall in Nicolson Street, Lady Rachel struck in with great keenness, saying, "What has he to do with evergreens? let him cover his walls with bacon, hams, and kippers." The strangers were confounded. *Facit indignatio versus!*
[1] In 1759-60, when Britain was victorious in every quarter of the globe, she

speak with reverence of her rulers, she could not speak of King William or of George II. and his Ministers but with wrath and contempt. Still, however, her particular circumstances afforded her an apology which few others could plead. Nor was it diminished by the opinion generally entertained of her goodness of heart.

When the disaffected began to court the favour of the reigning family, Lady Rachel was hardly in charity with the new converts who rendered that allegiance to George III. which conscience forbade them to swear to his grandfather, and imputed their conduct to evident interested motives. Nay, she was not disposed to approve of those who had changed from conviction, it being her maxim that all *new light* in these cases was derived from a crack in the skull, accompanied by a flaw in the heart.[1]

Of Lady Rachel's religious notions little need be said, as it was none of her common themes. Suffice it to say, she was all along a member of the nonjuring Episcopal Church. Though she did not love Presbytery,[2] or regard it as a religion for a gentleman,

said it was an easy matter to bake with other people's meal,—a proverbial expression.

[1] One day she had a spirited conversation with the late Mrs Dundas of Blair, a strongly marked character. The latter told her plainly that had she been a man at the Revolution she would have promoted it. "Madam," said Lady Rachel, with a sneer, "you were not always of that opinion." "Very true," replied the other; "but in those days I had not read history." As Mrs Dundas's father was one of the unfortunate sufferers after the Rebellion, one would hardly have expected this declaration from her.

[2] Her great-grandfather, Sir Alexander Bruce, afterwards Earl of Kincardine, was expelled the Scottish Parliament in 1702 for a violent attack on

yet when I knew her best she lived on a friendly
footing with some of the Established clergy. In
adhering steadily to the tenets and ordinances of a
fallen Church, she had the more merit that her father
was not thought to be more than partial to any
Church or sect. Like the ladies of the last generation, she was probably indebted to her mother, who
looked on religion as a cordial and luxury. It is,
however, well known that the clergy and laity of that
communion in the preceding generation grafted religion on the acid and unfruitful stock of politics.

At length the prospects of her family began gradually to brighten up, the reins of government being no
longer kept at full stretch. The annexation of the
forfeited estates, and the establishment of a board to
manage them, had not produced the propitious effects
that might have been expected. On the contrary, it
was supposed to give occasion to robbing and abuse.
It seemed, therefore, the general wish that they
should be restored to the nearest heirs of the attainted
persons. The ice was first broke in the case of General
Fraser, who in 1774 was restored by Act of Parliament to his father's estate. It was now taken for
granted that sooner or later the rest would be treated
with the same benignity. It is needless to add that
the American war and the fluctuations of Ministry
prevented the execution of a measure to which none

Presbytery "as inconsistent with monarchy," ranking it with vice and
hypocrisy. It gave occasion, he said, to the pride of infallibility of a pope in
every parish—an assertion sufficiently strong.

seemed to object. At last, in 1784, when faction ran mountains high, the restoration of the forfeited estates was carried through Parliament without a dissentient voice. None had more reason to rejoice than the lady under consideration, as it afforded her a prospect of seeing the family of Perth re-established in wealth and lustre. In whatever favour the former lords of that family might have stood with the Scottish monarch, to none of them were they so much beholden as Mr Drummond was to the King now on the throne. Nay, the violence and severity of his grandfather's Ministers turned out ultimately to the family's advantage; for had the estate been sold, like the low-country ones, it had been lost for ever. To one that can look back more than half a century, the whole looks like a tale of romance. It is not connected with my subject to tell what use has been made of the princely bounty by the families that received it : that will fall properly under the cognisance of some other historian of private life. It is sufficient to say that Mr Drummond made a provision for his sister which fully satisfied her.

In May 1796, when at Perth drinking Pitkeathly water along with Colonel Edmonstoune, I made her and her venerable aunt Lady Sarah a visit at Stobhall. Having gone to breakfast, it was some time before I was admitted, having been mistaken for another person. Nothing could be more gracious than Lady Rachel's reception. The house was mean and inconvenient, consisting of detached parts built at different times and pieced ill together. Everything about the place bore marks of forfeiture and the eclipse of the family. If the dining-room or parlour was small and low-roofed, it was garnished with pictures that commanded attention and respect. There was a picture of Cardinal Howard, grand-uncle to the Duchess-Dowager, and hard by it hung those of Secretary Maitland[1] and her brother, Chancellor Thirlstane,—an odd assortment of characters and principles. In a book-shelf stood a MS. copy of Lord Strathallan's ' History of the Drummonds,' a very interesting work, in which one finds more on the subject of manners and private life than is commonly found in such performances, which are often masses of dulness and vainglory, oddly huddled together. Near it were placed superb editions of Virgil and Horace, printed at the expense of Louis XIV. of France, never sold, but given in presents to ambassadors or the confidential Ministers of his allies. Assuredly, the family of Chancellor Perth had little reason to plume itself on its friendship and intercourse with that ambitious monarch.

After Lady Rachel had commented in her own style on the pictures, we sat down to a very good breakfast in great glee. The thing that appeared most new was a dish of wild-fowl's eggs, boiled hard, got from a loch in the Stormont. I forget the name of the bird, but its eggs had been a standing dish

---

[1] Lord Perth used to say that though descended from two Maitlands, he looked upon them as a couple of rascals : they were at least distinguished ones !

in the family, being accounted a delicacy which was
not the less valued for being rare.   Lady Sarah
was rather late of making her appearance, which was
the only mark of old age discernible in her, for she
was lively, cheerful, and attentive.   At the back of
her chair stood a comely barefooted girl, twelve or
thirteen years old, who, Lady Rachel said, was her
aunt's *page*.   She was niece or grandchild to one of
the Duchess's Popish domestics, who, after her decease, were retained by Lord Perth and his daughter.
I have been told they were valuable domestics, as
their master and lady did not plume themselves upon
their knowledge of the mysteries of domestic economy.
However, the damsel, who was as arch-looking as
any page, acquitted herself to good purpose, filling
the kettle, handing about the tea-cups, and going
messages to the housekeeper.   I was next taken
to see the family wardrobe, great part of which had
been embezzled or lost in the late civil wars.[1]

Yet even the remains were very interesting to an
antiquary.   Among them were the clothes of an Earl
John in James VI.'s time, which appeared more
fantastic than those of our *petits maîtres*, being
flounced and decorated with a profusion of ribbons and
fringes.   Then I saw in high preservation the official
robes of Lord Drummond, who had been Justice-

---

[1] It seems the Lundin family used to preserve in trunks their wedding
clothes. Mr Abercromby told me that when he used to visit there, the young
people sometimes arrayed themselves in these antiquated garments, which
made them look as if they were going to a masquerade. It was a good
habit illustrative of manners and customs.

General in the reign of James IV. They were of
black damask, richly embroidered with gold, similar
to those of the Lord Register and extraordinary
Lords of Session, which they wore in my younger
years. I was also shown a set of letters from the
Princess of Orange, daughter of Charles I., written
soon after her marriage, when under the control of
a stern governess.[1] They were perfectly girlish, ill
written and worse spelt, but anything from the pen
of King William's mother was a curious *relique*. It
was a proof that the *cacoethes scribendi* had by that
time seized princesses when imperfectly taught. I
was much pleased with some missals and psalters,
finely written and illuminated, which the family had
probably picked up when the great religious houses
in that country had been plundered and pulled down.
She spoke of the great losses in that way which the
family had sustained in the first half of the eighteenth
century. My wonder was that so much had been
saved in such over-zealous times. She then took a
full view of the house, of which she gave a chron-
ological and curious account. It seems the first
Protestant Lady Drummond, who was the daughter
of Lord Ruthven the great reformer, converted the
church into a kitchen, and a burial-vault into a wine-
cellar, with some other changes equally anomalous.
There were, if I mistake not, four separate houses, to
each of which there was a separate outer door, locked
at night. There were, however, more bedchambers

[1] To Lady Lillias Drummond, afterwards Countess of Tullibardine.

than could have been expected, furnished as that
venerable lady[1] had left them.

We afterwards sallied forth to survey the place, or
what the Scots call the *policy*. Though everything
without doors was out of order, one might see that at
some preceding period the lords of that family had
not been inattentive to embellishment and what
Milton calls "vernal delight." It could not be expected that any of them for fourscore years could
pay much attention to that matter.   The Duchess
cared not to spend anything in that way after the
attainder; and had Lord Perth attempted it, offence
would have been taken by the factors, in whom the Commissioners had implicit confidence. If, however, art
had done little, nature had been most bountiful in her
gifts. The house and garden overlook a long stretch
of the river Tay, terminated by a noble flow of water
at the Linn of Campsie. If, since the Rebellion, the
forest-trees which had afforded shade and shelter had
been wantonly or improvidently cut down by the
factors, there was a large natural wood to fringe and
enliven the prospect. It varied every step, and added
much to my pleasure. On our way up the hill, Lady
Rachel, pointing at the *wine*-well, asked if I spied a
bottle at the bottom. On saying I did not, she told
me that it had been the immemorial practice of the
Perth family to order a bottle of wine to be put into
it upon the arrival of strangers, apologising for the

---

[1] The Duchess contrived to save a great many articles in 1745-46, all
which she bequeathed to the Earl of Perth, as the representative of the family

omission. Before we went into the house, she carried me to see a small parterre-garden, edged with box, which lay under the windows. This, said she, the good Duchess[1] called her *drawing*-room, repairing thither with her guests after dinner, telling them she had no other drawing-room.

In short, I had a most delightful walk; but it may be affirmed that Lady Rachel's conversation and remarks upon persons and things were more interesting and picturesque than the finest landscape.

We then had a very pleasing dinner, where the two ladies appeared to great advantage, each in her own way. If the table was not an elegant one, it was good and plentiful. I did not relish it the less, that I understood Lady Rachel trod nearly in the steps of the venerable dowager. I should have liked to have met with some of the priests, who were in a manner inmates of the family. One of them, a sen-

[1] This excellent woman was of the Gordon family, a valuable specimen of the ladies of the last age. She bore the abasement of her family and the blasting of her fondest hopes with the heroism of a Roman matron, seeming to glory in them, and making light of imprisonment and of the insolence of office. The style in which she lived at Stobhall was kindly and dignified. Between that place and Edinburgh she spent her time. Though a zealous Catholic, she all along cherished the Protestant tenants of her locality lands, never obtruding persons of her own religion at the instigation of priests or favourites. A short time before her death she sent for James Moray of Abercairney, to give him some directions about her burial in the chapel at Innerpeffray. "Sir," said she, "you need not be afraid of any obstruction in performing this charitable office, for, be assured, the sepulchre of the family is not attainted, having never been surveyed." I had this from Abercairney. Not long before, the Justice-Clerk would not permit young Lochiel to be buried with his ancestors. To Lord Perth, the Duchess, and her daughter, Lady Mary left a considerable sum of money, with a great deal of furniture, plate, and trinkets. Proper care was taken of her domestics both by Lord Perth and his son.

sible well-behaved man, was brother to one of the servants. After passing a long day very much to my satisfaction, I returned in the evening to my friend at Perth.

In June 1792, when upon a jaunt to the north, I made these good ladies a second visit at Stobhall, and was not the less welcome for bringing the news of Tippoo Sultan's defeat, which made Lady Rachel shed tears of joy. I was happy to find them both in health and spirits. So many curiosities had I seen when there before, that I could hardly expect to meet with anything new; but I took a second survey of things still remaining there, for a number of them had been transported to Drummond Castle. The conversation of the two ladies was a great luxury, for Lady Rachel's information was equally copious and interesting. Nor could one expect to see extreme old age more placid, entire, and cheerful than in the aunt, who had always something apposite to say, there being no visible decline in her faculties or frame. In going through the house, I got some curious anecdotes relative to the statesmen of Charles II. not to be found in books. They were suggested by some of the portraits, that were more beauteous than good, if traditionary history may be trusted. My noble hostess took me then to see her *labouring* or farm, which was not in much better order than the *labourings* of our gentry fifty years ago, of which some account was given in the first part of this work. Whether it was lucrative signified little to her, who was quite at her ease, seeing it afforded her exercise and amusement. In truth, she had too much genius, perhaps whim, to succeed in the practical part of husbandry, which requires perpetual attention to little men and little things. She had no turn for business of any kind, and was guided by favourites, who are not always wisely chosen. From her brother's managers she might have got great help, but of them she was not over fond. On that subject, however, she said little. The wisest thing she could do was not to intermeddle in those matters. Indeed, had she obtruded her counsels, they would not have been listened to. Meanwhile she flattered herself that her *improvements*, though upon a very small scale, would benefit the estate of Stobhall, which was then mostly in a state of nature.

If Whig and Tory were by that time out of date, this good lady had got new subjects of fear and indignation. To the democrats and to Paine's levelling notions she was as hostile as she had ever been to the statesmen of the former reigns. The keenest Whig could not be more zealous for the constitution or for the prince that filled the throne.

I was very much pleased to see a portrait of Lady Sarah, which, if not good painting, afforded such a striking characteristic likeness, that one would have thought her in the act of conversation. She was averse to its being drawn, and could hardly be persuaded to sit. But her zealous niece overruled all her scruples by saying, with her usual keenness,

"Nay, madam, if you will not like that trouble now, you *shall* be drawn after you are dead." After spending a day at Stobhall, very much to my satisfaction, I took leave of the ladies, and set out next morning betimes on my expedition.

I regretted exceedingly that in June 1795, when upon a tour to Aberdeen, Peterhead, &c., I did not call at that place to have seen my noble friends in passing. The family surgeon at Coupar-Angus apprised me that they were both in good health. I might have considered how little the health of a nonagenarian's life was. I had hardly got home when I received an intimation of the good lady's having slept the sleep of death.

This event at any other time would have given a great shock to the mind of Lady Rachel; but her feelings were then less lively than formerly, owing to a bad state of health, which was not the less serious for being gradual. As long as she lived at Stobhall, one of her female friends stayed there, to be her companion; but for some years before she died, she was fond of shifting the scene, in hopes of some change to the better, from air, company, &c.

With this view she, and her aunt while alive, used to pass the winter in Fife among the relations of the Lundin family. And when the family was at home, she lived a good deal at Drummond Castle. I incline to think that Lady Rachel and I did not meet again after we parted in June 1792. That was owing in part to the death of some of her favourite friends in this country.

In the decline of her health, she thought proper, in spring 1797, to make a visit at Cardross, purposing to return to Stobhall as soon as she should get better. There, however, she grew worse and worse, her ailments being no less obstinate than complicated. Meanwhile, everything was done by the family to render her comfortable and serene. Since it was her fate to finish her course at a distance from her own home, she could not have found a more eligible situation. After languishing near a year under this hospitable roof, Lady Rachel breathed her last in the midst of a set of relations whom she loved and revered. To them her deathbed and the drooping of her spirits must have been very mortifying; but none knows what may be between him and the grave.

When this good lady was about to make her will, Mr Erskine entreated her to leave nothing to his family, in which he acted perfectly in character. After leaving marks of her esteem to friends and favourites,[1] she directed the residue to be applied to pay her father's debts that were still outstanding. This was a very honourable step, seeing these creditors were poor and friendless. From regard to the

[1] To Miss Rachel Erskine she left her library, which was not a very valuable one, consisting chiefly of romance, of which she and Lady Sarah had been exceedingly fond. If it was not very wholesome intellectual food, it was so far well, that it afforded them entertainment when they could not have company and conversation to their taste. To them it was innocent.

family, they had held off when others to whom it was
indebted had been pressing and harsh. In doing all
in her power to indemnify those people for their sufferings, she made charity go hand in hand with regard for the memory of her father, for which she had
all along professed the highest veneration. She was
buried with much pomp in the sepulchre of the
Perth family, a thing she much desired. Such was
the life and death of Lady Rachel Drummond. I
have endeavoured to delineate her prominent features
with truth and delicacy. In performing that task I
have done ample justice to her merits, which were
confessedly considerable. If her foibles and peculiarities are brought forward, they are not exaggerated,
but referred to circumstances which afford a sufficient
apology. If sometimes warped by passion or prejudice, be it remembered that in those things she rather
followed than led. Be that as may, the warmth of
her heart, the honesty and frankness of her nature,
superior to disguise and deceit, made those that were
best acquainted with her esteem her most. Her
faults and errors may be regarded as nearly akin to
original sin ; for she surely carried filial duty and
admiration sufficiently far. If that was the case, it
must be regarded with an indulgent eye, when we
take into consideration her father's embarrassments
and misfortunes, which claimed her sympathy and
support. She was sometimes apt to fly off at tan-
gents, nor was she always lucky in her counsellors

and confidants. In these cases the liveliness of her
fancy and the keenness of her temper, which scorned
all restraint, proved too hard for her judgment, and
even for the rectitude of her heart. And as she was
apt to take side-views of a subject, it was no easy
matter to do business with her. Had she been a
great queen, she was likely to have fallen under the
guidance of favourites. It was, however, her good
fortune that she was not called to act an arduous
part in the stage of time.

To conclude, Lady Rachel was perhaps the last
person of her rank in Scotland who retained the principles, or, in other words, the attachments and an-
tipathies of a great and numerous party, which had
for many years weakened the national strength, and
sometimes threatened to overset the throne when
filled with able sovereigns. But the people of whom
it was composed were more remarkable for good
morals and amiable manners than for political wisdom or enlightened patriotism. If, for a number
of years, she found it expedient to be more temperate in her language, the change appeared chiefly in
her silence ; for, as she made no recantations, it is
imagined she did not drop a single principle or prejudice which she had imbibed and cherished when
civil dudgeon ran high. And therefore she was better
entitled to the praise of consistency than a number
of her party, who found it necessary to bow the knee
to the reigning family. It cannot, however, be

denied that this good lady, both in her younger and more advanced years, was a decided aristocrat in manners, sentiments, and pretensions, which last, perhaps, she carried too high in times when the tide of opinion was setting in strong the other way, riches being in more estimation than lustre of birth.

CHAPTER X.

AGRICULTURE.

THE situation of Scotland for some hundreds of years was exceedingly unfavourable to agriculture, its inhabitants being almost constantly engaged in wars or violent factions. They had therefore no encouragement to cultivate the land further than necessity required. As far back as the public records go, the stewartry of Menteith, and the adjacent parts of Stirling and Clackmannan shires (to which our observations chiefly relate), were divided into *towns* or townships, occupied by two or more tenants and their cottagers. Their houses commonly lay close together, which was probably owing to their being of old obliged to defend themselves by force of arms against the Highland freebooters, who sometimes attempted to carry off their goods and cattle.[1] For

---

[1] Robert Buchanan of Moss-side was told by his father, then a tenant in Ochtertyre, that about the Revolution the M'Gregors came down and plundered my grandfather's house, and drove off his cattle and those of the tenants. They also carried him prisoner some miles above Callander, whither, upon the country taking the alarm, George Drummond of Blair followed them with a strong *posse*. Upon his arrival, the women were busy

the same reason the smaller gentry had their houses
and orchards in one of these towns, security being
then in more estimation than embellishment.

In the end of the last and the beginning of the
present century, the making and unmaking of kings,
and disputes concerning modes of worship or church
government, employed the attention of all ranks of
men. And hence the nobility and gentry had little
inclination to attend minutely to the management of
their estates, that matter being devolved upon their
people of business. But hard-heartedness towards
tenants was by no means the vice of those times.
Great bargains were often given, sometimes from
kindness and personal regard, and sometimes from
not knowing better.

Many of the more respectable farmers were probably descended of the *rentallers*, or *kindly tenants*,
described in our law-books, who formed in the middle
ages a very numerous and powerful body. But in
the course of the three last centuries the greatest part
of them became feuars or tacksmen. Though this
produced a general rise of rents, and other unpalatable
changes, some great families, either from policy or
tenderness, continued, almost to our own times, to
tread in the steps of their ancestors. They laid it
down as a rule, never to change tenants that behaved

cutting down the sheets and tablecloths. "Where are your sons?" said he
to the father of the ringleaders. "In the hill, I suppose," answered the
man. "If everything is not forthwith restored," said Blair, "I will raze you
and them off the earth." Their prisoner was released, and everything got
back but a favourite gun.

well; neither were the rents raised, they being satisfied with *grassums*, or fines, which Lord Stair observes
was always a mark of kindness.[1] But as that tenure
could no longer be depended on, it imported those
favoured tenants to have tacks in writing for a defi-
nite term of years. We have had these in this
country very far back, at a time when few countrymen
could either read or write. The hardships experienced by that class of people after the Reformation
made them solicitous to have legal security.

Whatever was their origin, we had lately in most
low country parishes tribes of husbandmen who prided
themselves not a little upon their old standing in
the barony.[2] Some of them are mentioned in the
king's rentals, or in other ancient writings.[3] There
was a set of rich husbandmen on the Perth estate in
this parish when George Drummond of Blair purchased it. And those of the good old families on
the banks of the Forth were in the same situation,

---

[1] Such was the practice of the Perth family till a little before the last
Rebellion, when the late lord raised some baronies very much. Neither had
it been confined to the Highland tenants, from whom military service was
expected; it extended to the low country ones, who disliked the civil and
religious principles of the family, and had an utter aversion to the use of arms
in any cause.

[2] The late Mr James Stirling, Keir's brother, being one day in the house of
one of the Mitchells at Old Keir (where he was not known), asked if they had
been long there, and was answered, " Longer than the laird."

[3] Among the king's rentallers in 1479 we find the Quhiteheads of Row,
whose descendants were tenants on these very lands twenty-five years ago.
The Spittals in Cercentully, and the Hendersons in Cornton, also mentioned
there, are still in the neighbourhood. The Chrysties or Chrystiesons were
kindly tenants in Ochtertyre to Forrester of Corstorphin, and in Craigforth
to the Elphinstones 200 years ago.

particularly the Earl of Moray's tenants in the Trews,[1] and the Earl of Mar's in the parish of Logie. Alexander Thomson, who knew the latter in their prosperity, told me they lived more like feuars than tenants. There was in those days a kindness and familiarity between the gentry and their people which proved very propitious [2] to the latter. The hardest masters were the lesser feuars, who, being themselves countrymen, knew the full value of the land, and had not the smallest scruple at racking their dependants. It has often been observed that there is no oppressor so unfeeling as a *bonnet* laird, or a tenant who has power to subset. But for many years back there has been a clause in most of our tacks prohibiting subsetting.[3]

Nothing proved more hurtful to tenants than the misfortunes which befell their masters, whether occasioned by extravagance or forfeitures. Hence the sale of lands and a rise of rents which, during the pros-

[1] In the last century, an Earl of Moray observing at an entertainment one of his Trew tenants dancing merrily at the age of seventy, said in a joke, "John, you are too rich and wanton; I must raise my land." "My lord, answered he, "it is not the land that has made me rich, but God's providence and the *change of wives.*"

[2] Let me here give an instance of tenderness towards a country neighbour. About seventy years ago, Charles, Earl of Moray, offered George Home of Argaty a feu, at the old rent, of the farm of Wester Argaty, which came close to his door. Though this was very convenient for him, he declined it, saying, God forbid he should ever hurt an honest countryman. He might doubtless have continued the tenant, but the scruple did honour to his heart and sensibility.

[3] The family of Moray have all along allowed it; but though calculated to keep the real labourers of the ground in poverty, it has contributed to raise the rents, regard being had in the new set to what the subtenants paid.

perity of the family, both parties would have thought enormous. In this view, the difficulty of bringing bankrupt estates to sale between the middle of the last century and the Union was of no disadvantage to the tenants.

Besides rentals and tacks, there were in former times other less liberal modes of letting land. When a specific rent in money or victual could not be had, the master received a full third of the corn crop, after deducting the tithe. And hence it was called *third and teind*. A few years before the Restoration, part of the estate of Tullibody, which then belonged to Mr Robert Meldrum, was let in this way. The last instance of it in this part of the country was about threescore years ago, in the lands of Row, belonging to Mr Foggo.[1] This mode is reputed very ancient, and may have been one of those by which the bondmen paid rent, before their entire manumission. This was probably done by some rule general or particular. And though *third and teind* was not fit for all sorts and situations, it was better than none, and far from being unsuitable to a low state of husbandry.

In other cases the lands were let on *steelbow—i.e.,* at the tenant's entry, the master ploughed and sowed the ground, and delivered a proper stocking of horses, cows, sheep, utensils, &c., all which the tenant became bound to redeliver in good order at the end of the tack. In times either of national or particular dis-

---

[1] Mr David Erskine says that within the last twenty years the estate of Newark in Fife, belonging to Lord Newark, was set in *third and teind.*

tress, when good tenants could not be had, this mode
was resorted to.   It was always the way to get a high
rent, and, of course, much practised where tenants
had liberty to subset.

And now of the husbandry which prevailed in this
country at the time when it can first be traced by
memory.   In this corner, where the chief dependence
was upon corn, each tenant had commonly a ploughgate of land ; but upon the borders of the Highlands
there were commonly four tenants to a plough, sometimes more.   In place of having their possessions
separate from each other, the whole was everywhere
in *runrig*—i.e., the several tenants had ridge about of
every field.

The grounds were further divided into *infield* and
outfield.   The former lay contiguous to the home-
stead, and was cultivated with great care.   In the
carses east by Stirling, on both sides of the river, it
has been divided, past all memory, into equal portions
of peas or beans, bear or barley, and oats.   But in
the greatest part of Menteith it was the practice,
within the last fourscore years, to take two successive
crops of oats after bear.

The whole dung was laid upon the infield, but it
being inconsiderable, much of the summer work was
bestowed on making earth *fuilzie*—i.e., composts of
earth made of dung or lime.   For this purpose our
tenants made no scruple of taking the soil off one
ridge to lay it upon another.[1]   In that way whole

[1] In the east carses, the deeper one goes the soil is the better, and there-

fields on most estates in this neighbourhood have
been stripped of the vegetable mould, and nothing
left but a bottom of till or gravel. It may from that
circumstance be referred to a very remote era. Yet,
abstracted from the loss of ground, it was an excellent
manure, serving both to enrich and thicken the soil of
the infield, and answering some of the purposes of a
fallow.

But the far greater part of the farm consisted of
outfield, managed in a very slovenly manner. In
some places it was the practice either to fold cattle in
summer, or in thin sandy soils to lay them under
water in winter. In general, however, it got no
manure, and after the ordinary time, it was broken
up for oats. There was some variety in the articles
of cropping and resting, but in the dry fields it was
usual to leave the ground lea for six years, and then
to take three crops of oats. And the people of the
carses rested two years and took two crops thereafter.

In the outfields upon both sides of the great mosses
a particular mode of improvement took place. Every
summer in the month of July large quantities of the
refuse of peat were led out to the adjacent field and
burnt. There is a tradition that before this practice
took place the moss was cast up in large heaps and
burnt down to the clay, after which the ashes were

fore little ground was destroyed. The scourings of the ditches sufficed to
manure one-sixth of their farms yearly. The enormous size of their ditches
shows it to have been carried to a very great pitch of old.

carried out and spread upon the land. Of old only
one crop of oats was taken after burning, but it was
commonly a great one, especially if the summer
proved wet and warm. But about seventy years ago
John M'Arthur, tenant in the Muir,[1] began to take
two; in order, however, to improve the quantity and
quality of the ashes, he made a few thin furrows
across the field, which were burnt with the peat.
The managing a third of the Moss-side in this way
occupied our tenants very fully three weeks every
year. There being a contention who should be first
done, they thought nothing of beginning work by
three in the morning, and continuing, with little in-
termission, till seven at night.

Beside getting ashes for manure, a ridge 12 or
15 feet wide was every year gained along one-third
of the Moss-side. This seldom failed to produce an
extraordinary crop the very next season. In this
way many hundred acres of the low moss, or *spread
field*, have been gradually converted into arable land.
Some notion of its progress may be formed from the
following circumstances: I heard my grandmother
(who was married in 1692) say, that when she came
to Ochtertyre her father-in-law told her the little hill

---

[1] He was originally my grandfather's servant, and afterwards his tenant.
From small beginnings he made a great deal of money for one in his way
I never knew a more sagacious, worthy, cheerful countryman. His neighbours called him John M'Industry, from an expression of his, "that man
might make industry, but it was God that gave the increase." It is said he
was kept from being an elder for doubting the story of Samson and the
foxes; on hearing which read he exclaimed, "Wa! wa! where would the
man get all these tods!" He died in 1764.

called the Naad was, in his younger days, surrounded
by the moss, which is now 350 yards distant. Janet
Mitchell, daughter of Walter Mitchell, tenant in the
Muir between ninety and a hundred years ago, remembered, when in her father's farm, there was only
a narrow slip of land between the moss and the ditch,
called the black *gott*. From its narrowness, it was
ploughed east and west, instead of north and south,
which is the direction of the ridges at present. And
George Bachop was told by a John Ramsay, who died
in 1790, aged fourscore, that Robert Bachop, George's
great-grandfather, said to him he remembered when
there was nothing but a loan between the moss and
the Carat Brae below the present highroad. By all
accounts, the tenants of the neighbouring proprietors
were equally assiduous and successful in their operations. But after all, the commencement and progress
of these can only be matter of conjecture, because the
depth of the moss is very different, and the manner of
working was by no means uniform. And in troublesome times little or no progress could be made.

Upon seeing the good effects of ashes, Robert
Buchanan,[1] in Scribetree, who had no share of the
Moss-side, burned, about ninety years ago, two patches
of outfield, which yielded great crops in the dear years.

---

[1] This was a remarkable man, both for sense and good fortune. Upon the
smallest of my grandfather's farms he made, in less than half a century, what
purchased lands of 1000 merks a-year, which he divided among his sons.
Besides this, he portioned several daughters. Indeed, he dealt deeply in
woods, cheese, meal, &c., but he was withal an excellent husbandman. He
ran three nineteen-year tacks of his farm, and more than doubled its rent.

It was, however, wretched husbandry in the long-run, the ground having been barren ever since.

The grain of this country in our fathers' time was very poor in quality. Even after the Union, *white* oats were confined to the infield of the best farms; but in muirland, and even some dry field ones, nothing was raised but the *black* [1] or the *grey*. Nay, within the last fifty years we had hardly anything else in the Moss-side grounds, it being imagined the white would not thrive. And in the best outfields of the Trew, *bruiket* oats—*i.e.*, half black and half white —were common much later.

Though barley was then raised in the carses of Falkirk and Clackmannanshire, yet to the westward of Stirling we had only rough bear, the quality of which depended much on soil and culture. It had not in those days become the staple of tenants, who valued it chiefly as the best preparative for a great crop of oats. [2] And as the demand for malt was inconsiderable in comparison of what it has been of late years, a great proportion of the bear [3] was manufactured into meal for the lower classes of people.

By a law of James II., every tenant who had eight

[1] It appears from the king's rental 1479, that the victual rent of the stewartry of Menteith consisted chiefly of oats, even in the best soils, as the Rows, Cardross, Cruentully, the Trews, &c. These were probably black or grey.

[2] William Mayne of Tower told Mr Abercromby, Tullibody, that towards the end of last century, John Burn in Blackgrange was the first tenant thereabouts that sowed barley.

[3] In the rich carses of the lordship of Stirling the king's tenants paid, among other things, bear or malt—Cornton, five chalders bear; Inverallan, 2 chalders bear; Manour, a chalder of malt.

oxen, was directed to sow yearly half a firlot of peas
and forty beans at least. Though Bishop Leslie takes
notice of the luxuriant crops of them upon the banks
of the Forth and Tay in his time, yet if we may
judge from the rental of the archbishopric of St
Andrews, they were little cultivated by the rich tenants of that see. For whilst the third of the wheat
payable by them exceeded seven chalders, that of the
peas and beans amounted only to one boll and a
third. Even within the last threescore years, when
their utility was confessed, very few peas[1] were
sown to the westward. And beans were very late of
being introduced into the upper carses.[2]

Forty years ago there was no wheat raised in this
country, unless a little of a red *bearded* kind that
grew in the dry fields of Aithray.[3] The reason given

[1] James Drummond of Blair had a field of peas in Daira, to which the
schoolboys of Doune paid frequent visits. This made old Brown in his Saturday's charge say to them, "Cavete ab aquis, ab equis, ab herbis, et præser-
tim a pisis Dairæ."

[2] John Forrester's grandfather was the first tenant in the Trews who attempted it. He used to say his sowing three firlots of beans was a three
days' discourse at the kirk of Kippen. Old George Bachop was the person
who introduced them here.

[3] It is probable the wheat payable by the tenants of the lordship of Stirling was either of the red or white *bearded* kind. Be that as it may, wheat
appears to have been cultivated there at a very early period. Robert the
Bruce in the twelfth year of his reign gives to the Abbey of Cambuskenneth
the teinds of the lands of Bothkennar and Aithray, "tam in frumento quam
in denariis—sicut percipere consueverunt tempore Alexandri predecessoris
nostri ultime defuncti." And David Bruce, in the sixteenth year of his reign,
fixes it at £8, 5s. in money and six chalders of wheat. It appears from the
king's rental 1479, that the Grange of Bothkennar paid, among other things,
three chalders of wheat ; the lands of Cornton, five chalders ; the lands of
Inverallan, two chalders ; Blair-Logie, one chalder ; Manour, one chalder. It
seems, however, to have been confined to the very richest soils.

for sowing it there was the looseness of the ground,
which required to be consolidated.[1] It was sown
about Hallowmas without either fallow or dung;
and a worse rotation of crops could hardly have been
devised—viz., oats, wheat, bear. But as both the
white and red *bearded* wheat produced very white
flour, the tenants found a ready market for it, either
in Stirling or Glasgow. It was, however, a hungry
thick-husked grain compared with the smooth kinds
that have lately been introduced into this country.
The hardiness of the former, and its requiring no
extraordinary manure, was probably its chief recommendation of old.

Within the last forty years, ploughs, harrows, and
other implements of husbandry were in general
made by the tenant or his servants. Of course they
were clumsy and ill constructed, though sometimes a
mechanical genius appeared. The plough *graiths*—
i.e., the timber of the plough—rough and unshapen,
were brought by the Highlanders to the Martinmas
Fair of Doune, and sold at 1s. or 1s. 6d. apiece.
Even *withes* or widdies were furnished from the same
quarter at the rate of two pecks of meal yearly. The
collars of their work-horses were made of straw, and
their other apparatus equally cheap and primitive.

[1] It well deserves consideration why the farmers of the Carse of Gowrie
have persevered in raising great quantities of wheat, when those of Stirlingshire have given it over. At what time the bearded kinds were given up by
the former for the smooth wheat must be left to those who are well acquainted with the Carse of Gowrie. But, in all probability, both were actuated by
self interest and common-sense.

The tenants' horses were generally small and weakly in this corner, where peas and beans formed only a small proportion of the crop.[1] In the eastern carses they were in much better plight, some bean-stalks being reserved for their summer food, but even there they were comparatively small-sized to what they are at present. And the prices were also very low,[2]—hardly one-half of what is now commonly given for such horses.

The tenant's carriages were also very primitive and cheap. They used sledges for leading corn; and in old times for carrying out dung, &c., recourse was had to *coups*—*i.e.*, panniers fixed upon a sledge. And though these have long been exploded in the carses, they were within the last twenty-five years retained by the muirland people, both in carrying dung and performing statute work.[3] In their room we substituted *tumblers*, a trifling species of carts which have for ages been used about Alloa for transporting coals to the shore.[4] As there was neither

---

[1] Robert Buchanan says, his father sometimes laboured the farm of Scribetree with four beasts not worth forty merks altogether ; and in the Muir there was a plough belonging to pendiclers, which, from the insignificance of the horses, was called the *dog*-plough of Ochtertyre.

[2] The first horse that Alexander Thomson bought after being a tenant cost him eleven *nobles*—*i.e.*, £3, 13s. 4d. By that coin people counted much of old ; thus the price of weaving a plaid was a noble. He was at a great fair of Crieff about 1730, when the best horse was sold at eighty merks, but now he would give £16 or £18 sterling. Even within the last thirty years, £100 Scots was thought an extravagant price for a farmer's horse.

[3] Robert Buchanan remembers when the Muir tenants made use of *coups* for leading out peat to their Moss-side grounds.

[4] George M'Killop, a tenant in the Drys, whose grandson lately died, aged seventy, is said to have been the first be-west the Drys boat that got a *tumbler*

spokes nor iron upon the wheels, which consisted of
one solid piece of wood, they were unfit for long
journeys, being principally employed in leading dung
or peats. In those days, indeed, victual, coals, lime,
wood, slates, and other things from a distance, were
generally carrried on horses' backs, in sacks or pack-
ages abundantly simple.

In this corner, and in most of the carses, the tenants' houses were mostly built with *fail* or *divot*,
which in a few years had the appearance of a wall of
clay. Yet, when properly thatched, they were warmer
and freer from damp than what was built of stone
and clay. Within my own remembrance the farmhouses of the Muir were all built with fail, the
last of them being pulled down only a few years
ago. The chief objection to this mode of building
was its uncovering so much ground. It accorded,
however, with the inclination our tenants showed to
save upon every article. The same simplicity and
parsimony appeared in other things, stable-doors
being made of wattles, and there were seldom any
locks upon the barn-doors.[1]

The great extent of the outfields, and the facility
of boarding young beasts on the muirs during summer,
enabled tenants to keep a large stock of cows and
sheep. But being housed all night in winter, and

cart. Being a half-witted fellow, on paying for making it, he exclaimed, " A
dear sled, i' faith !"

[1] George Bachop, who died an old man in 1760, never had a lock upon his
barn door. Yet in other things he had the good sense never to grudge expense when it was likely to make a good return, or prevent a probable evil

starved in summer, these were both soft and stunted in their growth. It produced, however, a considerable quantity of dung, upon which, particularly that of the sheep, much reliance was had. Between the ingathering of the crop and the month of May, the whole beasts of the country were allowed, in the day-time, to go loose as upon a common. Indeed, before the Act for winter herding was made, nobody could be constrained to keep his cattle off other men's grounds, trespasses being only penal in royal forests. But for many years that excellent law remained a dead letter; and even now, after all the changes that have taken place, it is far from being popular among our country people.

The most rigid economy appeared in the dress and domestic expenses of tenants. The clothes of the family, and even of the servants, male and female, were for the most part spun and dyed at home; and thus, though hardly anything was made for sale, the wife's thrift in a numerous household turned to excellent account, as it saved her husband from going to market for a variety of necessaries. In the last age, the most substantial farmers seldom had anything better than a coat of grey or black *kelt*, spun by their wives. Twice or thrice in a lifetime, perhaps, they had occasion to buy a greatcoat of English cloth, as what was homespun would not keep out rain. *Harn* shirts were commonly worn, though upon holidays the country beaus appeared with linen necks and sleeves. Among no set of people was female

vanity ever confined within narrower limits; even
marriage apparel being mostly manufactured in the
family, and their ordinary wear being only a few
degrees coarser and plainer.   The gowns of women,
old and young, were made by country tailors, who
never thought of changing or inflaming the fashions.
In point of equipage they were equally primitive,
few of the topping tenants having either boots or
saddles fifty years ago.   It was the custom for them
and their wives to ride upon *sods*, over which, on
occasions of ceremony, a plaid or bit of carpet was
spread.

And now of the food of our tenants, which they
ate in a truly primitive manner, at the same table
with their servants.   Oatmeal - pottage was once
esteemed a luxury among that set of people,[1] bear-
meal being generally used.   Pease or bear bread was
a capital article with them, wheat-loaves being now
more common in farmers' houses than oat-cakes were
formerly.   In times of scarcity recourse was had to
inferior kinds, which are now happily forgotten—viz.,
grey meal—*i.e.*, a species compounded of oatmeal
and mill-dust; others made use of *egger* meal, consisting of equal portions of oat, pease, and bear meal.
The latter took its rise from the beggars mixing
different kinds in the same bag.   To some palates it
is said not to have been unpleasant.

---

[1] In the end of the last century, as Robert Buchanan and James Chrystie,
tenants in Muir, were passing one morning through Stirling, they spied children
eating oatmeal-pottage.   "Ah!" said the one to the other, "when will we get
that to eat!'"

In every family water-kail[1] was a standing dish, being made without flesh, of greens and *grolls*—*i.e.*, oats stripped of the husks in the mill. Without it they did not think they could dine to purpose. If tradition may be believed, the country people of old ate very little animal food, except perhaps a few old ewes that would not sell, and were likely to die through the winter. Walter M'Killop in Blackdub[2] is said to have been one of the first tenants in the country that killed a cow every Martinmas; and Robert Buchanan says his father was in his remembrance the only tenant in Ochtertyre who had a winter mart. But for the last sixty years almost every tenant in tolerable circumstances killed either one or two.

When there was no flesh, *kitchen* of one kind or other was given after the kail—that is, either butter, cheese, eggs, herrings, and sometimes raw onions, which were annually imported from Flanders. To

---

[1] It would seem that green-kail are of great antiquity in the low country. In William the Lion's grant of the kirk of Kincardine to the Abbey of Cambuskenneth, we find mention made of yards — "Cum uno orto et unum loftum ad baculum S. Lollani, cum uno orto et unum loftum ad Campanam S. Lollani." And Verstegan says, "The Saxons called February *sproutkele;* by kele meaning colewurt, the greatest potwurt in time long past that our ancestors used. The broth made thereof was the chief winter wurt for the sustenance of the husbandman." In all probability the Lowlanders borrowed this article of food, as well as their language, from the Teutonic nations ; for the Highlanders of old abominated kail, esteeming them fitter for goats than men. There are still districts where greens are neither planted nor eaten.

[2] Walter complained to his wife that whereas formerly her lads gave over eating bread when the kail was done, they now resumed it to the flesh. The wife was said to govern Scotland ; she ruled her husband, who ruled Blair, who ruled Chancellor Perth, who ruled Scotland.

supper they had *sowens*, or flummery, a cheap and healthy dish. In summer their drink consisted of whey or butter-milk, and in spring a little milk. But hardly any ale was brewed, except on extraordinary occasions. Indeed, the chief beverage of our country people has always been the pure element. Upon the whole, it may safely be affirmed that there hardly ever was a set of people who lived more poorly and penuriously, yet were they in general well pleased with their lot. Whatever might be their grievances, the meanness of their food and raiment seldom gave them a moment's disquietude.

Such were the labourers of the ground, and such their situation in former times, so far as we can collect from the conversation of the aged. They appear to have been warmly devoted to the persons of their masters, and entirely subservient to them in everything where their own purse was not affected. Though by no means deficient in industry which would make a speedy return, they laid their account that any extraordinary exertion or outlay on their part would, in the long-run, redound as much to their master's profit as their own, and they had no mind to work for him. They therefore had a system of their own, founded on long experience, and suited to small capitals and tacks for nineteen years. From this they were unwilling to deviate, unless for some self-evident advantage ; and with all its defects, it is not easy to figure one by which the same quantity of grain could be raised for the same money.

Their aversion to enterprise and innovation was fortified by a principle which pervaded every part of their conduct—viz., the desire of saving and hoarding. Indeed, no set of men ever followed more invariably old Cato's rule, of being " vendaces non emaces." It is astonishing what sums of·money the tenants of the last age had out at interest with the gentlemen of the country. They and the burghers were of old the moneyed men, who supplied the demands of the nobility and gentry that were engaged in any expensive pursuit.

The use of lime as a manure produced in time very important consequences.[1] Walter Mitchell, my grandfather's tenant, formerly mentioned, had, it is said, the merit of introducing it into the land of Ochtertyre. In the time of King William's death, he limed a very broad and long ridge in the field called the Glus, on which he had so early and excellent a crop, that his master offered to take the produce of that single ridge in payment of his rent. After seeing how well it succeeded with him, his next neighbours, Robert Buchanan and James Chrystie, began to lime with great spirit; and in order to carry on their opera-

---

[1] Tradition is silent whence we in this country derived the knowledge of this excellent manure ; but it was practised in other parts of Scotland at an earlier period. About 1633, George Bruce of Carnock, in a process of valuation of tithes, claimed a deduction, on account of a lime-quarry which he had bought from a neighbouring proprietor, whereby he had raised the rent from 18 to 26 chalders. And in 1670, George Abercromby, who some time before had purchased the estate of Tullibody, let a small lime-craig at Cambus within water-mark, and fixed what his own tenants were to pay.

tions the better, the three agreed to drive for one
another alternately during the summer.[1]

George Drummond of Blair, who a little before had
acquired the ten-pound land of Kincardine, encouraged, with his usual sagacity, the tenants to lay on
lime. In this he was well seconded by John Win-
gate and James Richardson, two of the old wealthy
tenants in the Baad, who the moment the bear seed
was over, hired people to cast peats, and employed
their men and horses in driving lime from Swallowhaugh. About the same time, Robert Gourlay took
a farm in Chalmerston; and though it was almost
waste at his entry, yet by laying on a quantity of lime,
he made himself rich in the course of his tack. It
is marvellous how people contrived to drive so much
lime in these days. The quarry at Swallowhaugh was
the only one within our reach. It stood in a wild
glen, part of the estate of Sauchie, and was barely
accessible to horses with back loads. The lime was
of excellent quality; but the badness of the road,
both within and without the glen, and the inconvenience of the ferry-boats, rendered it an arduous
operation.

John M‘Ewen,[2] told me that before 1700, when

---

[1] At first they were derided by their money-scraping neighbours, one of
whom seeing them lay out all they could gather upon lime, said, he would
lay up his money in a kist nook, till he could make up fifty merks, to lend
to some honest man; but he lived to change his mind.

[2] I asked this man, who, at the age of ninety-five, was lively and entire,
whether the old or the present times were the best? He smiled and answered: "There were difficulties then, there are difficulties now, and there
will be difficulties to the end of the world." He died in 1783, the year after.

he was a mere boy, his father took a waste mailing from Graham of Gartur, who, by way of encouragement, promised him a quantity of limestones from the family of Menteith's quarry. But as nobody thereabouts knew how to burn or break them, Forrester of Polder got a man from Campsie to direct the operation, which, he remembered well, was a great entertainment to him and the other boys. This, he fancied, was the first lime laid on land in the parish of Port, though no doubt the great crops his father had after it made others follow his example.

Between fifty and sixty years ago, a capital improvement took place, which was not the less valuable for being cheap and easy. *Runrig* was abolished, and the townships divided, so that every tenant had his farm separate from the rest. In this country, the new ones commonly consisted of fifty or sixty acres; but in the richest carses be-east Stirling, they frequently did not exceed thirty. There was, however, a wide difference between our management and theirs. They had little or no outfield, the farm being divided into equal portions of beans, barley, and oats. This was an excellent style of husbandry, both for the land and the tenant. Whereas with us the infield was commonly the least part of the farm; and though some addition was made to it by degrees, the old slovenly system still preponderated. If there was a necessity for building some new farmhouses in more central places, it could be done at a very moderate expense. At that time, and even within

the last twenty-five years, a tenant who was getting
a nineteen-year lease would have undertaken to build
a complete steading for a hundred merks, beside the
great timber.   The materials were then very cheap,
and all their neighbours ready to help them with
carriages and workmanship.   The tenants who possessed the old infield paid a considerable augmentation from the very first ; and a progressive rise was
stipulated on the outfield ones.   By the unremitting
industry of the possessors, some of the latter are now
in high condition, though in general the ancient infield, which has been dunged immemorially, retains
its character for fertility.

James Drummond of Blair was the first among us
that practised this excellent improvement to any
extent.   He was, by all accounts, one of the most
accomplished country gentlemen in his time.   His
views and management were masterly, the result of a
sound head and heart.   His learning and abilities
would have fitted him for any station ; yet by remaining upon the head of his estate, he perhaps
benefited his family more than if he had enjoyed a
lucrative important office in public life.   Though no
man was better acquainted with all the little fetches
of country people to obtain their ends, he scorned
to turn their artillery against themselves, as some
selfish able men would have done, to their own emolu-
ment.   Probity and justice secured him the love and
reverence of the commons,[1] and was indeed much

[1] He advised his son, in dealing with them, never to be profuse of his

better for them than brilliant unsteady gusts of generosity. As a proof of the solidity of his schemes, the barony of ten - pound land, which his father bought about the Revolution at a rent of 3000 merks a-year, was let in 1765, at the death of his son, to a set of very thriving tenants [1] at 15,000.

About the year 1735, my father made a new division of his farms, which proved equally advantageous to himself and his tenants. The neighbouring proprietors, some earlier and some later, took the same step. In general, the augmentation upon the old rent was not equal to the advantages which accrued to the possessors of the lands.

It promoted population [2] exceedingly. In place of two or three tenants in a township, there were now four or five, each of whom had as many servants as the old ones. At that time, and till within the last twenty-eight years, our ordinary farmers' households

favours. For, said he, they will consider such a conduct as proceeding from ignorance or weakness, not from goodness of heart. Let them, however, have justice, and in a doubtful point, the cast of the scale. His son gave me the same counsel when I was beginning my course. It sounded harsh at that time, but the experience of five-and-twenty years convinces me of its solidity.

[1] I have heard the late Blair say he never lost £5 sterling by bad tenants. Both my father and I have been equally lucky, though we had commonly one in labouring circumstances, from the beginning to the end of the tack. Now and then he had a great crop, which cleared him.

[2] In 1651, Mr Thomas Forrester, minister of Kincardine, rated his parishioners at 450 examinable persons; whereas, in 1760, according to the late Mr Smith's roll, they exceeded 800. Perhaps the pestilence, dearth, and civil war had reduced Mr Forrester's flock considerably. The making of a new village at Thornhill, in the end of the last century, made in time a great addition to the numbers of our people. The other parishes in the country seem to have increased in the same ratio. Else how came the churches of old to contain the parishioners? Were it the *fashion* at present for the people to attend the parish church, it would seldom hold the half of them.

consisted of a *big* man, a *little* man, a *pleghan*—*i.e.*, a
lad of fifteen or sixteen years of age, who could drive
the plough or thrash occasionally—a little boy to herd
the cattle in the labouring time, and a couple of maid-
servants. What is most remarkable, a tenant in Blackgrange or Bothkennar had the same number, though
his farm seldom exceeded thirty acres. But the
procuring manure of one kind or other for a full
third of their grounds was exceedingly tedious and
troublesome. And with us the earth *fuilzie* and the
operations upon the moss required a number of
hands.[1]

But in those days there was a redundancy of
people, and little to occupy them but husbandry or
handicraft trades. Of course the wages of servants
were very moderate. About 1730[2] our best ploughmen had only forty shillings a-year, beside *bounties*
—*i.e.*, certain articles of apparel manufactured in the
family, which amounted to a third of the wages.
The little man had about £11 Scots; the *pleghan*
£5 or £6, and the maid-servants £8, exclusive of the
bounties.[3] But about fifty years ago the servants

[1] John Foreman in Blacklub having taken a new tack from the late Blair, told his wife that, in order to pay the augmentation, he would dismiss one of his men. To which she answered very sensibly, "Goodman, you had better keep a man extraordinary, to help to pay what you have promised the laird."

[2] It would seem there had been little rise on wages for a great while. Alex Thomson was told in his youth by very old men that they never remembered the ploughmen's wages under £20 Scots, unless in the dearth, when people were glad to take anything.

[3] We shall specify the bounties paid to the different servants. The big man had 5 eln of grey, and if he stayed a second year, as much black kelt or finer

entered into a combination to raise their wages. The epithets given to the ringleaders are still remembered by old people, and one of them, *Windy* Shaw, is still alive. Their demands at that time were, however, very moderate, being only £4 Scots of addition to the *big* man, and to the other servants in proportion. But in 1760, after several small rises, the ploughman's wages did not exceed £3 sterling, and the women's were about 20s. a-year.

Of old we had few day-labourers, there being no gentlemen farmers or public works to employ them. And hence barrowmen, or hands for occasional jobs, had poor encouragement. Between 1720 and 1730, a number of people were engaged in levelling the bank behind the house of Blair, who had only 5d. in summer and a groat in winter. Even at that low rate they were probably a dear pennyworth, from their awkwardness and unskilfulness. But in 1756, a labourer's wages were generally 6d. a-day in summer. When Alexander Thomson first remembered the world, tailors had only 2d. and 2½d. per day, besides victuals. They afterwards rose slowly to 4d., where they remained a number of years.

In 1740 there was an excessive bad crop. It was impossible to take a proper furrow at the ordinary time, from the ground being hard frozen till far in April. And the frost continued in the air till well in

grey stuff, 2 harn shirts, 2 pair of shoes, and 2 pair *plaiding* hose. The *little* man had 3 or 4 elns of *grey*, according to his size. The women a serge or drugget gown, 2 harn shirts, an apron, 2 pair shoes, and 2 pair stockings. The clothes were all made at the master's expense.

summer. It was remarked that, even when the days
were tolerably good, there arose at night a sharp
north wind, which chilled everything; so that there
was little kindly vegetation till the month of July.
It was one of these uncommon bad crops, which bore
equally hard upon the carses as the moorish grounds.
There was a penury of shaw as well as of corn; and
the excessive rains in harvest did material damage to
both. The distresses both of man and beast were
much aggravated by the severity of the next winter,
which was not many degrees milder than the preceding one. It is therefore not surprising that prices
should be immoderately high, though not equal to
those in the worst years of King William's dearth.
And there was a liberal importation[1] from abroad,
which prevented the miseries of famine and the exactions of the mealmongers. It was fortunately a
single year of scarcity; and if the sufferings of the
poor were grievous, these were soon compensated
by the universal plenty and cheapness of the very
next season.

The Rebellion of 1745 is a capital era in the husbandry and economics of Scotland. The observation

[1] Mr Alexander Hog, a Dantzic merchant, told me a curious anecdote with
regard to the keeping of corn. In the year 1709 or 1710, an eminent victual
merchant in that city made a vow that he would never sell his wheat below
a certain price. Markets, however, fell; upon which he ordered his heir, upon
pain of forfeiting his succession, to keep the grain in the granary till a certain
price could be got. The man being very rich, his will was executed to a
tittle; a great expense being annually incurred in ventilating the wheat, and
preserving it from vermin. There it remained, a monument of caprice and
hard heartedness, till 1740, when it was sold in very good condition at the
price the miser had set on it.

that the providence of God can bring good out of seeming evil was never more fully exemplified than upon that occasion. It would be foreign to our subject to trace its salutary effects upon government and police. But the money remitted, first to pay the troops, and afterwards to purchase the heritable jurisdictions, gave new life to industry and enterprise of every kind. Above all, it produced a liberal intercourse between the Scots and English, who, though subjects of the same king for a century and a half, and members of the same empire for almost forty years, still retained many of their ancient prejudices. At that time the people of Northumberland and the Merse, who spoke dialects of the same language, and were only separated by a river, had little more intercourse than those of Kent and Normandy. From this period, however, there was a constant resort of our countrymen to England, which gave occasion to many innovations in husbandry and among the labourers of the ground. Those preceding the peace of 1763 were not the less solid for being gentle and gradual.

The convulsions inseparable from civil war had no sooner subsided than the price of land rose considerably. As this produced ere long great revolutions in rents, and in the views and practice of the husbandmen, it will not be unseasonable to point out the causes of its having been so long low. In the course of the troubles in the reigns of Charles the First and Second, a very great proportion of our nobility and gentry were ruined. Indeed, in those times credit

was so low,[1] and the rigour of the law so great, that
by the caprice or cruelty of a single creditor, a respectable family might be brought to the very verge
of bankruptcy for a debt which bore no proportion to
the value of its property. Nor could a sale afford
relief to people in unhappy circumstances, there not
being money to buy the twentieth part of the land
in the market. And so great was the tediousness and
nicety of legal proceedings that half a century frequently elapsed before matters could be brought to
an issue. Yet those delays, so distressful to creditors,
proved the means of saving many worthy families.
Before the estate could be legally transferred, some
fortunate circumstance occurred, which enabled either
the debtor or his heir to pay or compound the debts.[2]

The numberless questions among creditors, upon
the nicest quiddities of the law, gave occasion to a
very iniquitous traffic—viz., the *buying of pleas.* In
it, however, after the Restoration, the practitioners of
the law, from the highest to the lowest, were deeply
concerned. Many a poor client, seeing no end of
litigation, was constrained to sell his claim for a trifle

---

[1] A great estate in the Highlands is said to have been first apprised for
payment of a lady's silk gown. And it is the tradition of this country that
in the beginning of last century the Norries of Norriestoun embarrassed their
affairs by a tedious plea with a neighbour about a greyhound or spaniel.

[2] In this view, the memory of a Lady Touch, whose maiden name was
Stirling, a daughter of Lord Carden's, is revered as a second founder of her
family. She opposed with great spirit a proposition to sell part of the estate
to make matters more easy. She would have attended the plough from morn
to night, with nothing but an onion and bit of bread in her pocket. Nor does
tradition disdain to tell how she made more bannocks out of the peck of meal
than any of her neighbours. She lived in the end of the seventeenth century

to some man of law, who knew how to make it effectual. In this way some overgrown fortunes were
amassed, not very honourably.[1] The lawyers seem to
have been the nabobs of the last age.

These practices having at length excited general indignation, an Act of Sederunt was made, discharging
the members of the College of Justice from buying
pleas, under the pain of deprivation. But so long as
a man could make his fortune by taking advantage
of needy ignorant litigants, he despised every sanction
of that kind. But in the reign of King William a
remedy was at last found, a law being made author-
ising the apparent heirs of bankrupt estates to bring
them to an immediate sale. Instead of battling for
a number of years about preferences and interim possession, the lands were to be sold at a fair auction,
and the price divided among the creditors by well-
known rules. Though the great dearth, and the distresses occasioned by the failure of the Darien Company, prevented the immediate operation of this
excellent law, yet in less than twenty years the
buying of pleas was no more heard of.

Yet for a number of years after the Union the
price of land was still very moderate. The reduction
of interest from 6 to 5 per cent[2] made moneyed people

[1] An eminent lawyer is said to have acquired an estate of six thousand
merks a-year for a scarlet cloak and a few dollars. Lord Kames, who gave
me an account of this matter, used to tell of a Lord of Session (he would
neither tell his name nor the time he lived in) that said over his cups, "Gear
ill gotten and well *hained* would always last against what was well come by
but ill guided."

[2] The exorbitant rate of interest was a great cause of the distress of

at length think of buying land. In these times, however, people were very cautious in purchasing, there
being as yet hardly any influx of foreign money into
Scotland; and they were suspicious of the late rises
of rent being unsolid. But they who ventured, within
forty years of the Union, to buy land, got excellent
bargains.[1] From the very first they had legal interest
for their money; and since that time most estates
have risen exceedingly, even when let to ordinary
tenants.

To return from this digression. Beside the money
brought into Scotland in consequence of the Rebellion,
other sources of wealth were now opened to our
countrymen. It was about this time that the first
of our Scottish gentlemen returned from the East
Indies, with moderate wealth fairly acquired. Others
made their fortune by prize-money, Government contracts, and other lucky hits which occur in time of
war. The trade of Glasgow flourished apace, and
everything appeared to be on the mending hand.
Being warmly attached to their native country, the
people who had made what was then accounted good
fortunes, did not higgle about a purchase, but were
satisfied to pay liberally for pleasure and convenience.
In the course of a few years, after the peace of Aix-la-

landed gentlemen. In 1597 it was 10 per cent; in 1633, 8 per cent; in 1649,
6 per cent, where it stood till 1714.

[1] A person who acquired a considerable estate during this period, by parsimony and buying land, being asked how he thought of venturing so far on
credit, answered that he never hesitated about making a purchase when he
had wherewithal to pay the writings. It was another of his maxims that
" any man who pleased might be rich—but he must worship a lawbee:"

Chapelle, a great deal of land was sold, currently from
twenty-five to thirty years' purchase. Though the
new proprietors could seldom be assured of 4 per
cent for the money laid out, few who bought between
1748 and 1762 had reason to repent of their bargains.
Many estates still continued almost in a state of
nature;[1] so that a purchaser, by means of a little
conduct, might in a short time raise his rents, and
the tenants be better off than they were when their
farms were injudiciously laid out,[2] and they had no
encouragement to lay on manure or improve. At any
rate, there was a moral certainty of a considerable
augmentation at the end of the present leases.

The introduction of carts with spoked wheels shod
with iron, among tenants, was a circumstance very
favourable for them. Before this time, indeed, the
roads were hardly passable for carriages. The excellent laws of Charles II. relative to the statute work,
had produced nothing but a few feeble attempts. But,
about 1747, the gentlemen of Perthshire, encouraged
by various motives and incidents, set themselves in
good earnest to execute those obsolete laws. Mr
Craigie, afterwards Lord President of the Session, had
great merit in laying down rules and establishing
order in the proceedings of our road meetings, which

[1] Within the last twenty-five years the lands of Greenock, belonging to
Lord Moray, and those of Craigarnal to Mr Robertson Barclay, were in
runrig.

[2] About 1750 or 1751, the late Blair bought the estate of Burnbank. The
possessors were very poor, and their farms in sad order. By a new distri-
bution of the lands, and getting proper tenants, the last were in a few years
much better off than their predecessors, who paid much less rent.

were indeed highly respectable and well attended.
And the leading men of the shire co-operated with
uncommon zeal.   Among them were James, Duke of
Athole, the Earl of Breadalbane, Lord Gray, Peter
Campbell of Monzie, David Smith of Methven, and
George Drummond of Blair,[1] all of them respectable
members of society.

To the late Blair we of this country owe great
obligations for first rendering the statute work effectual.   In his father's time it had been called out, but

[1] We have had few country gentlemen in our day more worthy, none more
useful and upright, than the last of these. His heart being warm and his
affections strong, few private men had a greater number of respectable minds
attached to them. There was, however, something in his manner that
created a prejudice against him in those who knew him imperfectly, and
made him an object of great terror to the common people. A labourer of
mine, a very impudent fellow in general, said God had never made a face of
clay that he was afraid to look at but Blair's. And Colbert the mason used
to take a dram extraordinary, before facing him. His economy within
and without doors was admirable; for whilst no man despised meanness
more, he knew the true value of money, and made his shilling go as
far as any man's. In letting land, he inherited his father's talent of
hitting the happy medium. His tenants and he agreed no doubt the
better that they confided in his rectitude, and knew they should gain
little at his hands by tricks. Harry Carr at Camsdrenny (whom he meant
to favour) having rued when his tack was going to be signed, Blair ordered
his farm to be advertised next market day. This made the other anxious
to hold the bargain, the failure of which, however, he imputed to his wife,
but he was told that, for his folly, he must pay two bolls of meal more,
besides the expense of the former tack. "An' like your honour, is there any
more?" said Harry, glad to find it was no worse. "Yes," said his master,
"a shilling for drumming you through Stirling." He was an excellent spirited
magistrate, though he pretended to little knowledge of law, leaving forms
to the men of business; and his care of the police of the country was un
wearied. No man was a bitterer enemy to jobs and jobbers of every de
nomination. Upon his death, every prejudice evanished; his friends and
country neighbours paid him the grateful tribute of their tears; whilst they,
who before disliked him, confessed now the respectability of his character.
He died of an apoplexy at Auchinfield, in March 1765.

little was done, though sometimes bread and ale were given by way of premium. But after most other men in his situation would have considered it as a thing impracticable, he persevered with all that steadiness which marked his character. By a proper mixture of soothing and severity, he first brought his own tenants, and afterwards those of his neighbours, to do their duty to the roads ; at last, the very servants wrought cheerfully.[1] If less was done in his time in that way than at present, let us consider that the making of roads was then little understood, and the tenant's carriages were trifling, compared with the present ones.[2]

Indeed, people's views concerning roads enlarged step by step. That Government might be prepared in case of another rebellion, military ways were made at the public expense from Stirling to Crieff and Inverary, a measure which gave great offence to every primitive Highlander.[3] In 1748 a turnpike law was

[1] This will not appear surprising, when we are told that the gravel for the Craigforth road, within the last sixty years, was carried from the mouth of Allan, across the Forth in sacks on horseback. It was the first part of our road to Stirling that was made, under the direction of Dr Murray, Craigforth's father-in-law.

[2] Even in 1763, when I first took any charge of the roads, the tenants of the ten-pound land generally brought nothing but *tumblers*.

[3] In 1761, I was in company with Peter Graham of Rudivous, a lively man past fourscore. The conversation turning on roads, he said he saw no use of them but to let burghers and red-coats into the Highlands, none of whom, in his father's time, durst venture beyond the Pass of Aberfoyle. He affirmed that when there were no made roads they had as few broken bones as now. Being at last sore pressed, he concluded with saying that if our roads were better, we had no such men to use them as were long ago.

obtained for the roads from Edinburgh to Stirling.
and from Glasgow to Falkirk. But the most important step towards the improvement of this country
was the opening in 1752 a road by the foot of the
Govan hills, which rendered it unnecessary any longer
to climb Ballangeich [1] with every carriage.

A piece of wholesome chastisement towards this
district in 1756 produced excellent effects. One of
President Craigie's regulations provided that if no
report of the last year's work was given in to the
general meeting, the district in fault should be sent
the current year to work at a distance. Blair being
that year in London, the report was somehow neglected, and we were adjudged to perform statute work
near Dunkeld. When the order was intimated at
the church doors, it alarmed the country people
greatly, as they thought that it must be literally
obeyed. With some difficulty it was recalled, yet
it made the people double their diligence, for whenever they appeared careless or refractory, they were
threatened with a migration to Dunkeld.

Carts, with spoked wheels and rings of iron, were
early used by the people employed in carrying goods
between Glasgow and Borrowstounness.[2] So long as

[1] In 1747 a wide road had been made up the hill at a considerable expense
to little purpose. James V., in his disguises, called himself the goodman of
Ballangeich.

[2] As early as the year 1730, the late William Stirling, merchant in Dunblane, had a cart with proper wheels for transporting goods to fairs, &c. And
a short time after, James Henderson, one of the Anthray feuars, got another,
which was much wondered at, being a new thing in the parish of Logie.

the inland tobacco trade went on briskly, there were a few in Stirling. And fifty years ago most country gentlemen had them; but being commonly made at Edinburgh, they were considered as beyond the reach of an ordinary tenant. Indeed, the people of Crieff and Dunblane had good stout carts some years before the Carse tenants, who, with a few exceptions, were satisfied with *tumblers* till about 1750.

It is, however, difficult to alter old customs. Thus, for some years after carts became common, coals and lime were usually carried home in sacks. Even now it is the practice of tenants to carry meal and beer to market on horses' backs; whereas upon carts one-half of the servants and horses would suffice.

It seems strange how of old gentlemen's houses and public buildings could be supplied with bulky materials. In our fathers' time, however, good neighbourhood abundantly compensated the want of carts. It was then the general practice for all the gentry within a number of miles to give a person who was building a new house what was called a *rake* of their whole tenants' horses with lime, wood, slates, or whatever material was nearest them. This continued to be given of goodwill for ten or twelve years after the Jurisdiction Act had taken away the exaction of services at pleasure. In this way, no doubt, the trouble and expense of building had been very much lightened of old. At length, however, the goodness of roads, and the facility of hiring carts, joined to a change in views and manners, put an end to this friendly custom.

Another fortunate circumstance for tenants was the great demand for black cattle. But here it will not be improper to mention some anecdotes relative to that trade in former times. Before the Union, our cattle were liable to pay duty in England; and in 1703, upon a misunderstanding between the two nations, they were entirely prohibited.[1] As soon, however, as all restraints were taken off, the supplying England with cattle became one of our chief articles of commerce. Yet for a good many years prices kept very moderate, droves of the best Highland cows selling, when fat, at twenty-four merks each, and as often under as above. Old dealers allege that fifty or sixty years ago cows were better in quality than at present. It is true the Highland pastures were in general *under* stocked, which was favourable to size and fatness.[2] And many fewer cattle were then reared than of late years.

---

[1] It was probably then that one M'Leran, at Bridge of Turk, a great dealer was forced to sell a dozen of prime cows at the West Port of Edinburgh for 4s Scots each, which was two-thirds of the common price. So John M'Kinlay in Auy was told by Donald M'Conrich, who was then M'Leran's driver, and who now, if he was alive, would be upwards of a hundred years of age.

[2] The low prices of Highland grass may be inferred from the following circumstances. Between sixty and seventy years ago the workmen of the Lothians were sent in great numbers, after the bear seed, to graze on Brackleny and the neighbouring hills. The pasture was excellent, yet all they paid was two merks a head, and twopence to the herd. There they remained till the crop was got in, though about Lammas they became unruly, breaking in amongst the corn.

Nevertheless, about the year 1747 things took a new turn. Owing partly to the wanton waste of the rebels' stocking in summer 1746,[1] and partly to the disease among the horned cattle in the south of England, the demand from Scotland next year exceeded anything ever heard of before in that way. In a very short time Highland cows gave currently from thirty-five to forty shillings. Though afterwards the markets took various turns, upon the whole there was a gradual rise, so that by 1760 the same kind of cattle were sold at fifty or fifty-five shillings, a great rise in less than thirty years from twenty-four merks ! The profits of these higher prices centred principally with the Highland breeders, yet the low-country tenants were also essential gainers. They in general bred more beasts than they could maintain. And notwithstanding these were of very inferior quality, yet in a brisk market everything sells to advantage.

Having thus taken a view of the circumstances which, after the peace of 1748, raised the spirits of

[1] In June 1746 a very great number of cattle being driven off the hills, and brought to Crieff by the military, Major Forrester (well known in the gay and literary world) was ordered to send for a justice of peace, that they who could prove their loyalty and property might have their stock restored. The only one that could be had in Strathearn was Baron M'Cara, a man of small estate near Abercairney, whom James, Duke of Athole, had put on the commission for a sally of wit. His figure and address did not prepossess the Major in his favour. It being, however, proposed to begin business, the justice said he could not proceed till a Bible was brought in. The Major became peevish, but the other was positive, and threatened to leave them. At last his demand was complied with, when he turned up the text, " Wilt thou slay the righteous with the wicked ?" The Major, who was a man of wit and humanity, saw there was more in his associate than he thought, and told him the making a discrimination was their business that day.

tenants, and facilitated their operations, let us next consider the benefits that a proprietor could derive from land in his own possession. These were no less flattering, and contributed not a little to raise the value of land, and, in time, to open the eyes of tenants.

The great demand for cattle to the English market gave occasion to a cheap and easy improvement — viz., the enclosing land in a state of nature,[1] for the accommodation of graziers and drovers. We must not, however, confound this with enclosures for policy or private convenience, which will be considered in the second branch of these sketches. Of all the methods used to turn land to good account, it afforded the greatest and most immediate profit at the least expense. The only thing required was the building a stone dyke, for it was not even necessary to sow grass-seeds. Yet the very next season it produced a moderate rent in grass, and in three or four years a very high one, when the pasture was excellent. The rich infield ground produced spontaneously rib-grass, white, yellow, and red clover, with the other plants of which cattle are fondest. And the

---

[1] This improvement had been carried to a great height in Galloway as early as 1720. The Lairds Heron, Murdoch, and Gillespie turned out a number of tenants, and enclosed tracts of country with enclosures, which were built with sandstones set on edge so homely that a touch of man or beast would make a gap. It occasioned great ferments, insomuch that men in women's clothes went about levelling the dykes. The gentlemen principally concerned did not make rich by their violence and precipitation, and it is said the country still feels the loss of the inhabitants, many of whom emigrated to America. It reminds us of what happened in England in Henry VII's time.

most wretched outfields were filled with what was no less useful to the grazier in its season — viz., plants which stand the winter,[1] and supply the outlying cattle with wholesome food when the finer kinds are over. It is no incurious part of the economy of nature that manure and high cultivation should banish those coarse hardy plants, and substitute the finer grasses in their room, in a scanty degree, which are commonly gone by November.

Besides affording double, triple, or sometimes quadruple the old rent, the ground was every year growing better from being rested and dunged by the cattle. And in six or seven years they were commonly broken up for oats, which produced rich crops at very little expense. When let out for tillage, they gave currently from 50s. to £4 an acre for three years, according to the quality of the ground and the age of the grass.

The last Newton was the first in this corner who profited considerably by making these enclosures. In a few years his example was followed by other gentlemen, but by none more extensively or successfully than the family of Auchleshy. Fortunately, however, in this country it was never carried to such

---

[1] The notions of the London Society of Arts, &c., would have appeared very strange to a Skye or Kintail grazier. They maintained that Providence had surely intended grasses for winter as well as summer. So far they reasoned well. But after much botanical research, they found out that burnet was the plant designed for winter food. Our countrymen, however, could tell them that their worst land produces, without cultivation, better winter grasses than burnet—viz., heather, rushes, bent, ling, cotton grasses, all of them acceptable at different seasons to cattle and sheep.

a pitch as either to affect population or alarm the common people.

It was indeed only a prelude to improvements upon a much greater scale. The English husbandry, and certain crops formerly confined to the garden, were gradually introduced into Scotland. And here it is worthy of notice that the last Duke of Perth leads the van among our improvers. Having spent much of his youth among the English, he was a professed admirer of their agriculture, and very solicitous of introducing it into his native country. For this purpose, some years before the Rebellion he brought down English servants and implements of husbandry to Drummond Castle, where a few trials were made of summer fallowing and sowing artificial grasses. And in some of his leases there was an embryo of the new husbandry. But, like other young men of high rank who commence improvers without experience, he went too fast, and aimed at too much. Neither had his schemes time to take root among his tenants, who disliked everything new, more especially from England. They, as well as the bulk of the neighbouring gentry, regarded these essays as the freak of the day, and of the same stamp with race or hunting horses. The goodness of this young nobleman's heart, and his public spirit, were ill seconded by those about him.[1] Better coun-

¹ M'Arthur Ban, his ground officer, and one Bowie, a fowler, had more to say in the management of his estate than his men of business. When the opposition to Sir Robert Walpole ran very high, the Duke and his retinue went one day to visit old Ardvorlich, a man of a very sarcastical turn. After

sellors and more experience would probably have made him an honour to his family and a blessing to his people,[1] had he not been cut short in his career.

After the Rebellion, a number of noblemen and gentlemen in different parts of Scotland amused themselves with farming in the English style. Few of them had studied it as a profession, either here or in England, the earlier part of their lives having been devoted to very different pursuits. As they had neither principles nor experience to direct them, their systems were of course various, and sometimes ill digested. Yet, under all the disadvantages to which new schemes are liable, especially when carried on by persons in easy or opulent circumstances, it soon appeared that the inferiority of our tenants' crops proceeded as much from a defect in cultivation as from soil or climate.

dinner, having called in M'Arthur Ban to get a dram, he said, with a sneer, " Come away, Sir Robert," and to Bowie, " Come, my Lord Islay." As might have been expected from such low unprincipled minions, these fellows deserted their indulgent master in his distress, and afterwards cringed as low to Barcaldine and Mr Small as they had ever done to him. Nor was he more lucky in his other favourites. One Cock, a manufacturer at Crieff, whom he had patronised, headed the rabble that plundered Drummond Castle. Men of all parties detested his baseness and ingratitude. Mr Russell of Dunblane, with whom he had some business, brought him in when it was over to a company at his house, and drank to him by name. Old Auchleshy, who was a man superior to all rule, said to him, " What, sir ! are you Cock of Crieff ?" " Yes," answered the other. " Go home, then, you rascal," replied Auchleshy, " and crow upon your own *midden-head*. How dare you be seen among gentlemen !" The wretch sneaked off, and the company were well diverted with their honest neighbour's blunt indignation.

[1] Till he doubled the rents of the barony of Callendar, which had been very low, the tenants used to pray for him, by name, in their grace to meat.

The late Lord Eglinton was one of the first that
carried improvements to a great height. He spared
no expense in getting English servants capable of
executing his plans in the completest manner. If it
helped to embarrass his affairs, he certainly showed his
countrymen what might be done by high cultivation.

Though some of his neighbours in the Merse farmed
upon a greater scale, no man perhaps did more to
introduce the new husbandry than the late Lord
Kames. As a philosopher and lawyer, his fame is
justly high in the literary world. And what is
more connected with our speculations, his friends and
neighbours will long remember the profit and pleasure
they derived from his conversation, which was lively
and original, suited to persons of every age and character. Improvements being one of his favourite
themes, he studied to inspire all over whom he had
any influence with a passion for them, founded upon
public and private considerations. And as the enthusiasm of such a man is always catching, he had
a goodly number of disciples. His excellency lay in
throwing out hints which duller men could pursue
and carry into execution. But the practical part of
husbandry was too gross an employment for his
brilliant talents. It was like taking a razor to do
the business of a knife or an axe. He sometimes misplaced his confidence both in persons and measures :
nor could he submit to those details which appear indispensable to men of less fancy and fewer avocations.
Having too little veneration for maxims founded

upon observation and experience, he displayed the
same ingenuity and love of innovation in farming
which distinguished his ·theories. Perhaps he imagined that nature would bend before him like an
argument in law and metaphysics. From his treading constantly in unknown paths, he was often
foiled; yet when nature and he agreed, his experiments led to useful discoveries. Sanguine in his
hopes of gain, and tenacious of money, he bore the
failure of his favourite schemes with astonishing
resignation, either returning to the charge with
double vigour, or devising something else. To the
master - passion indeed, all the rest are thoroughly
subservient. It may suggest ample matter for consideration, that his neighbour Lord Nisbet should
have succeeded to his wish in a very great scheme
of improvement, whilst he, with much better parts,
should have been generally a loser. Upon the whole,
it must be confessed that, as a gentleman farmer,
Lord Kames did a great deal of good in his day,
though not so much as he meant. By intention,
however, are men to be judged.

About 1749 or 1750, the late Mr Drummond of
Blair became an improver. Before that time he
had a farm or *labouring* (as it was called) managed
in the old style, with the addition of clover and rye-
grass for hay.[1] Beside Lord Kames, others of his

---

[1] As early as 1735, in his father's time, the little field to the north-east of
the house was laid down with clover and rye-grass. It produced hay successively for twenty-eight years. The first red clover in this part of Scotland was sown by Sir John Erskine of Alva about 1724.

friends had taken keenly to agriculture, it being now
regarded as connected with spirit and fashion.　But
as it was a business entirely new, he proceeded for
a long while upon a moderate scale.　He was very
fortunate in servants—Charles Farquharson his overseer being a modest, worthy, sensible man, warmly
attached to his master's interest.[1]　Though a stranger
to the new husbandry, he was very willing to be
taught.　Nor was it any loss to his master that his
zeal was tempered with caution.　In the common
crops, he combined the old *tids*, or times of ploughing and sowing, with English cultivation ; and in the
new ones, he punctually obeyed the directions of
his master's counsellors.　He was well seconded by
James Row, who was, first and last, thirty years
ploughman at Blair.[2]　Whilst a tenant's servant, he
was noted for that neatness and skill which denote
natural genius.　In matters which he thoroughly understood, nobody was more stiff or tenacious of his

---

[1] He had been Lord Perth's forester at Glenartney, and was by birth a
gentleman.　Being a Roman Catholic, the commonalty were at first preju
diced against him ; but in a few years, from their confidence in his integrity
and obliging disposition, they would have trusted him with their all　He
kept so clear of controversy, that a countryman said one day, he doubted if Mr
Farquharson had any religion, as he could never get him to *dispute*.

[2] James was a very valuable servant, but something capricious.　When
thirty years old he wanted to go to sea ; and though a favourite of his master,
was always threatening to go away.　On these occasions, Blair, who knew his
way, used to laugh him out of it, by asking him what voyage he meant to
take　Among his other peculiarities, he hated to drive a cart.　Being un-
married, he ate with the house servants, where the contrast between him and
the powdered footmen was very striking.　On Christmas day it was great
sport to the latter to see James fast, rather than partake of the superstitious
g...ee.

opinion. But when he saw how far the new modes
of cultivation excelled the old, he was very desirous
of being instructed in them. In 1750 or 1751, he
was sent over by his master to Ayrshire to learn
drill husbandry and the culture of turnips from
Lord Eglinton's English servants. He was so apt
a scholar, that the very next year he raised in the
crofts of Daira a field of very large turnips, which
were the first in the country. And they were as
neatly dressed as any in Hertfordshire. A single
horse ploughing the drills astonished the country
people, who till then had never seen fewer than four
yoked. A few years after, he learned from another
Englishman to plough with two horses without a
driver.

Blair's farm being within compass,[1] was neatly
and substantially cultivated. His crops, particularly
of wheat, turnips, and sown grass, generally answered
expectation. If, however, upon balancing accounts, he
was no gainer, it afforded him much amusement;
and he made fewer slips than most of his brethren.[2]
It is no wonder that his counsellors, who were strangers to the country, should now and then mistake the

[1] " Laudato ingentia rura, exiguum colito."—Virg.

[2] Soon after settling here, I happened to say to him I do not understand
this new trade of mine, for my servants and horses eat all that grows upon
the farm. " Oh ! " said he, " you are a special farmer ; mine eat a great deal
more." Towards the close of life he went upon a great scale of husbandry
in contradiction to his old maxims. Indeed he told me a little before his
death, that being *ill of a disease* (the dressing a large lawn) and finding the
ordinary means too slow for an old man, he had got a *doctor* to cure him
rapidly, after which he would return to his old scale.

nature of the soil and climate. But his own good
sense enabled him to correct what was wrong before
much mischief was done.

One of his chief advisers was Mr Charles Dundas,
a man well qualified to give useful hints. Having
been long in the dragoons,[1] he was well acquainted
with the richest counties of England. When his
brother officers were very differently employed, he
amused himself in studying the husbandry of the
countries where he was quartered. Being a man of
very sound understanding, he acquired in time as
thorough a knowledge of the business as one who
never had a farm of his own could do. He trusted
entirely to his own observation, or the experience of
practical farmers, not to the theories of the ingenious.[2]
Upon his return to Scotland, he was a warm advocate for the new husbandry, but sometimes forgot to
accommodate himself to a northern climate and a
poor people. And however acceptable his notions
might be to the persons with whom he associated,
they seldom had a fair trial. His temper was so
harsh, and his language so coarse, that the servants
who were to obey his directions loved to thwart him.
The dislike was indeed reciprocal. If they could
not endure his manners, he contemned them for ad-

---

[1] After quitting the Greys, he was a lieutenant in Lascelles's regiment.
Being taken prisoner at Preston, he told some of his brethren that at their
next battle he hoped the General would be lathered between the first and
second line of the army.

[2] He had a sovereign contempt for books. According to him, nobody read
but fools, and the best thing a farmer could do, was to put his books in the
midden.

hering obstinately to their own customs; for he had no allowances to make for hereditary prejudices. A more singular character has seldom occurred, his conversation and his actions being continually at variance. Spite of his integrity and knowledge of the world, his passion, which was unbridled, led him often to forget the language of charity. And the strength and poignancy of his sarcasms rankled as deeply as the strokes of the bitterest satirist. Yet with the semblance of a misanthrope, he was in truth a tender-hearted beneficent man, even towards those whom he disliked and reviled. It was enough to him that a person was in distress and without friends. And surely few men have done so much good with such slender funds. Nor was it to be seen of men; for he appeared more ashamed of being detected in a good-natured generous deed, than others are of their vices and follies. In a word, his virtues greatly overbalanced his foibles.

Another of Mr Drummond's counsellors in farming, was John Hunter of the Merse. From a ploughman, he became the late Mr Renton of Lamerton's overseer and confidant. In his service he displayed so much genius and activity, that the Earl of Home took him to oversee his great operations at the Hirsel. And afterwards he was assumed a partner by Mr Pringle when he got a tack of that place, in security of money advanced. He was a man of strong mother-wit, and well fitted for carrying on any great undertaking. No man knew better how, by

good usage, to get the most out of man and beast.[1]
He took just as much, and no more, of the new husbandry as was sufficient to correct the errors of the
old ; valuing a well-dressed field only as it promised
a better crop than one managed in a slovenly manner.   His chief excellence lay in his resources [2] and
foresight, which enabled him to outstrip his neighbours.   He was one of the very few that made rich
by extensive improvements, having at one time lands
in his possession to the value of £2000 sterling a-year.
It was, however, fortunate for him, in some of his
largest farms, to be in partnership with people who
could afford to lay out money liberally.   But though
a capital and successful farmer in the Merse, he was
much at a loss when he came to this country.[3]   And
he certainly erred in advising Blair to burn and pare
the plain of Courtry, which was then light land, or to
fallow the hill of Daira,[4] which was a shallow, grav-

[1] Charles Dundas, who did not like him, said he knew very little but a
stot and a marl-pit. And the little he did know was from Mr Pringle of
Lees and him at Mr Renton's, where John used to suck in information
greedily ; a very high, though involuntary, compliment to Hunter

[2] In a terrible drought, when, by the middle of June the grass was burnt
up, and many had turned their sheep into their oat fields, John foresaw he
must either lose a very valuable stock of cattle, for want of winter fodder
or sell them for a trifle in autumn In this emergence, he bethought him of
raising triple his ordinary quantity of turnips, which he accomplished by
hiring all the carts and ploughs in his neighbourhood By this stroke of
real genius, his profits were very great

[3] Though fond of Blair, he had a very mean opinion of his place, and of
the country where it lay Walking out one day in the fields, he said in
his Merse dialect, "I no think I ever saw so many tame hares as here   Said
Blair, I make the herd tame half a score every year   I believe that,
replied John ; I imagine it is hunger tames them

[4] Blair one day met John M'Arthur, who was a sort of favourite, and

elly soil. With all his merit, Hunter was very much spoilt by the notice taken of him by people of the first rank, whom he very familiarly called by their titles. They were diverted with his natural coarse sallies, which were sometimes downright brutal.[1] He died some years ago worth £8000 sterling.

Mr Seton of Touch became a keen improver much about the same time with Blair. Being intimate friends, they had the same views and advisers. Mr Seton went on much the better that Mr Charles Smith entered deeply into schemes of improvement, from a persuasion of its being a profitable trade.[2] His son farmed upon what was then thought a great scale. For a number of years he led a very pleasant respectable life at Touch, being seldom absent

finding he had been at Doune, buying a pennyworth of candles, alleged he had wore his shoes more than the value of his merchandise. "Well, well!" answered John, "your honour is *faughing* the hill of Daira for a crop of guild and broom."

[1] Hunter estimated the neighbouring gentlemen farmers by their practice, not by their speculations, which he held exceedingly cheap. He told Lord Kames most insolently in conversation, "My lord, to hear you talk of farming, one would think you had been born *yestreen*." One morning at Blair, an officer of the army, now a peer, happening to say that for a small wager he would walk sixty miles a-day, John, who was hardly known to him, said : "Colonel, I *no* think that, unless they were Indians at your back. I myself" (proceeded he), "once rode a mile in a minute; but it was from a battle, and yet a Colonel wan the race."

[2] Mr Smith used often to express a wish, while attending the reapers, that he had been bred a farmer. He was, however, too anxious in his disposition, for a business that depends so much on contingencies. Sir Hugh Paterson, who was of a very different temper, used to say, when he saw his friend fretting about little matters, "Lord help that poor man! He is no better than a herd about the place." Mr Smith also advanced a considerable sum to improve his son-in-law, Sir John Stewart's estate, under the direction of John Hunter.

when anything important was going on. His system was sensible and liberal, and he grudged neither expense nor pains in carrying it into execution. Indeed all his matters were so well arranged that they went on like clock-work, his people never appearing hurried or behindhand. Ere long he made a wonderful change upon the place: his fences were substantial and neatly kept; his fields rich and gay; the Carse of Touch, that had been proverbially bad, produced plentiful crops, by means of liming and high culture. He was without doubt an excellent farmer, having less whim than many of his brethren.

We are, however, to remember that both he and Blair were full of money, and, of course, under no obligation of attending to immediate gain. Though neither of them meant to be lavish, they were more solicitous about nice culture and the prospect of a rich crop than to the striking a balance at the end of the year. If their expenses sometimes far exceeded their returns, they were morally certain that, in the long-run, they would be well paid for their improvements. Amusement and the reputation of being good farmers were, in truth, their great motives. In the first stages of their operations they were objects of wonder rather than imitation to their country neighbours.

And now of two other gentlemen in this country, whose views and procedure were somewhat different —viz., Mr Graham of Meiklewood and Mr Callendar of Craigforth. Though exceedingly sanguine about the new husbandry, they both professed to follow it as a trade, which must make regular returns in proportion to their outlay and industry. Neither of them could afford to farm for pleasure or fashion. Mr Graham was the plainer and less costly of the two. Having been a summer at Bristol upon business, he conceived, from what he saw, a very high opinion of English agriculture; and hence, when it came into vogue, he entered into it with all that warmth which marked his character. It is believed he was the first in this corner who summer-fallowed for wheat, and had a proper rotation of crops, in which artificial grasses had a place. Beside the enclosures about his house, he took one of his farms on the north side of the Forth into his own hands, which he enclosed and improved to very good purpose. In the management of his Moss-side lands, which had been rendered almost barren by repeated burning, he struck a new stroke. The moss-sides were trenched two feet deep, and the deaf stratum on the top put into the bottom of the trench, from whence strong clay was taken to replace the other. By means of this operation—called by him *golling*— a new soil was produced, upon which, after being exposed to the winter frost and a thorough summer fallow, he sowed wheat. Nor did he content himself with improving his own farm in that way. For in making new bargains with the tenants of his other farms, he stipulated that they should, at a certain rate, trench their mossy grounds, and after a fallow and a certain quantity of lime to the acre, sow wheat.

It was his great object to banish by degrees the distinction between *infield* and *outfield*, that so every part of the farm might produce the same crops in course. However uphill work this might be, owing to the prejudices of the commonalty, he had the greater merit in being the first among us who thought of introducing the English modes of husbandry among tenants, for that was the likeliest way of improving a country. His crops were not the worse that, whilst he adopted the new modes with great fervour, he also paid attention to the common *tids* of ploughing and sowing. His farm answered very well so long as he was able to oversee it ; but he persevered long after losing the use of his limbs. And in his leases he erred in making his plan (which was rational, though a little complex) as invariable as the laws of the Medes and Persians.[1] A variety of incidents may at times interrupt the execution ; and then either the tenant loses heart, or the lease becomes a dead letter. But taking this gentleman altogether, few people in his day did more to improve his estate, or gave his country neighbours a greater number of useful lessons.

For some time after his marriage, Mr Callendar was deeply immersed either in music or in commenting upon Milton's 'Paradise Lost.' He is said to have sometimes spent fifteen hours a-day in his study, which had almost ruined his health. But

[1] A countryman, who wanted to take a farm from him, said his plan was like the Covenant of Works, which no mere man could keep.

about 1748 or 1749 he commenced gentleman farmer with great *éclat*. To devote himself the more effectually to husbandry, he dropped all intercourse with most of his neighbours. And for a number of years he wrought hard, holding the plough and sowing the seed.[1] He went about his fields in a fustian frock and a felt hat, dressed like a common servant. In general, he ate his victuals in the open air amidst his labourers, seldom breakfasting or dining with his family but on Sundays.

In his practice he disclaimed all home modes of husbandry, professing to borrow his whole notions from England. To assist him in carrying these into execution, he got people from that country.[2] Having a strong ambition to excel, he tried a variety of experiments, some of which were abundantly unpromising. He attempted oxen, both in the plough and cart, but soon saw that in a strong clay horses were greatly preferable. He was for some time very full of the drill husbandry, which, after the publica-

[1] This being one day spoken of in company, a gentleman farmer of very good sense said it was needless for him to work, as he would get a man for eightpence a-day that would do more with his hands than he could. It was the master's eye that was to forward the operations ; if that was not worth four men's labour, it was ill employed indeed.

[2] For a while, Mr Callendar was directed in his operations by one Hickson from Yorkshire, who had an allowance from some noblemen and gentlemen for his advice. Sir James Campbell gave him a carse farm near Gargunnock, and built him a house ; but he soon broke and left the country. To this farm he brought Joseph Dalton from Northumberland, an excellent ploughman and breaker of horses, who, instead of blows, used soothing and gentleness. Joseph went afterwards to Mr Callendar's service, and from thence to Blair's. By him William M'Ewen, my ploughman, was bred, and taught to plough with two horses without a driver.

tion of Tull's book, was a common theme of discourse. But after getting an expensive complicated apparatus, which he improved considerably, the wetness and tenaciousness of his soil made him relinquish it. There was hardly a plough or implement of husbandry which had any vogue in England, that he did not commission. It was in those days equally new and pleasant to see his four-wheeled waggons, with five or six sightly horses in a row, carrying the produce of his farm to market. Spite of his crotchets, which cost him much money at first, he is to be ranked among the most skilful and spirited cultivators we ever had in this country. For seven or eight years before he gave up farming, his management was judicious and his crops excellent. In 1763 he went to live at Edinburgh, at the very time when it was most his interest to have persevered in husbandry. The great expense being already incurred, his profits would have been sure and regular, and things might have gone on without either personal labour or slavish attendance. But he seems to have thought no more of his farm than how to make it give the highest rent. For this purpose, he let it to common tenants in tillage, without any restrictions. If they paid him a rent fully adequate to his inclinations, they in a few years run out the land. Of his enclosures, few of them either could or would avail themselves. It was, however, in his power to have set the lands in grass at a very high rent, from their vicinity to Stirling. Or he might have got good tenants, who would have submitted to restrictions in cropping that would, in the course of a nineteen-year lease, have been equally advantageous to themselves and the proprietor. It is very doubtful whether, at this moment, exclusive of his fences, the estate be intrinsically the better for all his improvements.

Having thus given some account of the introduction of the English husbandry into this corner, let us now see how it was received by the labourers of the ground. For a while they were at a gaze, and borrowed nothing from the neighbouring gentlemen farmers, considering their schemes as ideal and extravagant, at least for people who had rent to pay. To say the truth, neither party was free from prejudice. The notions of the gentlemen were often crude and fanciful, borrowed either from books[1] or from a superficial view of better countries; and many of them took it for granted that tenants were ignorant and faulty in every part of their conduct, because they wanted that neatness and dexterity which distinguished the English farmers. They did not, however, consider how difficult it is for men with small capitals all at once to exchange their own practice for that of a wealthier people. On the other hand, the tenants were doubtless obstinate and unjust in thinking whims and blunders part of the husbandry of the English, who

---

[1] One of our minor improvers having got a huge folio on husbandry, compiled by booksellers, made it his rule in all things. On a gentleman's asking one of his servants what he was about, the man answered, "He does everything by the *book*: he ploughs, and sows, and brews his strong ale by the book—but he *sticks* them all."

are as much guided by common-sense and attention
to interest as any people.

But by degrees both parties abated somewhat of
their prejudices. The gentleman improver found it
idle to sow as early as in Kent, or to import Lincoln-
shire barley, which, though an excellent grain, would
hardly ripen in time with us. After throwing away
much money upon new-fangled ploughs [1] and implements of husbandry, he was at last satisfied that those
of his own country, well made, would answer every
purpose in high cultivation. And in the important
article of *tids*, or times of ploughing and sowing, they
found it prudent to follow the practice of their country
neighbours, which in things within their narrow sphere
was founded in nature and experience.

In process of time, however, tenants came to copy
some of their masters' novelties in farming. They

[1] Once when I was dining with Blair, in company with Mr Charles Dundas
and John Hunter, the conversation turned on ploughs. Somebody asked Mr
Dundas if he had got anybody to work with his Suffolk plough. "No," said he.
"Sawney comes to the laird, clawing his head, and says, indeed it will not work
and the laird is seldom wiser than his man." Here Hunter interfered, saying,
"I have wrought with it, and could get my men to use it, but it is by no
means proper for us. If you are for an English plough, there is Lummel's."
"None but an idiot would say that," retorted the other. "Mr Dundas
answered Hunter, warmly, "when you have held your own plough on your
own farm seven years, as I did, you will be a competent judge of that matter.
I have tried all your English ploughs, but there is none of them so fit for a
soil and situation as our own, provided it be well made. You take a
your notions from the south of England; but these are too far-fetched for
us. In the Merse I am thought to know as much as my neighbours, but here
I find myself at a loss, and at Errol," whence he came. "I find I understand
nothing of the matter. You talk of English improvers. We had two of them
in the Merse brought down by Ker," Mr Ker of Moriston. "Though they
had plenty of money, nothing throve with them. I left the one in the Abbey
and expect the other will be gone thither before my return.

got better tools and tackle,[1] and the size and quality of their horses and cows were much improved. Between 1750 and 1760, some country lads who had been taught by the English servants to plough and manage horses in the new way; were hired by the neighbouring farmers, and helped to open their eyes. On the whole, if prior to 1760 (when the great changes commenced) our tenants did not make so much progress as they might have done, a number of them were at least disposed to learn, which was a great matter.[2]

It will not be improper to mention here two tenants who early adopted the new husbandry—viz., Alexander Galloway at St Ninians, and Henry Stirling at Park of Keir. There being a carse farm

[1] Since 1742, that Alexander Thomson came to Ochtertyre, he was repeatedly employed by Blair in making his ploughs. He himself was taught by William Headrig at the Miln of Aithray, and one M'Culloch, a servant of James Drummond of Blair, who had the chief repute in their day. But Sanders was born a mechanic. Thus, when a lad driving the plough, he used to put her to rights for the man who held her but did not know what was wrong. James Duncanson at Logie was the first eminent maker of ploughs for sale in this country. He was bred a smith, but having a strong bent to that branch of mechanics, he commenced plough-wright with general applause. After the great advance upon the price of Highland wood, he or some other of the trade was employed both by gentlemen and tenants. From having great stocks of timber on hand, they could afford the materials almost as cheap as the clumsy unseasoned plough-*graiths* brought to market by the Highlanders.

[2] Though fanners were used in mills as early as 1720, it was only about this time that our tenants got them for their barns. The winnowing of corn was of old a tedious and uncertain operation. Every mill had a *sheiling* hill, where it was performed in the open air. It is said the Anti-Burgher ministers testified against fanners, as a *creating of wind* and distrusting of Providence. They thought people should wait with patience for wind, as their fathers had done before them. But this scrupulosity being contrary to self-interest, made little impression on their followers.

below the town to let, the former, who was a considerable distiller,[1] went to the late Polmaise and offered for it. The laird, being heartily tired of broken tenants in that farm, was well pleased, and told him he should have it, provided he would take a two nineteen-year lease. The farm having been very much run out, Mr Galloway set about enclosing it: he then gave it a complete summer fallow, field by field, and after laying on plenty of lime and dung. sowed wheat.[2] In the important article of manure, he was no doubt luckily situated, the distillery giving him a command of dung, and having water-carriage for lime at hand. In assorting his crops, he had a large proportion of clover and rye-grass. The country people, who marvelled to find *him* following the *gentles* in their maggots, began to think more favourably when they saw his crops. No sooner was the land in good heart and the hedges fencible, than he let it off in pasture at a very high rent. And after being a proper time in grass, it was broke up occasionally for flying crops of corn, a species of hus-

[1] He learned the distilling business in Holland more than forty years ago, when it was little understood or practised in this country. In order to obtain admittance, he pretended to be an outlaw from Scotland, and putting on a barn frock, procured instruction from an eminent Dutch distiller, when he served as a labourer for some time. His spirits were all along the best in the country, and after making rich by the business, he gave it over in 1764 with a fair character.

[2] When he was busy dressing his first field of summer fallow, Thomas Buchan in Bandeath, a sensible old fashioned farmer, happened to pass by. The ground being rough and dirty, Thomas asked what was the meaning of ploughing at that season, and being told it was intended for wheat, he answered, "You may as well sow it in the crown of your hat."

bandry equally cheap and profitable. But pasture was his principal object.

In 1749 Henry Stirling got the farm of Park of Keir from the late John Stirling of Keir.[1] Being a connection of the family, it was meant he should have a good bargain. Nor did he disappoint the hopes or abuse the bounty of his patron. He became, ere long, an adept in the new crops and modes of cultivation, as well as zealous to promote their progress. As he is still upon the stage, it would be improper to enter into any detail concerning him. We cannot, however, forbear saying, that his fields and fences, his horses, cows, and implements of husbandry, his garden and dairy, remind one of England,—a country where neatness and plenty, and well-directed industry, go hand in hand with liberality and kindness on the part of the landlord. The more moderate the rent, the more anxious is the tenant to excel. We may safely affirm, that the spirited and successful exertions of Messrs Galloway and Stirling did more to give tenants a taste for improvements, than fifty gentlemen farmers, opulent in their circumstances, but rash or unsteady in their conduct.

In 1756 the crop failed over a great part of Scotland, owing to a very frosty spring and a wet cold summer, which retarded the ripening of the corn. The losses fell chiefly upon the late moorish counties,

---

[1] We should have mentioned in its proper place that Keir began much about the same time with his friends, Blair and Touch, to practise the English husbandry. But he died in 1757, before he could make much progress.

for in this neighbourhood, which is warm and early,
it was better than middling, and tolerably well got
in. Of course, our tenants were exceedingly well off.
The scarcity bore the harder upon the poor, that we
had a great and lasting storm of frost and snow in
the following winter. Nor did the crop 1757, though
a good one, bring down the markets so soon as might
have been expected. For they kept up till the month
of June thereafter, when wheat and other grain fell
near 50 per cent in the course of a few weeks.

The effects of the high prices of corn were somewhat alleviated to the poor by plenty of potatoes, a
root which twenty years before had been confined to
gentlemen's gardens. About 1746 or 1747, the Irish
method of cultivating them in the open field was
practised with great success in the neighbourhood of
Kilsyth. From thence it spread by degrees far and
near.[1] Upon the extension of their culture, it was
apprehended they would reduce the price of grain
under par. But those fears proved void of foundation, and they have long been the great support of
the labouring poor. In 1757 and 1758, amazing
quantities of them were raised in different places,
particularly in the neighbourhood of Callander, in

[1] In 1749 or 1750, George Henderson in Drys went to Kilsyth for a bag of
them to plant in the field. It succeeded so well, that many of his neighbours
cultivated them in the same manner. And they have ever since been a
stated part of the crop. Before that time there had been a few in tenants'
kailyards. Old George Bachop, a peevish crabbed man, being told by his
wife that she had got potatoes for his supper, said, "Tattoes! tattoes! I
never supped on them all my days, and will not to-night. Give them to the
herd, and get me sowens."

expectation of extravagant prices; but it produced
the very opposite effect.

The scarcity of 1756-57 was of too short duration
to produce important consequences. If the carse tenants fattened whilst labourers and tradesmen suffered
in proportion, the cheapness of the three following
years balanced matters pretty equally—wheat selling
at twelve shillings per boll, and other grain in proportion. There was, no doubt, a circumstance which
contributed to keep men temperate in their views
and actions: we were then struggling in a war the
most extended and hazardous of any in which the
country had ever been engaged. But about 1760
the scale turned decidedly in our favour, which gave
occasion to very new and extraordinary exhibitions.
In the course of an *over* successful war, princely fortunes were acquired with great rapidity by some of
our countrymen. Beside these blazing stars, which
eclipsed our first nobility, a number of handsome
though inferior fortunes were made by other Scotsmen. By this means vast sums of money flowed into
Scotland in the course of a few years.

All these fortunate adventurers hastened upon the
peace to invest their money upon land in their native
country. As was natural for men in opulent circumstances, generally past the prime of life, they were in
too great a hurry to higgle about the price; and there
being a choice of purchasers, land rose to a pitch
unknown in any former period. The money brought
home diffused itself by degrees among men of every

condition ; and they who had had no share of the
loaves and fishes, found means to procure ample credit.
It was now thought want of spirit for one to regulate
his conduct by the prudential maxims which had
passed current in the last generation. The prosperity
of so many individuals, joined to our smiling prospects at home and abroad, made a deep impression
upon the most sober minds ; whilst the sanguine
and inexperienced were in a state little short of
intoxication.

Among the various projects to which this fulness
gave rise, none was more fashionable and alluring
than farming and improvements. Here private interest and public utility seemed to go hand in hand.
And hence almost every country gentleman became
a professed improver upon a greater or lesser scale.

Precisely on the peace, the price of corn rose at
least a third above the ordinary conversion ; and for
a dozen of years it was often higher, never lower.
Amidst such a glare of prosperity it was not surprising that farmers of all denominations should ascribe
it to the flourishing state of the country rather than
the seasons. " Why," said they, " should there be
no advance upon grain, when black cattle and sheep,
though little affected by the weather, have almost
doubled within the last thirty years ?" They were,
indeed, disposed to consider it as their share of the
national felicity.

In a short time there was a pleasing show of industry and thriving among our tenants. They grad-

ually departed from the saving maxims of their fathers, and laid out liberally upon their farms. Before enumerating the alterations which took place in their husbandry, we shall mention the circumstances that either raised or depressed their spirits from 1763 to the present time.

After various lesser fluctuations in the sale of black cattle between 1760 and 1765, occasioned principally by the weather, the demand to England in summer 1766[1] exceeded what had ever been seen before, the dealers hardly knowing how much to ask. And in the three following years the markets continued extravagantly high. But in 1770 there was a considerable fall, though cattle were still beyond their value. Though there were various ups and downs in the course of the next ten or twelve years, prices never fell so low as preceding 1766, nor rose as high as in that and the three following years. Before the great start, the usual profit of a cow grazed in summer on a good Highland pasture was 10s., and of one in a low-country enclosure, 20s. Yet when the same beast, which twenty years before sold at 45s. or 50s., now fetched £3, 10s. or £4 sterling, the grazier seldom cleared more, often less, owing to his buying rashly at May-day.

It is not a little extraordinary that few of the

[1] In 1762 and 1765 there was excessive summer droughts, and in the latter a famine of winter fodder. Many people sold cheaper at Michaelmas than they bought at May-day. But their losses were made up in 1766. In June, Mr Stirling of Keir sold two draught-oxen at 20 guineas, which he thought a high price ; but before the end of the season they fetched £40 in England.

Highland breeders (with whom the profits chiefly centred) should have laid up money at the time that markets were exceedingly high, and their rents still upon the old footing. An enormous rise upon a commodity is indeed seldom advantageous, as it encourages jobbing and speculation, which frequently end in ruin. And in the Highlands it soon occasioned a rapid rise of rents, the consequences whereof were severely felt by tenants. Though the Lowlanders depended more upon corn than cattle, the rise upon the price of cattle was of great service to them. It made money plenty, and ensured them a good market for whatever they had to sell. The hopes of more profit made them think of paying attention to the improvement of their breed.

The rise upon horses kept fully pace with that on black cattle. And as it was now proper to have the former of a better size for carting, &c., a stronger and more sightly kind of stallions were by degrees introduced. Hence, in the course of the last twenty years the value of our tenants' horses has more than doubled. It was, however, no loss to them, as they mostly rear their own stock, and of course oftener sell than buy.

Between 1760 and 1770 [1] the carse tenants of their own accord gave over keeping sheep, from a conviction that more was lost by their nipping up the spring grass than was got by their dung and wool. They were, indeed, of very little value in low grounds.

[1] As early as 1741, John Stirling of Keir prohibited sheep on his carse farms.

About Michaelmas yearly, a man came from the muirlands who, from the colour of the sheep's eyes, pretended to tell which of them would not stand the winter. These were frequently sold at 2s. or 2s. 6d. apiece. Nor did the best country ewes and wedders give more than 4s. or 5s. They had formerly been boarded on the southern muirs from May to Michaelmas; but after the price had risen in the course of a few years from 3s. 4d. a score to 10s., it was at last difficult to get grass upon any terms. This was owing to the muirland men having got a more valuable stocking upon their farms. It falls to be reckoned among our improvements.

On dismissing sheep, the milch cows had better and earlier grass; and there being now an additional demand for butter [1] to tea in the neighbouring towns, the tenants' wives took more pains than formerly to make it sweet and clean. Since I remember the world, that article made in country houses would have turned stomachs the least squeamish.

The thriving state of manufactures not only increased the demand for yarn, but, by raising an intermediate order of men to plenty, gave tenants a ready market for everything their farms produced. And this, to people whose gains consist of a number

[1] The first dairy upon a great scale in this country was at Keir, in John Stirling's time, towards 1752. It was managed by Mrs Donaldson, who made it turn to great account. The butter was sent weekly to Edinburgh. Craigbarnet, whose remarks were seldom good-natured, said the milk to the tea at Keir was as blue as indigo, and the prints of butter no greater than his thumb.

of petty articles, was a matter of great importance.
Formerly, when the tradesman was poor and often
out of employment, he had some difficulty to procure
the necessaries of life ; but having now extended his
views, he was able to aspire at a few superfluities.

The facility of getting credit raised the spirits of
such tenants as were in haste to improve their farms.
In the former state of the country, it was no easy
matter to raise a sum, even where the security was
undoubted and the scheme rational. But now, since
the amazing extension of paper money, there were
people in most towns ready to advance cash, without
standing much upon security. It was doubtless not
a little hazardous both to the borrower and lender,
and in time produced very unpleasant consequences.
But whilst everything appeared prosperous, neither
party had any dread of a reverse of fortune.

But the circumstance which of all others contributed
most to the improvement of this country, was the
practicability of procuring lime to any extent. Tenants could do very little whilst they were confined to
Swallowhaugh and back-loads. In consequence of
good roads and carts, they now brought limestones
from Broomhall by water to Manour-pow[1] or some of

---

[1] William Mayne, Powis, told Mr Abercromby that, towards the end of last
century, John Burn in Blackgrange (formerly mentioned) was the first in
that neighbourhood who brought limestones from Broomhall by water. And
Alexander Thomson remembers the first limestone boat that went to the
westward of the Abbey Craig, it having been commissioned by Alexander
Galloway in Cornton, and landed at the Howford This was about 1719,
when Sanders was ten years of age. Of course, however, the use of limestones was long confined to the verge of the navigable river. Yet as early as

the neighbouring creeks, from which they could be easily transported in carts. After 1760, a man who formerly contented himself with laying on a few chalders yearly, for two-thirds of his lease, thought nothing of driving a quantity equal in value to the half of his rent. And instead of two or three chalders to the acre (which had been the old practice), it was found good husbandry to double the quantity.

It was extraordinary that for a number of years less lime in proportion should have been laid on by the farmers below Stirling, who could bring it to their doors, than by the people of Menteith, that labour under many disadvantages. Whilst the Trew tenants were making great exertions, the late Lord Elgin showed me fields within a stone-cast of his works which had not been limed within memory of man.[1]

Meanwhile, the demand for Swallowhaugh lime did not diminish.[2] Being the strongest in quality, people were glad to get it at any price. But about 1768, Mr Cheap, upon giving new leases of his estate, prohibited the tenants from burning or carrying lime

1742, John Chrystie, my father's tenant, drove a boatful of limestones from Manour-pow through Cornton and Greenock, partly on sledges and partly on tumblers, both of them very awkward vehicles.

[1] It may be expected that something should be said of marl and its effects, but of it in carse or tilly ground we have no experience. Colin Fairfowl used it at Breandam sixty years ago. It is most used in Strathallan and Strathearn.

[2] Between 1761 and 1767 there were frequently fifty or sixty horses here in a morning with back-loads of lime. The carriage, drink-money included, equalled the prime cost, and at Braco, where great buildings were then going on, it was fully double.

for sale.   They were, indeed, no better than carriers
for the whole country, doing nothing to their land
but ploughing and sowing it.   Fortunately for us,
Lord Elgin erected about this time great lime-works
at Broomhall, by which means either shells or
powdered lime could be had.[1]   But, in general, the
tenants in this corner prefer stones to shells, though
the latter require much less carriage.   They have not,
however, learned to put a proper value upon their
own labour.

For some time the driving limestones and coals
to the district south of Teith was confined to the
drought of summer, or to hard frost, when carts
could pass upon the ice.   The limestones were landed
at Manour-pow or Sheriff Muirlands, and carted in
dry weather through the lands of Cornton and
Greenock, across the Allan and Teith.   Though
carse roads and timber bridges were ill suited to
wheels, and the rivers proved often impassable, the
going by Drip coble was still less advisable, the Forth
being only fordable in very dry weather, and even
then the bottom was very rough.

But in 1770 those obstructions were happily removed by the building a stone bridge at the Drip.
It was set on foot by the tenants, who contributed
handsomely, and Lord Kames generously subscribed
£100 sterling, besides giving up the rent of the ferry.

[1] In Lord Elgin's minority, when nothing was sold but stones, the clear
profit of the quarry seldom amounted to £70 sterling ; whereas, from his
death in 1771, it has commonly exceeded £1000 a-year.

Since that time the Cornton road has been relinquished, somewhat imprudently, it being the nearest way to the Clackmannanshire collieries, from which we had been supplied for ages, and to which, in all probability, we must sooner or later have recourse again. The shore of Stirling became henceforth our principal port, and the bulk of our coals were brought from Bannockburn.[1]

The happy effects of good roads and bridges were soon apparent. In a few years after the Drip bridge was built, the tenants of this country drove more coal and lime between the end of October and March than used to be formerly through the whole year. And exclusive of the coals required for burning limestones, an ordinary farmer burned more in his house than a gentleman of moderate fortune forty years ago. It is true they cast a much smaller quantity of peats than they formerly did, which was surely no loss to them, it having been a tedious expensive operation. The winter-driving proved no doubt very hard upon the roads, but if the repair upon them was increased, the statute work turned to much better account, owing to better horses and carts. And the common people wrought with the greatest alacrity, being fully persuaded of the great utility of good roads.

We now proceed to a year of dearth and distress. From the beginning of the year 1782 to the end,

---

[1] It is said the Clackmannanshire colliers, in their Litany, used to pray for heavy rains in July, to spoil the west-country people's peats.

there was something dreary and judgment-like in the weather.[1] It was one of those memorable seasons which baffle the skill and labour of the husbandman, and which, happily for mankind, do not occur above twice or thrice in a century. It seems to have resembled the worst years of King William's dearth.

[1] In January hurricanes of wind, and, in the space of ten days, three great floods in the Teith, accompanied with an unnatural spring such as we seldom see in April. From 1st February continued frost for two months; and in the middle of March a prodigious fall of snow. In many places of this country it lay for a fortnight from two to three feet deep. But in the low grounds of the parishes of Lecropt and Logie, it was so light that it stopped the ploughs but a few days. By reason of snow or rain, very little oats or black victual could be sown here till the middle of April—most piercing cold winds in the end of that month and in May, and of course no vegetation. The barley got a dry but a very cold bed. By refusing to let more be sown till the weather grew milder, I succeeded better than most of my neighbours. Exceeding heavy rains in the end of May and beginning of June, which chilled the young corn. Ten days of hot weather about the middle of July, after which torrents of rain, attended with cold stormy winds, which lasted for six weeks with little interruption. It looked liker February than the warm month. Hurricane 24th August, which blew down a number of trees, and did much mischief to the wheat by breaking the straw. In the middle of September, notwithstanding a fortnight of fine weather, the oats in general green. 17th, Highland hills covered with snow; after some frosty mornings, boisterous wet weather to the end of the month. No oats ripe here till the first week of October; yet in Argyleshire they were a month earlier, which was a new phenomenon. Mornings of the 4th and 13th of October frost like mid winter, the ground being hard under foot till far in the day, and ice on the pools as thick as a crown-piece. It whitened the late corn and prevented its filling. Tempests of wind and rain and hail for a week after the 20th. Began to lead about midnight between 24th and 25th October in clear moon shine. All in 25th in the morning, two days before the great fall of snow. Melancholy to see at that season stooks and sheaves white with snow and stiffened with frost. Froze hard for ten days, with piercing north wind, which kept the snow from melting, and put the corn in excellent order for leading. Hardly ever less spoilt corn in a late harvest. In the high countries, covered with snow and not cut down till well in November. End of that month to beginning of December very deep snow, and the frost so intense that it threatened to set the mills, which would have heightened the distress of the country. Mild weather after the middle of December

Nor were its baneful effects confined to the fruits of the earth; for either in spring or summer, the human species, from one end of Europe to the other, was seized with an epidemical disorder, which, though not mortal in Britain, was attended with severe sickness while it lasted.

And now of the crop. The wheat was excellent; the oats in this corner better than middling, and tolerably ripe; the barley very poor; and the peas and beans mostly frost-bitten.[1] But nothing alarmed people so much as the risk which the potatoes ran. Till the beginning of November, everybody's attention was directed to the corn-crop. Indeed, had there been time to raise the potatoes sooner, they were not ripe. The frost from Monday the 4th of November to Saturday the 10th was so intense, that the most alert lost all that lay near the surface; and whoever persisted in lifting them towards the end of the week, had reason to repent their rashness. The highland and muirland grounds being covered with snow for weeks, it was concluded the potatoes would be entirely spoilt. But about the middle of December, when the weather became mild, the people were agreeably surprised to find a goodly number of them fit either for food or seed. The best way of preserving them through the hardest winter is to bury them in the earth so deep that the frost cannot penetrate. Amidst our wants and apprehensions, it was lucky

---

[1] In the carses of Logie and Lecropt, where, from the ebbness of the snow, people could sow early, there was a great crop of beans.

that the cattle had plenty of wholesome fodder to
eat.

Spite of our untoward prospects, the price of grain
continued almost stationary during the summer;
and luckily there was a great deal of the meal-crop
of 1781 still upon hand. On such occasions, it is
long before people allow themselves to despair of a
turn to the better. But by September the alarm
became general, insomuch that barley rose all at
once to 20s. from 14s., and other victual in proportion. Before Christmas it was apparent that our own
crop would not suffice to feed the inhabitants of
Scotland. And it seemed very doubtful whether
supplies could be procured from abroad. Being then
at war with half the world, we had, in a great
measure, lost the empire of the sea; and as the
enemies' privateers swarmed on the coasts, the loss
of a few ships might occasion a temporary famine.
But in the end of January those fears were happily
removed by a cessation of arms, which came in good
time to save us both from national bankruptcy and
dearth. During the winter, seasonable supplies were
obtained from the south of England, where the crop
had been good. And among the other good consequences of peace, a large quantity of peas provided
for the navy being now to be sold, was imported
into Scotland, where they proved a hearty acceptable food to many poor families. And no sooner
was the Sound clear of ice, than great numbers of
ships were sent to the Baltic for corn. That trade

being at present profitable and secure, the love of gain contributed for once to alleviate the rigours of scarcity.

The lower classes of people behaved with more cheerfulness and patience than could have been expected from their late giddiness. They were, indeed, sensible that the present calamity was not the work of man ; and every precaution which human wisdom could suggest was taken by their superiors to procure · a sufficient supply of provisions. If the market was much too high for their wages, meal could always be had for money, and most of them found means to get a little credit. And besides, there are astonishing resources in temperance and industry, which enable our hardy commons to bear up with fortitude under every temporary pressure. Though there were doubtless many sober meals among them at this time, yet, as far as could be observed, the virtuous poor were strangers to the miseries of want. And as butcher-meat was cheap and plenty through the winter, the tradespeople found it good economy to buy the coarse pieces. And bread made of flour and bran, as it came from the mill, turned out a better pennyworth than either oat-cakes or pease or bear bannocks.[1] Even the people who wrought in the Highland woods brought with them every Monday their coarse loaf. The dearth was not succeeded by any dangerous

---

[1] We must, however, remember that this corner was better off than many other parts of Scotland. In the north the crop failed so entirely that the tenants were neither able to pay rent nor buy seed. The poor people must have been miserably off indeed.

epidemical sickness, which affords a strong presumption that the poor were never reduced to eat of the unwholesome food said to have been used in the end of the previous century. Famine seldom fails of producing infectious diseases.

The humanity of the rich never appeared with greater lustre than upon this occasion. Besides what was given privately, subscriptions were opened all over the country for purchasing meal and selling it to the poor at or under prime cost.[1] And some towns gave premiums to the persons who brought meal to market.[2] Though this afforded no more than a temporary relief, it was in truth sound policy. As the belly has no ears and will not listen to reason, it is the duty of magistrates, in times like these, to soothe the known prejudices of the populace. Now nothing exasperates them so much as a penury of meal in the public market. Being always jealous of the malpractices of the dealers in corn, they think themselves entitled, upon such an emergency, to assume a sort of tribunitial power of searching for

[1] The gentlemen about Doune bought fifty bolls of oatmeal at 20s. a boll. which they sold in March and April to the tradesmen and labourers of the parishes of Kincardine and Kilmadock weekly, in small quantities proportioned to their families. Only a halfpenny was discounted, yet it was very acceptable to persons who had not money to buy more at a time, and who would have been at the mercy of the mealmongers.

[2] The magistrates of Stirling began with seizing all the meal passing through the town, which was sent to market and sold at *their* price. Had they persevered a little longer, it would have starved the town and occasioned much. But they very wisely revoked the order, and gave a premium for every boll of meal that was brought to the market. This produced the desired effect, the tenants being no longer afraid of being seized like criminals by the town officers.

meal and stigmatising delinquents. Their interference, however, is often productive of mischief and bloodshed, and generally increases the scarcity it was intended to remedy.

In May or June a sum of money was voted by Parliament for the relief of the northern counties, which were supposed to be starving. Of this bounty we received a share, as being on the north side of the Forth, though many places to the southward stood more in need of it. All praise is due to the benevolent intentions of our rulers; but there seems to be a fatality in everything where public money is employed. Notwithstanding the vote passed in time enough to have done great good, the meal commissioned by the Barons of Exchequer did not arrive till September, when all fears of famine were over. Indeed they had no occasion to import any grain, there being already plenty in the merchants' granaries, or on the way. The distresses of the poor arose chiefly from want of money to purchase it at the extravagant price then given.

Had the bounty of Parliament been applied in making up to the industrious poor the odds between 16s. the boll and the current price, it would have gone a very great length.[1] A labourer or tradesman may make a shift to live so long as oatmeal does not exceed a shilling the peck; but when it comes to 15d. or 16d., his wages must either be

[1] The labouring servants who had livery meal felt the dearth very little. It was also the case with day-labourers, who got it at 16s. a boll.

raised or he will soon be reduced to poverty. There
is, however, no benevolence more misjudged than
the raising of wages, for they seldom return to the
old standard when the emergence is once over.[1] It
is therefore the wisest policy, as well as the truest
charity, to give the labouring man assistance whilst
he is yet willing to struggle for independence, and in
fear of beggary as the worst of evils. These hints
were suggested to the Barons, but they thought proper to distribute their first and largest quantity of
meal gratis. But although a largess of corn may
render a man popular in a district of burghs, it
hardly ever proves a blessing to those that live by
the sweat of their brows. Whatever they get in that
way has a tendency to make them idle and improvi-
dent, in hopes of some future benevolence. It would
seem, however, that the Barons afterwards altered
their views in part ; for they directed their second
cargo of meal to be delivered upon payment of two-
thirds of the prime cost. By the time it arrived,
which was very soon after the other, the scarcity was
so much over, that some parishes in this neighbourhood declined to take their quota ; yet, two months
before, meal at a reduced price would have been exceedingly welcome.

Nothing was more inexplicable during the dearth
than the distilling business. Although barley sold

[1] In 1757 the late Blair, in compassion to the wants of the labouring poor,
allowed William Bowie, his undertaker for the great walk, to give the workmen 8d. in place of 6d. But the very next year, when meal fell nearly a
half, nobody would take the old wages.

mostly at 25s. or 26s. a boll, and the duties, which were before much too high, had been lately raised, more spirits than ever were made in Scotland. Yet a very small proportion of them was consumed at home, being mostly intended for the London market. It also surprised everybody that the prodigious quantity of grain used in that way did not occasion any violent ferment among the populace. This was owing to the prudence of the capital distillers, who took care to supply the neighbouring towns with meal upon easy terms. And, in their own justification, it was said that they only made use of English or foreign barley, which would not otherwise have been imported. And it was, they alleged, of little consequence to the poor whether the Scottish or the London distillers should convert it into spirits. How far this reasoning was solid, we shall not say; but surely it required a great share of address to reconcile the lower classes of people to such a waste of grain at such a time.

The prosperity of the stills induced certain bold adventurers to try a business which, the more it was fettered, appeared, against all probability, to thrive more and more. Some of them in this country went on for a while with great spirit; but after running their race of speculation, the folly and injustice of venturing so deep without a stock became apparent.[1]

[1] At that time, James Guild of Myreton and his sons stopped payment for £22,000 sterling, an enormous sum for a man who not very many years before had been a common tenant! Being a bustling fellow of good natural talents, and much insinuation and plausibility, he prevailed on his landlord, the last

About the end of April 1783, it occasioned the same
kind of convulsion among the men of speculation
in this country that the failure of the Douglas and
Heron bank did in the metropolis.   It gave a rude
shock to commerce and credit; but what was most
to be regretted, some honest simple men were entirely ruined by their engagements with those unprincipled fellows.   Towards the eve of their bankruptcy, it was no uncommon thing to discount forged
bills, when they could not prevail on a friend to join
with them.   It was, however, an advantage to the
country to be rid of a set of knaves or dupes, who
would have done much more mischief had they been
allowed a little more scope.

The ploughing and sowing time of 1783 was very
favourable, and the apprehensions of another bad
crop from the want of wholesome seed were speedily
dispelled.   Though the seed boll was extravagantly
dear, it could be had without difficulty.[1]   If there

Lord Cathcart, to give him a feu of the lands of Myreton, &c., upon very advantageous terms. He lost no time in dressing and enclosing the low grounds.
Had he stopped there, he might have been a prosperous man; but having
many irons in the fire, some of them could not fail to cool. At last, finding
his affairs embarrassed, he took a most desperate resolution. To each of his
sons he gave a farm, and built houses, distilleries, malt barns, &c., at enormous expense. By this means, however, he kept afloat a while longer, it
being impossible to distinguish between the property of the father and sons.
The young men went on longer than was expected; indeed their expense
without and within doors astonished everybody. It was entirely owing to
their credit with the Stirling bankers, against whom there were loud clamours
for their advancing such sums to known adventurers. And as the debts of the
Guilds had doubled in the course of a few years, it occasioned violent sus-
picions of usurious practices.

[1] By all accounts the want of good seed was the ruin of this crop in the
northern counties. Strange that the landlords were not at more pains!

was a scarcity of peas and beans of our own produce, English ones of superior quality were to be got from the victual merchants;[1] and it was an agreeable surprise to find potatoes cheaper in spring than in the beginning of winter. From the middle of June we had the warmest, most growing weather ever known. There was indeed little sunshine, the ground being covered till far in the day with a thick mist or haar, which moistened the earth and promoted vegetation as effectually as copious rains. Of course the harvest was early, and though rainy at first, the crop in general was got in with little loss. Wheat and oats proved only middling, but the black victual was good, and the barley most excellent. The common people were greatly rejoiced with a plentiful early crop of potatoes, which rendered them in some measure independent of contingencies.

And now of the crop of 1784. The preceding winter had been perhaps the severest since the great storm of 1740. Amazing quantities of snow fell in the month of January, particularly to the eastward and northward; and the frost continued with little interruption from Christmas to the beginning of April. In this country the snow did not lie after the first week of February; yet in the Lothians and the muirlands, it continued unmelted till the end of March. Never was it easier to labour the carse grounds; and the oats and black victual were mostly

---

[1] Wherever any doubt was entertained of the quality of the seed, care was taken to sow much thicker than usual.

sown in hard frost, the harrows making little impression till mid-day. Though April was blasty and bleak, the fineness of the month of May, after a dry seed-time, set all to rights. The prodigious quantity of rain that fell in June, joined to the coldness and withering winds in July, checked the progress of vegetation. About Lammas the crop promised to be almost as late as 1782 itself. From the end of August, however, we had two months of blessed weather which dispelled all our fears and ripened the latest countries. And though not cut down till far in the season, the crop was got into the barnyard in fine condition. It was a long time indeed before the tenants would admit the grain to be *true*, but they could not deny that there never had been a greater quantity of fine fodder.

To the great joy of the farmers, the demand for barley to Stirling in the beginning of winter, continued as brisk as ever at a guinea or 22s. a boll. The fall of oatmeal from 17s. to 15s. was the first symptom of the goodness of the last crop. The great distillers went on at their great rate, in hopes that the obstructions laid upon exportation might be made easy in the execution. But their expectations of home sale proved delusive, the penalties upon smugglers and their landlords having been suspended by an order from Treasury.[1] The small stills were

[1] Vi lent as the late Act might be deemed with regard to landlords, it seemed to point out the best cure for smuggling. While the matter was in suspense, hardly a drop was distilled, the gentlemen having seized the stills, but no sooner were the terrors removed than these were restored, and the

now resumed all over the country, and consumed a great deal of grain, though equally injurious to the revenue and the entered distillers. It proved, however, highly beneficial to the excise officers, who were promised a considerable premium for every unlicensed still they should seize. And the prime cost of these utensils being small, they laid hold of numbers, without discouraging smuggling in the smallest degree.

But in the month of January things took a very different turn. Hardly anybody would buy barley, and hence for some weeks there was no settled price. By that time the bulk of our tenants had sold their grain; and they that kept up in expectation of a still better price, met with little sympathy. It was a sore stroke upon the Stirling dealers, whose barns were mostly full of grain, or sold to persons whose credit was very suspicious. Besides the goodness of the last crop, other causes were assigned for this extraordinary stagnation. The capital distillers had of late contracted their operations, in consequence of two ships with Scotch spirits being seized at London for not complying with the regulations in the late Act. One Nimmo, a distiller at Blackgrange, who had once before stopped payment, now broke in good earnest, very much in debt to the victual merchants. Like the Guilds, he behaved most fraudulently; and, like them, he went off to America with

gaugers went through their customers to tell them they might go on as formerly, only they would seize the stills.

all the cash he could collect.[1]   And hence everybody
who had taken up the business without stock or experience, came to be somewhat suspected.

This check would soon have been forgotten, had
not the Commissioners of Excise issued an order
directing the traders to charge their stills four times
a - week, otherwise three or four gaugers, besides
cruisers (as they were called), would be stationed
upon each of them.   As it was not in the power of
the middling distillers to obey this mandate, most
of them gave over business in the course of a few
weeks, of whom some became bankrupts.

Though this measure excited loud clamours, there
were not wanting plausible topics to justify it.   The
numberless frauds committed by the small entered
distillers required, it was said, severity.   Nor could
the Commissioners employ their officers more usefully
than in detecting or preventing malpractices.   It
would be better for the revenue to have this business upon the same footing in this country as in
England, where nobody thought of it but men of
great capital.   All countenance was therefore due
to the few respectable traders, who paid Government

---

[1] Since the last peace, the emigrants from the country have been in general
such as could well be spared. In November 1784, James Belsh, a tenant of
Keir's at Calder (originally from this parish), having had a dispute with his
master, resolved to balk him. For this purpose he *ployed* his own or
threshed the best part of it, and then stacked up the straw. After selling off
his cattle and other effects, he embarked with his family for America, and
had sailed some days before being missed. All he left for the hypothec was
three or four old horses and some stacks of straw, under the charge of an old
woman

a very great sum of money, with little trouble to the officers of excise. And Scotland was very much beholden to these gentlemen for having rendered our spirits an object of commerce. In that way great sums of money had come into the country, which served to replace what had been sent abroad to purchase corn. It was ridiculous to impute the fall of barley to the late order—that being owing to the goodness of the last crop, which had produced similar effects in England about the same time. But if local causes must be assigned, the harsh restraints lately imposed upon the exportation of our spirits had already produced bad effects, and must in a short time affect the landed interest very sensibly. Were things restored to their former footing, there would be a constant demand for barley at an adequate price.

On the other hand, it was contended that this new regulation, which had no authority in law, was suggested by a few overgrown distillers, who, being balked in their views with regard to the London market, aspired now at a complete monopoly in the low country. But as they had, by aiming at too much, excited the jealousy of the English—a people of all others the least narrow-minded — so it was hoped this last attempt would at length rouse the landholders of Scotland from their lethargy. Whenever duties are nearly equal to a prohibition, it is impossible to carry on business without either indulgence upon the part of the Government or evasion on that of the trader. With all their boasted secrets, it was not pretended their rich rivals could perform impossibilities. Their favour with the board had indeed secured them from the rigid treatment which others had experienced. Thus, when half-a-dozen excisemen were placed to watch some poor men night and day, one single officer was thought sufficient for the vast works at Kilbogie. By this indulgence, however, the revenue lost nothing, as the stills paid a very large sum in duty. Let the middling ones be treated with the same lenity, and there was no doubt of their making up among them an equal, if not a superior, sum. Whether this was to be done by lowering the duty further, or by paying it on the size of the still, was left to their superiors. All they asked was some plain rule which would exclude partiality. It was neither expedient nor just to deprive some hundreds of bread, that a few might be enabled to live like men of fortune. The former would never have it in their power to enter into any combinations about the price of grain.

Soon after the peace of 1783, there was a brisk demand for black cattle to England, owing, it was said, to great numbers of horses being exported to France, which made it necessary to get other beasts to put upon the grass. Whatever was the cause, in autumn 1784 cattle were dearer than they had been since the year 1769. Horses, too, which had been a drag for some years, rose in the course of a twelvemonth nearly a third. And the Highland sheep, which were supposed to be over-multiplied, found a ready market in England, from whence, it is alleged, they were smuggled into France. It was discovered that these animals suffered as little from the journey as the Highland cattle. Those things, joined to the demand for our manufactures, brought large sums of money into Scotland, which promoted a quick circulation.

Strange as it may sound, nothing in our remembrance has either raised the spirits or bettered the circumstances of our tenants so much as the late dearth. Even in 1782, the prices compensated for the want of bolls. And in the two following years they were exceedingly well off. At last they seemed to think 20s. a boll ought to be the medium price of barley. Actuated by the hopes of present gain, they never dreamt of the train of bad consequences which would result from a continuance of great crops and great prices. Various classes of people, one after another, would have put in strong claims to a share of their additional profits.

It must, however, be confessed that the late prosperity of the farmers has been attended with some good consequences. They are at this moment straining every nerve to make the land to produce more abundantly; and hence the quantity of lime and coal driven within the last two years exceeds anything before known. Luckily for them, the late heavy taxes bear very light upon husbandry. We cannot help observing that there is at present a giddiness approaching to intoxication among the lower orders of men which greatly resembles what prevailed among their betters before the great convulsion of 1775.

It may perhaps be thought we have been too minute with regard to the three last years; but in a work of this kind, everything that related to the dearth, and to the causes or consequences of the late exorbitant prices, seemed to merit a place.

About the year 1771 our tenants were well disposed to the culture of turnips, nor did they grudge the labour necessary to dress and clean them. But the want of enclosures was an insuperable bar to their progress. Nothing indeed but a stone fence will keep out cattle that have once tasted that delicious root. For it every other food is loathed; and the moment they are turned out, they run straight to the turnip-field, and if access cannot be had, stand at gaze for hours. Some of our tenants told me their cows were more the worse than the better of turnips, from being hard hunted, and put off their usual food. The house-wives were, nevertheless, very fond of them, because they afforded a great deal of milk, which is doubly precious in winter.[1] Indeed, my tenants' farms, Broadford excepted, are too wet and strong for this crop. But wherever the soil is sweet and dry, it is excellent

[1] In 1763 I let Alexander Thomson about an acre of middling turnips. On asking how he liked them, he said, "Very well. We have now almost as much milk in winter as we used to have in summer; but indeed the whey is very ill tasted. Was it not for giving an ill example in my family, I would not drink it." For some years the Craigarnal tenants, whose land is enclosed and well suited to turnips, have had regularly half an acre of them for their milch cows.

husbandry. They should, however, only be given to new-calved cows or stall-fed oxen. The former is proper where the quantity is small; yet a field of four or five acres, well dressed, would generally double the quantity of dung, besides preparing the ground for a great crop of barley. It is less advisable to give them to cows heavy with calf, or to queys, as it makes the latter take the bull too early.

For more than twenty years our tenants have had spots of clover, first in their kailyards, and afterwards in the corner of an enclosure; but as they grudged the want of a corn-crop, it was seldom sown in their best land, or well manured; and there was commonly too much rye-grass, which is a robber of the ground, and fitter for hay than green fodder. Though the carse tenants had plenty of bean-straw for their work-horses, yet most of their brethren in this country had nothing to give them after midsummer but thistles, in pulling which the men-servants spent much time. But so sensible were those people of the benefit of clover, particularly to milch cows, that they never scrupled to take spots of it at a most extravagant price whenever the neighbouring gentlemen were disposed to let it.[1]

But within the last seven years a great change has taken place in their views and practice. Sown grass is likely to become a stated and important article in the crop of tenants. Indeed something was necessary to supply the want of lea in our low-country outfields.

[1] It was a favourite proverb that " grass is a poor crop at Yule."

At present it is by no means uncommon to have fields
of clover in open ground. Alexander Thomson and
James Chrystie first practised it about the year 1779,
and the land being in high order, and free from rooted
weeds, they had a most excellent crop. Instead of
the ordinary practice of keeping the clover two years,
they very wisely broke it up next winter. The expense of seed is trifling, and the crop the second year
seldom answers ; and what is extraordinary, the Muir
people's land is as much the better of one year in
grass as of half-a-dozen. Nor is it a small induce-
ment to them that they have thereby a moral certainty
of a heavy crop of oats.

About 1766, Mr Seton of Touch let a farm which
he had enclosed, and in some measure dressed, to John
Whitehead, who came from Colonel Edmondstoune's
estate. By the bargain, the latter was tied to a rotation of crops, a thing disagreeable to him, who had not
the smallest experience of the new modes of cultivation. But though in very moderate circumstances at
coming there, the man made rich in the course of a
nineteen-year lease. It is true, independent of the
rotation, it was held a great bargain at the time.
And as Mr Seton has all along proceeded upon the
same liberal plan with his other tenants, the estate of
Touch is at present in very high condition, the bulk
of it being enclosed.

Much about the same time the last Keir began to
enclose the lands of Luigs upon an extensive and
substantial plan. The neatness of his stone dykes

struck every passenger; and by rows of trees and
belts of planting, he in a few years warmed and
beautified a bleak country. It being in vain to alter
his tenants' system all at once, he was satisfied with
doing what was within his reach, and consistent with
their very limited ideas. The farms being extensive,
as well as easily rented, he was entitled to stipulate
that in future there should always be two-thirds in
grass and one in corn. In this way the ground could
not be run out, and by *lathing* and liming, more corn
might be expected from a third than from the whole
in the old way, when they were under no restraint.
As their lands are full of rooted weeds, they are sure
of good natural grass. Of this they could make
better use than when the fields lay open in winter and
spring to the whole cattle around. It may perhaps
lead in time to more solid improvements.[1] One would
imagine turnips and sown grass would thrive in their
haughs, which are of a sweet loamy soil.

In the course of the last twenty-five years the same
gentleman enclosed the greatest part of the lands of
Keir, both dry field and carse, either with stone
dykes or hedges, so that the tenants have it in their
power to sow what crops they please.

About sixteen years ago Mr Robertson Barclay
enclosed his lands of Craigarnal, and as he had quar-
ries in almost every field, it was comparatively an

---

[1] Mr Stirling had a farm there in his natural possession, in which, to show
his tenants an example, he tried the new husbandry, but, it is said, with
little success.

easy matter to enclose. His tenants discovered ere
long that artificial grass was likely to make a much
better return than ground left lea in its natural state.
They have therefore had, for some years, not only
green clover for their cattle, but also some hundred
stones of hay to sell.[1]

In proportion as the quantity of grass increased,
they bethought them of bringing in new land for
corn. A great part of their outfields had, past all
memory, been overspread with furze or whins,[2] which
afforded the horses and cows a scanty pasture in
summer, and a slender resource in winter, amid frost
and snow, by browsing on the bushes. It was,
indeed, next to impossible for a plough to have gone,
on account of a great number of large grey stones
which lay upon the surface, or immediately below it.
But now James Watson, a most spirited industrious
tenant, set about rooting out the whins and blowing
the stones with powder, which last were useful in
building his subdivision fences. In this way, in the
course of a few years, some fields which had been
waste for ages now produced corn in rotation. If the
crop was but moderate at first, it served to swell the
barnyard; and by means of manure and good culti-

[1] In 1780 and 1781, two troops of dragoons were quartered at Stirling, and
as they came unexpectedly, it was no easy matter to procure them forage.
Of this, as usual, advantage was taken, and the hopes of a high price and
ready market made people sow fields of clover for hay who had never done it
before.

[2] We have a tradition that the seed of the whins was imported and sown
as a profitable crop by one of the Dows of Arnhall in the sixteenth or seventeenth century. Few crops thrive so well as they have done.

vation, the land is gradually improving. The same thing has taken place in the neighbouring estates, so that ere long there will hardly be a spot of ground that is not arable.

There is within these few years a great change in the views of the tenants in this neighbourhood. They begin to have an idea of property in winter as well as in summer ; nor is it any longer thought bad neighbourhood to drive off cattle that are trespassing upon their winter crops. Being convinced of the benefit of these, they seem more desirous of having enclosures than their masters are of making them. Thus the Muir tenants have lately, of their own accord and at their own expense, made march-ditches and planted them with thorns. And James Chrystie, who had advantages above his neighbours, enclosed, some time before, ten acres of ground adjacent to the Blair enclosures. Whether their hedges will ever come to perfection is, however, not a little doubtful, the palings being very slight, and the cattle having access to crop the young shoots. Though it should be productive of no other good effect, it may be the means of introducing winter herding. In that way, at a very moderate expense, all the winter crops that tenants have occasion for might be preserved.[1]

---

[1] It is the practice of our tenants to dismiss the herd after the crop is got in ; nor does he return till Candlemas, when the plough is yoked. They only save his meat for three months, as they would get him for the same wages through the whole year. In the winter, however, the boys are not idle ; at that time they go to school, and hence one seldom meets with a country lad that cannot read.

The years 1797 and 1798 were nowise memorable. The spring of the former promised at first well, but from April till far in May the weather was cold and coarse, unfavourable for ploughing and barley-sowing. June was warm and growing, only too much rain and a good deal of thunder. In July, the crop, which promised to be luxuriant, was much lodged by heavy rains or thunder-showers. The weather in harvest was checkered, and sometimes threatened to break; but in the first and second weeks of October the crop in this corner was got in in good condition. In winter, barley sold much lower than in the former season, and other grain was moderately priced. At Michaelmas, cattle, large and small, sold at enormous rates.

1798, taken upon the whole, was a fine season. The seed-time was excellent, and May delightful, a thing not very common in our climate. Never did grass and corn look better than in the beginning of June. After some hot weather, and more drought than was agreeable, there came, in the end of that month, and in July, warm refreshing rains, followed by sunshine. August set in wet, but in a few days it cleared up, and we had near a month of very hot weather, accompanied with heavy dews. Reaping general from the 15th. In no harvest did less rain fall when that operation was performed. All cut down 4th September, and a good deal put in before the 12th, when excessive rains took place for two days. It produced a first-rate flood in Teith, a thing equally uncommon and unpleasant so early in the season. Yet little corn was swept off the haughs, it having been previously removed. In a few days the weather broke up, and in less than a fortnight the crop all over the country was secured without any loss. It was an abundant one, and the prices of grain in winter differed little from those of the preceding year.

I now proceed to another strongly marked season, whether we consider the weather, the crops, or the consequences. Upon my own mind it made an indelible impression.

1799 promised ill from the commencement of the ploughing season. No severe storm of frost and snow after Christmas; but after a week of piercing cold weather, with frost, an excessive fall of snow February 7. It soon melted, and was succeeded by cold, wet, blasty weather till the end of March. Of course the oat-seed time bad and late. Hard frost and snow 10th April when sowing oats. For four weeks, from the end of that month, much cold rain, there being hardly two days fair together, and hence barley was sown in very bad case. Great wind and rain 4th June. Dry pleasant weather for twenty days thereafter. Three very hot days about 22d, the warmest of the season. From the second week of July to the end of August, a succession of tempests of wind and rain, such as one would expect in February. The *worm* month—*i.e.*, from the 26th of July to the 26th of August, new style—to which the Highlanders look so much, was almost as stormy and ungenial as 1782 itself. Everything looking ill, there was much reason to dread a very late harvest. In the beginning of September, however, we had eight or ten days of fair sunny weather, that were of great use. Leaking weather afterwards, but the rains were not violent. Hardly any corn cut down hereabouts till 20th September, except some spots of bear or barley. Though the harvest was doubtless late and unpromising, the crop was at least a fortnight earlier than that of 1782. From that time to the end of October a good deal of rain, but little wind. Very hard frost in the first part of that month, which injured late corn by whitening it before being full. People who were attentive and cautious got in the crop in the beginning of November in tolerable order, but this corner is very early. Yet we found it necessary to open a number of sheaves that were beginning to grow. The most effectual cure for it is to expose them for some hours to the open air on a fair day. Owing to rashness or want of skill, many stacks were put into the barn-yard when wet or not fit to keep. Seldom has there been greater losses by victual heating than this year; and what was very tantalising, after stacks began to smoke, the weather was so close and rainy that people durst hardly turn them, which, in a better season, would have cooled the heat.

We, however, escaped easily in comparison of the moorish and late countries. From the beginning. of November to the middle of December there was

hardly a fair day, the rain being constant and soaking. Had the winds been loud and searching, the
wet would have done little mischief. They had
secured next to nothing before the weather broke
finally in November, and for six weeks there was
hardly a leading day. Over a great part of the kingdom, which used to produce a great deal of grain,
nine-tenths of the crop was completely rotted. Not
to lose *all*, some of the Cardross tenants thrashed out
their oats, wet as they were, and made meal of them,
the straw being fit for nothing but the dunghill. In
a word, towards the conclusion of this harvest, nothing
could be done by means of skill and care, which in
ordinary seasons do great things.

Had this year's crop been got in safe, it was much
superior in quantity and quality to 1782. Wheat was
in general excellent; barley middling; peas and
beans below par, owing to the coldness and lateness
of the season, and the severe early frost. But it gave
great satisfaction that the oats and potatoes in this
warm corner were, upon the whole, bulky and prolific.
There was too much reason to expect a scarcity, from
the great quantities of spoilt corn. Yet, in expectation of great prices, much meal was made early by
the tenants to the westward, and sent to Glasgow,
where, till December, no more was got than from 22s.
to 25s. a boll.

The bulk of them, however, were in less hurry, and
after Parliament met the cry of famine was very loud.
In the latter end of January oatmeal gave 30s. and

31s. 6d. a boll, but every week it advanced considerably. It was generally believed that if the victual merchants and farmers had brought forward their grain with discretion, there was enough to have served till supplies were got from America or the Continent. In April oatmeal had risen to 48s., and it advanced in May to 52s. 6d. Other kinds of grain were also very high, though oatmeal was most out of proportion. None could tell to what a pitch grain might rise in the present temper of the dealers' minds, which even famine prices could not satisfy.[1]

Nothing was left undone by Parliament to avert the miseries of famine. The distillery was early stopped, and restraints laid upon the trades which required a quantity of wheat or flour. Recourse was again had to large bounties, to be paid to the importers of wheat and other corn. But America was remote, and little could be had from the Baltic till the northern ports were free of ice. In these circumstances, apprehensions were entertained that in summer there might either be a deficiency of wholesome food, or of money to buy it at an enormous price. Loud complaints were made against forestallers and regraters; but to these our Ministers of State lent a deaf ear, it being their axiom that the prices of corn should be allowed to find their own level. That did not make victual merchants and farmers more popular or re-

---

[1] The mealmongers wished to take 4s. for the peck, which occasioned a meal mob, that was not easily suppressed. Though a desperate remedy, it kept prices where they had been for some weeks in Edinburgh.

spected; but owing to the Volunteers in towns, the persons and property of the former suffered very little, in circumstances which, at any former time, would have kindled the wrath of the mobility, which is often ill directed and unjust.

Meanwhile, meritorious exertions were everywhere made to alleviate the distresses of the lower classes of people, who, in ordinary seasons, required no help. In Edinburgh, Glasgow, and other considerable burghs, the magistrates and communities bought or imported quantities of grain, which they retailed in small quantities at reduced prices to their townspeople. In consequence of liberal subscriptions in the capital towns, public kitchens were set up, from which every day messes of excellent soup, made of cheap materials, were distributed to such as were furnished with tickets. By general consent the wages of tradesmen and manufacturers were raised to a rate which would procure them the necessities of life. In truth, a number of them were greater objects of charity than paupers, who must either be maintained by the parish, or beg their bread.

In this quarter, the virtuous poor that did their best were comparatively well off as long as their potatoes lasted. When these were finished, they had recourse to the inferior kinds of meal. Kail was to them a standing dish. All they desired was to get as much oatmeal as would make porridge, which afforded a most comfortable meal. By the end of May things had a gloomy appearance. Oatmeal bore

a most extravagant price, and was hardly to be procured in small quantities. The cargoes of Indian
wheat or meal belonged either to magistrates or societies, who had commissioned them for the use of
their own people. From a scrutiny made at the
request of the Duke of Athole, our lord lieutenant, it
appeared that the farmers of this parish had still on
hand in that month, according to their own computation, 106 bolls of wheat, 88 of barley, 84 of peas and
beans, 18 bolls of oat, and 14 bolls of oatmeal.[1] This
was more than could have been expected at that
season, considering the state of markets. Though
more than adequate to the wants of the parishioners
before harvest, it was continually decreasing, and
might be disposed of in a short time. Previously
provision had been made for the paupers; but there
was a class of people of a superior kind who were
perhaps in more distress, though they made no complaints. A calculation was exhibited of 179 bolls of
meal, that would be necessary to supply tradesmen,
moss-lairds, and labourers, till the potatoes and new
crop should be ready. This was evidently exaggerated, and therefore a middle course was held. The
gentlemen of this parish purchased a quantity of
wheat at £2, 14s. a boll, which was much cheaper
than barley at £2, 14s., or peas at £3 per boll,

[1] About that time his Grace gave notice to the several districts that he had
commissioned 4000 quarters of oats for the behoof of Perthshire. On account
of the distance, &c., we declined taking a share. Though bought when markets were comparatively low, the meal would have cost 3s. a peck, besides
carriage.

which the two last gave currently through summer.
When ground, the bran was not taken out of the
flour; but though less toothsome than oatmeal, it was
a wholesome nourishing food, though it did not, they
said, make good porridge; but necessity has no law.
Every week there was a little market, and the people
came with their bags; and what was pleasing, they
never wanted money, but seemed cheerful and contented.   There was at that time a vast quantity of
rice at Glasgow, which was much lower priced than
any species of corn.   Had it been attended to sooner,
it would have proved a most seasonable relief to the
lower classes of people, as four or five pounds of it,
with milk, went as far as a peck of oatmeal.   For
a while the benefit of it was little known.   In July
we got a hundredweight of it, which was distributed
in small quantities to the country people, who were
instructed how to boil and use it.   Such as had not
milk were directed to lay salt herrings on top of the
rice while soaking in the pot.   Rice by itself is somewhat insipid, but the herring would give it a taste.
Though a favourite dish with the West Indian negroes,
who fare better than many of our tenants did formerly, it was little relished by our people; but had the
scarcity continued, they would have been reconciled
to it.

Some time before Lammas a quantity of English
oats from the fenny countries was imported, and part
of it manufactured at the mill of Circentully, which
was of great benefit to the west end of this parish, to

whom it was retailed. The prospect of an early harvest, and the vast quantities of grain imported in
summer, dispelled all fears of famine, and made our
people look forward to better times. It said little for
the heads or hearts of certain tenants that when they
saw a prospect of markets falling apace, they were
more ready to sell oatmeal than others were to purchase; and therefore they sent it away *privately* to
places at a distance, where it sold highest. Had that
class of people manufactured from time to time meal
to accommodate their poor neighbours in small quantities, they would have lost nothing, and done much
good. Indeed, their greed and selfishness exceeded
all bounds. On the other hand, on the approach of
harvest, the common people became somewhat saucy,
and would hardly buy what had been provided for
them; but that was more than made up by their
quiet and orderly deportment.

Before the conclusion of the American war, wheat
and artificial grasses were as common in the carses
above and below Stirling as beans and barley, which
had been little cultivated till the beginning of the
eighteenth century. At present our good farmer
summer-fallows for wheat, and has a field of hay, with
a spot of red clover for milch cows. Besides lessening
the spring labours, which is a great matter, these
crops prove both lucrative and beneficial to the ground.
They succeed not the worse for grafting the new husbandry upon the old; and hence in ploughing and
sowing the several crops, our present tenants pay as

much attention to *tids*—*i.e.*, seasons, as their fathers. In truth, common-sense and long experience, connected with knowledge of soil and climate, have taught them excellent lessons which could not be learned from books, or from persons accustomed to countries very differently circumstanced. The contempt which our first gentlemen farmers expressed for the modes and sentiments of their country neighbours, which were sometimes sounder and better digested than their own, was one of the most common causes of the failure of some of their favourite schemes. By being either too early or too late in their operations, they at times had indifferent crops in fields which had been well manured and neatly dressed.

It is to be regretted that for the last twenty years turnip-husbandry has made little progress among the tenants of this neighbourhood, where soil is well adapted to it. At one time there was a prospect of its being as common as clover and potatoes. At present they are confined either to gentlemen's farms, or to fields substantially enclosed. If the culture of that excellent root were steadily persevered in, it would ere long make a great change to the better on the face of the country. It is surely the most effectual way of eradicating the rooted weeds that rob the ground and choke the crop. Either stall-feeding of oxen, or fattening sheep on the field by means of flakes, would make a great addition to the manure. If it requires high culture and a considerable quantity of lime and dung to ensure success, and the thinning and hoeing of the plants be tedious and expensive, it commonly proves a very lucrative crop and an excellent preparation for barley and grass seeds. As soon as our better kind of tenants are convinced that a crop is lucrative, and within their reach, they neither grudge labour nor cost. Nothing but want of proper fences prevented the people who first attempted this branch of husbandry from persisting in it. But it is next to impossible to preserve turnips from cows, either in open ground or on fields that are but half-fenced. Indeed, when tenants' cattle once get a taste for them, they loathe their other food.

Experience has at last convinced ordinary tenants of the benefit to be derived from winter herding. By means of it and unwearied attention, such as had no enclosures saved their turnips from cattle, notwithstanding their fondness for them. This was more than they who had only *half* fences could pretend to, and it extended to wheat and artificial grasses, two capital articles at present. Twenty or thirty years ago one who should have proposed it would have been laughed at; but if persevered in, and reduced to a system, it may do great things, and in moderately sized farms either save the expense of enclosing, or at least allow hedges to be raised without paling, which is hardly to be had. Much, however, will depend on circumstances, and sloth is of a contagious nature.

CHAPTER XI.

SOME SCOTTISH WORTHIES.

It will not be unacceptable to give an account of some gentlemen who, though born and educated in Scotland, seldom resided in this part of the country, even when they had estates. It will serve as a corollary to a former chapter, in which the gentry of the district were considered in connection with their country seats. Of some of the persons of whom I am now to speak, it is too late to look out for better materials than the memory of their neighbours and contemporaries who lived to talk of them. Suffice it to say, that in my youth and prime I have heard as much of their story as would have furnished ample materials for biographical sketches of the worthies that have been longest dead. All that I can give is a set of gleanings picked up in conversation from persons who had the best access to information, and never thought themselves better employed than in retailing anecdotes of persons who had made a figure in society in their time, though much older than themselves. I cannot recall the persons who could have given me fuller intelligence, but shall set down such anecdotes as I remember to have heard of the persons about to be commemorated, some of whom are on the very brink of oblivion.

James Spittal of Leuchat was the eldest of them. He was born in the year 1663 or 1664, though by the parish register he appeared to be two or three years younger. It was vitiated to save him from being fined for attending a conventicle. He married early,[1] but his wife died in a short time, leaving one son. The widower fell deeply in love with her sister, but no Protestant Church would allow them to marry. It was therefore concerted that Leuchat should go to Rome, and obtain a dispensation to marry his mistress.

In passing the Alps, he heard a woman in a tartan plaid singing " The Broom o' the Cowdenknowes." On inquiring what was her errand to Italy, she said her husband was a trooper in the Pope's guards. Soon after this gentleman's arrival at Rome, his sister-in-law fell into a consumption and died, which was very afflictive to him. It was a wild plan to think of changing his religion, and quitting his native country, in order to possess his mistress ; but in every age and country love plays strange pranks with its votaries—and the more sensible they are, the more absurd and headstrong is their conduct.

In order to get the better of his grief, and the

---

[1] His wife was the daughter of Sir James Holbourne of Menstrie. If I mistake not there were two knights of that name, father and son.

blasting of his fondest hopes, Leuchat spent a number of years in travelling through Italy, France, and Germany. Being a scholar and an accomplished man, he kept the best company wherever he went, to whom he was very acceptable, on account of the sweetness and simplicity of his manners, and the courtesy of his disposition.

At length, being tired of roaming abroad, and much importuned by his friends, he returned to his own country, where he met with a very gracious reception, being regarded as a man of fashion, who had studied books and men to excellent purpose. He was elected member for the burgh of Inverkeithing, which lay hard by his house of Leuchat in 1696 ;[1] and used to give precious anecdotes of the people who made a figure in the tempestuous debates which took place while the Union was under agitation. He was all along a Whig and Presbyterian, though he once meant to have solicited favours from the Roman Pontiff.[2] From that period he lived

[1] Besides Leuchat, hard by Donnybristle, he had the estate of Blair Logie, which had been long in his family. He told somebody, who asked him why he did not sometimes live at Blair, that he cared not *to shavel his shoon—i.e.,* to set his shoes awry on the declivity. While at Rome he chanced to be in company with persons of different nations, when the conversation turned upon striking prospects from mountains or hills. Each of them spoke of those of his own country. At last an old Scottish priest said the most picturesque, if not the most extensive, prospect he knew was from Topmiat [now spelt Dumyat], a hill within three miles of Stirling. After hearing his description, the company assented to his opinion. Though Leuchat was proprietor of it, he had never been there before his travels. He wisely kept his own secret, but one of the first things he did on his return home was to go to the top of Topmiat.

[2] A spendthrift relation of his, for whom he had procured a tide-waiter's

mostly at Leuchat, though he frequently made excursions to Edinburgh, where he was highly esteemed
both in the fashionable and literary circles. If he
took little share in the public business, or in politics,
he outlived the whole members of the Union Parliament.

Perceiving his son more fond than he wished of a
female cousin, he bought a cornetcy of dragoons for
him, thinking that the best way to break off the connection, which he imputed to idleness, ignorance, and
rawness. But a private marriage having taken place,
the young woman claimed her husband, and declared
herself pregnant. "Madam," said Leuchat, "what
shall I make of the cornetcy which I have bought?"
"Take it yourself, for you are much fitter for the
army than him." The son died a young man, after
his wife had brought him several children. The
father and daughter-in-law lived together very cor-
dially and comfortably for near fifty years, she being
at great pains to make him happy, by accommodating
herself to his ways. He was all along a very popular
character in town and country, there being something
fascinating in his conversation, which was unaffec-
ted and simple, full of nice matter. He often dined
at the Earl of Moray's house, which was within a

place, refused it with great indignation, saying. "What, sir! would you that
know the world have a *gentleman* give up his *liberty* for such a paltry place?"
Meeting Leuchat afterwards at Queensferry, when he pled poverty, he
extracted a *dollar* from him by his importunity. Coming up to that gentle
man's boatmen, he told them that they should not stir till they had got a
share of his cousin's dollar, which he meant to drink. The latter, who was im
patient to get over to Parliament, was obliged to wait till his charity was spent

bowshot of his own, and remarkable for mirth and primeval hospitality. He made it a rule to go home to his own bed, but as soon as he came in he cried, " Margaret, get the kettle." He had for many years a small sneaker of brandy-punch before retiring to his bedroom. He used to be much with Mr and Mrs Abercromby, first at Menstry, and afterwards at Tullibody, where he could commit himself safely, and find discourse to his taste.[1] It was the greater compliment, that in his latter years he was not fond of ladies and company, unless he was well acquainted with them. Though no man understood the art of conversation better, he seldom shone in mixed companies, and when *leading* questions were put he commonly said nothing; but in small or select parties nothing could be more delightful than his social hour.[2] In 1756 or 1757 I spent a very pleasing day with him at Tullibody, where he always found himself at home. He was the more kind to me that my mother had been one of his favourites. At the company's breaking up after supper, he took me to his bedroom, where he sat till three in the morning, talking over his travels, and of people who had made a great figure at home and abroad. I admired the shrewdness and *naïveté* of the remarks of a man past ninety, whose faculties were entire. In the

---

[1] He said one day to his friend, " George, the best of an old man's pleasures is the crack."

[2] Lord Edmonstoune, a very competent judge, used to say that, were he a very great or opulent man, he would give Leuchat a handsome pension to live with him, his company being great luxury.

morning he said to me, "O man, is it not hard for
one that has not a tooth in his head to be plagued
with the toothache?"   We afterwards met at Inverkeithing, but as the company was very miscellaneous,
he hardly opened his lips. He was a man of middling
size, of a spare habit, and thin face. I considered
him an excellent sample of the Scottish gentry at the
Union, who were much better acquainted with the
modes and manners of foreign nations, than with
those of England, for which in his youth and prime
his countrymen had no partiality.[1] I was assured
by a friend, who visited him a year or so before his
death, that he found him walking about his farm as
straight as a stick, giving directions to his servants.
Somebody observed that his daughter-in-law constantly wrought stockings to amuse her. "Why,"
said he, "it is a disease which has seized the poor
woman; and it is at least harmless, for she gives
them away to her friends."   Upon a person's asking
him about that time how he did, "I am almost
ashamed," answered the good man, "to say how well
I am."   He was at last gathered like a stalk of ripe
corn in its season. His last illness was short and
gentle. Had I turned my thoughts to that subject
somewhat earlier, ample materials might have been
had for a life of the amiable man.

[1] He spoke the most elegant Scots I ever heard, probably the language
spoken at the Union Parliament, which was composed of people of high
fashion. He said he never admired the English language so much as when
he heard it spoken by Rachel Pauncefort, Countess-Dowager of Kincardine,
a woman of family married in 1699.

Mungo Græme of Gorthie was the grandson of the Bishop of Orkney, who, being very rich, found it expedient to make his peace with the Covenanters by renouncing his function. I know not when he was born, but should imagine he was somewhat younger than Leuchat. Be that as it may, they met on their travels. The first Duke of Montrose brought him afterwards into Parliament.

To the first part of his life I am a stranger, and know not where to seek information. His chief, the Duke, being one of the heads of the Squadrone, obtained for him the office of Receiver-General of the Customs, which he retained long after his patron ceased to be in power. While in Parliament he lived in the Duke of Montrose's house at London, being the person on whom his Grace relied in matters of business. From what I had occasion to hear from people who were intimately acquainted with him, he was a man highly esteemed for his worth, knowledge, and strength of intellect. And his good qualities were not diminished by his having lived in first-rate company at home and abroad, and being well read in books. His chief infirmity was a sort of mental absence,[1] which made him sometimes forget time and place, and led him to be sparing of his words.[2]

[1] Being much tormented with the toothache, he went for a surgeon to pull one of his three remaining teeth. He pointed to the tooth affected, being a man of few words. On its being extracted he said very calmly, "Man, you are wrong," directing him to another. After it was taken out, he said, "You are wrong again, and now you cannot go wrong." It was a great proof of absence and self-command.

[2] Once when the first Duke arrived at Edinburgh from London, he asked

That, however, was constitutional, and to be found in persons of very good parts; and early habits are seldom lessened by time : suffice it to say, it lost him no favour with his patron and friends.

For a number of years he forbore visiting England, where the first and second Dukes spent commonly two-thirds of the year. Whether he ever kept house at Gorthie I do not know, but for a number of years he took up his residence at Buchanan [1] summer and winter, being the Duke's commissioner and confidential man, to whom the chamberlains made their audits and received their instructions. Whether he was an able prime minister I know not, but he was surely a sorry architect; for in building a new house

Gorthie to give him a list of the persons whom it was incumbent for him to visit, but at the head of the list were persons that had been dead for years. His Grace having one day asked an English member of Parliament to dinner, said that if he should be detained in the House of Parliament his cousin Gorthie would receive him. On being shown into the library where the gentleman was, he took no notice of the stranger, sitting with a leg on each side of the chimney. To try how far his absence would go, the new-comer sat down close by him and placed his own legs close by the other's without its being noticed. And in that posture did the Duke find them when he came into the room, and awakened his friend from his reverie.

[1] Lord Kames told me that when at the bar he chanced to be benighted near that place : on sending a servant with a message to Gorthie requesting a night's lodging, he received a kind invitation. On his arrival he was taken into Gorthie's bed chamber, where he usually sat, arrayed in his nightgown and slippers. He received Mr Home with great courtesy, and placed him as a stranger in the arm-chair. Kames said nothing could exceed the urbanity of his host, while his conversation became interesting and animated, turning upon topics which his guest wished to know. In this way did matters go on till the eve of supper, when Mr Duncan Macfarlane, the minister whom Gorthie did not love, opened the door. Thus, in a moment, dispelled the spell, and made Gorthie taciturn for the remainder of the night. Much did Kames regret the minister's intrusion. Gorthie's manner savoured, he said, of the old Court, of which he was a valuable specimen.

there he *forgot* the stair. Nevertheless, his maxims and manners of proceeding with tenants differed widely from those that are now in vogue. They probably differed little from those of the preceding age, when, if the *tenure of kindness* was not recognised by men of law or courts of justice, strong traces of it were to be found among landlords, and nowhere more than among great families. In his time the Montrose estate, both Highland and Lowland, was held, at what was then accounted moderate rents, by persons exceedingly attached to the family, who could boast of having stood by it in trying perturbed times. And a number of them had gentle blood in their veins, though little beholden to the goods of fortune ; the Duke, therefore, and his minister, used them with benignity and liberality befitting the feudal times. Their conduct savoured of the spirit of chivalry, even at a time when the feudal system and its appendages were exploded and ridiculed. It was the more meritorious, that in those times military service was not desired or expected from those favoured, I had almost said happy, tenants, who were at their ease, and gratified in their humble wishes.

It is foreign to my subject to institute a comparison between the landlords of the last age and their sons and grandsons. It is sufficient to say that during his administration the family of Montrose was prosperous, none living more like a great man than the last Duke, while he paid unwearied attention to economy. I have heard that in Gorthie's time the

Montrose rents were sometimes very ill paid.   Lenity
and forbearance may be carried too far.   That evil,
however, was completely corrected by his successor,
Mr Græme of Orchil, a dull plodding man, who went
on like clockwork.   Be that as it may, this gentleman
was well entitled to plead the merit of the best intentions.   I have been told by people who used to be
much with the Duke at Buchanan, that Gorthie was
all along in high favour with his Grace, and regarded
as an accession by the guests.   If he did not take as
great a share in the conversation as they would have
wished, what he had said was shrewd and sensible,[1]
and he had a vein of humour and irony peculiar to
himself.   It may, however, be taken for granted that
his fits of absence and spleen did not diminish with
old age ; but when he chose to commit himself his
company was highly pleasing.[2]   He died between
1752 and 1754, when, having been a bachelor, he was
succeeded by his cousin General Græme.

Mr Andrew Drummond, afterwards an eminent

[1] A hot dispute having taken place at the Duke's table about the number
of men in the Duke of Cumberland's army at the battle of Fontenoy, it was
referred to Gorthie. On the questions being stated once and again, he an
swered laconically, " More than he made a good use of ; " a decision which dis
pleased neither party.

[2] The late General Græme gave an account of a very pleasing meeting
which took place between Gorthie and Leuchat some years before the
former's death. He being obliged to go to Edinburgh on important business,
a party of his old friends met him at the tavern, where they had a good sup
per and genuine old claret. Leuchat, who was one of them, reminded Gorthie
of his having *walked into a canal* in Holland. " It may be so," said the other .
" but do you remember, Leuchat, that you bought a *fool* to carry you to
Italy ! " Nothing, the General said, could be more delightful than the con
versation of the two old men, who seldom had occasion to meet.

banker, is well entitled to commemoration, as being
a native of Strathearn, and the purchaser of his
brother's estate.   He was the second son of Lord
Strathallan, whose property was very moderate, being
confined to the estate of Machany.   That, however,
did not hinder him from making a very respectable
figure.   This gentleman was born between 1680 and
and 1685, and bred frugally and hardily, as was the
custom of those sober-minded times.   He told me, in
1758, that he had been 'prentice to what was called
a goldsmith, in the Parliament Close at Edinburgh.
"When," said the good man, "my time was out, I
was sent to London, mounted on a horse of my father's,
with a moderate sum in my pocket.   After selling
him, and paying the expense of the journey, I had
only ten guineas remaining, with which I was thrown
upon the wide world.   For some years I wrought
hard as a silversmith, and saved a little money; but
on Sunday I put on a good coat and sword, and kept
company that drank claret."   In this there was true
spirit and wise policy, as it enabled him to make
friends that might be useful to him when in a situation so ill befitting his noble birth.   I cannot give
any account of his progress for a number of years
after he came to London;   but he married when a
young man a Miss Strahan, a Scottish lady, whose
family was settled at London in trade.   To them
Mr Drummond was indebted for his first introduction
into business, though I cannot enter into particulars.
But he was under very high obligations to Mr John

Drummond, member of Parliament, who, on his
becoming banker, got Sir Robert Walpole to keep
money at his shop, which was a great matter to a
young beginner.

It may well be thought that his progress was slow,
for in these days speculation was in little repute. In
truth, his prosperity and future eminence were owing
more to his probity and firmness than to his parts
and knowledge, which were very moderate. He was
for a while in partnership with a Mr Walkinshaw,
but it did not last long. In 1745, owing to a run on
him by the bank, he was obliged to stop payment,
being suspected of sending money to the rebels, whom
his brother, Lord Strathallan, had joined. For this
charge there appeared to be no foundation on exam-
ining his books; and therefore, after paying principal and interest, in a few months he opened shop
again with great *éclat*. From that time he flourished
apace. In the first stages of his business he had been
rather lavish in his credit to his countrymen, some of
whom were in Parliament. If eventually he lost little,
the money was not recovered without much litigation
and delay.[1] This made him afterwards decline all
money transactions in Scotland. His son, a man of
parts and much address, married a niece of the Duke
of St Albans, which brought a great increase of
business to the house. Upon the sale of his brother's
estate, which had been forfeited, Mr Drummond be-

[1] This I was told in 1758, both by father and son, who felt sore at the way
they had been treated by some of their Scottish debtors.

came the purchaser at a moderate price. It gave
great satisfaction, as the family had been highly
respected.[1]   After a long absence from his native
country, he came and took possession of the purchase;
but his stay was short, for notwithstanding his fondness for the haunts of his youth, his business lay at
London; and when tired with it, he retired to his
villa at Stanmore, which had great amenity, besides
being within eight or ten miles of London.

Upon a trip to that place in spring 1758, my
excellent friend, Mr Drummond of Blair, recommended me to the father and son, who never forgot
their obligations to his uncle John.   And I was not
the worse received that my father had been long Mr
Drummond's man of business in Scotland.   Much did
I hear and see of their benignity and good deeds.
The connection was not the less agreeable that Mr
George, who had been my preceptor in 1745, was
their cashier, and in much favour with them.   By
that time they had a great run of business, the army
agents keeping cash with them.

Mr Andrew Drummond being about to pay a visit
to his friends and estate in Scotland, I was asked to

---

[1] I may mention as a caveat to the harshness and insolence of men in office,
that Campbell of Barcaldine, the factor, a man of excellent parts, but great
pride, had treated both the family and tenants harshly, obliging the tenants to
perform carriages to him from a great distance. A person connected with Mr
Drummond meeting a string of them with back-loads of coals, asked what they
were about. " Performing," they said, " heavy bondage to the factor." " That
must be from liking, for you have a new laird."   On hearing the joyful news,
they tumbled down the coals on the road, and galloped home to drink Mr
Andrew Drummond's health.

accompany him on the journey. The day before our
setting out, his son carried me in his curricle to
Stanmore, pointing out to me by the way Cannons,
the first Duke of Chandos's seat, then the property
of a citizen. There I saw the good old man to great
advantage, happy in his family and connections,
living in a great style, which he could well afford.
He was very vain of his place, which he had got
Capability Brown to dress up. It was not only
picturesque, but healthy, being hard by an extensive
common on an eminence. The good air and dryness
had, he told me, wrought cures on some of his city
friends, whom he invited thither to recruit. Before
dinner he proposed to show me *his* piece of water.
"What, sir! will you show a Scotsman water?"
And indeed neither the quality nor colour of the
water recommended it to me, being thick and yellow.
In the evening his son took me aside, and said,
"Though my father be an old man, he is a very
young, inexperienced traveller, having been little out
of London for many years ; and when he makes an
excursion, it is in the old slow style, taking regular
meals, and drinking liberally. I will tell you how
he will proceed. On coming into an inn where he
means to stop, he will bespeak a great dinner, and
sit so long after it as to leave little time to get on.
Will you try to get him to go 100 miles a-day?"
I should, I said, try, though it did not become me to
direct him, and my own experience was not great.[1]

---

[1] It was pleasing to see the good man take leave of his old domestics, who

It turned out as he said. On coming to St Albans, he bespoke a plentiful dinner, and drank two or three bottles of claret after it, being in high glee. On proposing to set out, he said, "Time enough, time enough." In fact we made only two stages after it. And he went on in the same way during the journey, seldom setting out earlier than nine o'clock, and making hearty meals. When I proposed to see any place, he cheerfully assented. I never saw a more pleasant companion; and he had none of the peevishness of old age. " In passing an insufficient bridge in Yorkshire on his way up to London, he perceived a fellow coming up to jostle him on the bridge. Being in those days, said he, a strong young fellow, and withal a good horseman, he put spurs to his horse, and met the man in full career, and fairly *canted* him over the bridge. None of them made any inquiries after the other, but the fellow got what he deserved." [1]

seemed to behold him with reverence. I considered him as a sort of city Sir Roger de Coverley.

[1] He paid a visit of two days to Mr Allanson of Bramsham-Bigging, not far from Witherby, a man of fortune, and a particular friend of Mr Drummond. After seeing some places in the neighbourhood, we dined there with Dr Drake, author of the ' History of the City of York,' and conductor of the ' Parliamentary History,' both voluminous works. He told us that when young he was member of a club at which treasonable healths were sometimes drank. This made them cautious about admitting visitors. One day a leading man introduced a stranger, whom he was at pains to accommodate. The preses then asked if he could answer for his friend. " Yes, sir, I can ; for this gentleman has stood twice on the *pillory*." On which the preses, filling a bumper, said, " Worthy sir, let me drink your health." This made Mr Drummond tell what passed at a mercantile club in the city, of which he and Mr Oliphant the hatter were members. One night the conversation turning on the extravagance of young merchants in the article of horses,

Going along at another time, he said to me with honest pride, "I have done great things, and have almost everything I could desire. My son is married into a noble family, and I have planted a colony of Drummonds round Charing Cross which appears to thrive." We had excellent horses, because my travelling companion gave the ostler and postilion double of what they got from other people. This made them tip the wink to their brethren. Vanity and haste were out of the question; but it was of a piece with his general conduct, which was generous and openhanded. He was accompanied by two servants on horseback. One of them, his body-servant, having no opinion of Scotland, in packing up the luggage put up a vial of ink, which broke loose and stained his master's linen, of which the poor man was much ashamed. We went to Dr Douglas of Cavers' parsonage-house, within ten miles of Durham, where he was one of the prebendaries. I accompanied them and Blair as far as Morpeth, from which they went to Kames, and I took the Berwick road. He took up his abode at Machany for some weeks, and enter-

some of them having two or three horses, Mr Oliphant said he thought nothing of that, for when he was young he sometimes kept five or six horses. The Londoners stared, thinking he had been wild and extravagant in his youth. In walking home, Mr Drummond said, "Fie, Oliphant! I always took you for an honest man, but am now ashamed of you. Where did you ever keep these same five or six horses?" "On the side of Corstorphine Hill, Andrew." When a boy he had been a herd there. His rise was not more wonderful or improbable than Mr Drummond's. Dr Drake, who was a lively, well informed old man, was very much diverted with that anecdote. He had, he told me, once been a high Tory, but was now looking forward to a change of men and measures like his brethren

tained his friends and neighbours handsomely and with great cordiality, though a stranger to the persons and manners of his neighbours. Indeed his ideas were all English, and he knew next to nothing of Scotland, having left it when a lad.

In the year 1764, when his friend Blair stood candidate for Perthshire, Mr Andrew Drummond supported him with great warmth. A noted minor politician of those times having proposed to *lye off* with him (a thing very desirable at his advanced time of life, and great size), he gave the gentleman to understand, that if he did not come precisely at a certain hour, he should set off by himself. And he was as good as his word, though the politician was only two hours behind the time.

An unlucky jolt having loosed his two remaining teeth, he made his man pull them out with a piece of pack-thread. He stood the journey well, and was not the worse of the bustle of an election. Soon after I paid him a visit at Machany, where he was his niece, Lady Strathallan's, guest. He was in great health and spirits, very fond of the place, saying with an emphasis, "Ay, it has capability." I saw him afterwards at Blairdrummond, and at this place [Ochtertyre]. From that time he was never in Scotland. He died in the summer of 1765 or 1766, full of years, and universally respected, more for the quality of his heart than his talents. Suffice it to say, that if he had only *one* he turned it to the best account. His son survived him but a few years. A blessing seems to have followed the colony of Drummonds planted by him at Charing Cross. It may with truth be said of him and of them, "*Sui memores alios fecere merendo.*"

James Stirling, manager of the Leadhills Mining Company, well deserves a place among the worthies of the last age. He was a strong, marked, and meritorious character in his day, and was the artificer of his own fortune.[1] He was the second son of Stirling of Carden, grandson of Lord Carden, who, in 1666, succeeded to the estate of Keir upon the death of Sir George Stirling. Being a handsome spirited boy, he was a great favourite of his mother, a strange woman, who too much undervalued her eldest son, a worthy virtuous man, saying in her coarse way that she had rather borne a *whinstone* than him.[2] James, the second son, was born in the year 1696. It matters little where he learned grammar, which was

---

[1] Carden informs me that, some years ago, he furnished Dr Hutton of Woolwich with materials for a life of this gentleman, he being employed in giving an account of the persons that had made a figure in the higher branches of the mathematics. Here he will be considered as a man of business, and a member of society.

[2] She exceeded everything in those days for coarseness and indelicacy. On the day of the battle of Sheriffmuir she was at Keir, within a mile or two of the field of action. An indiscreet person came suddenly into the room where the ladies were, and told them that both Keir and Carden were killed. The wife of the former, an amiable woman, and fond of her husband, shed a flood of tears on hearing these tidings. In a while Lady Carden exclaimed, "Madam, let us be thankful!" "For what?" said the other. "Because there is a hell for the Whigs." Once that a gentleman proposed to make her a visit, a person in company that was not well with her said he would go along. On their arrival the lady gave the one a kind reception, but took no notice of the other. On the latter's asking her, with great humility, how she did, she bade him go be d——d.

excellently taught at that period all over Scotland; but he was bred at the University of Glasgow, which gave him one of Snell's Exhibitions at Balliol College,[1] that was in their gift. Thither he went in 1712 or 1713, and remained there for six years, intent upon his studies. It was perhaps little against him that at that period these exhibitions were of much less value than they are now. Besides making a great proficiency in classical learning, he was esteemed a first-rate mathematician. He made friendships with learned and ingenious members of the University, and was introduced to the excellent Dr Arbuthnot, who was a man of science, as well as *belles-lettres* man.

In 1720 he accompanied the Venetian ambassador when he returned home, being promised the chair of Professor of Mathematics in one of the republic's universities. In that country he resided for five or six years. Though I cannot enter into particulars, he was by no means idle. Carden assures me that he was highly respected by the Italian *literati*, as appears by letters to him from them; and while in the Venetian territories he published a number of scientific tracts, copies of which he brought home; but the dampness of the house at Leadhills had spoilt both them and the letters, and he kept up a correspondence with the most eminent mathematical men both in Scotland and England, who rated him very high.

---

[1] Mr Stirling used to give a curious account of the modes and economics of Balliol at that time. Their trenchers were timber, and the knives and forks chained to the table. In July 1791, the rooms assigned to the Glasgow exhibitioners were mean and incommodious.

He was requested by some mercantile men to get full information with regard to the process of making mirror-glass, which was little understood at that time in England ; and it is allowed that he got them all the information they wanted.   To a man of Mr Stirling's turn of mind and course of studies, his long residence in Italy and intercourse with learned and accomplished men, must have been no less gratifying than useful, it being classical ground, of which he had read and heard so much.   It was likewise in his favour that he was in these days a handsome man of great address and conciliating manners, having studied books and men to great purpose.   From his long abode at Venice he was afterwards commonly called the *Venetian*.

Upon returning to England he was well received by his old friends.   I have heard that for some time he was employed in teaching mathematics at Wall's Academy, which was then in high repute, and numerously attended ; but when the opposition to Sir Robert Walpole ran exceedingly high, Lord Bolingbroke desired Dr Arbuthnot to find a person deeply learned in algebra and fluxions who could appreciate Walpole's financial calculations, which were regarded as profound and masterly.[1]   The Doctor recommended this gentleman as likely to spy flaws in them.   What he did in that way is not now known ; but opposition trusted more to wit and oratory, seconded by clamour.

[1] Of this I was assured by Mr Dundas of Man r, the intimate friend of this gentleman

than to arguments drawn from the sublime parts
of science. Mr Stirling lived for some time on a
familiar confidential footing with that noble lord
and his associates, whose parts were brilliant. At
their tables he saw the first-rate geniuses in the
kingdom. He used to say that his friend Arbuthnot and Dr Berkeley, Bishop of Cloyne, were the
most amiable and interesting of the whole group.
Of some of them that had a great name as authors
or orators he spoke with little reverence, they being
deficient in heart or in temper. Of these, when well
set, he used to retail interesting anecdotes. Meanwhile the people with whom he associated at that
period had little in their power, the loaves and fishes
being distributed by the Prime Minister and his colleagues. It therefore behoved Mr Stirling to look
out for an establishment which should render him easy
and independent. It was well for him that he had
formed friendships with some eminent merchants who
had heard of the useful information he had procured
from Venice, and had a high opinion of his abilities.
By this means he was appointed, in 1734, agent or
manager for the Scottish Mining Company, in room
of Sir John Erskine of Alva,[1] who found it necessary

[1] Though he was a man of genius and fascinating manners, nature never
intended Sir John to make a figure in business; for he had more wit than
wisdom, and more fancy than judgment or discretion. After the ruin of his
own affairs he betook himself to mining as a profession, he being thought very
learned in that matter. His operations were carried on for a while both
in the Isle of Man and at Leadhills, but they neither profited him nor his
partners. He acted too much on impulse, and was fond of expensive experiments; and he was too lively to keep regular books, or to attend to little

to retire, as the Company's affairs were in great confusion. The partners of this Company were opulent, respectable Englishmen, engaged in some branch of trade. They soon discovered that their new manager was not only a man of science, but also had a great turn for business. For the first years after his appointment he was but a few weeks at a time at Leadhills, in order to put the miners into order; but in 1736 he took up his residence there, never leaving it, unless on business, or when visiting his friends. At his entering on his office everything was in wretched order, and a heavy debt contracted; and though much metal had been got, it had hitherto turned to little account. The miners and labourers were thoughtless and dissipated; and if their wages were high, they could hardly live upon them. People in that state are apt to be mutinous and unmanageable; ere long, however, the new manager showed what great things could be done by a single man of superior understanding, regulated by discretion. He gradually paid off the Company's debts, and established its credit far

matters which, when neglected, cut very deep. Such, however, was Sir John's eloquence and address, that he persuaded the Company to adopt his plans, when it was obvious that they were likely to be losers by them. At last he seemed sensible that it was an undertaking beyond his strength; but in his adversity he kept up his spirits, and the part of a gentleman. Passing once in his way from the Isle of Man through Whitehaven, he heard a knot of people on the street, on seeing him and a couple of footmen well mounted, exclaim, "A new man, egad!" Being directed to an inn, an attorney came to tell him that the election might be carried at no great expense, the town being much dissatisfied with the Lowther family. With his usual courtesy the Knight said he could not have the honour of representing the borough, he being pre-engaged. He died in the Isle of Man in 1736. He called his sons, who were officers in the army, "Hanoverian rascals."

and near, whilst he put the miners and other workmen employed in the Company's service under regulations that were equally beneficial to themselves and
to their masters. He established a set of rules and
regulations which he did not suffer to remain a dead
letter. Nothing, however, did more to promote his
schemes than the unwearied attention paid by him to
their health and morals. Comfortable houses and
gardens were provided for them. In the latter they
raised potatoes and pot-herbs, besides passing their
leisure hours, which from the nature of their work
are many, with pleasure and profit; and while spir-
ituous liquors were reprobated as little better than
poison to people that wrought below ground, they
were allowed to drink porter and strong ale, whilst
they ate more animal food than people of their station
used to do at that time. As idleness and the want
of some rational employment for the minds of people
at their ease are sources of folly and abuse, Mr Stirling suggested the expediency of a library, to which
they should annually contribute a mite. This would
procure them wholesome and palatable intellectual
food ; and he recommended proper books, which
might instruct and entertain. Under his auspices
they provided funds for the support of the poor or
aged, he drawing up laws for the procedure of the
society. Nowhere, from every account, did strict discipline and subordination appear less burdensome and
grievous than at Leadhills, where this gentleman presided with dignity and benignity. Whilst matters

went on like clockwork, without hurry or constraint, the Company flourished apace. In forming his plan of operations, Mr Stirling had good information with regard to the lead-mines of England and foreign countries, taking care to adopt such parts of their management as were suited to Scotland.

In the meantime the Company was abundantly mindful of its obligations to their manager. Besides a share of their stock, the partners gave him a good salary, to which additions were made from time to time. And they built a good house for his accommodation, to which was added a farm hard by, to make him easy and comfortable in that bleak remote corner. They sent him all along presents which were useful in housekeeping; and oftener than once stocked his cellars with liquors. And when he began to decline, they kept a carriage for him. It was therefore their wish to make him easy and independent. They knew that it was necessary for him to live at a considerable expense; for, besides a numerous and respectable set of friends, curiosity, and the desire of seeing a man and place of which they had heard so much, induced literary and scientific men to visit him; and there were no inns [1] in

[1] Sauntering one day in an old coat a mile or two from his house, he fell in with an Irish student of divinity returning from Glasgow, who inquired who kept the best house in that vile country? "Sir," answered the Venetian with much humility and gravity, "I am the man, and if you please I will show you the way." On arriving at Leadhills, the man, astonished at what he saw, asked his host what he could have for dinner? "You shall," said the other, "have a share of my own dinner - a fowl, a leg of mutton, and some other little things." "That," replied he, "is more than I should have bespoke." After dining

the neighbourhood where they could put up. It accorded with his generous nature, and in those days hospitality was accounted a virtue and a luxury. I never was at Leadhills in his time, but have been assured by very competent judges that nothing could be more joyous or edifying than this gentleman's social hour. Besides being deeply read in books and men, he was one of those who could simplify science, and make philosophy speak the language of common-sense. And having lived long in first-rate company at home and abroad, he had the air and conversation of a man of fashion, together with a vein of wit and humour which was very acceptable. Nay, he could be frolicsome and humorous without lowering his dignity or giving offence. Hence he sometimes brought things to pass in a way that would not have occurred to anybody else.[1] To say the matter strong,

---

heartily, he was asked what he chose to drink. Seeing him hesitate, "Come," said the other, "let us have a bottle of claret, and as it is the first time you ever were in my house, I will treat you." Poor Paddy was delighted with his reception, and satisfied that his host was not what he at first took him to be. At parting, the latter finding him short of money, gave him a guinea by way of *viaticum*. In this fun was happily grafted on benevolence.

[1] One of his partners, with whom he lived in habits of intimacy, had an only son of whom little could be made—having no turn for trade or the learned professions, and a dislike for the army. In those circumstances he resolved to send the young man, when turned of twenty, to Leadhills, where he could have the benefit of the Venetian's conversation and advice, there being no man of whose understanding and resources he had a higher opinion. After the youth had been for some months an inmate in the house, his host wrote the father that though his son was good-hearted and well-disposed, he wanted strength of mind and address to figure in active or fashionable life. It would therefore be expedient to marry him to a woman of family and superior understanding, who should be not only an amiable help-mate, but set off her husband to the best advantage. If that should meet his friend's ideas, he had a woman in view who was likely to make an excellent wife, and was well connected, but

in a country to which neither nature nor art had been nowise bountiful, did Mr Stirling live for more than thirty years, highly esteemed and revered for the qualities of his head and heart. He was only once married, to a Miss Watson of Stirling, whose family had once a great sway in that country. I never saw her, but she died in the course of a few years, leaving an only daughter. It was necessary, in the way of business or amusement, to make frequent excursions to England or to different parts of Scotland to see his

slenderly provided. But as the young man was somewhat capricious, he must be allowed to do it in his own way. This proposition met with the old man's hearty approbation, and full powers were given to bring matters to a happy issue, want of portion being no objection. The Venetian (as he was called) contrived to give his guest a Pisgah view of his intended bride, who, if no beauty, was sensible and agreeable. For some weeks they did not meet. Meanwhile the lady was directed to assume the garb and appearance of an old gipsy, disguising her face and person so completely that her most intimate friends could not recognise her. She was introduced as a celebrated fortune-teller, whose predictions were often accomplished. Though dumb, she heard what was said to her, and gave her response in writing. The young man, though disgusted with her appearance, was persuaded to show her his hand. In her answer she told him particulars which he did not think she could know by natural means. She assured him, in enigmatical terms, that he would soon be married to a woman who would not only make him happy, but be acceptable to his father. Several interviews took place, in one of which she contrived to draw his own picture in flattering terms, declaring also some of his little secrets. At last she gave him the initial letter of his future spouse's name and abode, telling him that all depended on I. S. On asking her if she meant the Venetian, she said she did. Upon this the simple swain repaired to his host and laid the whole business before him. The latter said, "Miss W. of —— must be the person meant, and happy will be the man that gets her; for I know her to be worthy and amiable." "Then sir," said the other, "if that be your opinion, *I believe I must have her.*" The marriage took place soon after, and, however oddly brought about, proved very auspicious to her husband. The father was much pleased, and made ample provision for the young couple; and at his death they got a large fortune. I had this story from Miss Maddie Stirling, Keir, who lived then at Leadhills, and was privy to the plot, which was surely a laudable though somewhat —— ue.

many friends, among whom he could reckon persons
of first-rate parts or the highest rank, who loved his
company.   And of his relations in the country he
was equally fond and proud.   I had the good fortune
to meet him repeatedly at Keir, Cardross, or Touch,
as well as at Mr David Erskine's house.   I never
saw a man whom I liked more, or from whom more
was to be learned.   If sometimes a little sarcastic or
hasty in his repartees, it was only a temporary
ebullition, for he was well - bred and courteous.[1]
Nothing excited his spleen so much as sciolists in
science or literature.   For some years he declined
apace, but in December 1770 he died at Edinburgh,
whither he had gone to get medical advice.   It is
proper to observe that he had acquired, in the course
of his long and active life, what he regarded as a
handsome competence ; and it was not likely to wear
the worse for being honourably acquired.   Had the
love of money been his ruling passion, his sagacity
and steadiness would have stood him in great stead.

This gentleman may be regarded as an excellent
specimen of the Scotsmen of the last age, who began
their course without patrons and without money ; yet
being well taught, and obliged to avail themselves of
time and chance, their spirit of industry and address

[1] One day at Keir, G. E., a sort of rural Yorick, was so unadvised as to joke
the Venetian, who retorted, saying, "I spied yesterday among your father's
corn something like a scarecrow, a needless precaution where the crop was
bad ; but I begin to suspect it was you."   None laughed more at this sally
than poor Yorick.   At another time he abruptly asked a tedious story-teller
"If he ever kissed a bonny lass nowadays?"   "Sometimes! Mr Stirling,"
and then returned to his stories.

enabled them to surmount every difficulty, raising
them to eminence, and commanding the esteem of all
that knew them.   Nor was it aught against them in
their laudable struggle that they had gentle blood in
their veins, since that led them to act in a way that
should do honour to their birth.   The old French
used to say " *Gentilhomme, toujours gentilhomme.*"

Mr Stirling of Carden succeeded his uncle as manager for the Scottish Mining Company.   It was much
in his favour that he had been bred up under the
Venetian's auspices from a boy.[1]   He married that
gentleman's only daughter.   Of a man who is still
alive it would be improper to say much ; but it is
well known that he managed that Company's business for more than thirty years with equal ability
and success.

In the latter end of May 1790, Dr Stuart of Luss
and I, on our way to England, paid a visit to Carden,
being desirous to see a scene so much out of the
common road.   Everything I saw brought the Venetian to remembrance, who first brought the mines to a
complete state.   Of him, therefore, it may be said, as
of Sir Christopher Wren, " *Si monumentum quæris,
circumspice.*"   It will be a proper supplement to the

---

[1] The Company had for a number of years a lease of the Tyndrum mines
from the Earl of Breadalbane, in which a number of hands were employed,
but it not being a lucrative adventure, was at last given up. When Carden
was treating with Lord Glenorchy about a new bargain, his lordship insisted
that his lady should have, as usual a gown from the lease. "Look at her,
Mr Stirling ; does not she richly deserve a gown ?" "My lord," answered
the other, "for my own part, I should like her the better without a gown."
Carden managed them for a while.

foregoing sketch to set down a plain account of what I saw and what I felt on that occasion.

Although Leadhills has been a source of much wealth, and a motive for great exertions, the mines are situated in a bleak, barren spot. The manager's house and the village hard by are supposed to be the highest inhabited places in Great Britain,[1] being about 670 yards above the level of the sea, nearly of the same altitude as Topmiat [Dumyat] near Stirling, where none would attempt to set down a house. The hills around have not the grandeur or variety of the Highland ones. The soil, as far as the eye goes, consists of barren hill, rock, or short heath. No wonder, then, that vegetables should be raised with difficulty and be stunted in size. The few trees about the place were three weeks later of leafing than those about Glasgow and Hamilton, from whence we had come. Observing a clump of stunted firs set down to shelter the house from south-west winds, I was told that they had been planted by the Venetian about the year 1740; but so tremendous were the blasts of wind, that each tree was secured by three *hair tethers*, to keep it from being blown out at the root; and one would not have thought them more than twenty years old. Indeed, so tremendous are the winter blasts, that no *harling* with lime and sand can prevent the rain from beating through the walls; and therefore the outside of the windows was secured by thin plates of lead, which it is said answer better

[1] Tyndrum is of the same height.

than hewn stone or ashler-work.   Nor is the water
in the earth free from great drawbacks.   Above the
smelting - mills the water of the brook is excellent,
but is there impregnated with arsenic, zinc, and
sulphur, which render it poisonous to such as rashly
drink it.   From the particles of arsenic, &c., on the
surface of the ground, domestic fowls, cats, and dogs
do not thrive or live long at that place, and cows and
sheep seldom fatten on the pastures around the mines.
And till they were put under strict regimen, the
miners were subject to what is called the *lead-brash*:
and frenzy or idiotcy were not uncommon among
them, which were ascribed to the noxious effluvia of
the mines, seconded by improper food or liquors.   In
short, one would think that nothing but the prospect
of sharing in the hidden treasures which the hills contain could induce any person at his ease to take up
his residence at that place, seeing it has a number of
drawbacks and no amenity or fulness, the greatest
part of necessaries being brought from a distance at
a great expense.

But on going into the house every prejudice to the
place vanished, from the kind reception we met with.
Our host's conversation was truly interesting.   Well
acquainted with literary, scientific, and commercial
subjects, he contrived on all occasions to introduce
fragments of them which everybody liked to hear,
without a spice of pedantry or affectation; for none
dealt less in technical terms.   In a word, if he had
not his uncle's figure, address, or vivacity, he resembled

him in essentials; nor did the simplicity of his manners and discourse diminish them. The first thing he showed us was a small phial of a deep blue-coloured liquor, which contained a poison so strong that a few drops of it would poison the strongest animal. I exhorted him to break the glass. We next took a look of a MS. book, pointing out the progress of the Leadhills mines after they came into the possession of the Hopes, by marrying the heiress of Foulis of Leadhills or Waterhead, in the reign of James VI. How much earlier they had been wrought is not known, but tradition gives the merit of the discovery to one Mark Templeton, who lived in the beginning of the sixteenth century. It appeared from an entry in the book that after some progress had been made in it, a party of Montrose's troopers had laid hold of it, and carried it to the borders of England. They were probably little partial to the first Hopetoun, who was a son of Sir Thomas Hope, a man detested by the Royalists. It was, however, got back and continued. Though it contains facts that are curious and important to the proprietor and the miners, it bespeaks little knowledge of the subject. Carden said it was not true that before the great vein was discovered the miners begged of the then laird to be allowed to work on their own risk till it should be found out. At no time have those mines been so productive as in the time of the two first Earls of Hopetoun, who drew great sums out of them without great outlays. Their profits and proceedings were

the rules followed in the lease granted to the Scottish
Mining Company. Though in general lead was a
saleable commodity, it was a mere drug when the
trade with Holland was interrupted, vast quantities
of it being used in making white and red lead. Yet
when one market failed another was opened. Of
late the Russians had recourse to thin plates of lead
between the tiers of stone, by way of a succedaneum
for lime, the first being sometimes so strong as to
destroy the cement.[1]

In the afternoon we had a long walk, and took a
survey of the village and of its inhabitants, which
was a new and curious scene. The first thing that
struck me was the absence of the east wind, which
had been very keen and piercing on the banks of
the Clyde. This may be accounted for by Leadhills
being in a manner land-locked. However, on our
way to Dumfries we found it very bitter. We first
took a view of the smelting-mills and of the way
of thrashing lead ore, and saw on the other side
of the burn where the Susannah vein stood, from
which first the family and afterwards the Mining
Company had got great quantities of silver and lead.
The miners' houses in the village and its environs
were snug and comfortable, better than the great run
of tradesmen's and labourers' in corn countries. They
had large gardens planted with potatoes, and other

---

[1] One had calculated the amount of our yearly exports of metals, raw and
manufactured, to be at that time little short of three or four millions; and
he had access to better information with regard to commercial subjects.

kitchen stuff, and a number had cows fed in neighbouring enclosures. In short, their situation bespoke
fulness and attention upon the part of the masters.
If they have a particular look, it is owing to their
peculiar modes, and consorting mostly with one
another. Owing to the miners living so much under-
ground, without the benefit of fresh air, they have
somewhat of a sallow look, even when in good
health; but the same thing is observed of weavers
and other tradesmen, who are pent up in rooms
ill ventilated, and do not take regular exercise. It
being difficult to replace a miner, the Company was
at pains to preserve their health and cure their hurts.
A regular bred surgeon was entertained at its expense
to take charge of their people; and from what was
told us, he had much to do, and was very successful
in his practice. It seems he trusted fully as much to
regimen as to medicine, he being entitled to tell his
patients what to eat and drink, and also the articles
from which they must abstain. From whatever cause,
the men and women of Leadhills have not that
fresh blooming look which persons employed in husbandry, or out-of-door work, usually exhibit. It is,
however, well that the disease called the *lead-brash*
is less common among them than formerly, when it
often operated fatally when preceded by intemperance
or improper food.[1]   Be these things as they may, the

---

[1] If we may believe a life of John Taylor, the miner, Leadhills could boast
of the oldest man in the three kingdoms; but the account is evidently in-
accurate and inconsistent, such as might be expected from a man that had

people of Leadhills have a civility and courtesy somewhat systematic, little to be expected from persons of their profession, who are elsewhere rude and boorish, somewhat similar to colliers.   It affords a strong presumption that their government was both steady and temperate, working more by love than by fear.

We next took a survey of the library, which was in good order, and consisted of some hundreds of volumes of English books, divinity, history, novels, or travels.   If trash was sometimes admitted, it was to please individuals not free from prejudice.   What libraries, public or private, contain nothing but what is excellent or useful?   It was, however, a sure measure to give the miners, who have often much leisure time, wholesome and palatable food for the

lost his memory. Carden told us that when asked in what reign such an event happened, Taylor answered that he did not trouble his head with kings but that there was one of them, the one that dethroned his father-in-law, whom he should never forget ; for on his coming down to Scotland he was pressed and put on board a man-of-war. Taking all the circumstances together, he was probably twenty or twenty-five years younger than is stated. That tallies with his being employed in the Scots Mint, his marriage, &c. Nor is it credible that a man of ninety-seven years should have been taken into the Leadhill mines. I am very suspicious of tales of great longevity unless well authenticated. At Langholm, 17th May 1773, I was told by the landlord of a Mr Monat in that town, aged 130. I sent a message to the old man, wishing to see him ; and though gone to bed, he desired me to come to his room. On telling the meaning of this unreasonable visit, he started up in his bed and said the landlord was a great liar, for he was little more than 90. He was a lively old man ; yet a year or two after, the Annual Register set him down as aged 130. Hearing, twelve or fourteen years ago, of a beggar called Hozier, aged more than 100, I sent for him, and was convinced he exaggerated. As he was a native of the parish, I consulted the register, and found him to be between 80 and 90. For him it was sound policy, seeing he got shillings and half-crowns when others got halfpence. Old men wish to be thought older than they really are.

soul. From every account that class of people are better informed than people of their station in other parts of the kingdom. Reading is surely better than lounging in the ale-house or gossiping at home.

As the mines lie at a considerable distance from the parish church, there is a chapel of ease in the village, in which an ordained minister officiates, paid either by the Company or Lord Hopetoun. The minister was not at home, but we were told that he had a numerous attentive congregation. I wished to have seen them chaplainly convened, in their best attire. It was sure policy to give them wholesome spiritual food, to counteract vice and folly.

Next morning went to the mouth of one of the pits or *shafts*, and saw one company of miners come up and another descend. The clothes[1] of the former were somewhat wet with the droppings from the roofs of the mines, which are divided into chambers upheld with pillars of wood. The other party went down with alacrity—all of them being fond of the profession. They were warmly clothed, and had hoods and boots which enabled them to defy the damp of those subterranean regions. Dr Stuart would would fain have descended, but was dissuaded by our host, who told him that the scene differed little from

---

[1] Observing how well the miners were clothed, Carden told me that every year there came a set of *troquers* or *trockhers* [barterers, Fr. *troquer*] from Ireland with horse-loads of linen, which they bartered for the miner's old clothes. Though a strange traffic it must be profitable, else it would not be continued. One can hardly think the Irish have a market at home for ragged or worn-out clothes. Nowhere are rags more common than in that rich plentiful country,

the Tyndrum mines, only the pits here were deeper
and more disagreeable. It could only give entertainment to a fossilist, or hints to a cosmogonist. It
was to others gratifying an idle curiosity in which
there was some risk.[1]   It is proper to observe that, if
their work be hard and unpleasant, the miners work
only *six* hours out of the twenty-four, which is less
than falls to the share of other trades. In fact, they
have high wages and much time at their own disposal, and regard themselves as some degrees superior
to ploughmen or operative weavers ; yet few country
lads care to turn miners. We were next shown their
laws, which are *printed* on a sheet of paper, to which
an appeal is made in doubtful questions. They relate
principally to the funds provided for the maintenance
or relief of their poor, to which and the library every
one is bound to contribute by certain rules. The
disposal of it is vested in a general meeting of the
society. It may well be thought they do not interfere with the miners, &c., when they owe unreserved
obedience to the manager and his deputies. Indeed
they breathe somewhat of a republican spirit, which
wishes to set bounds to the power and encroachments
of their superiors. They anxiously stipulate, that on
no pretext shall the Earl of Hopetoun and his factors,
or the Company's manager or deputy, attempt to

[1] We were told that Mr David Erskine had wellnigh stuck by the way.
The late Lady Hopetoun and Dr Walker of Moffat having gone down without
taking the usual precautions, her ladyship's clothes and head dress were much
spoiled, while the good Doctor's locks were dishevelled, and he came up drip-
ping like a merman.

influence the proceedings or resolves of the society. It is further enacted, that if the preses shall either absent himself from the meeting, or fail in his duty, he shall pay a fine of sixpence *toties quoties*.[1] They reminded me of the laws of the republic of San Marino, of which Addison gives a pleasant account in his travels. Yet in their *proper* business they were obliged to give up their *natural rights* and obey the commands of their superior, without calling them in question. It was, however, well for all concerned that in no society, great or small, was there ever less caprice or oppression than at Leadhills.

In a place so wild and sequestered, one would think it difficult to procure the necessaries and conveniences of life; but in fact they are better off in that respect than could be imagined. Well-directed industry and commerce on a great scale can produce plenty and propriety in a wilderness. Nowhere can the comforts and luxuries on which men pride themselves be had better or more expéditiously procured than at Leadhills. The great number of carters employed in transporting lead to a seaport gives the manager and people of the village a chance of carriers cheaper and more expeditious than ordinary ones, because they wish to oblige the manager or better sort of miners. Both the Mr Stirlings got butcher-meat, fish, garden stuff and fruit, mostly from Edinburgh or Leith, where they had correspondents. The carters were at times

---

[1] The surgeon, who had been often preses, told us that he had repeatedly incurred the fine for not complying with the statutes.

employed in bringing meal or necessaries from Lothian, Lanark, or Dumfriesshire, the managers entering into contract with country gentlemen or merchants. Sometimes, however, the snow lay so deep that carts could hardly pass; but even then care was taken to open a passage for carriages, to which, for their own sakes, the people of Leadhills were disposed to lend their helping hand. For six weeks or more travelling was sometimes dangerous or unpleasant. However that might be, it was the practice of the two Mr Stirlings to make up their books and annual accounts in the dead season of the year, when they could not go abroad with comfort, or expect visits from their friends and acquaintances.

So much for what I saw and heard at Leadhills, where I spent the best part of two days very pleasantly. In our way to Sanquhar in the afternoon, we called at Wanlockhead, where there are valuable lead-mines belonging to the Duke of Queensberry, carried on by a company that seemed to proceed on as great and liberal a scale as the Scots Mining Company, in buildings, machinery, and numbers of people. We saw both the minister and surgeon. The celebrated Linnæus, in his 'Amœnitates Academicæ' translated by Stillingfleet, speaks of the advantages to be derived from men's travelling in their *own country*. There is indeed no province or district so wild and remote from which a person intent on studying manners, customs, and pursuits, may not derive profit or pleasure from conversing with the more intelligent inhabitants, and discriminating their characters. It enables the natural philosopher or historian to trace the Author of nature in His ways and works, which are as conspicuous in an alpine barren country as in one which lies in more fertile regions. Nay, the man who is fond of discovering odd and original characters, of which there is a great diversity, is as fond of a Will Wimble or a Tom Touchy, as of a Sir Roger de Coverley or a Sir Andrew Freeport.

In that point of view I am led to give some account of John Williamson of Moffat, the neighbour and often the visitor of Mr Stirling, whose ruling passion was the investigation of the mineral kingdom. If his discoveries were not great or striking, he deserved much praise for his zeal and perseverance, and for his disposition to serve his friends and neighbours. In a word, he may be considered as a kind of philosophical Will Wimble, who, like him, was always busy and benevolent, though his industry and bustle did not turn to much account. His father, a tenant in the neighbourhood of Moffat, left him in possession of a sheep farm well stocked, on which he might have lived comfortably and creditably had it not been for his wild crotchets. To put the matter strong, the person under consideration had more book-learning than common-sense, and what was unfortunate, he was rather a sciolist than a proficient in the sciences to which he pretended. Nothing could be more absurd than this poor man's tenets. Early in life he embraced with all the ardour of a new convert the opinions of Pythagoras and the Brahmins with regard to the transmigration of souls and the duty of abstaining from animal food, as conducing to the health both of the body and the soul. It is needless, indeed too late, to inquire from what sources he imbibed doctrines which ran counter to the sentiments not only of his countrymen of all ranks and sects, but to those of the most civilised nations of Europe. Much, however, might be learned from Ovid, and travels or histories relative to the East Indies. The Hindoos of modern times, who thought nearly in the same way with him, were so taught by their priests and philosophers, who had a great ascendancy over the minds of both high and low, whereas John was perhaps the only person in the three kingdoms who held these doctrines. It showed that his mind was strangely configured, and had a strong tendency to paradox. To prove that he was perfectly in earnest, he endeavoured to reduce his theories to practice, without attending to his own interest. At selling sheep and lambs, he made it part of the bargain that on no account should they be slaughtered. As he sold lower than other people, the purchasers were little scrupulous of making promises which they did not mean to keep. When the Earl of Hopetoun (the second) heard of this absurd conduct, he thought it time to deprive him of the farm, but as he had a favour for the man, gave him a small annuity, which he enjoyed as long as he lived.

He afterwards led a wandering life, which accorded with his favourite pursuits. Moffat, however, was henceforth his home. There he had time and opportunity to study books which might confirm him in his opinions, or increase his stock of knowledge, which was greater than he could digest. Indeed he was singularly unlucky in the choice of the books he read. Being passionately fond of mineralogy connected with chemistry, he fell in with the performances of the alchemists. These coincided with his chimerical notions. And to complete the jumble, he was much enamoured of the writings of Jacob Behmen, a German fanatic in philosophy, who dealt deep in what his countrymen called *theologia recondita*, in which met scholastic notions, later Platonism, and Jewish cabalism, intelligible to none but adepts. Unluckily for this poor man, some of Behmen's treatises had been translated into English, which he devoured with an ardour proportioned to their mysticism and absurdity. It may be thought odd how he should fall in with those strange authors; but as his crotchets were abundantly known, he found people who readily supplied him with rare and eccentric books which seemed to accord with his views and pursuits. Be these what they would, all his studies were directed to mines and minerals, in which he hoped to make great discoveries which should better his fortune and procure him celebrity.

Like some oriental theologists, he thought that the Almighty ought not to be worshipped in houses made with hands, but on a mountain or hill which presented grand or picturesque views of the works of creation.   Such, he said, was his own practice, for he did not attend church.   It was alleged, however, that in his Sunday's pilgrimages he used to take a peep of the metals and mineral waters by the way ; but he was never regarded as a profane or impious man, though, like the celebrated Sir Harry Vane, he was a man above ordinances.   Among other strange notions, he was (in theory) a strenuous advocate for a plurality of wives, holding that every healthy man who could afford it ought to have *three* wives.   For this he assigned both physical and political causes, which it is by no means necessary to enumerate here.   This heresy having come to the ears of the women of Moffat, they threatened to mob him.[1] John was neither idle nor stationary, being for great part of the year in search of mines and minerals in different parts of Scotland, where he had a numerous

[1] On a visit to Mr Stirling, Leadhills, where he used often to be, his host said, " Pythagoras, why do not you, who are of an amorous complexion, take a wife ! "   " Because, sir, the women of this age and country are such abominable flesh eaters that I cannot think of any serious connection with them." The other told him that within a few miles of that place there was a young woman that would answer him to a T., seeing she could not be prevailed on to eat animal food, living chiefly on milk and vegetables.   " Have you any objections to visit her ' "   They accordingly went, and the girl having got the cue, behaved like a Pythagorean, reprobating flesh   Poor John was perfectly charmed with her, and disposed to cultivate her acquaintance.   But ere long he came in great haste to tell the Venetian that Jenny   had gone off with the soldiers.   Intent on some abstruse problem, Mr Stirling was fretted to be disturbed, and said, when John was admitted, " that it did not surprise him, for women were not always what they professed to be ; and it now appeared that she had a strong hankering after the flesh."   John went away in high dudgeon at having been played on.

acquaintance who either had, or thought they had, the prospect of veins of lead or copper in some part of their property. And as none is more given to castle-building than mineralogists, he did not discourage their hopes, laying hold of every circumstance which might induce them to make the trial. This, of course, made him an inmate of a set of respectable families, who listened to his lectures, and thought he might stumble on something of great value on their estates. Nor was he the less acceptable that he made no charge for his trouble or loss of time. They took care, however, to make it up to him in another way, either making him a present or inviting him to stay with them. That was very flattering to a man fond of society and slenderly provided. If his conversation was not like that of any other man, it was modest and unassuming, while his notions were so wild and absurd, that they carried their reputation with them ;[1] neither was there any danger of his making prose-lytes, he being rather a dogmatist than a close rea-

---

[1] One of his favourite haunts was Alva, with the Lord Justice-Clerk or his son Baron Erskine, both of whom were very desirous of recovering the vein of silver, out of which Sir John Erskine had got much of that metal. George I., on hearing of it, said it was what the miners called a *nest*. In fact, no traces of it remained, and no discoveries were made. At their table John met sometimes with antipodes to himself. Dr Dundas of Alva told me that he one day dined there with John and a Harry St Clair, youngest brother of Lord St Clair, one of the greatest gluttons of the age ; for he sometimes ate a sixpence loaf, &c., to breakfast, and a leg of mutton or a goose to dinner ; but he could eat anything, were it crows or *water-kail*. He was a poor thin-looking man. John eyed him with equal scorn and indignation, and declaimed against flesh-eaters. In his latter years, Harry, who was a weak man, lived with Mr Campbell, minister of Alva, who, he alleged, gave him nothing but *prayers and porridge*.

soner.   Be that as it would, he had no interested
views in suggesting those plans to his friends.   His
over-sanguine temper might at times warp his judgment and make him deceive himself, but he was none
of these that wished to gull or fleece the people that
sought the benefit of his skill and counsel.   If he
did not do all the good he meant to have done, few
projectors in mines ever did less mischief.

In rambling through the mountains and glens near
Moffat, John Williamson had the merit of discovering
the Hartfield Spa, in a place seemingly accessible only
to a goat or a fox.   It proved a very valuable mineral water, being esteemed little inferior to Pyrmont
in Germany; and when properly corked it suffered
nothing by long carriage or keeping.   Being esteemed
a powerful medicine in certain diseases, the demand
for it for a number of years was very considerable.
With equal benignity and justice, the late Earl of
Hopetoun gave the profits to the discoverer as long as
he lived, which mended his slender income, and flattered his vanity.   That the well might be accessible
to invalids and strangers, his lordship ordered it to
be enclosed, and a good road made to it through a
wild glen.

In 1753 and 1754, I met this extraordinary man,
first at Menstry and then at Tullibody.   Thither he
had come in the course of his peregrinations to see
Mr Abercromby, who was well acquainted with him
in Dumfriesshire, where he used often to be.   That
gentleman was almost as sanguine in his expectations

of mines and minerals in the Ochils as his neighbour
the Lord Justice-Clerk. Neither of them, however,
was disposed to launch out far in quest of hidden
treasures. John excited much attention from his
host, by assuring him that he had read in an old
mining MS. in the Advocates' Library, that in the
burn of Auldwharry, which rises in the Menstry
estate, there was a vein of native cinnebar. As that
was a rare and valuable metal, seldom found in Britain,
Mr Abercromby was very desirous that John should
make diligent search for it. Accordingly, he discovered in that place a species of ore metal that was
new to him, which, with the credulity of a mineralo-
gist, he supposed to be the precious metal he was in
quest of. I well remember that the discovery occasioned much joy in the family; upon the faith of
which both young and old were disposed to amuse
themselves with castle-building. But on its being
tried by a chemist at Edinburgh, it was found to
be only iron ore of a rich quality, but in too
small quantity to be of any object. Be that as
it may, it ensured John a kind reception in that
family.

In August and September 1757, I went to Moffat
with the Kennet family for the recovery of my
health, being advised to drink the Hartfield Spa, in
order to remove stomachic complaints. Many a long
walk had John and I together in the environs of that
romantic town. Though he seldom avouched his
wild opinions in mixed companies, he disclosed them

to me without scruple. Well acquainted as I was
with his character, he sometimes made me stare at
his singular notions.   Besides retailing with great
enthusiasm the doctrines of the Pythagoreans and
Brahmins, he expatiated with great fervour on the
bad effects which resulted from monogamy—such as
superfœtations, abortions, &c., &c.   I told him these
things were above the ken of bachelors.   He likewise
declaimed against the use of spurs and whips, as
being cruel and unnecessary to that valuable domestic animal the horse ; for he had no objection to his
being employed in ploughing or travelling, if he were
treated well.   He said none could tell but that the
soul of a near relation or intimate friend might animate the horse he treated harshly and unjustly.
And he lent me the treatises of his favourite author
Jacob Behmen, which he regarded as worth their
weight in gold.   It was plain that John had a mist
in his brain ; but it was fortunate that it neither
spoilt his morals nor diminished his goodwill to man.
   At that time he appeared to be near forty years
of age, middle-sized, rather lean, but muscular and
active.   There was something queerish and sombre
in his face ; but in these cases one connects the person's countenance and crotchets, which is no sure
criterion of his mind.   His Brahminical diet had not
impaired his health or strength, for he still under-
went much fatigue in his researches after mines and
minerals.   In point of figure, dress, and deportment,
he resembled the miners whom I saw at Leadhills in

1790. Nor is that surprising, as with that class of
people he often consorted, their ideas and pursuits
being nearly akin. And as they were somewhat on
a par in point of fortune, he adopted their modes
and manners. To conclude, John Williamson was
one of those eccentric characters which do not occur
often in any age or country. If his foibles and
oddities were great and unaccountable, they hurt
nobody but himself, and he wished well to the best
interests of society. The discovery of mines and
minerals, which was his ruling passion from youth
to age, cannot be condemned by the most rigid mor-
alist, seeing it bids fair to give bread to numbers of
labouring men, whilst it adds to the national wealth.

At length he paid the debt to nature. After his
death a monument was erected to his memory, with
a suitable inscription, by the late Sir George Clerk of
Penicuik, who, as he was always kind to John, lived
for a number of years in the vicinity of Moffat. In
fact, that gentleman was as great an enthusiast in
mineralogy as Williamson, and what is more, as little
successful in his theories and operations.

James Graham of Kilmardenny was a strong-
minded man, much admired for his wit and convivial talents. As he has been dead more than
seventy years it is too late to attempt to trace his
progress from youth to age. All that can be done
is to record a few anecdotes which I have heard
in my younger years. My uncle, Mr Dundas of
Manor, told me that he sometimes met with him,

either at Edinburgh or in the west country. He described him as a bulky, coarse-featured man, with an enormous nose, studded with carbuncles. In fact, his person and countenance might be regarded as indexes to his mind and modes, which were rough and antiquated, yet well suited to the age and country in which his lot was cast. With the Keir family, which resided mostly at Calder after 1715, he lived in great intimacy, his company being very acceptable to John Stirling of Keir.

He was a gentleman of small estate in Kilpatrick, a district of Dumbartonshire. Owing either to embarrassments, or a desire of bettering his fortune, it behoved him to push his way in the wide world when outlets for young adventurers were comparatively rare. Whether he was bred a sailor I know not; but in the memorable Darien expedition he was lieutenant of the Rising Sun, one of the Scottish ships that conveyed the colony that was to be planted in Darien, or, as our countrymen phrased it, Caledonia. From it they expected wealth and territory which should put them somewhat on a level with the English, of whom at that time they were exceedingly jealous; and it would appear that the latter were no less narrow-minded than spiteful. It was at best an ill-concocted scheme, beyond the strength of a poor divided country to execute, and might be regarded as a species of castle-building. Into it, however, the Scots entered with great enthusiasm. It is needless to go further into that measure, which proved inglorious and disastrous to all that were concerned in it. Suffice it to say, that Kilmardenny had a full share of the hardships and mishaps of his countrymen who had embarked in that ill-fated enterprise. That it did not better his fortune, or lead to promotion, is well known; but the scenes he witnessed in the course of that expedition made a deep impression upon his mind, and if they did not teach him better lessons, afforded him never-failing topics of discourse, which the older he grew were the more acceptable to his friends and acquaintances that he gave them in his own drapery and colouring.

It would seem that, upon giving up active life, he took up his residence at Kilmardenny, where he spent the residue of his long and checkered life amidst the companions of his youth and the connections of his family. It is well known that he outlived all his associates in the Darien enterprise. That did not make him enlarge less on his favourite topics, which it was supposed he rather amplified. When his young friends seemed to doubt of his stories, he said, *"Back-speer* [cross-examine] me now, lads, if ye can"[1] He seems to have dealt deep in rodomontade, or *white lies*, which mean nothing wrong, and at least amuse, while none think it necessary to believe them. He said that part of their provisions consisted of *Jews' flesh*, which was known when they came to the *giblets*. Speaking of bees in Darien of enormous size, and

---

[1] I had this from Lord Kames, a great friend of John Stirling of Keir.

of their hives, he was told they could not get access.
"Oh," said he, "let the bees see to that." Talking
of a great mob at Edinburgh in 1695 about Darien,
he said he saw a fellow thrown into a bonfire, who,
on being taken out, ran down the street burning like
spunkie in a winter night. Somebody observed that
woollen cloth never blazes in a fire. "Ay," said the
wit, "but the fellow was a candlemaker." Indeed
he never wanted a loophole to creep out at. One
of his female friends reprehending him for going
seldom to church, he answered, "Madam, I myself
am nothing the better of going, and my mare is
much the worse." It was one of his singularities
that he never took a *lift* at burials, which was done
by all ranks of people. "Did you," said he to somebody, "ever see a coffin lying on the road for want
of people to carry it?" Talking of the absurdity of
the burghers of Edinburgh in the last century, who
walked at the Cross arrayed in jack-boots, spurs, and
tie-wigs, he said he remembered the time when the
children were children in jack-boots, spurs, and tie-
wigs. This was in the true spirit of hyperbole.

One day in harvest while attending his reapers,
very ill dressed, a person of a decent appearance on
horseback accosted him, asking *supply*. He told the
man that he was going to breakfast, where that
matter should be settled. "Eat," said he to the
stranger, "and welcome. I know it is our duty to
feed the hungry, and clothe the naked, but nowhere
are we enjoined to give money. There you see

butter and cheese, eggs and cold salt beef—make
therefore a hearty meal, and much good may it do you ;
and if you should like my coat better than your own, I
am willing to exchange." The *gentle* beggar went off
(*re infectâ*).   These gleanings show him to have been
a man of wit and pleasantry, whom it was difficult to
entrap.   He was for many years considered as a most
pleasant companion—one of those that could set the
table in a roar, and add to the intellectual feast.
Kilpatrick was in his time the seat of a number of
families of moderate fortune, who lived together in
great cordiality, without ceremony or *fracas*.   The
bottle was their great bond of union, and in liquor
they were not more than nice ; any more than in their
talk, which was coarse and free, going even beyond
their neighbours on the water of Endrick.   It even
extended to the ladies, who, though virtuous, did not
plume themselves on delicacy.   In that school the
Duchess of Douglas was bred.   No wonder, then, that
this gentleman should be in high favour with a jovial
free-hearted race of people.   Nor would he be the less
acceptable to his compotators that he had no reverence for the memory of King William or his English
ministers.   On the whole, he was a character which
one would wish had been portrayed by some of his
contemporaries that had lived in habits of intimacy
with him.   I imagine he died between 1730 and
1740.

Baron Maccara had a small property near Abercairney, from which he got the name of *Baron*, a title

not peculiar to him in that country. In whatever
way he acquired it, whether at college, or by reading, he had more knowledge and ingenuity than fell to
the share of a number of wealthy proprietors. But
the thing which got him a name, and made his company acceptable, was a vein of wit and humour, in
which there were no traces of rudeness or ill-nature.
His sallies bespoke much vivacity, combined with
common-sense. No wonder that his flights of fancy
should be much admired in a narrow circle. James,
Duke of Athole, made him a justice of peace, for
a profane jest not worth recording. In that capacity he had once an opportunity of combining wit
and commiseration together, in a way that did
him honour, and, what is less common, produced
the desired effect. In the summer of 1746, when
the Highlanders' cattle were driven off their farms
and collected near Crieff, loud complaints were
made that the innocent were punished with the
guilty. Numberless complaints being made to Lord
Albemarle at Perth, he directed Major Forrester
(author of 'The Polite Philosopher') to get a justice
of peace to examine into the facts, that so the cattle might be restored to such as could prove their
property and loyalty. The Baron was the only one
that could be had. Having come on foot, the Major
was rather prepossessed against his appearance.
" Well, Mr Justice, shall we begin business?" " As
soon as I get the Bible." " The Bible!" said the
Major; " I thought my orders were the only things

for consideration to-day." The Baron was positive, and threatened to go away. "Well," said Forrester, "since the justice is a humourist, let him be indulged." The Bible being produced, he turned up the verse in Genesis, "Wilt thou also destroy the righteous with the wicked ?" The Major then saw there was more in his coadjutor than he expected. He told the Baron that their sentiments were nearly akin. In a word, the business went on swimmingly, and the greatest part of the cattle was restored. At the burial of James Graham of Braco, which took place in the end of August 1745, the Baron was by general consent appointed toast-master, but enjoined to give no healths that would give offence. His first toast was the King *abroad* (George II. was then at Hanover); the second, the Prince at *home;* the third, the Duke *abroad;* and the fourth, the Land of Cakes and a good *Stewart* to divide them. To these the party itself could take no exception.

In these days religious controversy was a frequent theme of discourse among his neighbours. Tired one day with a hot dispute about Church government, he told the company that, after having studied the matter with great diligence, all he could discover was "that St Peter was a Roman Catholic, St James an Episcopalian, and St Paul a Presbyterian. In short, I did not find that dipping deep into religious controversy makes people wiser or better." It being said that old Lady Balgowan had all the faiths on her finger-ends, "Methinks," said the Baron, "a thimble would fit them fully as well." At that time the *usages* had occasioned great divisions among the Episcopalian Nonjurors.

It may well be thought the Baron was a frequent guest at Abercairney, being greatly in favour with the Laird and Lady Frances, a well - bred lively woman, who read a great deal, and knew well what was going on in the literary as well as the fashionable world. Abercairney told me that once the Baron happened to be there when Mr Home, afterwards Lord Kames, was at the bar. They got into a warm dispute about some abstracted point; for the Baron had a metaphysical turn, as some people have a turn for poetry, or an ear for dancing. Whether it was that the Baron thought himself treated with too little respect, but at last he said the highest *upper storeys* were not always the best furnished. When Mr Home's Essays were published, Lady Frances loaned them to her friend the Baron, knowing that he had a turn for such reading. "Well, Baron," said she, the next time they met, "what do you think of this performance; do you understand it?" "Why, madam, I wish its author may understand it. Sure I am it is some points above my reach."

It is now too late to give more of this gentleman's strokes of wit, which showed him to be no ordinary man. More culture and better company would have enabled him to figure in a higher line, and to improve his fortune. Wit is not always a blessing to the person that possesses it, being a two-edged tool.

It made him too fond of company and his bottle, which embarrassed his circumstances. At length he sold his lands to his great neighbour Abercairney; and being appointed a stamp-master, took up his residence at Auchterarder, where he died between 1765 and 1770.

Of the following anecdotes I have no reason to doubt, and they are worth preserving in a work of this kind. In autumn 1746, Clerk Miller of Perth, a very able but unpopular man, much trusted at that time by the king's servants at Edinburgh, seeing Mr Anderson, factor to James Moray of Abercairney, on the street, beckoned to him. Taking him aside, he said, "Anderson, do not you remember being in this town a year ago when the Highlanders were here?" "Really, George, my memory is not so good as it has been." Said the other, "I will refresh it. Do you not remember carrying one thousand guineas to the Prince, and making a speech to him in your master's name?" Mr Anderson, who was a shrewd worthy man, got away as soon as he could, and mounting his horse, galloped home. On hearing what had passed, Abercairney said, "Let my horses be got ready; I will set out directly for France or Holland." "That I hope," said his sagacious factor, "will be unnecessary. Take your bed and play the part of a sick man, to which your friend, Dr Smith of Perth, will give countenance, and leave the rest to me." The good doctor entered readily into the plot, and pronounced his patient to be in great danger.

Meanwhile Abercairney directed George Miller to
be sent for in great haste. On his entering into
the bedchamber, the supposed sick man addressed
him thus in a tremulous voice, "My dear George,
thinking myself a dying man, it is most proper that
I should settle my worldly affairs. In your abilities
and integrity I have full confidence; let bonds of
provision to the younger children, and a nomination
of tutors and curators be drawn as soon as possible.
I mean to make you factor on the estate till the heir
be of age. Nor shall it be in the power of the tutors
to remove you from that office." The deeds were
drawn, for which Miller received fifty guineas and
then went home. In a competent time the laird recovered, and it may well be thought that for some
months George was a frequent and welcome guest
at Abercairney. Anderson judged soundly. Miller,
who was sheriff as well as town-clerk, and supposed
to be officious and over harsh, took no steps to in-
vestigate Abercairney's conduct in September 1745.
When the Act of Indemnity passed, in which he was
not an excepted person, he sent for his friend Miller;
but after giving him a good dinner and plenty of
wine, loaded him with abuse, and then kicked him
to the door. The person from whom I heard this
story had good access to know. On my asking
Abercairney if it was true, he laughed and said,
"Hypocritical scoundrel! he went and said no man
had ever used him so ill as I did." In giving a sop
to this ministerial Cerberus, Anderson discovered orig-

inal genius and sound policy. Other people gave
him, it was said, a sop to soften the evidence.[1]

Abercairney and Lady Frances told me that some
weeks after the battle of Culloden, Secretary Murray's
wife, the daughter of a Colonel Ferguson, made her
appearance one evening seemingly in great distress,
being disguised. In respect of her situation, she
met with a gracious reception from that hospitable
family, which was warmly attached to the exiled
king and his grandson. At parting, after supper,
Lady Christian and Lady Frances accompanied the
disconsolate stranger to her bedroom; but in the
paroxysm of her· sorrow she bestirred herself so
much that a large quantity of gold, concealed
about her clothes, broke loose and rolled about the
room, which made it necessary to summon the Laird
to collect it. It may well be thought Mrs Murray
did not feel very pleasant on the discovery. A few
weeks after her unworthy husband was taken in
Tweeddale and sent to Edinburgh, where he betrayed
his master's secrets. From him it is probable Miller
derived his information second-hand. These two
anecdotes may be regarded as two political interludes
exhibited in one family in the same year. Let me
also mention a third one of a ludicrous nature which
took place the same year. At a time when such
edifices were either rare or mean, Mr Moray of
Abercairney erected in a corner of his garden, hard
by the house, a spacious and elegant temple to

[1] Ballochellan, &c.

Cloacina. When the king's army marched north against the rebels in February 1746, General Hughes and some other officers of rank were billeted on him, who gave them a courteous reception, with plenty of meat and wine ; but nothing pleased them so much as the temple, which was so clean and sweet. "Why, sir," said he to me a number of years after, "if I had written 'Paradise Lost,' I could not have received greater praises than were paid me by those military grandees whose national prejudices were abundantly strong."

In a collection tied to no rules, I will set down a little incident relative to this family. The Archbishop of York was at Dupplin in the year 1764. The gentry of Strathearn said that he gave them better *cracks* and more wine than his brother the Earl [of Kinnoull]. In returning the visits of the neighbours, the Archbishop stayed a couple of days at Abercairney. In the forenoon, Mr Moray being called out on business. his son Alexander, a weak *matter-of-fact* lad, thought it incumbent on him to entertain the stranger. "My Lord Archbishop," said he, "can you tell me whether the Duke of Kingston keeps Miss Chudleigh?" "Sandy," answered he, "how come you to know anything of that matter?" On quoting his authorities, his Grace said these things lay somewhat out of his line ; but he believed if the Duke ever kept that lady, he kept her still. Anthony Moray of Crieff told me he was present when this notable question was put. The rest of the company did not know how to look.

Before passing to other topics, let me pay tribute to the memory of the father, in whose company I passed many pleasant hours, either in his own house, or those of our common friends. He was one of those who combined hospitality and good neighbourhood with that meritorious economy which seeks to save that it may have the more to spend. In a house much too mean and incommodious for his estate (part of it being built of clay plastered over) he found means to entertain much good company; and to friends and neighbours his door was ever open. He kept a plentiful genteel table, suited to the number and quality of the guests. Neither did he balk them in the article of liquor, which was then regarded as the great cement of society. Though in compliment to the company he often drank hard, it mattered little what was the liquor, for he could hardly distinguish one from another from a defect in his palate; he was therefore obliged to trust to the opinion of some friend. Meanwhile, while keeping what would now be accounted open house, he was satisfied with moderate rents, not wishing to be thought a squeezer, though he meant to take the value. Yet he had a considerable sum of lying money, ready to answer future exigencies, or to make convenient purchases of land. If no man read less, or spoke less of books, his conversation was very entertaining; for he knew well what was going on in the busy or gay world; and his *ex re fabellæ* showed that he had lived much in good company. Perhaps his mirth was sometimes too noisy, but that accorded with the taste of the neighbours with whom he associated. Sir Ralph Abercromby, who was an excellent judge of character, used to say that he looked on Abercairney as a pattern for country gentlemen that wished to maintain their state without hazarding their independence, or splitting on the rocks and quicksands that proved fatal to their brethren.

A little must now be said of this gentleman's eldest son, of whom very sanguine expectations were formed. In the beginning of the year 1758, before his education was finished, as he was threatened with a consumption, the physicians recommended him warmer climate. With this view he was sent first to Lisbon, from whence he travelled by land to Gibraltar, having letters to the Earl of Home, the governor, who gave him a very kind reception, but was very much dissatisfied with a Mr Lunan, his companion, who was an awkward pedantic man, very unfit to be a travelling governor. If I mistake not, he succeeded James Elphinstone, the translator of Martial, a pedagogue; and it is sufficient to say, that they were of the same principles. And therefore the first thing the Earl did was *to ship off* Mr Lunan for England, sending Abercairney a bill of boarding for him. Young Mr Moray was sent soon after to Nice, where he and Sir Archibald Stewart's son were to be under the charge of Dr Dundas of Alloa, a well-bred pleasant man, from whom young men could learn excellent lessons. The climate agreed well with them,

and in spring they made an excursion to Rome and
Naples, with which they were much gratified.[1]

Poor Stewart died soon after; but Moray, after
passing some time in Britain, returned to the Continent for the confirmation of his health, which was at
best delicate. For Italy, its modes and manners, he
had a great fondness; and during the war of 1756, the
British were excluded from France.

In the spring of 1763 he was either at Rome
or Naples, whither his father, attended by Dr
Dundas, went to fetch him home. I supped with
them at London the night before they set out.
Though they had a pleasant and prosperous journey, Abercairney's pleasure was confined to his
eye on the bottle, speaking only English. All the
French he learned was *doucement*, when the pos-
tilions were driving furiously, and *toute à l'heure*,
when impatient for his meals. At Rome he met
with people of his own sentiments, and, if I mistake
not, was one of the last who kissed the exiled king's
hands,—an unmeaning compliment, but a proof of
zeal and consistency. He sufficiently undervalued
classical scenes; for when a shallow traveller harangued in a drawing-room upon the *Elysian* fields,
Abercairney said, "Stinking fields, ladies." After
spending some time in Scotland, he went in winter
to London, where he had a number of friends of the
first rank and fashion whom he had seen in Italy.

[1] On entering Rome, Stewart exclaimed, "Moray, saw you ever such
a crop!"

He grew exceeding fond of a London life. Being an elegant-mannered man, of the most amiable disposition, he was received into the fashionable circles and the club at Almacks. These things, however pleasing, did not confirm his health, but impaired his strength, preventing his marriage to a fine young woman with a large fortune. I saw her repeatedly at Blairdrummond or Abercairney in 1764 or 1765, and was delighted with her manners and conversation, which were fascinating and instructive. He was not more than fond of home, and very anxious to get into Parliament. It may well be thought he lived at great expense, which his father paid without a grudge, being fond of a son that bid him fair to be an honour to his family. He died in the summer of 1767 on shipboard, his constitution being quite exhausted. He was an inexpressible loss to his family and to the country.

CHAPTER XII.

EXPERIENCES OF A LANDLORD.

Whilst it would be ill-natured and unpardonable to speak of living men, there is nothing to hinder me in a work like the present, which is really akin to memoirs, to give a plain and candid account of the style and principle on which I proceeded in managing my small but sweet inheritance, which, however, suffices my wants and wishes. It is the more proper, that I have been all along much censured by my neighbours for want of judgment and inattention to my own interests. If in dealing with tenants I have been over moderate and self-denied, I certainly could not plead in justification *defendit nummus*. Upon reviewing my course, which is now far run, I feel not the least compunction, on a retrospect of this part of my conduct. It is well, however, when a man acts up to his maxims and professions, which are sometimes powerfully counteracted by selfishness or vanity. And hitherto I have had wherewithal " to maintain my state, and send the poor well pleased from my gate."

Upon coming of age, I found the tenants possessing by tacit relocation, on a tack granted by my father in 1735 for nineteen years. In imitation of some of his ablest friends and neighbours, he had a little before divided his runrig farms into separate ones. If by the new leases the tenants paid an augmentation, that was more than compensated by the new division. But though an indulgent landlord, it was by no means his intention to let his lands below value. From all I can collect at this distance of time, his rents were upon a par with those of his most sensible and skilful neighbours. At that period bankruptcies were not uncommon in the country; and hence it became necessary to use legal diligence, a measure from which the master derives neither pleasure nor honour. With great good sense, therefore, my father, who was easy in his circumstances, forbore to squeeze his people.

Although my father's leases had expired at Martinmas 1754, no steps were taken for five years to renew them, which was against the lands, and little in favour of the tenants, who gave over liming, a thing much against their own interest. It was, no doubt, too important a transaction to be hurried over. Being disposed to think well of a set of people whom I had known from my earliest years, I wished to treat them with kindness, without neglecting my own interest. It was, however, difficult in my then situation, an entire stranger to country business, to hit the happy mean. Besides the estate, my father had left me a considerable sum of lying money, which he had made with a fair character in the course of his practice. That circumstance did not warrant my treading in the steps of certain well-known money-scraping neighbours, who proved generally heirs and executors to their tenants, whose bargains were regarded as very hard. I had at that time faithful friends capable of giving me sound counsel with regard to the let of lands. They declined, I know not for what reason, to take any active hand in that business. Yet they put me on my guard against some of the then present tenants, of whom they judged more soundly than I did. And knowing a little of my temper and turn, they earnestly dissuaded me from being too generous towards country people, which, they assured me, would turn to little account.

In those circumstances I was forced to form a plan for myself, the execution of which was committed to Mr Moir at Doune, Lord Moray's factor,—an honest, fast-headed man, and an excellent judge of the value of land, and of the character of countrymen, whose arts and subterfuges he was perfectly acquainted with. The taking of *written* offers for farms was by that time much in vogue, he himself having conducted the set of the Earl's lands in that way with great ability and address. If the new rents of the feus, &c., were then considered as very high, Mr Moir was not to blame, because he acted according to instructions from Lord Moray and his ministers. He was therefore directed to receive offers from the tenants, but to prevent a sort of roup, not of the best kind, he was not to admit strangers to bid upon them. That would not be tried till they had made their highest offer. After a competent time he transmitted to me a set of offers which rather exceeded my expectations, after the language the tenants had held to me and my late factor, who was no better judge of that matter than myself. I therefore signified my approbation to Mr Moir. I must, however, do him the justice to say that he thought the offers much too small, and offered, if I inclined it, to give me higher rents and good tenants, provided I would let him take his own way. And of his own accord he sent me an offer for one of the farms much higher than the present tenant had made, and if that did not satisfy me more would be given. He thought the man entitled to less favour that he had been troublesome and uncandid in his communications.[1] But I declined it, thinking I had enough. Nay, so much was I convinced of this, that at signing the tacks in 1760, I gave Doune, by a note subjoined to them, £5 of what had been offered, apportioning it to their situations. In this it must be confessed there was little wisdom, for it had been better laid out in premiums. It was, however, entirely my own doing, not the

[1] When John Macarthur, a primitive venerable man, was told I had given him an abatement of twelve shillings, he said he would pay what he had promised, but no abatement. On the other hand, another of them, a modern Naball, when quarrelled for not performing some of the carriages stipulated by his lease, told me, very insolently, that he did not think himself much indebted to me, seeing I had done more for others than for him. This was provoking, but I was not implacable : *Ignoscenti, ut ignosceratur.*

effects of teasing or solicitation. If ever a person
was to exceed in goodwill to the members of the little
society over which he presided, it was at the age of
twenty-three, when his prospects were fair and flattering, and his ambition very limited. Had my disposition been more flinty, who does not know that in
those days it was more difficult to get a crown of
augmentation than a guinea at the present time?
The tenure of *kindness*, though no longer recognised
by courts of justice, or men of law, was not at that
time totally eradicated from the minds of proprietors
and tenants. Besides, at the time when these tacks
were granted, victual markets were exceedingly low,
bear and meal selling currently at ten or eleven
shillings the boll, sometimes under it. The former
rental converting the meal at £100 per chalder, did
not exceed £ [1]   . Besides this, there were eighteen
acres of enclosed land that had been in my father's
natural possession. They had been set yearly by
roup for pasture at about 20s. an acre, which was
reckoned a high rent, when the best carse farms
hardly gave so much.

On settling at Ochtertyre in 1760, I took a farm
contiguous to the house and the enclosures into my
own possession. Nearly £30 of augmentation was
got upon the other seven. Moderate as it surely was,
yet could the price of necessaries, and of luxuries that
cannot be wanted, be reduced to the rates then given,
it is not clear whether I should not be as well off

[1 The figures are left blank in the MS.]

with the old as with the new rents. Nor must it be
omitted that, two years after giving these leases,
victual markets rose considerably, and for thirteen
years the average price of barley and meal was nearly
a third higher, and sometimes more, than in 1760.
That circumstance, joined to a glut of prosperity
public and private, unexampled in Scotland, got an
elation of mind amongst all sorts and conditions
of men, which was not always regulated by discretion, and none felt its influence more than the labourer
of the ground. In the meantime, with one or two exceptions, which no prudence could prevent, my tenants
throve apace, to which they were the better entitled
that they were very industrious and skilful. And
therefore it could not be said of them that the
easiness of their rents had made them slothful or
sparing of cost which promised a good return.

Even in this happy period bankruptcies took place.
In 1770, owing to indolence and want of conduct,
one of my people found it necessary to surrender his
tack. The farm was immediately let to a good
tenant, who paid little less than a half more than his
predecessor. And had the other farms been out of
lease, they would, without any hardship, have been
let in the same ratio. But by that time circumstances
were wonderfully changed to the better from what
they had been ten years before.

In 1778 I opened a treaty with my people for new
tacks. I wished to prevent their scourging the land
in the last year, which, as matters then stood, could

neither be prevented nor redressed. If experience
had not made me more worldly wise, it was not for
want of counsel. After full consideration and advising with judicious people, I made the tenants
two offers : first, to make the money rent fluctuate,
according to the Mid-Lothian fiars of oatmeal, our
best barometer of the price of corn, estimating every
10s. 5d. of the last rents at a boll of oatmeal; the
second, for every 10s. 5d. of their rent to take 13s.
4d. A victual rent, payable in kind, would have been
the most unexceptionable, and, as things afterwards
turned out, the most lucrative. To that, however,
there were strong objections, and tenants can always
sell better than their landlords. My people chose the
last, which gave me a little more than a fourth of ,
augmentation. Had it not been for a great stagnation and depression in the price of grain for some
years preceding, I would have demanded 15s. instead
of 13s. 4d. for each 10s. 5d. of the preceding rents.
And as grain fell very low in 1780 and 1781, it was
doubtful whether I had not done better than those
who had squeezed their people without mercy.
Knowing that the tenants were treated liberally, I
thought it a proper time to prevent in future, if
possible, a set of abuses in culture and cropping, for
which there was no legal remedy. Yet were they
confessed by even judicious husbandmen to be as
much against their interest as their master's. A set
of rules were therefore drawn up which allowed the
tenants a proper latitude, while they were restrained

from malpractices which would be condemned by
nine-tenths of their brethren.   They differed little
from the hints suggested in an earlier part of this
work, and being assented to by them all, were engrossed in the leases, which were revised by my excellent friend Mr David Erskine, who put them into
business language.   Better ones, perhaps, might have
been desired, but it was well that in the whole course
of that tack I had not a single dispute about their
import.   And what was very gratifying, all of them
that I had any opinion of did more than they were
enjoined to do by their bargain,[1] whilst it gave
me great satisfaction to see one and all of them
laborious and successful.   Still, it was the general
opinion that I had been too moderate.[2]   But as I
had formed my plans of life, in which vanity and
dissipation had no place, my income was the more
likely to suffice that my farm and garden, which had

---

[1] Joseph Ferguson, who was an idle dissipated fellow, possessed in terms of
the articles during pleasure. He broke in 1781, but his trustees fulfilled the
conditions. He might have made as much as would have bought his farm.

[2] So little vindictive was I, that even Nabal, notwithstanding his petulance
and ingratitude, was permitted to make an offer. But besides being rich and
skilful, he had also the merit of having lately improved his moss-side land to
great purpose. Yet perfectly in character, he could not forbear giving a
sample of his spirit. At revising the lease, he began to carp and joke at some
of the conditions to which he had consented. I asked him what he meant.
"Did he not wish for a tack?" He said he did not much care; on which I
bid him begone, and I should find another tenant. Two days after he came
back very penitent. In respect of his folly and insolence, after keeping him
awhile in suspense, I made him pay 18s. a year more than he would have done
but for this ebullition. And he was given to understand that the law should
henceforth be my rule. I was obliged afterwards to take legal measures,
which soon brought him to his marrow bones, and he was quiet during the
remainder of the tack.

cost a great deal of money, were by that time finished or reduced to a stated charge. Owing to these and other causes, of which I had no reason to be ashamed, my *impedimenta virtutis*, or riches, as Lord Bacon calls them, were much diminished from what they had been at my outset.

In my justification, however, it might be pled that nobody could foresee a set of events that fell out in the course of the new tacks, which raised the spirits of farmers, and gave people new notions with regard to the value of land. The first of these was the extravagant prices at which grain sold in the years 1782 and 1783, in consequence of the very bad crop in the first of these years. It was regarded by most of them as a propitious event. The French Revolution also contributed to keep up the markets, nor were these depressed by the war that broke out soon after, which enhanced the price of everything. But above all, the scarcity in 1795-96, though in some measure artificial, made proprietors hardly know what to ask for lands out of lease. In matters of that kind, however, a man must be directed by present circumstances, and not look forward to contingencies which may never take place.

In the summer of 1797, the last year but one of my current leases, I entered into treaty with the tenants for a renewal of them. I was well apprised that the situation of my tenants and estate warranted a considerable augmentation, which was the more requisite that the value of money had fallen exceedingly in the

course of the last nineteen years. Ill-used as I had
been by some of my people, who could hardly have
behaved worse had I pared them to the quick, I was
determined against *rack* rents.   In this I was at least
consistent; for I had from the commencement of
my course wished for thriving, well-pleased tenants,
as one of the most rational luxuries that a country
gentleman could have.   It caused me much time and
thought to form a plan to please myself.   Whatever
opinion may be formed of it, after five years' trial,
and two years of exuberant prices, I still think it was
right to make the rent depend in some measure on
the price of oatmeal, which has long been our staple ;
but independent of that, a considerable increase was
stipulated.   Yet even such as are satisfied with the
leading principles may think that much too moderate.   Nay, the progressive increases, according to the
Mid-Lothian fiars, might have been made somewhat
higher without injury to the tenants.   But in not
making any classes above 20s. per boll, I can hardly
be blamed ; for to have made provision when the fiars
should be at 30s. or 40s. would have shown an
inclination to profit from times of dearth and calamity, while there was little chance of my ever being a
penny the better for that provision.   Yet in less than
three years from the time of opening this treaty, oatmeal sold currently from 40s. to £3 a boll; and
never were rents better paid than during the dearth.

Yet, however much I may have been under the
mark, it must be acknowledged that a decent attention was paid to my own interests.   The seven farms

which, prior to Martinmas 1760, paid only £ [1] converting [1] bolls of meal at the ordinary conversion, had risen in 1779 to £168, 15s. 7d., besides 52 bolls of oatmeal paid in kind, and 8 bolls of barley, besides kain and carriages. It was now proposed that the money rent should fluctuate from £224, 11s. to £259, 1s. 6d., to which should be added 59 bolls of oatmeal and 9 bolls of bear or barley. This was exclusive of the farm in my natural possession, which was valuable and productive. I acknowledge, however, that much more might have been got by playing the usual game of admitting strangers to bid, or cajoling the tenants; but my nature revolted at having recourse to such mean arts. That much greater rents than what I demanded would have been paid regularly for any length of time, depended upon circumstances that were not at my disposal. In fact, an avaricious unfeeling landlord may impoverish his tenants, and prevent their doing justice to his lands, which will ere long affect his patrimonial interest.

In conducting that business, I took the assistance of Mr Burn of Coldoch, because he was not only able and upright, but also revered and trusted by his country neighbours. I cannot, however, shelter myself under the sanction of his opinion, for he thought I ought to have taken higher rents. But as I had in a great measure made up my mind upon that subject, nothing remained but to carry the plan into execution, taking care to obviate some objections.

[1 Blank in MS.]

The tenants acceded cheerfully to the proposals made them, which they knew to be connected with kindness. On that occasion I endeavoured to rise superior to passion and prejudice ; for in spite of all the provocations I had met with, even Nabal himself was admitted to come forward on equal terms with his brethren. I ought perhaps to have removed him ; indeed very few men in the country would have given this man three nineteen-year tacks. But he had more affection in his nature than could have been expected from the pruriences of his language and the peevishness of his temper, over which he had no command. In a word, he had a number of good points ; and his infirmities, which sometimes fretted me, were become as familiar to me as my own. It is by no means expedient to turn out *old* tenants for slight offences, because they are the best acquainted with marches and those circumstances which a proprietor ought always to keep in view. However, had the leases expired in 1800, I should assuredly have invested on higher terms, without losing sight entirely of kindness and moderation.

When the offers were signed, I told my people that it was not my practice to give a missive of acceptance. The true way of completing the bargain was to enter into a tack upon the conditions demanded of them, as none could tell what might happen in the meantime. In fact, in a few months after the communing, I found it necessary to get rid of a tenant of whom, till then, I had the highest opinion. But the rash step taken by James Christie rendered him a most improper tenant for me.

Before speaking of this man's wild schemes, let me speak of his character and conduct while one of my tenants. In fact, his good properties and foibles were strangely blended together in a way not to be accounted for. It would require the pencil of Lord Clarendon to trace him through all his lights and shades. If he had had a regular education, and been called to act a part in public life, his language and conduct would have displayed a motley mixture of genius and caprice. There is, however, nothing to hinder biography from being extended to persons in the vale of life that possess talents to make them conspicuous among their contemporaries. None will assert that it ought to be confined to warriors, states-men, or literary men. Every traveller is struck with the late Lord Gardenstone's gallery of village por-traits, and disposed to compare them with the orig-inals whom he sees walking the streets. In sketching out the prominent features of the person under con-sideration, no injustice will be done him, it being my purpose to represent him in his genuine colours, without concealing his good qualities or exaggerating his faults.

He was the second son of a tenant in the Muir of Ochtertyre, whose predecessors, with the exception of one or two generations, had been seated there since the end of the sixteenth century, when they were called in writing Christiesons. The elder

brother John succeeded his father as tenant, and
had at one time two contiguous farms from my
father; but not finding it to answer, he gave up the
easter one. Having in my minority married the
widow of a tenant in the estate of Keir, he thought
proper to remove to her farm, leaving his brother
James in his own farm by way of *locum tenens*.
John was no eligible tenant: for though a man of
good understanding, his temper was harsh and liti-
gious, which proved ruinous to the poor man in the
long-run.[1] He being therefore out of the question,
his brother James made, in 1759, an offer to Mr
Moir for the farm, showing that he was able to stock
it. Though not accounted substantial, he proved
industrious and enterprising, which was the more
meritorious that, owing to his brother's deserting it,
the farm was not in good condition. In the year
1765, in common with his neighbour, he suffered
exceedingly from violent rains in the oat seed-time,
which were succeeded by some months of violent
drought, which stunted the crop, and stifled a great
part of the corn in the ear. By mere accident, I
had the good fortune to procure James £20, 11s.

---

[1] John had an unhappy quarrel with Archibald Stirling of Keir. Being
refused his wife's son's farm, he scourged it by taking a universal crop of
oats the year of the removal. For that and cutting wood, Keir prosecuted
him before the justices, and recovered high damages, which were suspended.
Wishing to save the man, I interposed with his master, who would have been
more gentle to him than he deserved; but the man was too high-minded to
stoop. The process went on, and if the damages were *modified*, he saved
nothing as the expense was enormous. I would have got him off for a third
or half of what it cost him.

from an uncle of his wife, which came in great stead to him at that critical time.[1] Next year we had a double crop, which made us forget the former one. From that time James throve apace, which he deserved the better that he lived liberally, and cultivated his farm to great purpose. The thing most against him in his first lease, was the asperity of his temper, which, joined to the hardness of his work, made it difficult for him to get servants when these were both cheap and plentiful; he was therefore glad to take up with such as none else cared to take: but he made the most of them. By degrees his children grew up, by whom he was both ably and cheaply served; and as he was at great pains to teach them, they were very docile. He made his sons successively hold the plough when only twelve or thirteen years of age; and there was hardly any out-of-doors work proper for them that his sons and daughters were not employed in. He had therefore no occasion for servants, or the occasional aid of strangers. At last they cut down the whole crop with expedition and effect. A more handsome or spirited band of reapers was seldom to be seen than James's progeny. If he kept up the *patria potestas* to the full, love was mingled with awe.

Though a prosperous man, encircled by a smiling

[1] One day that the late James Russel dined here, he mentioned how good Mr Andrew Kinross, an Episcopal clergyman that kept an academy, had been to his relations about Dunblane, who had in general turned out ill. I mentioned James's wife as a deserving person. Ere long, Mr Russel returned and made her and her husband very happy with good Mr Kinross's bounty.

It was, however, chiefly during the second lease
that James's genius and increasing diligence turned
to account. His eldest son was esteemed one of the
best ploughmen and best dressers of ground in the
country. It was astonishing how much work he
could put through his hands. Though he received his
father's *dicta* as if they had been oracles, the latter
paid him much deference, as he sometimes suggested
excellent hints. And for more than ten years they
had marvellous crops, everything going on like clockwork. Nor was it any reflection against them that
they commonly went further than they were bound by
the lease, being never below the standard prescribed.[1]

Yet at the very time when things seemed to go to
his mind, he sometimes suffered from obstinacy and
greed ; for oftener than once he kept his grain for a
couple of years rather than sell at the market price.
Though that is not a wise measure, he assured me
that he was no loser by it, owing to a turn of markets. In a word, I was vain of having such a tenant,
and never disposed to take an ungenerous advantage
of his exertions.

When his children grew up, James met with demands on their part which could hardly be evaded.
His daughters expected clothes and decorations to

but on being set loose they got home sooner than their master, being as positive as himself.

[1] Ere long, it will hardly be believed that James, at getting a new tack in
1779, *cheerfully* agreed to build a complete new steading for £100 Scots and
the timber. What was more, he and his sons moulded and burnt the whole
bricks, and built the office houses without the help of a mason.

put them on a footing with their neighbours—for
companions were out of the question.   The sons, too,
looked for a recompense for their long services.
Some of the latter he bred to business; and to such
as continued in family with him (who did not eat the
bread of idleness) he gave every year bills for their
wages.   Though there was justice in this, it might in
time have led to disputes and quarrels.   The eldest
son had surely the heaviest claim upon the common
stock, to the increase of which he had greatly contributed.   A more singular and deserving family,
conducted in a way peculiar to itself, is seldom to be
met with in any country.[1]

Although James was reputed obstinate and dis-
putatious, I saw nothing of it in the thirty-eight
years that he was my tenant, and that when some of
his brethren were troublesome and captious.   If sometimes paradoxical in his talk, and a little metaphysical in his ideas, I had no reason to complain of his
temper or procedure; on the contrary, he was ever
as ready to do his duty as I was to require it.   Our
only dispute did not last two days, when he submitted with a good grace to my demands.   If this did
not flow from gratitude, there was a vein of good
sense in it; for it behoves every wise tenant to be
upon good terms with his landlord.

---

[1] During the first tack he fed a cow on turnips and sold her by *living*
weight, as it should be ascertained by Mr Blackadder's machine.   The butcher
and he having differed, *toto cœlo*, the matter went to the Court of Session,
where, after a proof, the question was given for the butcher, to James's great
loss and sorrow.

The very circumstances upon which, with good reason, this extraordinary man plumed himself, involved him at length in difficulties from which it was no easy matter to extricate himself.[1] If he had already set off colonies of sons, there remained more than he had work for. His present farm was even too small to contain him and his eldest son, who was tired of having been long a servant, and desirous of having a farm of his own where he could marry and exert himself for his own behoof. Had the father judged wisely he should have resigned the farm to his son and have betaken himself to a pendicle or moderate farm, where he might have spent the evening of life in peace and independence. It is no easy matter to say whether James had realised much money towards the close of the second tack. The largeness of his family, and the expense of putting some of them in a way to do for themselves, were much against him. And be his funds what they would, he was certainly debtor to his sons for the bills given them in lieu of wages. From what he told me of the matter, had he himself been cut off suddenly, it would have been no easy matter to arrange his affairs.

In these circumstances the times when James and his eldest son resolved to take an extensive farm is uncertain, though from some incidents to be after-

[1] Mr Abercromby told me he was one day at Clackmannan with Colonel Dalrymple, when a tenant deep in arrears entreated for a delay till his sons should grow up, when he hoped to pay all. "Oh, man," said the Colonel, "I never knew what difficulties were till my young men grew up."

wards mentioned it would seem they had it in con-
templation for some time. But it was kept a dead
secret from me, who he knew was no friend to
deep speculators. When the conferences for a new
tack opened, James came forward with his usual
frankness, acceding readily to the conditions proposed; and had higher rents been asked he would
probably have been the foremost in his compliance.
If I had had the smallest suspicion of his design, I
would have excluded him from making an offer, however much I might regret the loss of such a tenant.

Somewhat more than three months after finishing
that conference, the farm of Raplock, belonging to
Cowan's Hospital, was let by public roup. That is no
eligible way of letting land in any case, but the more
reprehensible in a community which was already
too rich. There were several offerers, but James
Christie, jun., being the highest, was preferred, having
bid £3, 10s. 8d. per acre—which was about thirty
shillings higher than the former rent. In terms of
the articles, which required a cautioner, the father became surety for the new tenant. The vicinity of the
farm to Stirling and to water-carriage, were doubtless
great advantages, had not the land been in wretched
order—great parts of it being rendered *deaf* and
loose, from having been for ages manured with coal-
ashes dung. This was a very untoward circumstance
for a tenant, because it rendered summer fallow of
little use, ground in that condition spewing up the
roots of wheat and clover in severe frost. But the

capital objection was the size of the farm, which contained a hundred acres, which, at the enormous rent offered, was seemingly too great an undertaking for father and son, neither of whom was supposed to have a large capital. As an encouragement to the future tenant, he was assured by the articles of roup that the Hospital should build a mansion-house two storeys high with suitable offices, besides dividing the farm into fields and enclosing them with hedges, protected with palings and ditches. It is supposed that little less than £1000 has been laid out in that way since the tenant's entry, which must curtail the Hospital's profits greatly.

It is needless to inquire whether this bold and unadvised plan was devised by father or son, for both of them had a very teeming imagination. One thing is certain, the former entered into it with zeal and alacrity. He told me afterwards that everything had been arranged before the roup. It was indeed easy for them to obtain, a considerable time before, notice of the period at which it would be let. It was part of these plans that the old man should remain in my farm, while the eldest son and some of the brothers should migrate to Raplock. The taking these strong measures without my privity or consent was a very ungrateful return for all the kindness I had shown him from first to last, of which till now he seemed abundantly sensible. It was in truth an attempt to run my cheap farm against a very dear one. But the finest spun schemes sometimes fail, from not paying

proper attention to obvious circumstances. When
taking this seemingly desperate step, the father forgot
that his bargain with me was not concluded ; and
from what he knew of my sentiments and motives,
he could not be ignorant that he now stood on a
very different footing from what he had done at the
time of our communing.

I was equally astonished and offended upon being
told of the conduct of the father and son in that
matter, which savoured of infatuation and despair.
So far from being likely to better the family by
relieving it from difficulties, it was by most people
considered as a rash and ruinous bargain. But the
remedy was obvious, and however unpleasing it
might be to one of my disposition, there could be
no doubt of its being efficacious. I directed Mr
Burn to let James Christie know that I now considered the treaty for a renewal of his lease as at
an end. The very extraordinary step that he had
lately taken justified me, both in law and honour,
to remove a man who was no longer, from his other
engagements, fit to do justice to my farm. I was
therefore determined to get quit of him, be the
trouble and expense what it would. If that should
prove very hurtful to him, the fault was his, not
mine. He was, however, given to understand that
I wished to part with him in peace, since he could
no longer be my tenant. I was therefore inclined
to make him a present, in consideration of the
hedges he had reared, and of the high order into

which he had put his farm. He was at first stubborn and sulky, seemingly disposed to try the question. Having taken the best advice, I directed him to be served with a summons of removal. He then requested a conference, at which he behaved better than I expected; for after some conversation, he gave me to understand that he did not wish to keep the farm against my inclination, and was ready to sign an obligation to remove at the next Martinmas, provided all his claims should be referred to Mr Burn, my own man of business. I readily agreed to that proposition, which was evidently advantageous to all concerned; and after some bad humour on his part, we met at Stirling and signed the proper papers. At the conference his demands were not exorbitant, but hearing of new claims every day, I left the matter entirely to the arbiter, who I knew would do justice to the parties. In the course of that business James Christie displayed a very bad spirit, unlike anything I had ever seen in him before. I knew him to be wrong-headed and capricious, but was disposed to think better of his heart.

After his first claim and my answers had been laid before the arbiters, he gave in a very extraordinary paper, in which, to my utter astonishment, the man claimed from £400 to £500 for what he had done to a farm for which he had hardly paid £30 sterling. It was difficult to conceive how a number of the articles could enter into the imagination of any man of common-sense. He demanded large sums for having altered ridges, for not doing what he might have done, and for doing things beneficial to the farm, which he was not bound to do. They were so absurd and inadmissible, that I left them to the arbiter with very little argument, knowing that he would examine everything with his own eyes. I represented, however, that my consenting from the very first to make him an allowance for the hedges he had raised was an act of mere grace and favour on my part, seeing that in making these enclosures he had not complied with the letter or spirit of the tack of 1779, for he had neither asked nor obtained my consent. After the parties had been fully heard, Mr Burn pronounced his decree, rejecting all James Christie's claims except for the hedges and some houses, for which I was decerned to pay something more than £40. I thought myself very fortunate in escaping a lawsuit with a man who would have stuck at nothing to carry his point by false colourings and unfounded assertions. It was most fortunate that I did not accept of the offer made by him, but left matters open till the lease should be signed.

In the course of winter and spring, proper attention was paid to his method of cropping, being determined to prosecute him if he should transgress the rules prescribed by his lease in any material article. It was then discovered that this singular man had had windmills in his head for years; with much perverse in-ingenuity, and little to his own advantage, he had

contrived, in his removing crop, to have the greatest
possible quantity of land in oats that could be had
without transgressing the *letter* of the articles.   Had
I been disposed to try the question, he was in some
things within the lash of the law ; but it was surely
more dignified not to dirty my fingers with such a
man.   His devising a method of evading to a certain
extent the regulations prescribed by his tack may
show how difficult it is to guard against *collar policy*,
which is better calculated to gratify spleen or spite
than to fill the tenant's pockets.   It affords a hint in
future leases to provide that upon no pretext shall more
than a certain number of acres be cropped with oats,
particularly the removing crop, when tenants are commonly in worst temper.   And it shows the wisdom of
not entering too early into a treaty for a new lease ;
for had that been attempted without effect in this case,
James's genius for evasion and injuring his ground as
much as possible would have had more ample scope.
Indeed, such was the son's rapidity in ploughing the
farm after the crop was got in, that I found it no
easy matter to ascertain the kinds of grain that had
been sown the preceding season.

About the time that the arbiter pronounced his
award, James Christie sustained one of the greatest
afflictions which could have befallen him in this world,
by the death of his eldest son, whose youth and
vigorous frame seemed to promise long life.   Having
some complaint, the latter was advised to try the
effect of sea-water, which is at present regarded as a

specific for all diseases. At his bathing-quarters this poor young man was seized with a violent fever which baffled all medicine, his abundance of flesh and blood adding fuel to the flame. Neither did his having been till then almost a stranger to sickness render him the better patient. With hereditary positiveness, he insisted upon returning to his father's house while the fever was at its height; but having been conveyed home in a cart, he died a day or two after. I lamented the untimely fate of this young man, who, with a better education and better opportunities, might have figured in husbandry. It is sufficient to say, his virtues were his own; his foibles and peculiarities were derived from his father. Ill as I had been used by him, I commiserated him upon this occasion, seeing it had blasted the poor man's fondest wishes and views, whilst it subjected him to a load of care and fatigue which a person well advanced in years was not able to sustain; but being a man of strong nerves, he bore his loss with fortitude and equanimity, and prepared to remove to his new farm. Everything being at length adjusted, he carried off in a few days, with the help of his neighbours, a very abundant crop, which proved exceedingly advantageous to him. In this he acted according to his lease, which allowed the tenant at his removal liberty to sell or carry off the crop.

As soon as it was known that James was to go away, I had a number of applicants, to whom nothing could be said till the arbiter had pronounced his decree.[1] I then canvassed the merits of the candidates, and pitched on one that was likely to copy the former possessor in things laudable. And as I chose for myself, I likewise fixed the rent, Mr Burn having declined it as being connected with the new tenant. It was stipulated that the incoming tenant should pay five pounds a-year more than Christie had offered. He became also bound to pay the lime laid on by his predecessor in terms of the bargain. I have no reason to repent of my choice. If Christie did not do the farm justice the last year, his successor soon found means to put it into high order, which consoled me for the loss of an excellent tenant; and it is no less true than extraordinary, his crops have been all along equal, sometimes superior, to Christie's at Raplock. My farm was in great heart, the other in miserable order at his entry. The son, whose ardour of mind and skilful cultivation might have put a new face on it, was gone. As George Macgowan hardly pays 20s. an acre, whilst his predecessor pays £3, 10s. 8d., that is sufficient to explain the mystery.

It is needless to pursue this man's story any further than to mention some characteristic circumstances. He was doubtless well off during the three years' dearth and exorbitant prices, at which, in common

---

[1] When we met at Mr Burn's house to sign the papers, James said to me with great keenness, "Now, sir, do not let this farm for nothing, but make the most of it." I thanked him for his counsel, but said I would take my own way. Yet I assured him none should have it as cheap as he might have had it. It reminded me of the fox in the fable, who, having his tail cut off, wished his brethren to be treated in the same manner.

with most of his brethren, he rejoiced immoderately.
And it is allowed none carried his greed and harshness
further than he did at that calamitous season.　His
doubling the price of milk did not render him more
popular ; and if he charged carters, &c., extravagantly
high for hay, straw, chaff, &c., they retorted on him
by raising their dung in the same ratio.　So strong
indeed was the prejudice to him, that he found
great difficulty in getting hands at any price to
work for him.　And as soon as plenty was restored
by a fall of markets, none would deal with him that
could be supplied elsewhere.　Neither did his crotchets
about keeping up victual desert him at his new
habitation, for his barnyard and hayricks showed
all along his disposition to wait much too long for
a rise of markets.[1]　Had grain fluctuated between
25s. and 40s., this man might doubtless have paid
his present rent, he being *rendax non emax*.　What
effect three years of comparatively low prices may
have had on him I do not know, nor is he likely to
tell.　He has sufficient fortitude and pride, grafted
on obstinacy, to put a good face on the matter ; but
no man can achieve impossibilities.　It is very
doubtful whether he or his sons will be able
to hold the lease to its conclusion, as that depends upon circumstances.　But it may be safely

---

[1] While solacing himself with famine prices, he said one day, with equal folly
and falsehood, that he had made more in one year at Raplock than he had
done at Ochtertyre during nineteen years.　Had it not been for my systematic kindness and moderation, this ungrateful man never had been in a
condition to take his present farm.

affirmed that James would have been a happier and more respectable man, and probably a much richer one, had he not, in an evil hour, adventured beyond his depth at the instigation of his eldest son.[1] Although James Christie's spirit and manners seemed to have a strong tinge of republicanism, it savoured more of the sour leaven of the Covenanters in 1649 and 1650 than of Tom Paine's 'Liberty and Equality.'[2] Whatever might have been his sentiments upon politics, he did not join any of the democratic societies, or do anything not becoming a good subject. At the same time people's conduct and character are regulated by situation and example. Had my late tenant been born and bred in New England or Virginia, at the time "civil dudgeon first grew high," and men revolted they hardly knew why, he was likely to have taken the side of the insurgents with great zeal and pertinacity.

[1] Hitherto his exertions have neither been great nor costly, in point of time or cultivation. Possibly his failures in wheat and sown grass may have discouraged him ; and as men grow old they do not become more venturous. By all accounts he has incurred no expense in buying furniture suitable to his new house, and he is not likely to exceed in entertaining company, which costs other great farmers, who have good houses, much time and money.

[2] In 1792, hearing that James had been studying Paine's 'Liberty and Equality,' I exhorted him strenuously to keep aloof from clubs of pretended reformers, which he promised to do. The thing he seemed most disposed to rebel against was the town of Stirling's customs, which he evaded or disputed, little to his profit. No consideration would have made him take the constable oath, not even an absolution from his ministers, which quiets the consciences of other Antiburgher constables. In our last conversation, I entreated him not to quarrel rashly with his new masters, who, having a heavy public purse, might crush him even if he were right. And what was hardly to have been expected from a man so positive, he has hitherto lived on good terms with them.

Perhaps too much has been said of a man whose rank and education do not entitle him to be the subject of a biographical sketch ; but there is none from whose story landlords and tenants may draw more useful and instructive lessons. The former will see from it the expediency of keeping to forms with countrymen, who are wonderfully ingenious in finding loopholes at which they may creep out, and give trouble and disquietude to their superiors that were disposed to serve them. And it may teach husbandmen not to give too much way to whims and crotchets in the conduct of life ; for these, when carried far, and persisted in with obstinacy and spleen, are apt at times to make good parts useless or mischievous to the person that possesses them. Nor can it escape observation, that in giddy pragmatical times, the labourers of the ground cannot bear a full cup with more equanimity than persons of higher rank. And in treating me in the manner he did, my late tenant not only behaved with gross ingratitude, but also hurt his own interest materially. As far as in him lay he deserted his brethren. It discouraged landlords from being liberal or self-denied towards tenants, lest the latter might tread in his steps ; nay, it afforded them a plausible pretext to take the highest offers that were made them. Men who act under the influence of the selfish passions are so glad of any apology, that they are disposed to draw general rules and maxims from very sorry precedents when these support their systems.

It is painful to say that since that man left me
two other of my tenants have, like him, taken large
farms upon very high terms.   One would almost
imagine there was something in the air of Ochtertyre
to encourage the mania of speculating deep on land,
with little prospect of succeeding in their schemes.
But after having enlarged so much upon James
Christie, I shall be brief with regard to the other two,
who differed as much from him as from each other.

One of them concluded a very indifferent bargain
for a farm without consulting me.   It was the less
pardonable that his venerable father in his settlements
had enjoined him to take no steps of consequence
in his affairs without being advised by me, whom
the good man affectionately styled " his honoured
master." [1]   Indeed the only apology that can be made
for the son is his being headstrong and conceited—a
kind of man very likely to deceive himself when acting, as he imagines, most wisely.   Had he missed one
bad bargain, it was ten to one but he might have got
a worse one somewhere else.   Indignant as I was at
the conduct of this man, he was less in my power
than James Christie, for he had got his tack more
than a year before.   All that I or my heir can do
is to enforce constant residence on the part of the
tenant.   Though the clause for that purpose be clear
and explicit, yet at present none can say what effect

[1] It was observed before the old man's illness and death, that if he could
bequeath his mother-wit to his sons, it would be of much more advantage to
them in the journey of life than all his lying money.

the Court of Session, acting as a Court of Chancery, would give it. That, however, is of the less consequence to me, that the present tenant is likely to outlive me.

The other, who is a man of sound understanding, and one of the most spirited tenants in the country, acted a more candid and consistent part than the other. Both before and after getting a new lease, he avowed his intention to take another farm for one of his sons. To this there could be the less objection, that he was able to make ample provision for them without neglecting my farm. Having a great regard for the man, I earnestly beseeched him to act with caution at a time when proprietors, the best thought of, contended who should take the highest rents. Were he to act as rashly and absurdly as some of his neighbours, he would hurt himself and his family more than me. He might be assured that the infatuation which at present possessed landlords and tenants would ere long receive a rude shock, and therefore he had better have patience till he saw a decent bargain. When he informed me that he was in treaty for the farm which he afterwards took, I told him I did not know its value; but a person who buys at an extravagant rate must endeavour to make the most of it. I likewise disliked its size and situation, and reminded him that, as he was getting fast into years, he could no longer exert himself with his usual skill and energy. And if it was too great an undertaking for himself had he been in his prime, what must it be to his second son, a raw lad, if he should be cut off? He took my counsel in good part, but told me he had taken his resolution, and would close the bargain. That, I said, was his affair, not mine; it was my duty to express my real sentiments, and therefore nothing more remained for me but to wish him health and success. Two years ago he removed to his new farm, leaving his eldest son behind him in mine. To that young man, who is since married, he has conveyed the lease and stocking. It is hard to say what shall be the effects of those three men's conduct to themselves and their families, but it is hard that I or mine should suffer for their folly and precipitation. In that case, I may say with truth, I have been "more sinned against than sinning." It was one of those evils against which it was impossible to provide. Men whose stocks and attention are divided, cannot do proper justice to their original ones. Had they not fallen into this snare, they might have hurt themselves more essentially by becoming caution for other people; and therefore the landlord who is most solicitous to promote the interest of his tenants, will sometimes find his philanthropic purposes counteracted in a way which he could neither foresee nor prevent. Even parental care and guidance cannot prevent children from folly and excess; and the better provided they are, the greater in many cases is their peril.

Thus have I given a full and undisguised account of the way in which I have managed my small estate

for more than forty years. One would wish for something of the same kind, twice or thrice in a century.
Landlords and tenants might learn good lessons from
a review of the way in which the predecessors of the
former comported themselves in dealing with the
labourers of the ground, who constitute a useful and
important body in society.   A country is to be de-
nominated rich or poor, industrious or slovenly, from
its condition.   In some things I have perhaps gone
wrong; for he who is too solicitous to avoid certain
rocks and quicksands, is likely to incline too much to
the other side.   That I meant excellently well to my
family and people, will hardly be disputed by those
who are least partial to me and my maxims.   At my
outset in life, I endeavoured to tread in the steps of
my wisest and worthiest neighbours, who, whilst they
never lost sight of their own interest, retained some
of that kindness towards tenants and dependants
which had been one of the prominent and interesting
features of the nobility and gentry of former times.
I afterwards endeavoured to suit myself to circumstances; for I have lived in times when all ranks of
men have been changing their modes and manners
and sentiments, some for the better, and others for
the worse.   During my course there have been new
maxims laid down by proprietors and men of business
which sounded to me harsh, precipitate, and unpolitic.
Indeed for near twenty years after I commenced a
country gentleman, no character was in lower repute
than that of a harsh and avaricious landlord, it being

confined to a few persons whom nobody thought of
taking for their oracles. In those days it could not
be foreseen that the time would come when the raising
of rents should occupy the attention of proprietors
great and small. If this be at present the ruling
passion of that description of men, it surely does not
savour of heroism or patriotism. Without a portion
of self-denial and benevolence, neither public nor
private virtue can be very pure or attractive. What
a miserable state of society would it be, were it
creditable for every man to make as hard a bargain
as he could with his inferiors and dependants! It
must necessarily abound in poverty, rancour, and
chicane. No man, then, who wishes well to his
country, would like to see that vile spirit predominate
among his neighbours high or low. It would, if
carried to a great pitch, make the world little better
than a purgatory.

As far as concerns myself, I have found little inconvenience from the line of conduct pursued by me
from first to last. My income, moderate as it was,
enabled me to improve the place where I spent my
boyish years, and where I hope to draw my last
breath in peace. Nor have I been at a loss to entertain relations, neighbours, and friends, in the way
that became and pleased those whom I was chiefly
solicitous to please. Now that old age and infirmities
are fast approaching, there are certain luxuries which
at present rank among the necessaries of life. But
however desirable these may be, I can do without

them.   I should spurn a carriage which could not be
set up without overstretching rents.   In fine, had it
not been for the repeated fleeces of exorbitant taxes.
and what perhaps has been as distressful to persons
of moderate fortune, the great depreciation in the
value of money of late years, I should have been easy
if not rich.   If I have been treated with ingratitude
by tenants whom I wished to befriend, it affords no
good reason against my general views.   As well might
one declaim against friendship or kindred, because
these do not always answer our expectations.   The
causeless or capricious alienation of persons or families,
to whom one was long warmly attached, is one of the
evils of life that a mind of sensibility is least prepared
to bear up against.   But after the first emotions are
over, one must make the most of it, conscious that he
has deserved a very different treatment.

Fastidious or prejudiced readers will doubtless be
much disgusted with the egotisms which run through
this branch of my retrospects ; but should these lucu-
brations afford any useful hints to persons in the same
situation, commencing their course with good dispositions, I shall not think my labour lost.   If I have
censured the conduct of many landed men with
a degree of asperity, I have spared their persons.
Appello posteritatem.

CHAPTER XIII.

THE HIGHLANDERS.

AT present [first years of the nineteenth century] there are hardly any chieftains who live with their clan upon the old footing of familiarity, or who profess general hospitality. And a few years more will remove every person who remembers their little courts, or has seen them in the field in all their state. Ere long it must be the province of the antiquary to describe the life and manners of a real Highlander.

Their domestics of old were very numerous, though of a very different cast from the powdered lackeys of their successors. The industry and real usefulness of both were perhaps equal; yet were it possible for them now to meet, they would stare not a little at each other's dress and deportment. In every great Highland household, whether of a chieftain or a nobleman, besides a crowd of common servants, there were certain officers who contributed not a little to their master's dignity, and to the pleasure of his guests and retainers.

Anciently the first of these officers was the bard, who sometimes conjoined the office of *sennachie* or historian to that of . bard.   Highland bards have gradually declined for nearly two centuries, and are now utterly extinct ; excepting Neil M'Vurich, who lately officiated in that capacity to the Laird of Clanronald.

It appears strange that the bards should have been discarded at a time when ancient manners and customs of every kind were carefully cherished by the Highlanders. It could hardly proceed from economical motives, as the portion of land and other perquisites assigned the bard were inconsiderable.   They probably flourished most during the greatness of the Lords of the Isles, whose court resembled that of an old Gaelic Scots or Irish king.   And in the middle ages they were also entertained in the families of the territorial lords who held the countries of Atholl, Badenoch, Mar, Argyle, Ross, Sutherland, &c.   Notwithstanding their being mostly of Low-country extraction, yet in process of time they adopted the language and manners of their Highland vassals, in whom their strength consisted.   Upon the fall of the Lords of the Isles, their bards would find an asylum with some of the neighbouring chieftains who were not involved in their ruin.

At length the power of the Crown became very great, in consequence of which the nobility were induced, from motives of interest, to live much at Court.   And as Highland manners were in no estimation there, it behoved them to copy the modes and opinions of people of fashion in the Low country. At the Reformation, a tincture of letters was reckoned indispensably requisite both for them and the more considerable chieftains, in order that they might judge in the controversies about religion which then agitated the minds of men. The indifference of the nobility to the bards and their productions is not surprising, when we find persons of the same profession stigmatised by Act of Parliament *as idle and strang beggars*. Nothing damps the poetic fire more than the coldness of the great.

In a certain period of society the poet and musician were one and the same; and thus we see, both in Homer and in Ossian, that the bards accompanied their poetical effusions with the harp. In process of time, however, they became two distinct professions, little perhaps to the advantage of either. We cannot pretend even to guess at the era of this separation in the Highlands. But if we may believe tradition, there was, some ages ago, a harper as well as a bard in every great household in that country. At Duntulm Castle, the old seat of Lord Macdonald's family, is a window called the "Harper's Window." But there have been none of that profession in the Highlands for upwards of a century past. And it is the general opinion that they and the bards declined about the same time. The last Highlanders who played on the harp were two gentlemen of Atholl—Robertson of Lude and Stewart of Cluny.

For some ages past the piper seems to have been
a great favourite with the Highlanders. In time of
war he attended the clan, and roused their spirits by
his martial music. In peace he played every morning
before the chieftain's windows, strutting with stately
steps to and fro; and at meal-times, he regaled him
and his guests with favourite tunes. When the young
people were disposed to be merry, they danced with
great alacrity to his music. On solemn occasions, his
pipes were nicely ornamented with flags, on which
were painted the arms or device of his master. The
more considerable chieftains had three pipers at least,
by whom they were accompanied in their progresses.
being indeed a great part of their equipage.

The piper, as well as the other officers, had an
allowance in land, and the more eminent ones had
also a salary. There were two families at the head
of the profession — viz., the M'Rimins and the
M'Aslans, both of the Isle of Skye. One of the
former is said to have composed a song well known
in the Highlands, the burden of which is :—

" Oh for three hands !
One for the claymore, and two for the pipes !"

By them many who resorted from every part of the
country were bred, which probably gave rise to the
stories of a college of pipers in Skye.

The following anecdote, which a friend of mine
had from Lord John Drummond soon after the
circumstance happened, shows how much veneration

was paid a celebrated piper by his scholars. In the last rebellion a body of loyal Highlanders was defeated at Inverury, and the laird of M'Leod's chief piper, one of the M'Rimins, taken prisoner after a stout resistance. Next morning the rebel pipers did not play through the town as usual; upon which Lord John, who commanded, sent for them, and asked the reason of their neglect. They answered, that whilst M'Rimin, their master, was in captivity, their pipes were *dumb*, and nothing but his release could make them do their duty.

The more considerable chieftains had their principal standard-bearers and quartermasters, who were continued in some families from father to son.

"The latter (says Martin, speaking of Sir Donald M'Donald's quartermaster) has a right to all the hides killed upon any of the occasions mentioned above (the young chieftain's first military expedition and his inauguration as chief), and this I have seen exacted punctually, though the officer had no charter for the same, only custom.

"There were also (proceeds Martin), a number of young gentlemen called *Lucktarth*, or *gard de corps*, who always attended the chieftain at home and abroad; they were well trained in managing the sword and target, in wrestling, swimming, jumping, dancing, shooting with bows and arrows, and were stout seamen.

"Every chieftain had a bold armour-bearer, whose business was always to attend the person of his master night and day, to prevent any surprise, and this man was called *gallowglath*; he had likewise a double quantity of meat assigned him at every meal. The measure of meat usually given him is called to this day *beyfir*—that is, a man's portion, meaning thereby an extraordinary man, whose strength and courage distinguished him from other men."

The common men-servants, or *gillies*, were of old little employed within-doors; for the work presently performed by footmen was then the province of the maid-servants. Unless in a few chieftains' houses where Low-country manners were adopted in part, the latter waited at table and upon strangers. The men-servants were indeed principally employed about out-of-doors work, and in the chieftain's military progresses, or on visits. These customs were entirely similar to those of the heroic times, when the domestic offices were mostly performed by females, being esteemed too mean for any man that carried arms. It appears that the maid-servants attended the men even while they were bathing or dressing, a practice seemingly inconsistent with the modesty of the sex. Even the venerable Nestor was attended by a damsel in the camp.

The perquisites given of old to the several domestics when a cow was killed were as follows: the bard had the rump; the piper the udder; the *gallowglath* the great gut; the smith the head; the cook the skin; the weaver the neck; the butcher the brisket.

Not only the *duinewassals*, but strangers and travellers, were welcome, uninvited, to the chieftain's house and table. And occasionally the better sort of commons had access, and were treated with kindness; the chief distinction consisting in the liquor allotted to them, and in their place at table. According to tradition, those primitive manners subsisted in some noble Highland families as late as the middle of the last century, and they remained in all their purity among the remote chiefs within the last fifty years.

The cordial kindness with which guests of every denomination were received, must have afforded high entertainment to a sentimental traveller. Though his host might be rough and unpolished on other occasions, he suffered not the angry passions to enter under his roof; there he was all peace and love. He was indeed utterly a stranger to that disguise and self-command which constitute so capital a part of modern manners. If on some occasions they seem hardly compatible with truth and sincerity, they at least contribute to make men live quietly and easily together. The chieftain's affection to the members of his little community and his hospitality to strangers were warm and unrestrained as his enmities, public and private.

It is no wonder, then, that the manners of the old Highland gentry should differ materially from those of the present generation. The *duinewassals* and commons being bred together in the same sports and pursuits, and having the same friends and enemies, lived on the footing of familiarity which nowadays would be considered as mean and unbecoming. In every age and country, children, left to themselves, pay little regard to external circumstances. Spirit, generosity, and complacency of manners are the qualities that cement their young hearts. But in the Highlands the gentry, arrived at a state of manhood, carried those primeval manners a step further. In their social hours, when no strangers of distinction were present, the accidental differences of birth and fortune were sometimes forgotten, at least suspended. On these occasions, good sense and pleasantry of humour took the lead, however humble their possessor might be. And indeed, in troublesome times, every man's personal character was known, and a brave, a sagacious, and a faithful commoner was sure of the esteem and confidence of his superiors.

In this there was nothing unnatural or immoral. Men were originally on a level, and the distinctions introduced by degrees into society were so many infringements of the natural rights of mankind. And hence among every primitive people we find their rulers at pains to reconcile inferiors to their lot by kindness and familiarity.

We have hitherto viewed the familiarity which subsisted between the Highland gentry and their dependants in a favourable light; let us now consider the disadvantages that ensued from it. By conversing chiefly with inferiors, the chieftains and *duinewassals* were exposed, especially in their youth, to flattery and mistaken notions. Yet what state of society is so happily constituted that power and influence will not be haunted by sycophants, who study by insidious arts to mislead the youthful and the unwary? The company of equals and superiors has doubtless a happy influence in forming the tender mind, and in banishing that arrogance and self-conceit which are too often the effects of a domestic education.

But by means of this familiarity, the manners of all ranks of people in the Highlands were more upon a level than is usual in other countries. The gentry could hardly fail of borrowing some vulgarisms and oddities of behaviour from the commons, in whose company a great proportion of their time was spent.

In former times, however, these peculiarities remained almost unheeded. The chieftain and *duinewassals* lived much at home, and were little desirous of associating with their fellow-subjects of the south. Indeed they sometimes met in the camp, but there the former were chiefly distinguished by gallantry and spirit, and there was no leisure for intercourse or conversation. In their own country they had a standard of their own, by which men and women estimated each other's deportment. And whilst that was kept up to, there was no danger of any person's appearing awkward or ridiculous in the eyes of those whom he was most solicitous to please. The censures or contempt of the *Bolach Gald* (as the Lowlanders were termed in derision) gave the Highlanders little concern.

But the commons profited greatly from their familiarity with the gentry. They formed themselves on

the model of their superiors, and endeavoured to
adopt their manners and sentiments. And hence that
class of men in the Highlands have always been more
courteous and intelligent, more gallant in their manners, and more scrupulous about personal honour,
than persons of that humble station in other countries.

The last rebellion, however, gave occasion to memorable changes of every kind. Many chieftains lost
their lives either in the field or on the scaffold, or
were forced into exile, and their estates forfeited.
The whole weight of Government, for a number of
years, was employed to dissolve every tie between the
chief and the clan, and to abolish all distinctions
between the Highland and Lowland Scots. Even the
gentry who had not been engaged in the rebellion,
found it expedient to drop some of their national
customs, which either gave offence, or were prohibited
by law. It was doubtless with reluctance that people
advanced in life complied with these innovations.
But these old-fashioned gentlemen being now mostly
gone, their successors have no longer the same attachment either to their people or to ancient modes of
life. They affect the manners of the Lowland gentry,
but in general they retain their hospitality and courtesy to strangers, especially those that come properly
recommended.

The middling and inferior classes of Highlanders,
who have been little out of their own country, retain
the domestic manners of their forefathers in great
purity. In the remote countries, apart from military

roads, the traveller will meet with hospitality worthy
of the patriarchal or heroic times. The being a
stranger entitles him to a kind reception, provided
he comes not to molest or dispossess the old inhabitants. While the gentry entertain him with their
best fare, and convey him from place to place, he will
hardly pass a cottage without being offered something
to eat and drink; and the commons desire nothing in
return but news and a little tobacco. An old *duine-
wassal* tenant told me once with great simplicity,
that he allowed nobody to pass his house without
bread and cheese and a drink of milk or whey; but
if a gentleman or minister came into the glen, he
killed a lamb or a kid. And another of them hearing
of some gentlemen being landed from a boat, waited
some hours to invite us to his house, and was much
mortified at our having taken another way.

Such manners would please among savages, but in
the Highlands the traveller will meet with intelligent,
well - informed persons, whose conversation would
please in any country. And the Highlander, well
advanced in years, is never more agreeably employed
than in describing those modes of life which prevailed
in his youth, but now exist no more. To a well-disposed mind, kindness will more than compensate for
the want perhaps of a few superfluities that are the
boast of nations among whom hospitality is either
obsolete or unnecessary.

Their kindness also extends to mariners ship-
wrecked on their coasts. When a vessel is dis-

covered in distress, the inhabitants send out boats to
her relief, and try to bring her into harbour. If she
is driven ashore they do what they can to save the
crew and to secure the cargo for the owners. And
the unfortunate sufferers are afterwards billeted,
according to their rank, on the neighbouring families
till they are in a condition to proceed homewards.
It is unnecessary to quote Martin with regard to a
fact universally known.

Their conduct in this respect forms a notable contrast with that of the inhabitants of the more civilised
parts of the kingdom. The latter too often make no
scruple of plundering, nay, sometimes of murdering,
persons whom distress has driven on their coasts.

It will perhaps be said that hospitality is the virtue
of every sequestered people. Be it so; but this will
hardly account for the kind reception they give forlorn mariners whom they are probably never to see
again, and whom they might plunder with impunity.
It seems rather a branch of that primeval charity
which shines to greatest advantage among a simple
sequestered people, whose hearts are unspoiled by
commerce and its inseparable attendants, luxury and
selfishness. What interested motive will the lover of
system assign for the conduct of the Camerons, who,
in spite of the frowns of those in power, met the son
of their attainted chieftain in a body on his return
from France, and with many tears made him a
present of some hundred cows! Every feeling heart
will surely regret the necessity which constrained the

virtuous and enlightened statesmen of the last reign
to wage war with so noble and generous an attachment. Nay, a few years after, they thought proper
to refuse this very gentleman a grave among his
ancestors.

In a word, hospitality was regarded by the Highlanders as a first-rate virtue; and a man by shutting
his door against the meanest stranger would not only
have forfeited the esteem of his neighbours, but have
run a risk of being ill received wherever he or the
story was known. And by practising it universally,
even to the beggar in rags, valuable connections were
sometimes formed. The strangers, especially if under
circumstances of danger and distress, retained a lively
sense of the favour; and there are traditions of
attachments in the Highlands, founded on hospitality,
that are equally romantic with the story of Glaucus
and Diomed.

If, however, selfish motives must be assigned for
this virtue, none is more obvious than the amazing
thirst of the Highlanders for news. As there were
no periodical papers of intelligence amongst them,
they naturally expected much precious information
from a guest who came perhaps from a far country;
and thus a number of years ago a notorious criminal,
being brought to the place of execution, happened to
spy as he was mounting the gallows a man coming
towards them in some haste, whereupon he earnestly
requested the judge to be respited for a few minutes
till he might speak to that man,—which, being

complied with, all the wretch said to him was,
" What news ? "

Indeed the inquisitiveness of the common Highlanders is perhaps the least pleasing part of their
manners to a stranger. They stop passengers on the
road, asking them whence they come, where they are
going, what are their names and business ? But one
learns to evade them by answering their questions
indirectly, as they themselves constantly do. For
however curious a Highlander may be in other men's
matters, no man can be closer with regard to his own
affairs.

It must be confessed, nevertheless, that within these
few years the hospitality of the Highlanders is somewhat on the decline. The publication of books of
travels will, in this view, do no good, being likely to
make people artificial in their behaviour, and suspicious that their guests come to spy and tell of the
nakedness of the land. Gentlemen are not fond of
having their domestic economy disclosed, or of its
being published in print that they eat with horn
spoons. This, however, is chiefly confined to the
gentry and commons that live in the neighbourhood
of the military roads upon which there are inns for
the accommodation of travellers. To ensure a good
reception in private houses within reach of them,
acquaintance or recommendation is necessary —
circumstances never thought of in the more distant
countries.

At the first setting up of inns there were several

great originals among the publicans. A few of them
had some drops of gentle blood in their veins, which
they imagined could not be better evidenced to their
guests than by reversing the manners of their country. In place of being generous and disinterested
towards strangers, they thought too much could not
be charged; from being troublesomely kind and
officious, they were proud and inattentive.

A number of years ago I happened to be in a
Highland public-house, the master of which was more
high and mighty than the Duke at whose gate he
dwelt. An Anglo-Scots lady of the company was
so ill-advised as to reprimand this gentleman for the
dirtiness of his house and his assurance in taking the
first glass of wine to himself, upon which he and his
servants disappeared on the eve of dinner; and we,
who had fifteen miles to return in heavy rain, and
across a rapid river, were likely to have fared very ill.
But luckily for us, a person of the country came in,
and hearing from our host how ill he had been used
in his *own house*, procured us dinner and a night's
lodging, on condition the lady should ask pardon.
Mortifying as it was, she submitted to make concessions. And some years before, another of these gentlemen who condescended to sell whisky on the road
to one of the inland forts, refused a company admittance till they should give their word of honour not
to complain of any treatment they might meet with
in his house.

These inhospitable publicans are now dead, and

their successors have no pretensions to family pride. On the Highland roads there are at present some excellent houses, kept by persons properly educated, for which the traveller is indebted to the noble proprietors of the country.

I would, however, caution the English, and even my countrymen the Lowlanders, not to form any character of the Highlanders from the specimens they meet with in those inns. It is no pleasing view of human nature that men in their advances towards civilisation imbibe with more facility the vices rather than the virtues of an improved state. And in no capacity does the native Highlander make a worse figure than as an innkeeper, an ostler, or a waiter. He too often ingrafts pride, and sloth, and contempt of cleanliness, on the worst qualities of an English publican.

Yet a tour to the Highlands, though only to see the face of the country, will please every stranger who has taste to relish scenes of simple nature, in many of which there is a mixture of the great, the new, and the beautiful. Even they who connect health and poverty together, will find somewhat to admire in Taymouth, Dunkeld, and Blair, where nature is nicely smoothed and ornamented, and everything as neat as the citizen's villa of half an acre.

They, then, who only mean to pass through the Highlands, will do well to be in good-humour while on their journey. They are soon to revisit their own country, which abounds with every comfort and convenience of life. The little crosses and deficiencies that occur in their progress will be matter of merriment to themselves on their return home. Meanwhile, let them consider that the Spanish landlord is more proud and inattentive than the oldest-fashioned Highlander, and that the accommodation in many parts of Italy is more intolerable than the worst of our public-houses.

Nor were the southern parts of Scotland famous of old for inns. Moryson, who travelled through that country in the reign of Queen Elizabeth, says: " I never did hear or see that they had any public inns with signes hanging out ; but the better sort of citizens brew ale (their usual drink) which will distemper a stranger's body ; and the same citizens will entertain strangers or acquaintance on entreaty. Their bedsteads were then like cupboards in the wall, with doors to be open'd and shut at pleasure, so as we climbed up to our beds. They use but one sheet, open at the sides, but close at the sides and so doubled. "

Till of late years hunting was the favourite diversion of the Highlanders of every rank, and indeed their country was formerly well stored with venison and wild fowl. However strict great men might be with regard to their forests, they were at little pains to prevent interlopers from killing the feathered game, or even deer or roes, without the boundaries allotted for their own sport, or for supplying their kitchens.

Before the Disarming Act took place, when there

was no military expedition in view, both gentry and
commons spent much time in fishing and fowling,
accounting them manly and healthy exercises. But
of late years a number of Highland forests have
been disforested, and stocked with animals that
would sell at market. It seems strange that grouse
and blackcocks should be so much diminished of late,
when the Highlanders were disarmed, and none permitted to shoot but gentlemen, and that only at certain
seasons of the year. It is, however, owing partly to
the increase of sheep, and partly to the superior skill
of modern fowlers.

The great Highland families, both lords and chieftains, upon extraordinary occasions held what they
called *huntings*, to which their friends and neighbours were invited, and vassals and dependants were
bound to give suit and presence, in their best arms
and equipage. Martin tells us "that the chieftain is
usually attended with a numerous retinue when he
goes a-hunting the deer, this being his first specimen
of manly exercise. All his arms, clothes, and hunting
equipage are upon his return from the hill given to
the forester, according to custom." These *huntings*
were generally held in some wild forest remote from
the castle; and the victuals were prepared and
served up to the company in temporary houses or
huts, sometimes in the open air. There are curious
accounts of the *huntings* of the old Earls of Athole
and Mar to be found in Pitscottie's History and
in Pennant's 'Last Tour.' They were sometimes

political; and thus the first rendezvous of the Rebellion of 1715 was concerted at a great hunting on Mar; and a little before that of 1745, Lord Perth had numerous and splendid ones in his forest of Glenartney, in Strathearn.

One of Sir Duncan Campbell of Glenorchy's regulations in the year 1615 directs every tenant on his estate to make five *croftails* of iron for slaying the wolf, yearly. We know not the meaning of the word *croftail*. But the last Scotch statute about wolf-hunting was enacted in 1457.

Fairs may be classed among Highland diversions, being formerly attended by people of every rank. Though business was transacted at them, and every article bought which the country did not afford, yet pleasure and the hopes of meeting their friends and acquaintance were the true errands of most of the company. As in the Low country, they were generally held upon saints' days, especially that of the tutelar saint of the parish. In the Popish times, divine service preceded the business of the fair; and so deeply was this notion impressed on the minds of the remote Highlanders, that even of late years it was with difficulty they could be prevented from converting the Monday after the Communion into a market for the accommodation of the crowds assembled on that occasion.

The fair of Mull is the most considerable one in the West Highlands. It is held in August, upon the side of a high hill, four or five miles from any houses.

Thither great numbers of persons resort from all the
Western Isles and adjacent countries; and it is attended
by pedlars from the Low country, and sometimes from
Ireland.   It lasts a week ; and though it is now less
frequented by the gentry, it is still a season of great
festivity with the commons.   People who come from
a distance are obliged mostly to eat and sleep in tents
or temporary huts, where droll adventures often occurred.   In such a multitude of people quarrels were
unavoidable, though since the Disarming Act less
dangerous.   But of old, they sometimes occasioned
bloodshed ; for in a broil occasioned either by liquor
or ancient feuds, the contending parties were sure
to be assisted by their own clans ; and when blows
once began, it was no easy matter for any one to
be neutral.

In former times the young men, in their leisure
hours, employed themselves in wrestling, leaping, and
pitching stones; and much of their time was also
spent in learning their military exercises.   Hence.
shooting at marks with the bow or the gun, and
fencing with the broadsword, were considered rather
as business than a pastime.

Both sexes were passionately fond of dancing, which
consisted chiefly in reels and other simple figures.
The style of it is too well known to need any illus-
tration, being indeed more remarkable for the spirit
and agility of the performers than for its elegance
or grace.

On particular occasions the young people used to

perform a sort of Pyrrhic dance, which was exceedingly violent, in the course of which drawn swords were alternately flourished and leapt over.

But till of very late years a peculiar strain of conversation was the great amusement of all ranks and ages of people. In it the whole family, seated by a cheerful fire, contrived to pass the long winter nights with pleasure, without the aid of books; and through the day the old folks, who had no longer any relish for country sports, frequently met each other half-way, to talk over the feats of their youth, or the tales of other times. Little more than forty years ago it was the custom in some countries on Sunday, when there was no sermon within reach (a thing not uncommon), for the whole men of a valley to assemble dressed in their best clothes and arms. They then repaired in a body to the sunny side of a hill, where they sat for hours discoursing with great delight on various subjects.

Their conversation turned on the traditional knowledge of the Highlands in general, and of their own clan and country in particular. The genealogy of every man, from the chieftain to his lowest follower, was kept by memory alone, with a precision inferior only to that of the Jews. They had numberless anecdotes relative to the past and present times, together with other local topics, of which a polished commercial people can have little notion. In discussing these, an idle and illiterate, but acute and intelligent set of men, contrived to pass away their time, if not profitably, at least very much to their own satisfaction.

The old men communicated with the utmost care their histories and traditions to the rising generation, as they had received them from their fathers ; and nothing could exceed the avidity with which young people sucked in and retained this interesting information.

Their popular poetry was surely well suited to a country where little more than threescore years ago every person wished to be thought a soldier—husbandry, and even pasturage, being followed no further than necessity required. And till very lately, sheep and goats were regarded as the property of the wives, being beneath the attention of their husbands ; and the lowest fellow would have thought himself dishonoured by entering a byre or assisting at a sheepshearing.

A great proportion of the poems in question is said to have been composed in the course of the last three centuries by well-known Highland bards or rhapsodists, who made a livelihood by reciting poetry among their countrymen. And from time to time private persons indulged in poetical effusions to please themselves or their friends. Notwithstanding the coldness and neglect of the barons and chieftains towards their bards and their productions, the bulk of the gentry and people took great delight in their national poesy. The Highland muses are said to have drooped their wing more since the last

rebellion than at any preceding period. This is by
no means surprising when the changes that have
taken place in that country are considered. Something like a new state of society has been introduced,
which has given a different cast to their sentiments
and pursuits. The Highlanders have got a set of cares
and grievances unknown to their fathers, which are
very unfriendly to original composition. Their popular poetry might, with great propriety, be termed
pastorals for warriors. And great was their influence
upon the Highlanders of both sexes, from the highest
to the lowest. Their poetical tales, breathing a warlike spirit, were well calculated to inspire the men
with an ardent desire of imitating, on some future
occasion, their ancient worthies. The women, too,
who were passionately fond of them, regarded the
martial virtues as essential in a son or a lover; and
in every age and country, the wishes and sentiments
of that sex have a surprising dominion over the men.
When these circumstances are considered, can we be
at a loss to account for that heroic bravery which
distinguishes Highlanders at their first entering upon
action? These precepts and examples, which are set
before them in the engaging dress of poetry, aided by
congenial music, teach them that generous contempt
of danger, and even of death, to which the common
people of commercial countries seldom attain till they
have been thoroughly disciplined and familiarised
to war.

Even such as are most sceptical with regard to

Ossian must admit that, in the end of the sixteenth century, the Irish bards still made a considerable figure; and as their language and national features nearly resembled those of the Highlanders, so at a very *early* period their poetry was probably akin. Spenser the poet has indeed drawn a frightful picture of the morals of that order of men. Yet he admits "that some of their compositions" (as translated to him) "savoured of sweet wit and good invention, but skilled not of the goodly ornaments of poetry; yet were they sprinkled with some pretty flowers of their natural device, which gave good grace and comeliness to them, the which it is great pity to see so abused to the gracing of wickedness and vice." The acrimony of that author's language with regard to the Irish shows him to have been actuated by prejudice and personal injuries. National antipathy in a great genius is a sad proof of the weakness of human nature in its brightest form.

Over all the Highlands and in the Isles there are various kinds of songs which are sung to airs suited to the nature of the subject. But on the western coast, from Lorne and in all the Hebrides, *luinneags* are most in request. These are in general very short and of a plaintive cast, analogous to their best poetry, and they are sung by the women, not only at their diversions, but also during almost every kind of work where more than one person is employed, as milking cows and watching the folds, fulling of cloth, grinding of grain with the *quern* or hand-mill, cutting down of corn, or peeling oak-bark, and hay-making. The men, too, have *iorrams*, or songs for rowing, to which they keep time with their oars, as the women likewise do in their operations whenever their work admits of it. When the same airs are sung in their hours of relaxation, the time is marked by the motion of a napkin which all the performers lay hold of. In singing, one person leads the band, but in a certain part of the tune he stops to take breath, while the rest strike in and complete the air by pronouncing to it a chorus of words and syllables, generally of no signification.[1]

These songs greatly animate every person present, and therefore, when labourers appear to flag, a *luinneag* is commonly called for, which makes them for a while forget their toil and work with redoubled ardour. In travelling through the remote Highlands in harvest, the sound of these little bands on every side, " warbling their native wood-notes wild," joined to a most romantic scenery, has a most pleasing effect on the mind of a stranger.

The more tender and delicate airs were probably composed for the harp at an early period. There is a striking resemblance between them and the Irish harp

---

[1] Whoever desires more information with regard to the state and nature of Highland music, may consult a collection of Highland vocal airs published by Mr Patrick Macdonald, minister of Kilmore, in 1784, chiefly from his brother Joseph's MSS. Dr Young of Erskine, an eminent musician, superintended the publication and wrote the preface, in which the airs are classed and characterised. In it is inserted a beautiful letter from Joseph to his father. The dissertation, " Of the influence of poetry and music on the Highlanders," was furnished by me.

tunes. If the former are more short and simple, it is probably owing to the want of harpers for many years past, and to their being transmitted by tradition alone. Whereas the great old Irish families continued to the last to cherish their national music, for which purpose they entertained harpers in their households.

The St Kildans, who are great lovers of poetry and music, have a number of reels for dancing, which are either sung or played on the trump or Jew's harp, their only musical instrument. One or two of these sound uncommonly harsh even to one who can relish a wild Highland reel. Some of the notes seem to have been borrowed from the cries of the sea-fowl, which visit them at certain seasons of the year, and are considered as their great benefactors. But their elegiac music is in a more pleasing and natural strain, pathetic and melancholy, but exceedingly simple.

At the conclusion of the fishing season, when the winter store of their little commonwealth is safely deposited in a house called *Tigh-a-bharra*, its whole members resort thither, as being the largest room in their dominions, and hold a solemn assembly. On that occasion they sing with gratitude and joy one of their best reel airs to words importing—" What more would we have ? There is store of *cuddies* and *sayth*, of *perich* and *aluchan* (names of fishes), laid up for us in Tigh-a-bharra ! " Then follows an enumeration of the other kinds hung up around them.

For some hundred years the bagpipe has been the favourite musical instrument of the Highlanders. We cannot, however, ascertain by whom or at what period it was introduced. Perhaps it may have been brought in by the northern nations whose viceroys resided in the Western Isles for some centuries. Whether it be the *chorus* of Geraldus is submitted to those that are learned in musical antiquities.

A species of martial music sometimes sung, but more frequently played on the bagpipe, was in the highest estimation with all ranks of people. Even nowadays a *pibroch*—*i.e.*, a march—though it may disgust a delicate ear, rouses the native Highlander in the same way that the sound of the trumpet does the war-horse. It even produces effects little less marvellous than those which are recorded of ancient music. At the battle of Quebec in Sept. 1759, while the British troops were retreating with some precipitation, a field-officer of Fraser's regiment came up to the General and said with some warmth he had done wrong in forbidding the pipers to play that morning, since nothing animated the men so much on a day of action. The General bade him do as he pleased; and the pipers being ordered to play a favourite tune, the Highlanders who were going off returned to the place where they heard the music and formed with great composure.

The music of the bagpipe was not more in request with warriors than with the fair and the gay, who danced with great alacrity to any cheerful tunes the nature of which is generally known. They form a great contrast to the melancholy airs before mentioned, insomuch that one would hardly imagine them to be the same national music.

A considerable part of the pipe music has already perished, owing to its never being noted down, but played by the ear; and ere long the remainder is likely to be either lost, or performed in a slovenly manner. Formerly the want of notation was supplied by the earnest desire which every piper had to play with taste the tunes which he knew to be most acceptable to his patron.

In twenty years more it would be in vain to attempt a collection of the popular music of the Highlanders. Enough, however, remains to point out its spirit and tendency. To allow such a monument of antiquity utterly to perish would be a reflection on the taste and liberality of the present age. Though its intrinsic or comparative merit may not be great, it is nevertheless valuable as a specimen of the music which delighted the Gaelic Scots a thousand years ago, and which they probably derived from the Druidical bards. The music of the Thracians, and the airs sung by the Sicilian and Arcadian shepherds of old, were, it is imagined, much inferior to the compositions of Handel and Corelli. Yet every person of real taste would readily grasp at such precious fragments of ancient times, could these now be obtained.

The Highlanders were also passionately fond of

sgealachda, or romances, which were mostly in prose, though in a figurative and animated style. They are full of giants, necromancers, fairies, dragons, &c., such as we find in the 'Arabian Nights' Entertainments.' "Such hold" (says Mr Macpherson) "do they take of the memory, that few circumstances are ever omitted by those who have received them only by oral tradi- tion. What is still more surprising, the very language of the bards is still preserved."

One cannot forbear a wish that some of the best and most striking ones were collected and faithfully translated before they be irrecoverably lost. By this means many curious interesting anecdotes relative to the ancient Gaelic Scots might be rescued from oblivion. Less than half a century ago, when reading was little in request, these tales were listened to with the utmost avidity by persons of all ranks; and of later years they have been one of the chief entertain- ments of the common people.

These customs, however, are at present very much on the wane. Traditional history only subsists by means of a few old people who have outlived their contemporaries; and though poetry and music, as well as the *sgealachda,* may be retained a while longer in a few sequestered districts, they are likely to decrease every year. This has already taken place in countries where Gaelic is the mother tongue. The people of Breadalbane, Rannoch, Atholl, and the southern parts of Argyleshire, seldom sing *luinneags* at their work, though, little past memory of man, their forefathers practised it as constantly as the north-west Highlanders do at present.

Nor are those changes surprising. In most parts of the Highlands the young people of any substance are remarkable for motley ill-according manners. It is impossible for them to divest themselves of certain national peculiarities; yet they would fain copy the manners and customs of their commercial neighbours. They therefore affect to despise the tales and traditions of their fathers. Besides, high rents, and other cares and pursuits, unknown to the Highlanders of old, have given the minds of the rising generation a very new turn. Most of them are now strangers to that pastoral vacancy which is indispensably necessary to the acquiring by oral tradition a great stock of poetical or historical knowledge.

CHAPTER XIV.

HIGHLAND SUPERSTITIONS.

THERE are few countries in which there is a greater variety of superstitious practices than in the Highlands and Isles, notwithstanding the many changes which have taken place within the last thirty years.

Many of the peculiar customs and superstitions of the Highlanders seem to have been derived from the Druids, the priests of their forefathers. Upon the arrival of the Christian clergy the inhabitants would naturally listen to their doctrines and precepts, which had the charms of novelty and good tidings to recommend them. We may, however, reasonably suppose them warmly attached to many of the customs and opinions of their ancestors. An uncommon discernment and strength of mind are surely requisite to conquer those prejudices which have been imbibed in infant years. The clergy would be glad to have people embrace Christianity, trusting that in process of time a more thorough change would be effected. These notions were, however, too deeply impressed to be removed without a

violent change in manners and circumstances. And
hence it became necessary to connive at such of them
as were not ascribed to impious means.

The marriage contracts of the Highlanders were
settled in a singular manner. The men of both families assembled, attended by a number of their friends,
and the chieftain or landlord was commonly present
to do honour to his dependants. While it was the
custom to go armed on all occasions, they sometimes
went to the place of meeting in a sort of military
parade, with pipers playing before them. A hill or
rising ground was always chosen for this purpose,
generally half-way between the parties. As soon as
the bridegroom and his retinue appeared, an embassy
was despatched to them from the other party, de-
manding to know their errand, and whether they
meant peace or war. The messenger was told in return that they attended their friend, who came to demand a maid in marriage, naming the young woman.
This being reported, her father and those of his attendants who were advanced in years went aside and
considered the demand in form, though that matter
was commonly settled beforehand. After weighing
the young man's circumstances and connections, they
sent to let him know that her father agreed to the
match. This, however, produced a second message
from the bridegroom, intimating that he expected a
portion with the bride, upon which a conference was
proposed and accepted. The two companies joined,
and many compliments passed between them. The

spirits and shell were produced, and business began. There was no small address shown, and much time spent, in adjusting the articles; though, perhaps, a parcel of sheep or goats, a few cows, or a horse or two, were the subject in dispute.

There was no occasion for a conveyancer, for in that country, till very lately, all their contracts were verbal. The provisions upon both sides were easily remembered, and, in case of any dispute, could be adjusted by the witnesses that had been present. Nor did this often happen. A people who transact their business verbally are commonly more tenacious of their word than those among whom writ or oath is requisite. In such a case breach of promise would subject the party that failed to infamy and shame. And besides, in the Highlands, where the laws were little powerful, he would have been liable to private vengeance, without possessing the esteem of those who would have befriended him in almost every other cause.

If the preliminaries were adjusted, the whole company repaired to the bride's house, where an entertainment was provided. Then it was she made her first appearance, for before agreement it would have been reckoned indecent, and even ominous, to have seen her, or to have entered the house where she was. The bridegroom stayed in her house all night, and the day of marriage was fixed. Though some of these ceremonies are now performed in a loose manner, it is still the custom to meet upon eminences to settle their contracts of marriage.

From these ceremonies, one would conclude that in the Highlands fathers had an unlimited power over their children's affections. But there is hardly any country where parental authority is more passive than there. People marry very early, and without much regard to circumstances; and hence their union is generally the effect of mutual liking, seldom proceeding from interested motives, such as in commercial countries frequently influence one of the parties. Their pastoral life, and the strain of their poetry, contribute not a little to promote love-marriages. In following their cattle during the summer season, the young people of both sexes have opportunities of familiar undisturbed conversation, which, from their manners and climate, are seldom abused. Their songs and other poetical compositions abound also with examples of disinterested love. Nor have parents the same reasons for crossing their children's affections as in countries where there is a greater inequality of circumstances. They have little to give them in portion, and can seldom form plans of marrying them with a view to honour and interest. It is, however, reckoned dutiful to consult them before entering into that state, because they may thereby expect their blessing, and a share of the little they have.

A ceremonial so stately and cumbrous as the one we have described affords a presumption of its antiquity, and connection with laws and policy that have long been obsolete. There is a passage in Cæsar which may perhaps give us some light into its origin.

In describing the manners of the Gauls, he tells us—
" Viri quantas pecunias ab uxoribus dotis nomine ac-
ceperunt, tantas ex suis bonis, æstimatione facta, cum
dotibus communicant. Hujus omnis pecuniæ con-
junctim ratio habetur, fructusque servantur. Uter
eorum vita superavit, ad eum pars utriusque cum
fructibus superiorum temporum pervenit." From this
passage we may conclude that the Druids, who were
magistrates as well as priests, did not allow a matter
of such importance to be transacted without their
intervention. And as all their judicial proceedings
were held upon eminences in the open air, so marriage
articles would be adjusted in the same manner by
their authority.

In these times parents were probably intrusted
with the disposal of their children only in subordination to the Druids. The whole strain of their laws
and policy, as far as we are acquainted with them,
is of the most interested and oppressive kind. Now
nothing could tend more to establish their dominion
than such a regulation, by which they were enabled
to gratify, in a high degree, their favourites, and to
oppress in an equal proportion those they disliked.
We may, however, presume that when interested
motives did not occur, they would pay regard to the
inclinations of parents.

It seems likely that in the Druidical times marriages were consummated the same night the articles
were settled. This accounts for the modern custom of
the bridegroom's staying all night in the bride's house.

Upon the people's conversion to Christianity, they would be taught to honour their parents, and, as a proper expression of it, to consult them in their marriages. And hence there was an additional motive to continue the ancient ceremonies, in which that principle seemed to be enforced. The benediction of a priest became thereafter the essential part of marriage rites, in consequence of which another ceremonial was established, which differed little from that of other Christian countries.

At the celebration of marriage there was a custom in some parts of the Highlands of leaving the latchet of the bridegroom's left shoe loose, and of putting a piece of silver under his heel. The purpose of it was to prevent the effect of charms and incantations.

The birth of children is another event too capital to pass unmarked by religious observances expressive of gratitude and joy, and imploring the divine blessing upon the mother and the child. What wonder, then, if a lot of idle unmeaning ones should be superadded by a superstitious people?

There are certain rites practised in the Highlands on these occasions, which, as they are unconnected with Christianity, may be deemed remnants of paganism. Thus it was a received notion that a lying-in woman should never be left alone, for fear the fairies should steal her away, and substitute something in her room. Yet this notion, though seemingly ridiculous, was in the main sensible, since it secured her against the giddiness or neglect of her attendants.

Before the Highlanders were disarmed it was common to have a broadsword half drawn at the head of the bed or below the bolster. And on the north-east coast it is the first business of the midwife to set a lighted candle at each corner of the bed; whilst in other countries she takes a light or fiery peat and draws a circle thrice round the lying-in woman, moving it *deiseil*—*i.e.*, according to the course of the sun. This rite was not, however, peculiar to this occasion, being used by the Highlanders in many of their superstitions.

In some districts, so soon as the child is born the midwife ties a straw round its middle and then cuts it in three pieces. A live coal, or some sparks of fire, are commonly thrown into the water in which the infant is first bathed; and in Skye they throw a little of the water into the fire. It is usual in Breadalbane to put the end of a new-cut ash stick into the fire, and to receive with a spoon the juice which gushes out at the other end, a little of which is the first liquor put into the mouth of the new-born infant. It is uncertain whether this was done medicinally or with a superstitious view.

The burial of the dead gave occasion to a set of rites and customs which merit a more full investigation. A very considerable change in funeral rites must have taken place upon the conversion of the Gaelic Scots to Christianity. People were no longer permitted to bury their dead in cairns scattered through the fields, as that would have been looked on as a proof of paganism ; but they were directed to deposit the body in holy ground near some church or chapel. It was, however, necessary in these new places of sepulture to disturb the remains of the dead in order to make room for other inhabitants. But that the prejudices of the living might be as little shocked as possible, persons of the same family were commonly buried in the same spot. And thus they gratified the pleasing imagination that those who had been intimately connected in life, by blood or alliance, should again be united in the tomb.

Yet, notwithstanding the style of monuments was thus changed, the Highlanders were still passionately fond of having some memorial of their fame set up after their death, but we can only guess at the nature of their sepulchres for some ages after their conversion.

According to tradition, the following mode of interment was used in the Isles. They had no coffins, but built up the ends and sides of the grave with stone, and the bottom was flagged. The corpse was carried on a bier made of boards, and laid in its dead-clothes in the hole. After covering it up with earth there was a thick plank of oak laid above all, which was called *Daraga Sleigh*. There is one of these in the island of Lismore, where the Bishop of Argyle had his residence, and also another in a churchyard in Skye. The wood in both is almost consumed, and there is no tradition with regard to the people interred under them. Mr Macpherson gives an account of another manner of burial which took place in other parts of the Highlands. These primitive modes of burying have been long in desuetude.

In the churchyard of Luss, a parish inhabited in the last century mostly by Highlanders, there are some stone coffins, consisting of two pieces, which are shaped so as to receive a human body. They belong to some old tribes that have resided immemorially in that parish; but they can give no account at what period the coffins were made, nor of the persons for whom they were originally intended. The lids of them are ornamented with some rude carving, and they are probably two or three hundred years old.

Most of the Highland tombs are large stones laid flat upon the grave. These in general are plain, though others of them are adorned with hieroglyphical figures. Hard by the old cathedral of Lismore are some curious gravestones. One of them is over Steuart of Invernachyle, who lived about the middle of the sixteenth century; and upon it is the figure of a two-handed sword, which seems to have been the favourite weapon of the ancient Scots. On one side of the sword is a lion and on the other a unicorn. Below the point of the sword have been other figures, but they are now much defaced, and nothing can be made of them. Near Invernachyle lies his *caoll*, or foster-brother, who, as well as his master, is famous in the traditions of that country. There are several other stones in the churchyard with figures of animals engraved on them. They are, however, generally much defaced, and of such antiquity that neither their age nor the families for which they were intended can now be traced. Being at Killechrenan, upon the side of Lochow, I sent for an old man who was said to be well versed in tradition. In that churchyard are several hieroglyphical gravestones, though the two-handed sword is the capital emblem. My conductor told me that under one of these stones lay the Knight of Lochow (ancestor of the family of Argyle), who fell some hundred years before in a battle near the Loch. Here, said he, lay Baron M'Corkadale, and there Baron M'Arthur, giving some account of their families and fortune. The same kind of tombstones may be seen in the churchyard of Balquhidder in Perthshire, where some old tribes of Highlanders bury, particularly that branch of the M'Gregors of which the famous Rob Roy was descended. The stones laid over him and his family are indeed of that antiquity, that tradition is silent with regard to the era when they were made. Numberless instances of such monuments might be collected upon a survey of the burial-places of the Highland clans.

This practice, though a singular one, was nevertheless well suited to the ancient Highlanders. An epitaph could have contributed little to fame, since the persons in whose esteem the dead man wished to live could seldom read. Indeed at Icolmkil, where a number of ecclesiastics had their residence, it is not surprising to find inscriptions on a few tombs. But in the countries where all ranks of people were equally

illiterate, the connection between the emblems engraved and the character of the deceased would be
seen and confessed by his contemporaries. Thus a
lion or a two-handed sword were significant of valour,
an elephant of wisdom, or a dragon of a fierce and
implacable enemy ; and a hunter would be fitly characterised by hounds or deer. These figures, in con-
junction with the poetical tales of their bards and
sennachies, were so many helps to remembrance.

But for more than a century back emblematical
gravestones have been discontinued, and at present people in the remote Highlands content themselves with plain stones ; but wherever Low-country
manners preponderate, inscriptions are adopted.

While primitive customs were retained among that
people, no sooner did a person die than those about
him lifted the body from the bed. And after being
stretched, it was laid at full length on a board or
plank of wood, set either on stools or two timber
pins placed on the side of the wall ; and above it, at
some distance, another board was suspended from the
roof, over which a plaid or piece of cloth was thrown,
which hung down like a canopy. When it became
dark, candles or lights were set on the upper board.
And it was also the custom to lay some iron, cheese,
a plate with salt, and sometimes a green turf, on the
dead person's breast. Some of these things were perhaps used to prevent the corpse from swelling ; but
the salt, the iron, and the cheese, intimate some purpose of superstition. Of late years it is the custom

to lay the body on an ordinary bed; yet the practice
under consideration explains a phrase common on the
borders of the Low country with regard to an un-
buried person—viz., "that he is under the *boird*."
And *marbh thaisy ort*—*i.e.*, wishing one under the
canopy—is one of the most usual imprecations in the
Gaelic language.   It was the custom to burn the
straw or heather of which the dead man's bed was
composed, and this was commonly done on some
eminence at hand, and was considered as a signal of
death, and a summons to repair to the house.

Between this period and that of the interment,
the friends and neighbours of the deceased assembled
at night in the chamber where the corpse was laid.
This was called *Faire-mhairbh*, or the late wake.
The manner in which the Highlanders formerly behaved on these occasions must appear to strangers
indecent and unnatural.   During this period nothing
went on in the house of mourning but dancing and
other amusements.   Not only the men, who might be
supposed possessed of superior strength of mind, but
also the women, laid aside that decorum and melting
tenderness which are so becoming in the sex.   Even
the ties of nature and affinity seem to have been suspended: for a widow who had just lost her husband,
her own and her infant's only support, was constrained by the fashion to suppress her sorrow, and to
join in expressions of joy and merriment.   The nearest relation of the deceased, together with the stranger
of most distinction, commonly began the dance.   A

gentleman of Lorne told me that a good many years ago, being at a tenant's late wake, he was taken out to dance by the widow and her daughter; and I was also well informed that at another late wake a widow of the same country called out to the piper to play a merrier tune, for indeed her heart was like to break.

Till about twenty years ago, this custom subsisted in great purity in the West Highlands and Isles; but it is almost threescore since the eastern Highlanders carried it to the same pitch of extravagance. There were, however, strong traces of it among them, and even among the bordering Lowlanders, not long ago.

Upon the day of the burial, both men and women attended in great numbers. In old times it was the practice in the West Highlands (as it is still in Ireland) to hire women as mourners at the funerals of people of distinction. The females who were invited commonly sat in a cluster by themselves upon a neighbouring eminence till the corpse was brought out and laid upon two stools at the door. As soon as it appeared the women flocked around it, clapping their hands and raising hideous cries. And many of them tore their hair or head-dress, and shed tears plentifully.

The corpse was then put on a bier and carried successively by four men on their shoulders; the rest followed—a piper, or perhaps a number of pipers—playing some melancholy tune all the way before them. The chieftain's march was commonly the first played after they set out, and the last was one pecu-

liarly plaintive and suitable to the occasion, called
Cha till mi tuilich. The burden of this song, when
rendered into English, is, "In peace nor war shalt
thou ever return!" The women kept behind the
men, bewailing at intervals, in broken extempore
verses, the dead man; and praising him for his birth,
his achievements in war, his activity as a sportsman,
and for his generous hospitality and compassion to
the distressed. This was called the *coronach*—*i.e.*,
the dirge. The women of each valley through which
they passed joined in the procession, but they attended but a part of the way, and then returned. Even
female passengers who accidentally met the funeral
joined in the *coronach*, though perhaps strangers to
the deceased.

As it often happened that people made it their last
request to be buried at a considerable distance from
the place where they died, so on these occasions the
funeral procession made an odd appearance. The
whole company seemed to be running; and wherever
they rested, small cairns or heaps of stones were
raised to commemorate the corpse having halted on
that spot. It was reckoned decent and benevolent
for passengers to throw a stone into the heap.

As soon as the burial people approached the place
of interment, two men were despatched before to mark
out the grave. And when the corpse arrived, it was
carried *deis il*—*i.e.*, according to the course of the sun
—around the spot which had been chosen. After this
ceremony, the body was laid down hard by; the

pipers then gave over, the grave was dug, and the tartan plaid or other covering taken off. When the body was put into the earth, the women raised the *coronach* for a few minutes louder than ever, and then were silent. And after the grave was closed, the whole company sat down in the churchyard, and every person was served with meat, and liquor out of shells.

The *coronach* seems to have had no connection with that mode of Christianity which was professed by the Highlanders before the Reformation. On the contrary, we are told the Popish clergy were at pains to discountenance it, as being highly indecent. Indeed, religion was none of the topics employed in it.

The *coronach* is not practised now in any part of the Highlands or Isles. Upon the west coast, and in the neighbouring islands, it was common forty years ago; and it is said to have been last used in South Uist, which is inhabited by Roman Catholics. There is no tradition of its having been performed in the east Highlands for a century past. They have, however, some remains of its spirit in Mull, Skye, and St Kilda. In the two former, the nearest female relations mourn in the house in extempore verses. We shall here present the reader with an elegy from St Kilda, which breathes the spirit of the ancient *coronach*. It is the composition of a young woman who lost her husband by a fall from the rocks, when employed in catching fowls. In the original it is in verse, and sung to a plaintive tune which is much admired in the neighbouring islands.

"In yonder Soa[1] left I the youth whom I loved. But lately he skipped and bounded from rock to rock. Dexterous was he in making every instrument the farm required, diligent in bringing home my tender flock. You went, O my love! upon yon hanging cliff, but fear measured not thy steps. Thy foot only slipt—you fell—never more to rise! Thy blood stained yon sloping rock; thy brains lay scattered around; all thy wounds gushed at once. Floating on the surface of the deep, the cruel waves tore thee asunder. Thy mother came, her grey hairs uncovered by the *curch*;[2] thy sister came: we mourned together. Thy brother came; he lessened not the cry of sorrow. Gloomy and sad, we all beheld thee from afar. O thou that wast the sevenfold blessing of thy friends, the strong *Ton*[3] of their support! Now, alas! my share of the birds is heard screaming in the clouds, my share of the eggs is already seized on by the stronger party. In yonder Soa left I the youth whom I loved."

Critics who judge of other countries by the manners of their own may be disposed to doubt of the authenticity of this little poem—at least of its being composed by an illiterate woman. The friend who furnished me with it got the original in Skye, from people in whose veracity he had full confidence, who had no doubt of its being genuine. Besides, Martin, in describing the St Kildans, says: "These poor people do sometimes fall down as they climb the rocks, and perish. Their wives on such occasions

[1] Soa, a small rocky island near St Kilda.
[2] *Curch*, the head-dress of the Highlanders and the St Kildans.
[3] *Ton* is a rope of raw hides used by the St Kildans. It is the most necessary part of their furniture, and a young woman possessed of one is reckoned well portioned. In searching for fowls and eggs, one or two men take hold of the one end of the rope, and another is let down into the clefts of the rocks by the other end.

make doleful songs, which they call lamentations.
The chief topics are their courage, their dexterity
in climbing, and the great affection they showed
their wives and children."

Upon the western coast, and in the islands, pipers
still play at burials ; but it is upwards of thirty years
since women forbore their attendance on these occasions. In the eastern Highlands, funeral rites are
now as simple and naked as in the rest of Scotland.
If the pagans, and some denominations of Christians,
have carried them to an extravagant height, we perhaps
err on the other extreme. In performing the last
duty to our friends and neighbours, the consolations
of religion would make a deep impression on every
feeling heart ; and though prayers on such occasions
cannot benefit the dead, they might surely profit the
spectators.

In some Highland countries, the vulgar believed
that the ghost of the person last buried watched the
churchyard. Indeed no people were more convinced
of the existence of ghosts and apparitions than they.
There is, however, no occasion to enter into any detail of their notions on that subject, as they are the
same with those of the Lowlanders.

In every part of the Highlands, the less enlightened
of the people believe still in fairies. Their Gaelic
name, *Siochraidth*, seems to be a primitive word in
the language. Small green eminences are frequent in
that country, in the middle of which they are believed
to have their abode. Some old persons pretend to

have heard the noise of their pots and pans, and others the most ravishing music.

In Mull, Morven, and Breadalbane, when young children do not thrive, it is a prevailing opinion that exposing them a whole night on the top of an eminence will afford them *an dara cabhair*—i.e., the one relief or the other : soon recover them, or soon make an end of them. And it is believed that the exposing them in this way, forces the fairies who have substituted a shadow in their place to restore the real children. Some eminences are more famous in this way than others. They come still at the distance of several miles to expose their children at *Lochan-nan-lanh* in Breadalbane.

This is another remnant of paganism which is common to the Highlanders with most other European nations. Indeed the fairies have a near affinity to the nymphs of the woods, mountains, and rivers which occur so often in the classic writers, particularly in Ovid, whose 'Metamorphoses' is full of their amours and adventures with the people of the heroic times.

The various configurations in the fire are also supposed to be a species of spirits. They are called *Corracha capull*—i.e., the spectres or spirits of the hearth. The bluish appearances excited by stirring the embers are reckoned the signs of their existence. In the winter nights, it is still usual to frighten children with them ; and when such appearances abound, they are supposed to forebode bad weather.

In Skye and Raassa, the *Gruagach* seems to have
been a deity, or superior being, to whom some worship
was paid. We know too little of the mythology of
the Druids to be able to say what was his rank or
office among their gods. In the Isle of Skye there
is in Trotaig, near Aird, a round horizontal altar, called
Clach a Gruagaich—*i.e.*, the altar or stone of the
Gruagach. It is about five feet in diameter. There
are several others of the same kind in Skye and
Raassa. In the latter, there is a well called *Tobar a
Gruagaich*—*i.e.*, the Gruagach's well—to the east of
which there is a heap of stones. This being, it is said,
has often made his appearance; and he is described
by Martin with loose flowing hair, and a wand in
his hand.

Upon every Saturday, or on removing from the
winter-town to the *shealing*, the superstitious vulgar
never fail to spill some milk on the *Clach a Gruagaich*. Nor are libations confined to these islands.
When it blew a hurricane, an old man in Harris was
wont to pour water with some solemnity into the sea,
thinking thereby to appease its rage. The only
reason he could assign for this practice was, that he
had seen his father and grandfather do so before him.

In Breadalbane and Morven, it is customary to
pour upon the ground a little of the milk that is
brought to table. In Breadalbane, though the dairymaid has through negligence spilt milk or cream upon
the ground, it is reckoned ominous in the landlady
to make words about it. It is a common proverb,

"Perhaps there was a needful mouth waiting for it."
We cannot even pretend to guess for whom the last-
mentioned libations were intended in the pagan
times.

Besides the days set apart for the solemnisation of
marriages, births, and burials, there are in most
countries stated times for performing the more sacred
rites of religion. It is still practicable to trace the
Druidical festivals among the Highlanders. And
indeed those we are about to describe have either no
connection with Christianity, or are observed with
rites which plainly denote their origin.

The least considerable of them is that of midsummer. In the Highlands of Perthshire there are some
vestiges of it. The cowherd goes three times round
the fold, according to the course of the sun, with a
burning torch in his hand. They imagined this rite
had a tendency to purify their herds and flocks, and
to prevent diseases. At their return the landlady
makes an entertainment for the cowherd and his
associates.

The last day of October is another of these festivals. It is termed in Gaelic *Samhain*—i.e., a time
of rest and pleasure. And, indeed, it was so named
with propriety. The labours of the husbandman
were concluded for that year, a circumstance highly
agreeable to a people who were never famed for industry. At that time, too, they fared better than at
any other season, cattle and venison being in their
prime, and a fresh store of corn laid in. The ap-

proach of winter was no disagreeable prospect—the nights being spent beside a cheerful fire, in conversation, or in singing songs and telling tales.

On the evening of that day the young people of every hamlet assembled upon some eminence near the houses. There they made a bonfire of ferns or other fuel, cut the same day, which from the feast was called *Samh-nag* or *Savnag*, a fire of rest and pleasure. Around it was placed a circle of stones, one for each person of the families to whom they belonged. And when it grew dark the bonfire was kindled, at which a loud shout was set up. Then each person taking a torch of ferns or sticks in his hand, ran round the fire exulting; and sometimes they went into the adjacent fields, where, if there was another company, they visited the bonfire, taunting the others if inferior in any respect to themselves. After the fire was burned out they returned home, where a feast was prepared, and the remainder of the evening was spent in mirth and diversions of various kinds. Next morning they repaired betimes to the bonfire, where the situation of the stones was examined with much attention. If any of them were misplaced, or if the print of a foot could be discerned near any particular stone, it was imagined that the person for whom it was set would not live out the year. Of late years this is less attended to, but about the beginning of the present century it was regarded as a sure prediction.

The Hallowe'en fire is still kept up in some parts of

the Low country; but on the western coast and in the Isles it is never kindled, though the night is spent in merriment and entertainments.

On the west coast the following festival is, however, more attended to than in the more inland countries. On the evening before New Year's Day it is usual for the cowherd and the young people to meet together, and one of them is covered with a cow's hide. The rest of the company are provided with staves, to the end of which bits of raw hide are tied. The person covered with the hide runs thrice round the dwelling-house, *deiseil*—*i.e.*, according to the course of the sun; the rest pursue, beating the hide with their staves, and crying, "*A cholluinn, so cholluinn, so cholluinn a bhuilg bhui bhorcionn, buail an craicion*,"—that is, "Let us raise the noise louder and louder; let us beat the hide." They then come to the door of each dwelling-house, and one of them repeats some verses composed for the purpose.

When admission is granted, one of them pronounces within the threshold the *beannachadth-urlair*, or verses by which he pretends to draw down a blessing upon the whole family :—

> "Gum beannaichrad th' Dia
> An ligh 's na th' ann
> Eadar chuallaich
> Cloich as chrann
> Tomadaidh bidth
> Brat as cudach
> Slainte dhaoine
> Gu raibh ann," &c.

That is, "May God bless the house and all that belongs to it, cattle, stones, and timber! In plenty of meat, of bed and body clothes, and health of men, may it ever abound!" Then each burns in the fire a little of the bit of hide which is tied to the end of the staff. It is applied to the nose of every person and domestic animal that belongs to the house. This, they imagine, will tend much to secure them from diseases and other misfortunes during the ensuing year. The whole of the ceremony is called *Colluinn*, from the great noise which the hide makes. It is the principal remnant of superstition among the inhabitants of St Kilda.

On the morning of New Year's Day it is usual, in some parts of Breadalbane, to take a dog to the door, give him a bit of bread, and drive him out, pronouncing these words: "*Bis à choin duibh a' h uil eug carrchal a biodh a sligh gu coann bliadhna gu raibh a' d' chreubhaig.*" "Get away you dog! Whatever death of men, or loss of cattle, would happen in this house to the end of the present year, may it all light on your head!"

But the most considerable of the Druidical festivals is that of Beltane, or May-day, which was lately observed in some parts of the Highlands with extraordinary ceremonies. Of later years it is chiefly attended to by young people, persons advanced in years considering it as inconsistent with their gravity to give it any countenance. Yet a number of circumstances relative to it may be collected from tradition, or the conversation of very old people, who witnessed this feast in their youth, when the ancient rites were better observed.

This festival is called in Gaelic *Beal-tene*—*i.e.*, the fire of Bel. It may be thought improbable that the inhabitants of any part of Britain should worship by the same name the great deity of the Phœnicians, Syrians, and other Eastern nations. We are, however, informed that several branches of the Celtæ adored the sun under the name of Belenus. This appears from the following passage in Ausonius :—

> " Ætate quamquam viceris doctos prius,
>   Patera, fandi nobilis ;
> Tandem quod ævo floruisti proximo,
>   Juvenisque te vide senem,
> Honore mæstæ non carebis næniæ,
>   Doctor potentum Rhetorum.
> Tu Boiocasses, stirpe Druidarum salus,
>   Si fama non fallet fidem,
> Beleni sacratum ducis e templo Genus,
>   Et inde vobis nomina :
> Tibi, Paterne, sic ministros nuncupant
>   Appollinares Mystici ;
> Fratri patrique nomen a Phœbo datum,
>   Natoque de Delphis tuo."

The similarity of the names is obvious; though the Romans, from whom we derive our information, generally disfigured those of the Gauls which they had occasion to naturalise.

The tenets of the Druids are too much involved in darkness for us to ascertain the nature of their religious belief,—whether, like the Persians, they con-

sidered the sun to be the purest and most perfect
manifestation of the Supreme Being that was visible
to men ; or whether, like the grosser idolaters, they
imagined it the residence of a particular deity, who
animated its orb in the same manner that the soul
does a human body.

The first of May was surely a most proper time for
the more solemn adoration of the sun. Then the
vegetable and animal world felt in a peculiar manner
the genial influence of that planet. Everything in
that delightful season seemed to invite men, who
were strangers to true religion, to pay homage to that
beneficent being which was the apparent source of
light and heat.

Like the other public worship of the Druids, the
Beltane feast seems to have been performed on hills
or eminences. They thought it degrading to him
whose temple is the universe, to suppose that he
would dwell in any house made with hands. Their
sacrifices were therefore offered in the open air, frequently upon the tops of hills, where they were presented with the grandest views of nature, and were
nearest the seat of warmth and order. And, according to tradition, such was the manner of celebrating
this festival in the Highlands within the last hundred
years. But since the decline of superstition, it has
been celebrated by the people of each hamlet on some
hill or rising ground around which their cattle were
pasturing.

Thither the young folks repaired in the morning,

and cut a trench, on the summit of which a seat of
turf was formed for the company. And in the middle
a pile of wood or other fuel was placed, which of old
they kindled with *tein-eigin*—*i.e.*, forced-fire or *need-
fire*. Although, for many years past, they have been
contented with common fire, yet we shall now describe the process, because it will hereafter appear
that recourse is still had to the *tein-eigin* upon extraordinary emergencies.

The night before, all the fires in the country were
carefully extinguished, and next morning the materials for exciting this sacred fire were prepared. The
most primitive method seems to be that which was
used in the islands of Skye, Mull, and Tiree. A well-
seasoned plank of oak was procured, in the midst of
which a hole was bored. A wimble of the same timber was then applied, the end of which they fitted to
the hole. But in some parts of the mainland the
machinery was different. They used a frame of green
wood, of a square form, in the centre of which was an
axle-tree. In some places three times three persons,
in others three times nine, were required for turning
round by turns the axle-tree or wimble. If any of
them had been guilty of murder, adultery, theft, or
other atrocious crime, it was imagined either that the
fire would not kindle, or that it would be devoid of
its usual virtue. So soon as any sparks were emitted
by means of the violent friction, they applied a species
of agaric which grows on old birch-trees, and is very
combustible. This fire had the appearance of being

immediately derived from heaven, and manifold were the virtues ascribed to it. They esteemed it a preservative against witchcraft, and a sovereign remedy against malignant diseases, both in the human species and in cattle ; and by it the strongest poisons were supposed to have their nature changed.

After kindling the bonfire with the *tein-eigin* the company prepared their victuals. And as soon as they had finished their meal, they amused themselves a while in singing and dancing round the fire. Towards the close of the entertainment, the person who officiated as master of the feast produced a large cake baked with eggs and scalloped round the edge, called *am bonnach beal-tine*—*i.e.*, the Beltane cake. It was divided into a number of pieces, and distributed in great form to the company. There was one particular piece which whoever got was called *cailleach beal-tine*—*i.e.*, the Beltane *carline*, a term of great reproach. Upon his being known, part of the company laid hold of him and made a show of putting him into the fire ; but the majority interposing, he was rescued. And in some places they laid him flat on the ground, making as if they would quarter him. Afterwards he was pelted with egg-shells, and retained the odious appellation during the whole year. And while the feast was fresh in people's memory, they affected to speak of the *cailleach beal-tine* as dead.

This festival was longest observed in the interior Highlands, for towards the west coast the traces of

it are faintest.   In Glenorchy and Lorne, a large cake
is made on that day, which they consume in the
house; and in Mull it has a large hole in the middle,
through which each of the cows in the fold is
milked.   In Tiree it is of a triangular form.   The
more elderly people remember when this festival was
celebrated without-doors with some solemnity in both
these islands.   There are at present no vestiges of it
in Skye or the Long Island, the inhabitants of which
have substituted the *connach Micheil* or St Michael's
cake.   It is made at Michaelmas with milk and oatmeal, and some eggs are sprinkled on its surface.
Part of it is sent to the neighbours.

It is probable that at the original Beltane festival there were two fires kindled near one another.
When any person is in a critical dilemma, pressed on
each side by unsurmountable difficulties, the Highlanders have a proverb : *The e' eada anda theine
bealtuin*—*i.e.*, he is between the two Beltane fires.
There are in several parts small round hills, which, it
is like, owe their present names to such solemn uses.
One of the highest and most central in Icolmkil is
called *Cnoch-nan-ainneal*—*i.e.*, the hill of the fires.
There is another of the same name near the kirk of
Balquhidder ; and at Killin there is a round green
eminence which seems to have been raised by art.   It
is called *Tom-nan-ainneal*—*i.e.*, the eminence of the
fires.   Around it there are the remains of a circular wall about two feet high.   On the top a stone
stands upon end.   According to the tradition of the

inhabitants, it was a place of Druidical worship; and it was afterwards pitched on as the most venerable spot for holding courts of justice for the country of Breadalbane. The earth of this eminence is still thought to be possessed of some healing virtue, for when cattle are observed to be diseased some of it is sent for, which is rubbed on the part affected.

It is probable that, on the fall of the Druids, the stated sacrificing of men ceased; though, as Beltane had been a grand festival, the people were indulged in the performance of all the ancient rites except the death of the victim. And on the introduction of Christianity these were perhaps tolerated by the clergy, with a view of impressing on the minds of the laity a grateful sense of their deliverance from a cruel and bloody system of superstition.

It was, however, no easy matter to eradicate from the minds of the superstitious people notions which had taken deep root in their imaginations. Although in peaceable and prosperous times they were doubtless well pleased to be freed from stated sacrifices, it seems to have been their firm persuasion that the violent death of a man, upon any extraordinary crisis, was productive of the happiest effects. Nothing, it was imagined, would more infallibly stop the progress of a contagious distemper. Of these sentiments there are many traces in the *sgealachda* or romances of the Highlanders, which are valuable chiefly on account of their describing antiquated opinions and usages. And some stories of this kind, said to have happened in the Highlands somewhat more than a century ago, though perhaps false, show the general sense of the people. One of the more ancient traditions on this subject is recorded by Dr M'Pherson, who tells us that, "Columba understanding in a supernatural way that the sacred buildings he was to erect in Iona could never answer his purpose unless some person of consequence undertook voluntarily to be buried alive in the ground which was marked out for those structures, Oran with great spirit undertook this dreadful task. He was interred accordingly." Ridiculous as the whole tale is, it affords evidence of the notions of the ancient Gaelic Scots upon this head.

The *clordhe'-seunta*, or enchanted sword, so famous in the before-mentioned romances, which killed a man at every stroke, had its virtue communicated to it by the smith's piercing some person through the heart.

The violent death even of a brute is in some cases held to be of great avail. There is a disease called the *black spauld*, which sometimes rages like a pestilence among black cattle, the symptoms of which are a mortification in the legs and a corruption of the mass of blood. Among the other engines of superstition that are directed against this fatal malady, the first cow seized with it is commonly buried alive, and the other cattle are forced to pass backwards and forwards over the pit. At other times the heart is taken out of the beast alive, and then the carcass is buried.

It is remarkable that the leg affected is cut off, and hung up in some part of the house or byre, where it remains suspended, notwithstanding the seeming danger of infection. There is hardly a house in Mull where these may not be seen. This practice seems to have taken its rise antecedent to Christianity, as it reminds us of the pagan custom of hanging up offerings in their temples.

In Breadalbane, when a cow is observed to have symptoms of madness, there is recourse had to a peculiar process. They tie the legs of the mad creature, and throw her into a pit dug at the door of the fold. After covering the hole with earth, a large fire is kindled upon it; and the rest of the cattle are driven out, and forced to pass through the fire one by one.

The other festivals observed by more ignorant Protestants without any religious purpose, owe their origin to Popery. We shall mention some of them that seem peculiar to that people.

On the western coast and in the Isles, it is reckoned lucky to kill a goat at Christmas.

Upon the night before Candlemas, it is usual to make a bed with corn and hay, over which some blankets are laid, in a part of the house near the door. When it is ready, a person goes out and repeats three times, "*A' Bhrìd, a' Bhrìd, thig a sligh as gabh do heabaidh*,"—that is, "Bridget, Bridget, come in; thy bed is ready." One or more candles are left burning near it all night.

On the Thursday before Easter, it is customary in some parts of Breadalbane for the landlady to send out the boys to carry home a stick of rowan-tree.[1] Plenty of barley is boiled in a pot, and meal is added till a thick pudding is formed, which is always stirred about with the rowan-tree stick. And when the sun begins to set on the dunghill, the landlady looks out for fear of any spectator; then takes the stick with as much of the pudding as will adhere to it, and buries it in the top of the dunghill. This, it is thought, will add much to its fertilising qualities. The pudding serves the whole family for supper, and next day for breakfast.

Both the last-mentioned customs seem to have been originally pagan ones, though afterwards engrafted on Popery.

Among other ancient customs which, though exploded among civilised nations, are observed by the Highlanders, may be reckoned that of lucky and unlucky days. The first day of every quarter, Midsummer and New Year's Day, are reckoned the most fortunate times for accomplishing any design. Such as dealt in charms and incantations took care to rise for that purpose before the sun.

In Mull, ploughing, sowing, and reaping are always begun on Tuesday, though the most favourable weather be in this way frequently lost.

That day of the week on which the 3d of May falls is reckoned unlucky through the whole year, it being

[1] Sorbus Aucuparia, quicken tree or service tree.

believed that the spells of witches have more effect
then than at any other season.

In Morven, none will upon any account cast a peat
on Friday. And it is reckoned unlucky to number
the people or cattle belonging to any family, but more
particularly upon Friday. The cowherd knows every
creature committed to his charge by the colour, size,
and other particular marks, but is perhaps all along
ignorant of the sum total of his flock. And fishermen
do not care to confess the number of salmon or other
fish which they have taken at a draught or in a day,
imagining that this discovery would spoil their luck.

The age of the moon is also much attended to by
the vulgar Highlanders. It is alleged that in the
increase everything has a tendency to grow or stick
together. And hence in Skye, dykes of feal are only
made at that time. But peats are neither made nor
stacked then, even in favourable weather. There is a
foolish notion in some places that if a house takes fire
in the increase, the family to which it belongs will
thrive; but if it happens in the decrease, that they
will decline in their circumstances from that time
forward.

The belief of witchcraft and of the operations of
evil spirits gave occasion to pretenders of another
kind that were little less contemptible and flagitious.
Availing themselves of the credulity of their countrymen, these persons professed to counteract charms
and incantations. And, indeed, it is surprising that
any mischief should ever have been apprehended

from witches, since the Highlanders were provided with a variety of exorcisms and counter-charms, to say nothing of those of Popish origin.

There were, however, certain superstitious usages among them which, notwithstanding their pagan original, were practised without scruple or examination by persons who had the utmost abhorrence at necromancy of every kind. But the Highlanders appear to have entertained certain traditions of specific virtues and hidden qualities which, though false and frivolous, were implicitly believed by a rude people.

If we may indulge conjecture, the Druids considered the circle as the most sacred as well as the most perfect figure. They probably looked on circular motion as an expression of homage to the sun, which was one of their chief deities. It appears, however, that most of the remnants of Druidism retained by the Highlanders are performed *deiseil* — i.e., according to the course of the sun. It even enters sometimes into business. Thus in a great part of their country, when a horse is sold, the delivery is performed in this manner. As soon as the price is agreed on, the seller turns the horse round *deiseil*, and then puts the halter or mane into the purchaser's hands, together with a wisp of straw or grass, called *sop-seilbth* — i.e., the symbol of possession. He then retires; but if he happens to touch the horse even with his clothes, the delivery must be repeated. It is remarkable that Lord Seaforth's factor in Kintail continues to give possession merely by delivering before witnesses a *sop-seilbth* into the hands of the tenant.

The circle is also employed in rites of an opposite nature. When a Highlander is desirous that his curses and imprecations should take full effect, he turns round on his heel in the contrary direction to the sun. This ceremony is called *Tual*, and was of old practised by the pretenders to witchcraft. It is likely this was part of the ceremonial used by the Druids in pronouncing those sentences of excommunication which were so terrible and oppressive to the laity. Whatever be the origin of that rite, the vulgar Highlanders entertain notions regarding curses and execrations which are highly repugnant to the divine nature. They imagine that when pronounced *tual*, these are to be dreaded, whoever the person is that pours them forth. But those of the poor, the widow, and the fatherless are supposed never to miss their effect, even when uttered without just cause.

Some ailments were supposed curable by pronouncing certain *ubs*—*i.e.*, mystical rhymes, of which some persons pretended to be possessed. And it was a vulgar notion that the fox and other vermin might be driven away by the same means.

In Breadalbane, when a person is seized with a lingering fever, it is usual to lay him for a few minutes under clods of earth. The cure must be repeated thrice before or after sunset.

In Morven and Mull there are thin ledges of rock near the sea in which are large holes. Consumptive people are brought thither, and the tops of *nine* waves are taken into a dish, and thrown successively over the sick person's head. The top of the tenth is taken and thrown on the ground. Afterwards he goes thrice through the hole, taking care to go *deiseil*.

From these and other instances which occur in the course of these speculations, it would appear that, at some remote period, *three* and *nine* were considered as sacred numbers. And the modern Highlanders are at least disposed to consider them as the most fortunate.

The curing the diseases of cattle gave occasion to a variety of gross superstitions. Thus, although the *tein-eigin* be no longer used on Beltane day, it is still resorted to when the *black spauld* breaks out. The ceremonies before described are then practised—only it is made at the house where the disease first broke out, the fires of *nine* families having been previously extinguished. The cattle are then forced to pass through a fire kindled in this way; and every person carries home a portion of the *tein-eigin* to rekindle his fire.

Indeed, that people entertain a superstitious veneration for the element of fire, there is a proverb "that no ill comes from it"; and hence it is usual to put a few sparks into their vessels before they brew or churn, and also into their chests or repositories before they use them.

The *Leugh*—*i.e.*, a sacred stone—is another engine

of superstition derived from the Druids, which is used
by the Highlanders as well as by some other branches
of the Celtæ. The Highland ones are generally larger
than a hen's egg, and of much the same shape. Some
of them are of a substance like crystal, and others of
a sort of half-transparent pebble. There are few old
families of any consideration that have not one of
them in their possession. Various are the virtues
ascribed to them—some being accounted efficacious
in curing diseases, whilst others are supposed to
secure people against dangers. And therefore, not
many years ago, it was customary to lustrate persons,
who were about to go on a military expedition, with
water into which the *leugh* had been dipped.

Mr M'Dougal of Dunolly, a gentleman of Lorn, is
in possession of one of the most celebrated of these
stones. According to tradition it once belonged to
M'Dougal, Lord Lorn, a great family forfeited by
King Robert Bruce, of which Mr M'Dougal is reputed
the representative. Its fame for curing the diseases
of cattle is still very high with the common people of
Argyleshire; and long ago the first people of that
country sent for it on extraordinary occasions, and
gave their obligation to restore it under a severe pen-
alty. It has a flaw, concerning which they have a
foolish tradition. It had been lent, say they, to
somebody at a distance, with a strict charge to put
it in a clean place, instead of which it was put into a
sack of wool. This offended it so much, that it gave
a loud crack and flew home. Ridiculous as this may

seem, the same locomotive powers are ascribed by the Highlanders to other *leughs*, as well as to St Fillan's bell.

It is somewhat remarkable that the Highlanders should have no tradition about the misletoe, which was in such request among the Druids of Gaul. It seems probable, however, that the rowan-tree (of which we took notice before) was esteemed sacred by the Scots Druids. That tree is indeed often found hard by their cairns and circles of stone, and in modern times it is used by the Highlanders in some superstitious usages.

Thus on Hallowday and Beltane the people of Strathspey make a hoop of rowan-tree, through which all the sheep and lambs are forced to pass evening and morning. And in Breadalbane it is the custom for the dairymaid to drive the cattle to the sheals with a wand of that tree cut upon the day of removal, which is laid above the door until the cattle be going back again to the winter-town. This was reckoned a preservative against witchcraft.

It is likewise the practice to make that pin in ploughs and water-mills upon which the greatest stress is laid, of rowan-tree. And in Mull, Morven, and Breadalbane, some part of the churn is made of that timber.

Even human urine is supposed to be endued with hidden virtues. Thus in Breadalbane, when the plough is first yoked, it is the custom yearly to sprinkle the horses and then the coulter with it.

And the wisp of straw used for that purpose is thrown between the mould-board and the beam.

Upon the evening of every day at the end of a quarter of a year, and sometimes oftener, it is also customary to take a wisp of straw, dip it in human urine, and sprinkle all the cattle in the byre with it.

In Glenlyon, the landlady takes care to rise early on the morning of New Year's Day. She ties together some straw in the form of a brush, and sprinkles urine with it upon the whole family as they are getting out of bed.

In Morven and Breadalbane, the old woman who officiates as midwife commonly sprinkles the bed of the lying-in woman, and sometimes every person in the room, with the same liquor.

We learn from Strabo and Diodorus Siculus that the Celtic and other barbarous nations made use of human urine in their lustrations and lavations—a circumstance which these authors mention as a proof of the savage state of society in these nations.

Some virtues are likewise attributed by the Highlanders to silver and cheese. The former is reckoned a preservative against charms, and is applied to cure cutaneous eruptions. And they esteemed cheese a security against wandering in mist, from which they often run much in danger whilst passing over trackless muirs and mountains in foggy weather.

Iron is believed by that people to be possessed of certain virtues. We have already observed that a sword or other piece of iron is commonly laid under the bolster of a lying-in woman. And it is reckoned lucky if, at the beginning of any enterprise, a person happens to find any bit of iron. It was some time ago the practice of the Highlanders to swear by applying the hand to a bare sword. *Air an iarum nahomh—i.e.,* "upon the holy iron"—is to this day a common oath in the Western Isles.

In Breadalbane, when the black cattle are first housed, the sock of the plough, or some other piece of iron, is put in the door, and the cattle are made to pass over it.

They paid much attention to certain exterior signs and appearances. And thus omens which are exploded in more civilised countries, were not many years ago considered in a most serious light.

If the sportsman saw any person stepping over his gun or fishing-rod, he presumed but little on that day's diversion.

It was reckoned unlucky if a person, on setting out upon a journey or enterprise, stumbled over the threshold, or was obliged to return to the house from having forgot anything.

Sneezing is also deemed ominous. If it happens when one is making a bed, a little of the straw or heather is taken out and thrown into the fire, that so nothing may disturb the rest of such as sleep in it. The vulgar Highlanders believed that when a person sneezed, he was in danger of being carried off by fairies or spirits. To prevent this, it was common for some other person to say immediately, *Dia leat—*

i.e., "God preserve you." If one sneezed when alone, he must either *seun* or sanctify himself in the same way, or draw a circle about him with the point of a sword.

Much of the success in any work or enterprise is believed to depend on the *comhlaiche*, or first person or creature that presents itself. Thus upon going to sport, it is reckoned lucky to meet a horse, but very unfortunate to see a hare if she escapes. And on meeting any person or animal whom repeated experience has pronounced an unlucky *comhlaiche*, it is deemed some remedy if a stone is rolled towards him or it. We cannot help observing that among the Greeks, the way to avert an omen was either to throw a stone at the object, or, if it was an ominous animal, to kill it outright, that so the evil portended might fall on its own head.

The motions and appearances of the clouds were once considered as certain signs by which the skilful diviner might attain to the foreknowledge of futurity. On the evening before New Year's Day, if a black cloud appeared in any part of the horizon, it was thought to prognosticate a plague, a famine, or the death of some great man in that part of the country over which it appeared to set. Such a cloud was often thought to resemble a bull or the head of a bull, and therefore called *tarbh-coinnle.* About a century ago, it was customary in the Highlands of Perthshire to watch the motions of this cloud, even during the whole night, if it happened to continue so long visible in the hemisphere.

Another method of prediction common among the
Highlanders seems to be derived from the practice of
consulting the entrails and bones of such animals as
were sacrificed.   The different configurations observed
upon the transparent bones of beasts are attended to,
and conclusions are drawn much in the same way as
by reading tea or coffee grounds.   The scapula or
shoulder-blade of a black one-year-old sheep is commonly preferred.   The part ought to be boiled, so as
all the flesh may come easily off; and the bone must
receive no bruises or scratches.   The moon must not
change between the death of the creature and the making this use of its shoulder-blade.   About a century ago,
one of the fore-feet of the sheep devoted to this use was
cut off when alive.   In later times a certain portion of
the shoulder-blade was appropriated to every clan.

Not long ago there were many who pretended to
great skill in this sort of divination, some of whom
were persons of good moral character.   Several seemingly well-attested stories are still handed about in
which there is a surprising coincidence of the event
with the prediction.

The most striking remains of divination among the
Highlanders are, however, to be referred to that
branch of it which proceeds from supernatural impressions on the mind.   There are various kinds of
them—some more impious and absurd, and others
which are considered to be either harmless or else
unaccountable warnings of futurity which imply no
imputation of impiety.

In the most vigorous and striking exertion of all
the active powers, the discerning mind pierces not
with any certainty into that which is future; yet it
is imagined by the less enlightened of most countries,
that in a sleep, a swoon, upon the approach of death,
or in a fit of terror or fury, man is permitted to make
nearer approaches to his Maker; that he sees and can
foretell the most accidental events. A human creature, complete in every limb and organ, has no uncommon qualifications; while the vulgar believe that
the dumb, the deaf, and the weak are possessed of the
divine gift of prescience. Hence sprang the great credit
which was given to many of the prophecies and oracular
responses among the Greeks and Romans, and to the
responses by *taghairm* among the ancient Highlanders.

This word seems to be derived from *tù*, which in
some parts of the Highlands is still used for a spirit
or ghost, and from *ghairm*, calling upon or invoking.
It signifies, therefore, necromancy, or an invoking
of spirits.

There were different kinds of *taghairm*. One of
them was used in Skye not many years ago. The
diviner covered himself with a cow's hide, and repaired at night into some hollow - sounding cave,
whither the person who wanted to consult him followed soon after all alone. At the mouth of the cave
he proposed aloud the questions of which he wanted
a solution, and the man within pronounced the responses. Indeed the awful silence of night, the gloom-
iness of the place, and the sounding of the cave, must

have often produced in both a fit of terror not less suspensive of the due exercise of reason than fury or madness. I need hardly remind my learned readers that some of the most celebrated heathen oracles were given in caves.

Another species of it is called *taghairm an uisge*—*i.e., taghairm* by water. It was last used by a tenant of the name of M'Curdhean, whose predecessors were also farmers, for that art. He lived in the isle of Skye, near a beautiful cascade, on the water of *Easbhercraig;* and when consulted on any matter of consequence, he covered his whole body with a cow's hide, and placed himself between the water of the cascade and the rock. Another man attended with a heavy pole, whose office it was to give repeated strokes to the water and to the man concealed behind it, crying now and then, "*An maide fearna so?*"—*i.e.,* "Is this a stock of arn?" This operation was continued till it was perceived that M'Curdhean was frantic or furious; and he was then thought in a condition to answer the most important questions. He was frequently consulted about futurity, and his responses were attended to, as proceeding from something more than human. A degree of frenzy seems to have been affected by those Highland seers not unlike the description we have of the Sibyl:—

> "At Phœbi nondum patiens immanis in antro
> Bacchatur vates, magnum si pectore possit
> Excussisse deum : tantò magis ille fatigat
> Os rabidum, fera corda domans, fingitque premendo.

Various are the arts used by the younger people of
both sexes for discovering their future spouses. Whatever may have been their origin, they are performed
of late chiefly with a view of gratifying idle and
youthful curiosity. Halloween is reckoned the pro-
perest season for performing these rites, though the
last night of the year, or any night at the end of
a quarter is supposed to answer. And from the time
any means are used till the conclusion, silence and
gravity are reckoned indispensable. As these are
probably remnants of Druidism, we shall describe
some of them.

It is customary for young men and women to drop
the white of an egg into a glass of water, and from
its configurations in the water they guess at the
trade of their future spouses. If it can be had, a
hen's first egg is preferred. The yolk is then mixed
with oatmeal, and a great quantity of salt or soot;
and a trencher is laid on the back of a young maid,
and on it they bake the mixture into a cake, with
one foot within and the other without the threshold.
Where girdles are used, the cake is fired on the wrong
side. Upon going to bed, they eat part of it, and
put the remainder under their pillow. It is expected
that in a dream they shall see their future spouses
giving them drink.[1]

In the night-time it is customary for young women
to go thrice round the dwelling-house, according to
the course of the sun, holding a drawn sword in one

[1] Breadalbane, Mull, Skye.

hand and the scabbard in the other; or for young men to go in the same way, with a distaff or a spindle. It is believed that their future spouses will take the sword or distaff out of their hands, and restore it again. The sword is returned sheathed.[1]

Young men and women leave their shoes near a large fire, get to the top of the house, and look down through a silver brooch, or through a piece of cheese. It is thought they will then see the persons they are to marry removing their shoes from the fire; but no other body must be in that part of the house at the time.[1]

Young people go privately to hearken at their own or their neighbours' windows; and the first man or woman's name they happen to hear is reckoned that of their future love. This operation they call *far-clais* or *faire-cluais*—i.e., watching by the ear.

They go about sunset to pull three twigs of gall, pronouncing these words every time they pull one:—

"*Gaisean ruagh roid*
Dean damh gnothuch grad
Fios mo feanaen as mo ni
Chrad oi' choidfeas mi;"

that is, "Brown twig of gall, execute speedily my wish. By the dreams of this night may I certainly know my future lover and fortune." The twigs are brought home and set above the door; and the name of the first he or she that comes in is that of the future spouse. Upon going to bed the *gall* is

[1] Breadalbane.

put under the pillow, that the sweetheart may be dreamed of.

There yet remains a species of divination which, in modern times, seems peculiar to the Highlands and Isles. It is called *ta-shios* or *taibhse*—*i.e.*, the second sight. They who are reputed to possess this faculty can give no account how it was communicated to them; neither was it ever imagined to proceed from necromancy or other impious means, being esteemed an extraordinary and ineffable impression of futurity upon the mind. Most pretenders to it regret their possessing such a talent, and many of them are shy of confessing it. They seldom attempt to profit by their prescience, for that would be sufficient to discredit their pretensions.

In order to explain this matter, it will be proper to give an account of some peculiar notions held by the Highlanders. It is the popular belief that every person has his *tarbhs*—*i.e.*, spirit or *wraith* (as the vulgar call it) which attends him through life, and is sometimes visible in the same likeness and dress with the person whom it represents. It is also imagined that the spirits of such as are much attached to one's interest in this present world flock about his *tarbhs* upon the eve of any extraordinary emergency, particularly before death, when the spirit is supposed to hover about the grave. These incorporeal beings were said at times to attack the traveller by night, but none more severely than the persons whom they represent.

It is by the agency of these that the *tais-dear*, or person endowed with this faculty, is supposed to see future scenes and occurrences exhibited. And when any person's death is thus foretold, the funeral procession is sometimes beheld, in which every person is in the same dress and situation as at the real burial. At other times the shroud is observed to cover the body more or less, as death is at a greater or less distance. And if it is the fate of any to fall in battle, or by accidents, they appear with these very wounds which afterwards prove fatal.

At a period noways remote the second sight was believed by persons of every rank, not only in the Highlands, but also in the low country. And even at this day it has not lost its credit with a considerable proportion of the Highlanders. However incredible it may appear to strangers, a person well acquainted with that people will soon perceive that among them it is no reflection upon one's education or understanding to yield it a full assent. A number of stories, some of them recent, are in everybody's mouth, where the prediction and the event corresponded exactly. And in a few of them there is also evidence that the prophecy was known some time before it either took place or appeared probable. The characters of some of the witnesses appealed to set them above suspicion of being influenced by the prejudices of their illiterate countrymen. If it was a delusion in the *tais-dear*, they were led to credit him from the striking conformity betwixt the presage and its accomplishment—a species of evidence that is almost irresistible. They that are desirous of being informed of the nature of such tales may find a variety of them in Martin, and in a publication by one M'Leod.

Indeed, taking this pretension in the most favourable light, it must be owned that there are no slight presumptions against its existence. All the other faculties with which man is endued tend evidently to promote his happiness; this, however, can have no other effect but to make him more miserable. The pretenders to this talent uniformly own that they can seldom or never prevent their own fate, or that of others. As that ignorance of futurity which it is intended to remove is a principal source of these hopes and fears, that activity and diligence, upon which human happiness so much depends, so nothing could more effectually embitter the cup of life than a foreknowledge of future events, without any possibility of avoiding them.

But however unaccountable the second sight may be upon philosophical principles, it is no easy matter to withhold our assent to conclusions founded upon facts seemingly well authenticated. It was on no better evidence that Lucretius himself was forced to admit the reality of ghosts and spectres, though his principles led him to deny the existence of incorporeal beings of every kind.

Walking with the late Earl of Breadalbane at Taymouth in July 1769, and talking of the second sight, he told me of a very interesting conversation the late

Lord Lyttleton, the historian, &c., &c., had had with
him when his lordship made a visit at Taymouth
some years before.   Upon the Earl's saying that
there was much reason to believe the second sight a
delusion—at least, it could answer no good purpose
—Lord Lyttleton replied that his natural brother,
Admiral Smith, a man of great worth and sense, told
him a story which he was as well disposed to believe
as any matter of fact, and could he get another as
well vouched, he should, for his own part, believe
that there was such a faculty, let philosophers say
what they would about final causes and hypochondriac
humours.   The admiral said that once, when he commanded a squadron of observation in the Bay of
Biscay, there was a midshipman on board whose
father was a Highland gentleman.   It was his custom
to make the midshipmen dine at his table by turns.
One very fine day he made a signal to the captains of
the fleet to come and dine with him.   They came on
board, and after dinner, when conversing cheerfully
over their bottle, the admiral observed the young
Highlander, who was a fine spirited lad, staring very
strangely at the gentleman that sat next him, and
turning away from him with a look of aversion.
When the captains returned in the evening to their
ships, Mr Smith sent for the Highlander to his cabin,
and asked him what ailed him at the gentleman who
sat immediately above him at table ?   "How, admiral,
could I do otherwise, when he appeared to want his
head ?"   The admiral told him that was some of his

nonsense about the second sight, and such behaviour might involve him in quarrels. A day or two after a ship appeared in the offing, and a signal was made to the captain to chase. On coming up with her, a single broadside was fired before the strange vessel struck, which carried off the British captain's head.

Lord Breadalbane then begged leave to tell Lord Lyttleton a story that happened a few days before the battle of Culloden, which he had from the gentlemen of the Argyleshire Militia. Captain Campbell of Ballimore, a nephew of Sir Duncan Campbell, had a half-witted fellow in his company, a great pretender to the second sight. He said to some of his companions, " What can be the reason that my captain has a stream of blood running down his brow ?" This story was whispered through the troops, and at last came to Captain Campbell's ears, who made light of it. Towards the end of the battle, the Argyleshire Militia were ordered to pull down a park wall on the flank of the Highlanders to admit the king's cavalry. In performing this piece of duty, Captain Campbell received a musket-shot in his brow which killed him. And in the month of August of that year I saw, at Mr Campbell of Aros's house in Mull, a daughter of that gentleman, who assured me of the truth of that story in all its parts, which was known to her family and all Argyleshire. These two stories are better authenticated than most of them that used to be told. I shall leave them to the reader without further commentary.

I shall tell a third one, which I had from the late David Home Stewart of Argaty, who was neither a weak nor superstitious man. Coming one day into the kitchen at breakfast - time, his *herd*, who was supposed to have the second sight, threw a dish from him, which had nearly hit his master. "What do you mean by that, you rascal?" said Argaty. "Oh," said he, "my fellow-servant is plaguing me with plunging in the water." In a few weeks news came that the poor man had been drowned in fording the Teith at the ford of Torry.

It is certain that hardly any are said to possess this faculty, but the illiterate, the ignorant, and the superstitious. Nor is it confined to the human species, it being a received opinion that dogs and horses also enjoy it. Thus when a dog howls, or a horse starts aside in the night time without any apparent reason, it is believed to proceed from a vision. The very pretensions to it die away in the same proportion that knowledge acquires footing. And many who were once famed for their gifts are now ashamed to own that they ever pretended to it. If at any time, from the hopes and fears of the people, the demand for diviners was great, they were found to multiply in proportion. And thus in the year 1745 the Isle of Skye swarmed with prophets.

Their predictions were generally conceived in ambiguous terms, and limited to no precise time. If the events happened within a twelvemonth or two, it was reckoned sufficient. Besides, death, which was the principal object of them, is the most uncertain as well as the most capital event that can befall man. There are several chances that the most healthy person may die within a year or two; and therefore it is not surprising if, in many instances, the prophecy should be verified, and that in a few there should be a remarkable coincidence of circumstances with the presage. Those stories are handed about, and establish the belief of the second sight; whilst the numerous predictions which never came to pass are either unheeded or soon forgot.

Like Mahomet's visions, the second sight seems to have derived much of its credit from certain fits of convulsion, to which the most celebrated pretenders to it are often subject. The very first appearances of that disorder are presumed by the spectators to arise from that horror which some extraordinary vision excites. And there are few Highlanders who had not rather acquiesce in the imputation of this talent than own themselves subject to such a loathsome distemper. Of this fact several examples could be given.

As convulsive diseases are sometimes hereditary in families, it is observed that pretensions to the second sight are also transmitted from father to son. And as it is uncertain when the convulsive fit may seize them, so the persons who claim this faculty confess that a vision comes of itself, and that they can never command one at pleasure.

It is little to be doubted, however, but that many persons of a weak complexion actually imagined they saw those very scenes which they pretended to describe. Skye, which has long been the favourite abode of those visionaries, seems well fitted for producing such habits of mind. It is seldom free from rain, and never almost without mist or hazy fogs. The persons that are most famous for their predictions are often observed to have something wild and uncommon in their appearance; their face being an index of a disordered imagination.

In the year 1769, I had an opportunity of seeing a pretender to the second sight at a gentleman's house in Appin. His name was M'Coan, a native of Mull, about thirty-seven years of age, a sort of vagrant, who subsisted by his pretensions to divination and the knowledge of herbs. There was something singular and uncouth in his appearance, which made it probable he might have a tincture of the visionary and hypochondriac in his disposition. At the same time he was by no means deficient in low cunning and the other arts which are necessary to cozen credulous men; and instead of affecting a degree of modesty with regard to his gifts, as was done by those who had any reputation, he boasted of his prescience, and imputed his cures to supernatural means. Indeed his credit was very low with the gentry and better sort of people; yet they who understood no English became dupes to his pretended skill in curing or preventing disease in cattle.

It being a wet afternoon, I had him examined in the Gaelic language by two gentlemen of character; and the substance of what he said interpreted and reduced to writing. He not only pretended to the second sight, but to a power of preventing the operations of witches and spirits; which last, he affirmed, he often saw and conversed with. He denied his using charms, though indeed the simples and herbs applied by him would have no effect in another person's hands. He said he never ate meat at burials, because the substance of it is consumed by spirits, of whom there is always a number present. Being told that there must be some substance in burial meat, since people sometimes live on the fragments for some days, he said that those who had not the second sight, like him, might *think* they reaped nourishment from it. He was then asked how people came to be intoxicated at funerals? to which he answered that he never saw spirits taste either whisky or other strong liquors. He also professed to restore the substance of milk and malt when taken away; for he admitted that it was not the quantity but the quality which was diminished by witches or spirits. And he produced certificates of the feats he had performed in that way. Though he could apply his cures at other seasons, yet the most efficacious times were the first days of the four quarters of the year. Being asked whether his parish minister knew of his pretensions; he said he did, and what could he say to them? I was very anxious

to learn when the violent rains would cease; but he
did not pretend to foretell anything relative to the
weather, nor to his own person : though if he had
cattle he could cure them.

At last he grew suspicious that we wanted to entrap him, and would answer no more questions. In
short, this creature, though deemed an impostor even
by those who firmly believed the second sight, was
so far valuable, that he spoke without disguise the
notions which a century before had passed current
among the Highlanders of every rank.

The little skill of the Highlanders in physic and
natural philosophy gave occasion to many absurd and
inexcusable superstitions. Their cures were chiefly
effected by simples, which frequently failed in an
acute or complicated distemper. And when their
cattle, in which the wealth of an uncultivated country consisted, were seized with a pestilential disorder
which threatened general ruin, how natural was it
for credulous, ignorant men, who despaired of relief
from natural means, to resort to unhallowed rites !
In sickness, too, the friends and families of the person
in distress thought it lawful to preserve by every
method a valuable life; for these the goodness and
innocence of the end seemed to excuse and sanctify
the means.

Indeed there is an unaccountable propensity in
ignorant unprincipled minds to believe the marvellous, and to imagine that on extraordinary occasions
some powerful invisible being will interpose in their

behalf. And when particular persons were reputed, by the general voice of a country, to be possessed of the means of obtaining such precious deliverances, we cannot wonder that these delusive arts should be in high estimation.

One cannot help wondering that the Highlanders who embraced the Protestant faith should have been allowed to persist so long in the use of such superstitious practices. But the Reformed clergy, in times of danger and alarm, were chiefly solicitous to root out the errors and corruptions of Popery. They were, indeed, too few in number, and too widely scattered, to be able to eradicate from the minds of a people, overrun with prejudices of ancient standing, false notions of every kind. In spite of all their care and attention some Popish usages were retained in sequestered districts. Though disposed to give heed to the injunctions and admonitions of their spiritual guides, they would have listened to them with disgust had they all at once prescribed a set of rules which they esteemed salutary and efficacious when labouring under disease or apprehension.

Let us also remember that the clergy at and since the Reformation, being natives of the Highlands, imbibed insensibly in their younger years a degree of veneration for the peculiar notions and customs of their countrymen — a prepossession which even the strongest, best-informed minds are not prepared to reject. In polished commercial nations, superstitious unmeaning usages and opinions are chiefly to be found

among the lower classes of people.   If the children of
persons of rank and education hear many ridiculous
tales in the nursery, then wrong impressions are soon
effaced by means of reading and keeping good company ; whereas in the Highlands, less than a century
ago, the gentry were as much infected with superstition as the vulgar.

Upon the whole, if the modern Highlanders be
more superstitious and credulous than the Lowlanders
or English, many of their peculiarities have of late
years received a rude shock.   Their country is now
accessible to strangers, who have introduced new manners and ways of thinking among them.   Such Highlanders as went abroad to push their fortune met with
much ridicule on account of their prejudices and prepossessions.   Not being able to answer the objections
to them, they began to waver, the rather that nothing
of the same kind was to be seen in other countries.
Upon their return home they were disposed to ridicule
their friends and neighbours.   If it be difficult to
make persons advanced in years relinquish opinions
sucked in with their mother's milk, these are now, in
a great measure, given up by the rising generation.
Meanwhile, in the Popish counties, and even in some
sequestered Protestant districts, a degree of superstition will continue to lurk, until prudent and effectual
measures shall be taken to undeceive and instruct the
Highlanders in their duty.

CHAPTER XV.

THE HIGHLANDS AND THE REBELLIONS.

THROUGH the greatest part of her reign, Queen Anne appears to have adopted her predecessors' plans with regard to the Highlanders. They had no personal dislike to that princess; on the contrary, they revered her for her father's sake. As she was childless, the adherents of the abdicated family entertained all along the most sanguine hopes that at her death the crown would devolve on the lineal heir. Meanwhile, though continually engaged in plots to procure a restoration, it was none of the least happy circumstances of her glorious reign that its peace at home was never disturbed by open rebellion. Yet the settlement of the crown on the house of Hanover, and the union of the kingdoms, were exceedingly offensive to the bulk of the nobility and gentry of Scotland; and had the Queen been less popular and powerful, their discontent might have occasioned a formidable civil war. But even the bitterest enemies to those measures looked on them as the deeds of her Whig Ministers, to which she had unwillingly consented.

Her conduct for the last four years of her life makes it likely she wished her brother to succeed her.

It is not surprising, therefore, that when George I., who was a stranger to the persons and language of his new subjects, ascended the throne, the ferments that had been so long smothered should burst out with violence. A rebellion broke out the year after his arrival, which required all the wisdom and vigour of that magnanimous prince to encounter. It is true he was powerfully supported at home and abroad, a great majority of the English, and the whole Presbyterians of Scotland, being zealous in his cause. But he had only an inconsiderable standing army to oppose his enemies; and it required time before he could raise more troops or get foreign auxiliaries.

The insurgents consisted of people who till then had seldom acted in concert. The Highlanders and the avowed partisans of the family of Stuart were joined by disgraced or discontented courtiers, and by noblemen and gentlemen, numbers of whom had taken the oaths in the two last reigns. They were all of them, however, great enemies to the Union, and some of them much connected with the late Tory Ministry. The bulk of them, also, were much dissatisfied with the Established clergy, and earnestly wished to see Episcopacy restored. Yet numerous and respectable as the Lowland part of their army was, its principal force lay in the Highland clans, which consisted of men fit for immediate service. And if they had been commanded by generals as able and decisive as Montrose and Dundee, they might, perhaps, by a forced march to London, have accomplished a revolution before the new king had time to collect his troops. But as they loitered too long after taking arms, so the severe and seasonable checks given them at Preston and Sheriffmuir, joined to the defection of Lovat and his friends, broke all their measures, and dispersed a most numerous and formidable army in a few months. On this occasion, however, Government was ably seconded by those Highland noblemen and chieftains who all along professed revolution principles.

George I. did not surely make a cruel or intemperate use of his victory. Little blood was spilt on the scaffold; and though the leading men, and many of their associates, were attainted, a number of them, in very respectable circumstances, found means to make their peace. The forfeited estates were often saved by means of settlements or fictitious debts, which were not violently contested by the Crown lawyers. And in other cases, the friends and relations of the family were allowed to purchase the lands at very low prices. The sale of some capital estates to the York Building Company bore, however, exceedingly hard on some noble families.

None escaped better on this occasion than the Highland chieftains who had been engaged in the rebellion. The bulk of them held of subjects, to whom the lands returned, in virtue of the Clan Act, on the attainder of their vassals. If the superiors

took possession to prevent the interference of the
Crown, they allowed the family to receive the rents.
And even where vigorous measures were attempted,
the factors and officers of the law were resisted,
unless when acting under the protection of a military
party. But sooner or later, according to circumstances, the whole of these forfeited estates were
granted in ample form to the families. The superiors,
whose attachment to the family on the throne was
unquestioned, had the more merit [1] in this generous
conduct, that they had no reason to think it would
change the principles of the persons that were to
taste of their bounty. Thus the very circumstances
which at first sight seemed to threaten chieftains
with poverty and ruin, proved their safety. It only
shows that the manners and principles of a country
are more powerful than its laws or the dictates of
party and avarice.

The same law that gave loyal superiors the estates
of their vassals that should be convicted of treason,
held out rewards to the lower class of people. It was
provided that all such tenants as did not rise in rebel-

---

[1] John Duke of Argyll, though much incensed at the conduct of his vassals,
never pocketed any of the forfeited rents, conniving at their being applied for
the family's behoof. But he could never be persuaded to give charters, for
which he was much blamed by Lord Ilay, who declared that, if he survived
his brother, that should be one of his first acts. And accordingly, after Duke
John's death, the writings were directed to be made out. His man of business having drawn up an elaborate preamble stating his motives, he, like
a real great man, dashed it out, and wrote on the margin with his own hand,
"And seeing I wish to do to others as I would be done by; therefore, &c."
Some of the people to whom he acted this noble part thought proper to
engage in the Rebellion of 1745, for which they were attainted.

lion with their masters should possess rent free for
two years.   But it produced no effect.   In those days
a Highlander could hardly be neutral; and the desertion of his chief or landlord, when the country was up
in arms, would have subjected him to a degree of infamy and contempt which no bribe could compensate.

To show that all were not, however, disposed to
show the same clemency and equity to their unfortunate fellow-countrymen, I may here give some account
of Patrick Haldane of Bearcrofts, latterly of Gleneagles, who, upon the death of his brother Mungo,
made long a great figure in the political world, without improving his fortune or his character.   Being a
younger son, he was bred to the law ; and, from the
pregnancy of his parts, very sanguine were the expectations of his friends.   I cannot assign the reason
why he was so late of putting on the gown, or say
how he was previously employed ; but not long after
he was elected member of Parliament for the Cupar
district of burghs, and took his seat soon after the
suppression of the Rebellion of 1715.   There, it
was alleged, he made speeches which made him
odious and unpopular for the greatest part of his
life.   He was accused of saying that he hoped
to make a fortune out of the ruins of his country.
Not long after he was appointed one of the Commissioners of Inquiry, with a handsome salary, at
a time when money went very far.   This was, at
best, an ungracious office for a Scotsman ; but if we
may trust to tradition, he rendered it still more un-

gracious by the harsh and intemperate manner in
which he discharged it. Being better acquainted with
the law of Scotland and the circumstances of the
attainted families than his English brethren, he naturally took a lead at that Board. This led him,
perhaps contrary to his inclination, to take a more
active part in seizing estates and rejecting claims
than a good-natured man would have wished. As
party spirit ran very high at that period, so, like an
aspiring man who had his fortune to make, he thought
he should recommend himself to the Administration
by the exuberance of his zeal. But he overshot his
mark; for while the Jacobites hated him with perfect
hatred, he was much disliked by many of the friends
of Government, who disapproved exceedingly of the
rigour and severity with which the rebels and their
families had been treated, when no longer objects of
jealousy and terror. They were, indeed, the more
entitled to commiseration that their private character
was fair, and they acted upon principle, which, even
when misguided, is entitled to esteem. And they
were nearly related to a number of Whig families,
who entered warmly into their interest, and, of course,
were exceedingly dissatisfied with Mr Haldane for the
part he had acted. Yet, spite of the clamour against
that gentleman, it is now well known that a very
great proportion of the attainted persons saved their
estates by means of conveyances or fictitious debt.
At these he must have connived, from some motive
or other. In such cases, however, a hundred instances

of mercy and favour are speedily forgotten in a
country convulsed with faction, whilst a passionate
speech, or a few acts of rigour, strictly legal, are
remembered to his disadvantage. When the Board
of Inquiry was dissolved, Mr Haldane found it necessary to return to the Bar, where he had not practised
much. There he met with little encouragement from
the men of business, there being a strong prejudice
against him. As the fees came in very slowly, he
found it would be his wisest course to get upon the
bench. In 1722, on the death of Lord Fountainhall,
he obtained the king's letter; but upon presenting
it, a harsh and cruel attack was made upon him.
The Faculty of Advocates and Clerks presented a
petition in the Court of Session, setting forth that
Mr Haldane could not be a judge, in respect he had
not been a practising lawyer for five years, in terms
of law. A proof was allowed, from which it appeared
that he had only attended the bar for thirty months.
The Lords found by a majority that he could not be
admitted; but on an appeal by Lord Advocate Dundas, the judgment was reversed by the House of
Peers. That did not mollify his opponents, for the
Duke of Hamilton and a number of others concurred
in a petition to the Court, representing that no man
ought to be made a judge who was not of *entire
fame.* That Mr Haldane was a bad man, in so far
as he had, in the first place, carried his election for
the burghs by bribery and corruption; 2d, he had
caused four deacons or councillors of St Andrews to

be imprisoned on a pretended charge of high treason
because they would not vote for him, and the moment
his purpose was served they were let out, without
insisting on the charge; and 3d, they offered to
prove that he was a Jacobite, and had repeatedly
drunk the Pretender's health upon his knees.   Though
no direct charge of infidelity or immorality was
brought, stories to his prejudice, some of them very
ridiculous, were circulated with great industry.   The
Court allowed a proof in 1724, but before it could be
advised a great change took place in the Ministry.
The Squadrone party were turned out, and succeeded
by the Argathelians.   In consequence of this Mr
Haldane's nomination was recalled, and Lord Milton
presented the king's letter.   But a law was made
depriving the Court of Session of the power of rejecting persons named by the Crown, leaving it nothing
but the power of remonstrating against an improper
choice.   There are few instances of more general
odium against any man,[1] he being execrated by Whigs
and Tories, Episcopalians and Presbyterians.

In spite of a repulse which would have broke
most people's heart, he continued to practise at
the bar under great disadvantages, his popularity
being irrecoverably gone.   He was allowed to be
not only the best election-monger, but also the best
election lawyer of his time.   To that subject, as ac-

[1] The Dalrymples, who had a great sway on the bench and bar, were his
bitter enemies.   For a while, when the nine of diamonds was turned up at
cards, it was called Peter Haldane, or the Curse of Scotland.

cording with the bent of his mind, he seems to have devoted his time and thoughts. The many struggles which took place between the friends of Sir Robert Walpole and his opponents gave him frequent opportunities of displaying his electioneering talents to great advantage; and lawyers are never paid so handsomely as in election causes. Although it is believed he commonly sided with the Administration, it was not thought prudent, in the present temper of the country, to make this gentleman a judge. Detested by a great part[1] of his countrymen, and neglected by the statesman of those times, his situation and prospects were far from being pleasant. At length, upon the removal of the Marquis of Tweeddale by Mr Craigie, he was made Joint-Solicitor with Mr Home. This was done to make him some reparation for former suffering and services; for he added nothing to the strength of the King's Counsel at a very critical period. His appearances in Crown causes between 1752 and 1755, which I had occasion to witness, conveyed no high idea of his abilities, his pleadings bespeaking neither eloquence nor vigour of mind.[2] When opposed, in the absence of the Lord

---

[1] The late George Drummond told me that when a young man he passed an evening in the tavern with his uncle, William Drummond, a writer in great practice, Gleneagles, and Mr Haldane. Having drank hard, Mr H. had the meanness to upbraid Mr Drummond for never employing him. The other, who was in liquor, answered he never would consult a man for whom he had no regard. On which Gleneagles (the most popular of the brothers) said, —"Peter, Peter, often have I told you your behaviour to the unfortunate families would stick to you like a Burgundy-pitch plaster."

[2] In 1753 I was present at a Michaelmas head court at Stirling, where he took a very active part and was perfectly master of the business. I admired

Advocate, to Lockhart or some other advocate, his
arguments reminded one of Priam's javelin hurled
with a feeble hand.   In great causes it became necessary to call in eminent lawyers, for his brother solicitor was no orator or deep reasoner.   In 1755, when
much broken, he resigned on a pension.   From that
time he ceased to appear in court of justice and
public meetings.   While leading a retired life, he
received a dreadful shock through the death of his
only son, the Governor of Jamaica, in whom all the
hopes of retrieving the family of Gleneagles centred.
It heightened his grief and distress that his son's
debts could not be paid without selling the estate of
Gleneagles, to which he had lately succeeded.[1]

It was, however, well that his brother Robert was
able to purchase it.   After losing his only surviving
child, Mrs Barclay Maitland, he went to live with Mr
William Bennet, minister of Duddingston, who had
been his son's governor.   There he passed his last
years with comfort, in the company of a sensible.
worthy man, forgetting and forgotten by the political

his great command of temper ; for while friends and opponents were exceedingly keen, he seemed to contend rather for peace than for oratory?

[1] He [the younger Haldane] was long a Colonel of the Guards, and being esteemed an excellent officer, was in high favour with the Duke of Cumberland.
What was more extraordinary, he was also much liked by the Jacobites, some of
whom he persuaded to support his uncle in the memorable Stirlingshire election of 1754, which ran within a vote.   He represented the Stirling district of
burghs for more than ten years, and though no orator, was well heard in the
House   Had he been able to square his expenditure to his income he must
have risen very high in the army ; but his luxury exceeded all bounds, and
involved him in difficulties.   To extricate himself, he solicited the Government of Jamaica, but died in 1758, a few months after his arrival in the
island.

world; and there he breathed his last at a good old age in the year 1769.[1]

In the year 1719 a body of Spaniards landed in Kintail, and were joined by some of the clans. They were, however, soon defeated by the king's troops, though much superior in number. It showed our Ministers the necessity of being on their guard against a warlike disaffected people, who were ever ready to expose themselves, even where there was no prospect of success. Poor as was the figure they made on this occasion, they would have been most useful auxiliaries to the Spaniards, had not their fleet been dispersed in a storm. The clemency of Government to the insurgents was great and unexampled, none being executed or attainted for this desperate attempt.

In the year 1726 military roads to the principal Highland forts were begun at the public expense. It was a measure that did great honour to the statesmen and generals of those times. Though its immediate purpose was to facilitate the march of troops into the wildest and most remote countries, it was also well calculated to promote civilisation and commerce. It gave the natives a high notion of the power and wealth of Government, before which nature was obliged to bend, and lay open those fastnesses which, till then, had been deemed inaccessible. And

[1] Maitland of Pittrichie, in the delirium of a fever, amused himself with sending his acquaintance to heaven. "Ay," said he, "Archie Murray will be of the number; but heaven will not be heaven to Archie, for there he will not get Peter Haldane to walk with him,"—alluding to their diurnal walks in the Meadows by themselves after the house [Court of Session] rose.

strangers were thereby encouraged to visit, with
safety and satisfaction, a country of which, and its
inhabitants, they had heard so much. It was, perhaps, the first considerable attempt of its kind that
had taken place since the departure of the Roman
legions from Scotland, and may be regarded as a prelude to the turnpike laws, which have rendered travelling so commodious, and done so much to improve
husbandry and manufactures.

About the same time a set of independent companies were raised in the Highlands, the command
of which was given to gentlemen who had either
been useful to Government, or from whom good service was expected. It being understood that they
were not to be sent abroad, the commissions were
looked on as sinecures or retaining fees, to which
every loyal chief or proprietor might aspire. As it
was little customary at that time for the younger
sons of Highland gentlemen to enter into business at
home or abroad, lieutenancies and ensigncies in those
companies were eagerly sought after. And for the
same reason, the sergeants, corporals, and even a
number of the private men, had a portion of gentle
blood in their veins. By all accounts, they were for
a number of years a very handsome, well-behaved
body of men, animated with a high sense of honour
and propriety. Being in some measure stationary,
and under the observation of their countrymen, they
did not cease to be citizens by becoming soldiers.
The being subjected to military discipline made them

more orderly, as well as better qualified to serve their
king and country when there should be occasion
for it.   Meanwhile they overawed the disaffected
and unruly, being much fitter than the regular
troops for any service which required expedition and
knowledge of the country.   They were of great use,
particularly in repressing theft and apprehending
criminals, with whose haunts and devices to elude a
search they were well acquainted.   In short, it was
a measure that produced important consequences,
both immediate and remote, for it gave our Ministers
of State a lesson how they might most easily destroy
disaffection in the Highlands.

Spite of all this vigilance and zeal, the people of
that country, fifty years ago, were only half subjects.
The law of the land, both civil and criminal, had little course among them, when not enforced by a military force.   Even the well-affected clans paid more
regard to the mandates of their head than to royal
authority.   Their old Government, with its train of
good and bad consequences, subsisted entire amidst
all the convulsions which had befallen the country.
Being trained to arms, and connected with one or
other of the great national parties, every one, from
the chief to the commoner, looked for some occasion
when it would be his duty to take a decided part.

At length the Rebellion of 1745 broke out, and,
contrary to expectation, was attended for a while
with brilliant success.   It is unnecessary to enlarge
on a subject so well known; yet a few observations

will not be improper. The strength of the rebel army lay in the clans, there being a much smaller number of Lowlanders engaged than in 1715. Some powerful chiefs, whose people made a great figure at that time, had either changed sides or remained neutral. Indeed the ruin of that cause was principally owing to the treachery or fickleness of some leading men, who failed in their engagements. The reigning family owed also the highest obligations to Lord President Forbes, who, though a gownman, well advanced in years, was exceedingly active in collecting a body of loyal Highlanders. These hung on the rebels' backs, and prevented many from joining them. By his persuasive eloquence and honest policy, he revived the drooping spirits of the friends of Government, and confirmed such as were wavering. If the honour of the latter received an indelible stain, he put them on a way to save their lives and fortunes.

It surprised nobody to see the clergy of the Established Church make the most vigorous exertions on behalf of Government, and that when the rebels appeared to carry all before them; and at that critical juncture, beset as the nation was with foreign and domestic foes, this was of great service. In the south and west of Scotland, they continued to have a great sway over their parishioners. And even in those parts of the low country that were disaffected, there was generally a number that sided with their ministers in politics.

Wherever Presbyterian principles had taken firm root, the people breathed a loyal spirit. Even the Seceders, spite of their late peevish, petulant language, now stood forth in defence of Government with spirit and effect. If they would not abjure the Pretender, for reasons that sounded strange to other Whigs, none were more hostile to him and his cause. Notwithstanding the aversion of the Lowlanders to arms, they, by the persuasion of their ministers, raised some companies of militia. These consisted of sober, resolute men, who enlisted from principles, not for pay, like the bulk of soldiers. Nothing was wanting to make them useful and formidable but discipline and a little expense, and had the war lasted, their enthusiasm and fidelity would have been of the utmost consequence to the cause. It now appeared that the statesmen had acted wisely in not tampering rashly with those wild well-meaning religionists as long as they did not disturb the peace and order of society. The likeliest way to secure the aid of such men in time of need is to let them alone for a while, if in a state of fanaticism. It is, however, not incurious, that a great majority of the insurgents were nominally Presbyterians. But as the common Highlanders had no mind of their own, they never entered deeply into controversies about modes of worship or forms of Church government. It is no incurious feature of that singular people, that in all the political revolutions that have taken place in Scotland for the last 150 years, they have conformed cheerfully to the religion of the State. They have, at the same time, all along been a serious, devout people, who wished for nothing more than good instructors,—none more affectionate and devoted to their ministers, or less disposed to cavil at their sermons and admonitions. From their sequestered situation and want of letters, they were chiefly attentive to the great doctrines of Christianity, having no cause or inclination for metaphysical disquisitions. As they never entered into the views of the Covenanters, the secession never made any progress among them. With all their veneration for their spiritual guides in matters of religion, the Highlanders did not think it necessary to embrace their political creed. In that they were implicitly directed by their chieftains or landlords.

Rob Roy Macgregor made an eminent figure in the first part of the century. He was a gentleman by birth, in a clan where every man, however poor, finds no difficulty in making out a long and honourable pedigree. His father was a Lieutenant-Colonel Macgregor *in* Glengyle, who, though only a tenant of the Montrose family, found means to distinguish himself, first in the civil wars, and afterwards under the Marquis of Athole, in an expedition to Argyleshire in the year 1685. The son in his early years was more in the world than most of his countrymen, and being a man of insinuation and strong mother-wit, was in such favour with the first Duke of Montrose that he obtained a feu of the lands of Craigroyston for himself, and of the farm of Glengyle for his nephew. For some time he was a great dealer in cattle; but having quarrelled with the Duke about money lent to him, his affairs went into disorder, and his lands were adjudged from him. It matters little which of the parties was right or wrong in this transaction, but Rob thought himself oppressed, and regarded his title to the lands as indefeasible. Being now desperate, he carried on a sort of predatory war against the Duke, his tenants and friends. This was the more extraordinary, that the scene of his numerous exploits lay at no great distance from the castles of Stirling and Dumbarton, at a time, too, when the Ministers of State were exceedingly spirited and attentive. It is, however, commonly believed that John, the great Duke of Argyll, secretly protected Rob, in return for some good offices he had done that nobleman when accused of a sham plot by the Squadrone party, of which the Duke of Montrose was one of the heads.

Be that as it may, the violence and wantonness of Rob's attacks upon the latter look as if he knew he should meet with powerful support. At one time he seized Mr Graham of Killearn, the Duke's factor, while collecting the rents at Chapel Lairock, and after robbing him of the money, carried him away prisoner to another part of the country. By the way, Rob, who was a big man, made the poor gentleman carry him on his back across the burns, which were then high. He used also to lay hold of the Duke's *girnel*,[1]

---

[1] Store of meal collected from the tenants.

and obliged the servants to carry the meal on horses' backs to his house in the Braes of Balquhidder. There, however, he gave them good words and plenty of meat and drink. And to complete the whole, he gave receipts to Killearn and them for what he had taken, which he was ready to allow the Duke at settling accounts.

This extraordinary man, for the age and country in which he lived, seems to have formed himself on the model of former times, when such characters were common. He even affected somewhat of the state of a chieftain, which he could the better do that there was no longer a Laird of Macgregor to head the clan. At the battle of Sheriffmuir he headed a considerable body of men, his nephew, Glengyle, being then young. But on that occasion he is said to have acted more cautiously than became a hero—being, indeed, never distinguished for personal courage, though his course of life surely required it. After the Rebellion, he continued to have a number of loose people in different parts of the country ready to receive his orders for whatever purpose. It was necessary for him to change his place of residence, according to circumstances, it being in Strathfillan or Argyleshire, but most frequently in the Braes of Balquhidder, which, in case of alarm, lay not far from a very wild country. There he lived for a number of years, a merry if not a creditable life, in great fulness, than which nothing could be more acceptable to his myrmidons, who had all their several parts assigned them. At length, to

the great reproach of Government, he died in his bed
at his house in Balquhidder, having a little before
become Roman Catholic, partly to quiet his conscience,
and partly to make his court to the family of Perth,
from whom he expected great favours to his son and
kinsmen.

Rob Roy contrived to make most of the gentry in
the neighbouring shires pay him black-mail, which
perhaps brought him more money than his depreda-
tions; and as he took care to secure the contributors
and their tenants from all harm, it was in those times
a provident measure, though contrary to law. He
had his own people in most complete subjection, nor
durst interlopers from other countries prey within his
precincts. Being an overmatch for any straggling
parties, he would have given them a very bad reception, and made a merit of delivering them into the
hands of justice.

After he died, his sons went on in his steps, but
the Rebellion of 1745 checked their career. One of
them committed a cruel murder, and the rest were
accused of houghing and maiming the cattle of people
that had incurred their indignation. For this some
of them were tried at Edinburgh, but acquitted for
want of evidence. But what was strange indeed, the
last Duke of Perth, who was then a youth, was so
ill-advised as stand in the panel with those worth-
less fellows. It was one of the bad consequences of
his politics; for the people who had then his care
persuaded him that the Macgregors were an oppressed

people, principally on account of their attachment to
the Stuart family, whose standard they would join
with a numerous body as soon as he should set it up.

Contemporary with Rob Roy or his sons, there were
a very few Highland gentlemen that kept bands of
loose people, equally ready to rise in rebellion or to
sweep away the cattle of an estate. Macdonald of
Barrisdale also was a very noted character in his day,
and is said to have drawn ten thousand merks a-year
in black-mail or contributions from the Lowlanders
of the northern countries. So much was his protection valued, that even Lord President Forbes found
it expedient to pay him black-mail, to prevent his
tenants from being plundered and oppressed.

How humiliating those practices were to them that
were obliged to follow the example of the first law
officer of the kingdom! There was in the conduct of
Highland thieves, in those times, a strange mixture
of virtue and vice, of honour and meanness. By all
accounts, Rob Roy valued himself highly on the *point
of honour* and the character of a gentleman, and that
at the very time when he was leading the life of an
outlaw and felon. Nay, he even pretended to patriotism, being a strenuous assister of the independence of
his country, and a decided enemy to the Union. He
certainly deserved credit for restraining the unprincipled bandits that were about him from injuring
those whom he had engaged to protect.

The Young Pretender owed his safety to a set of
the most notorious thieves in the Highlands, who

had no pretensions to the character of gentlemen. They knew, however, that they might have got their pardon, and thirty thousand pounds, by delivering him up. A London highwayman, or thief, would have broken the whole Decalogue, nay, betrayed his bosom friend, for the hundredth part of that sum. Some gentlemen who fled to the wilds of Rannoch, after the battle of Culloden, were protected by Sergeant More Cameron and his gang, with a courtesy and generosity not to be expected from a set of the worst desperadoes in the Highlands. In 1752 the sergeant was hanged at Perth for murder and theft. On the ladder, he declared no gentleman could accuse him of having stolen lambs, or kids, or calves; nor had he even, to his knowledge, taken a cow from a widow or a poor man.

I had an anecdote from James Menzies of Culdares, which marks very strongly the inconsistent conduct of those unhappy men. One of the Rannoch thieves, who, it was alleged, had refused great offers from the Breadalbane family in a lawsuit about a forest, was afterwards imprisoned for theft at Inverness. There not being sufficient proof against him at his trial, he was acquitted. No doubt being entertained, after suitable admonitions, he was asked by the Court whether he could find bail for his good behaviour. He answered without hesitation that the Laird of Culdares would be good for him. The Judges, Lords Strichen and Drummore, on their return, fell in with that gentleman at Sir

Robert Menzies's house, when Lord Drummore rated Culdares severely on a connection so notorious. The latter replied with some warmth : "My lord, I know the man, and from what I know of him, could give bail to present him at your lordship's bar though he was sure of being hanged next day. But for all that, I would not promise but he might steal the first parcel of cattle that fell in his way." This unfortunate man came to the gallows at last.

The heat of a civil war seldom affords materials for a dissertation like the present. There was, however, an incident that happened at that time, which shows what loose inadequate ideas the Highlanders entertained of criminal laws. A few days after the battle of Falkirk, as one of the Macdonalds of Clanranald was discharging heedlessly, in the street of that town, some muskets dropped by the King's troopers in their flight, he chanced to kill a near relation of the Laird of Glengarry, who happened to be standing opposite to him. The friends of the latter ran to arms and demanded the immediate execution of the manslayer. In vain did the gentlemen who were not connected with either party remonstrate with the Glengarry men that the thing was purely accidental, and where there was no malice there could be no murder; but there was no convincing them, and therefore, to prevent the desertion of a powerful clan, the unfortunate man, who was a *duniewassal* tenant, being tried by a court-martial, was sentenced to be shot, which was carried into

execution a few days after, in a field not far from
Callendar House, to the great indignation of all un-
prejudiced men. The clan of the deceased submitted
sullenly to his fate, conscious that they would have
acted the very same part had they been in the other
people's place. It proves that fierce ill-instructed
men cannot, or will not, make the proper discrimination between the various kinds of homicide. Upon
the slaughter of a near relation, nothing will satisfy
them but blood for blood. There was no time to
mediate a reconciliation by means of money, as the
Glengarry men, acting on the impulse of the moment,
had unluckily the power in their own hands of ex-
torting what they called justice. Invernachyle, who
witnessed the execution, said that nothing throve
with their army after it.

Though only part of the clans engaged in the Rebellion, the whole kingdom was convulsed; nor was
it suppressed without a great expense of blood and
treasure. Its breaking out amidst a just and necessary war with the house of Bourbon excited the
indignation of every man that loved his country.
And it was a bad return for the mercy shown to the
insurgents in the years 1715 and 1719. Can we
wonder, then, that a young prince, flushed with victory and applause, should make an intemperate use
of his success? And as the lenient measures of the
preceding reign had done no good, harsh ones were
now resolved on in the Cabinet. A greater number
suffered the cruel death appointed for traitors than

was sufficient to strike terror and satisfy the demands
of justice.   The burning of the rebels' houses and
plundering their effects, though warranted by many
precedents at home and abroad, bore hardest on the
innocent wives and children.   There was also a seeming absurdity in wantonly destroying what would
soon become the property of the Crown.   And many
cruelties are said to have been committed which
nothing could justify or palliate if they were done
by authority.

However that may be, we must not too rashly con-
demn Ministers for a degree of rigour on that occasion.   In every age and country high treason has been
esteemed a crime of the deepest dye, especially when
committed against a just and gentle Government.
The present rebellion being attended with circumstances highly provoking, self-preservation warranted
every measure which was likely to prevent a repetition of the late calamities.   In short, passion and
reasons of State were somewhat mingled at that
period.   In these circumstances it is difficult, with
the best dispositions, to hit the proper medium between justice and mercy.

It is easy for us, whose angry passions have
got new objects, to find fault with the proceedings
of the Ministers of those times.   We shall indeed
admit that a degree of sympathy and compassion
was due to men that acted on a set of principles
sucked in with their mothers' milk.   In everything
but politics their conduct had been irreproachable.

Attachment to the royal family, in the lowest ebb of its fortune, was in itself a noble principle; nor could anything justify a departure from it but the preservation of liberty and religion. In the conduct of our modern cavaliers there was indeed little worldly wisdom. Yet the risking their lives and fortunes in what they thought a good cause entitled them to esteem. Upon tempers like theirs, persecution was not likely to effect any change of sentiment or conduct. Well-timed acts of mercy, joined to a just and steady administration, might have operated many conversions upon people of that romantic turn.

However much we of the present age may be disposed to censure the statesmen and generals of George II. for their severity towards a fallen enemy, the former deserve all praise for their unwearied endeavours to better the condition of the Highlanders. From excessive zeal they may in some points have mistaken the means, but even party itself will not *now* refuse them the merit of excellent intentions. To cut the evil up by the roots, and to ensure the public tranquillity, the old connections between superior and vassal, landlord and tenant, were done away, that there might no longer exist any temptation to rise in rebellion. With this view military service and attendance at huntings were taken away, and an allowance in money given in lieu of them to the superior. The heritable jurisdictions, which subjected the lives and properties of vassals and tenants to the pleasure of the great and to the injustice and caprice of their illiterate deputes. were likewise abolished, not only in the Highlands but over the rest of Scotland. Ample provision was made for the establishment of learned judges in those parts where the law had hitherto little course. In order to enforce obedience to the civil magistrate. detachments of troops, more numerous than formerly. were stationed in the wildest and worst affected counties to overawe the inhabitants. To extinguish the hopes of the chief promoters of the last rebellion. all their estates in or bordering on the Highlands were, by Act of Parliament, unalienably annexed to the Crown. But to prevent all collusion between superiors and vassals, the former was allowed a sum of money in place of the property. The rents were appropriated for the improvement of the country and its inhabitants, in religion, husbandry, and manufactures. It was doubtless a most benevolent law. which might have done a great deal of good, both in public and private life. There was perhaps a degree of wrath mixed with policy in this measure. yet eventually it proved the means of preserving a number of families. The forfeited estates in the low country were sold by auction, and such of them as were not purchased by the friends of the attainted person were for ever lost to his representatives.

---

[1] The magnanimity of Archibald, Duke of Argyll, in surrendering a princely jurisdiction for the public good, ought to endear his memory to us. Had he been as adverse to it as some other great men, the bill had never passed.

As the habitual and indiscreet use of arms had promoted their warlike spirit, and been a source of much evil, public and private, the laws disarming the Highlands and the bordering counties were revived and strictly executed. That the pride of the Highlanders might be exceedingly mortified, and one of their most striking distinctions taken away, their favourite dress was likewise forbidden, under severe penalties. Nothing, indeed, seemed to hurt their spirits more, or to give them a meaner appearance, than this regulation, the wisdom of which might be questioned. At any rate, there ought to have been an exception in favour of the loyal clans, who were exceedingly attached to that ancient garb. Clad in it, they had oftener than once signalised themselves in behalf of the family on the throne; and indeed there was no more treason in tartan and the belted plaid than in Sir Thomas More's beard.

The attention of the Legislature was not confined to men's actions or external appearance, but extended to matters of conscience. Government oaths were now imposed, not only on voters and persons in office, but also on numbers that might have exercised their professions without endangering the constitution. But this neither improved morals nor increased the fast friends of the reigning family. A good many conscientious people chose to lose their bread rather than take the oaths; whilst others, with a versatility that did them no honour, swallowed those bitter pills without changing a single principle or prejudice. By way of apology, it may be alleged that ever since the civil wars about the Covenant, tests have been imposed by Government on certain classes of the people.

The shutting up of the Episcopal meeting-houses, and denying Nonjuring ministers that were ready to qualify the benefit of their orders, did more hurt to religion than good to the prince on the throne. They were indeed zealously devoted to the exiled family: but being a clergy equally pious and rational, respected by those that were not of their opinion, it was wrong to drive them to despair. It was possible a time might come when they would see things in a new light. The rigorous treatment a few of them met with neither diminished their flocks nor incomes. If it kept some of the gentry from attending on public worship, it redoubled the zeal and attendance of the females, who in every society have a wonderful sway in all matters of party. Meanwhile every minister fined or imprisoned was revered as a confessor in politics. The bulk of the Highland gentry were, no doubt, of that persuasion; but it is somewhat singular that, amidst all the changes of Government that have taken place within the last century and a half, the common people have regularly attended the Established Church.

The application of so many violent and bitter remedies at the same time could not be agreeable to the Highlanders. In fact they were treated like a conquered people, whom it is necessary to keep under restraint. They could not be persuaded that the in-

tention of their rulers, in the late innovations, was to
make the misfortunes of their leaders redound to the
good of the whole. Indeed it required time before
the salutary effects of the new regulations could be
plainly perceived. What wonder, then, that the families and friends of those that had lost their lives and
estates for adhering to the Pretender should brood
over those private calamities? They censured, with
almost equal acrimony, every measure, good and bad.
But, both in the natural and moral world, the providence of God brings good out of seeming evil. Had
it not been for the hardships and afflictions they lately
endured, that people might have continued for ages a
prey to anarchy, and a dead load on Government. It
is curious as well as melancholy to see what wrong
estimates ignorant men are apt to form of their own
situation. There was no constitution, ancient or modern, which the Highlanders of all ranks would have
exchanged for clanship, which vested the chief with
unlimited power. They regarded subordination to
King and Parliament as a state of abject slavery,
to which no generous spirit would willingly submit.
The perverseness of their notions, and the ruggedness
of their temper, upon which neither severity nor mercy
could make any lasting impression, served to irritate
the officers of State, and made them sometimes have
recourse to measures that hurt their private feelings.
Indeed, for ten or a dozen of years their attention
appeared to be engrossed with the affairs of the Highlands.

504 THE HIGHLANDS AND THE REBELLIONS.

By degrees, however, great alterations took place. Every year almost abated somewhat of the virulence of party and of the rigour of Government. Though the disaffected still complained of various grievances, they began to relish the blessings of peace and order. They saw justice ably and impartially administered to rich and poor: none had anything to dread from the law but the rebellious and dishonest; whilst liberty of speech, in its full extent, was allowed to people of all parties. Oppression was punished with great severity, especially when committed by landlords on their tenants; and where the party aggrieved was poor and friendless, the prosecution was carried on at the public expense. The crimes which had formerly been a reproach to the country and its rulers became comparatively rare. In a few years the banditti who had done most mischief were brought to justice, which made the young people likely to have followed their example (if things had remained in their former state) betake themselves to honest industry.

In the beginning of the war of 1756, Archibald, Duke of Argyll, recommended the raising of Highland regiments to serve in America. In proposing this plan, he had not the ordinary views of providing for his own friends and dependants, but a more patriotic one —namely, to destroy disaffection by indirect means. Accordingly, the command of one of the regiments was given to the Master of Lovat, who had received a pardon; and a number of the other officers had either been engaged in the Rebellion or were the sons

of fathers who had figured on that occasion. In the
course of that glorious war a number of Highland
corps were raised, among whom there were not a few
officers whose attachment to the family of Hanover
was very small; yet Government had no cause to
regret this confidence. Those gentlemen did their
duty on all occasions like men of honour. They, like
the Swiss, considered themselves as soldiers of fortune,
whose duty it was to be faithful to the prince whose
bread they ate. Ere long this honest policy produced
a great revolution in the sentiments of the Highlanders. With whatever intemperance the ladies and
the men advanced in years might talk, the younger
part of the family began to look up to Government
for military preferment. They now with great reason
chose rather to go into the British service than into
that of France and Spain, whose conduct they at last
saw in its true colours. Meanwhile the officers and
soldiers serving abroad formed useful connections, and
had their minds expanded by mixing in scenes of
more polished life.

The period between 1747 and 1769 was upon the
whole a propitious one, particularly to Highland tenants. If public affairs were not just in the way they
wished, they enjoyed the comforts of social life in a
perfection they never before experienced. They retained their peculiar manners and customs in great
purity, freed from those infirmities in point of conduct which had flowed from the nature of their former
government. Notwithstanding all they had lately

suffered, their attachment and love for their chief continued unabated, even when stripped of his estate and
in exile.[1] The spirit of clanship still maintained its
ground, though being divested of its sting. It no
longer disturbed the peace of society. The gentry
that retained their estates were still as kind and
moderate in their views as ever—partly from habit,
and partly from the hopes they entertained of a return to the old system. They were not, however,
disposed to grant leases to their tenants, for fear of
losing their influence and being treated with ingratitude. If the latter were neither rich nor industrious,
they were at least cheerful and much at their ease.
And at a time when rents were very little raised, the
high price of cattle gave them great joy. Amidst all
the late innovations, the warlike spirit of that people,
both high and low, was rather damped than extinguished, and might easily have been revived, as the
country was full of men. Upon the accession of his
present Majesty, the maxims of the former reign
seemed to be inverted—disaffection being no longer
a bar to promotion or Court favour. Even such as
were too old to make an open recantation of their
principles, had no longer any objection to their children going over when it should be their interest.

[1] In the year 1758 or 1759, Lochiel's eldest son, having quitted the French
service ... the plan of promotion at home, made a visit to the Highlands.
On ... parts of the country the clan met him in a body, forgetful of ...
... congratulate ... and, with a mixture of grief and joy, presented the ...
of their ... enriched with two hundred cows. This alarmed the servants of
the Crown who, some time after, most deliberately refused to allow this poor
gentleman to be buried among his ancestors.

At length, however, an unexpected change took
place in the temper and conduct of Highland proprietors, owing to the very circumstances which
flattered the hopes of tenants. Ever since the last
rebellion there had been a great demand for black
cattle to England, and a gradual rise in their value;
but in 1766 and the three following years the prices
exceeded anything that had ever been known before,
which raised the spirits of dealers in cattle to a great
height. This, of course, *raised* the value of Highland
grass, and made everybody wish to enlarge his farm or
obtain a lease. Some of the more considerable tacksmen very unwisely took that opportunity of squeez-
ing their sub-tenants in a way never before known;
others, still more culpable, wanted to supplant the
present possessors by offering much higher rent. By
this time landlords began to have new views, and
to think themselves well entitled to a share of their
tenants' profits from the breeding of cattle. In the
course of twenty-five years after the Rebellion a number of noblemen and gentlemen, whose estates lay
in the Highlands, had died, and were succeeded by
young men of very different manners and sentiments.
Some of these had been educated in England and the
low country, where they had formed new friendships
and connections. They had been accustomed from
their infancy to hear their country vilified and ridiculed
by all about them. No wonder, then, that they should
return prepossessed against it—a species of prejudice
of all others the most unfortunate to a man's self and

his dependants. To the persons and pretensions of their tenants, as well as to their language and customs, they were in a great measure strangers. Instead of treating such of them as were supposed to be of the same lineage with themselves in the manner their fathers used to do, they affected to estimate them by their dress and economies, which were indeed abundantly homely.

Other circumstances concurred in promoting a universal change in the views and dispositions of Highland proprietors of all descriptions. As they had no longer any hope, and few of them any desire, of returning to the old system, it was not necessary to secure the aid and affections of their people by means of bargains of land, that were always understood to be cheap. They thought it therefore time to compensate the loss of power and dignity by increase of revenue. It was a most favourable conjuncture for gratifying this wish. The Highlands were now perfectly quiet, and property as secure as in any part of the kingdom. By means of the military roads which were now completed, the country was accessible to strangers, a few of whom by this time had settled on the skirts of it. A decrease in the value of money, occasioned by national prosperity, had doubled the value of cattle in the course of thirty years. The amazing sums of money that flowed into Britain upon the close of an *over-successful* war, had produced a *South Sea* spirit among all classes of men. And when rents everywhere else were rising in an unheard-of proportion, the proprietors of Highland farms would have been wanting to themselves had they not put in for a share of the benefit. And as the tenants seemed exceedingly anxious to have leases, their known attachment to the place where they were born rendered it probable they would readily give a great augmentation. This was the more reasonable, that the way in which the gentry now lived required a much better income than that of their fathers.

Had the business been conducted with temper and address, they would have got something handsome without injuring their people or raising any ferment. But the avowed contempt some of them showed for maxims once held sacred, and the little value set on hereditary attachments, gave more offence than even the *sudden* rise of rents. Some well-meant but impracticable schemes of improvement in the more remote countries contributed to sour the minds of the inhabitants. In the course of two or three years some great estates were let at double rent, or more, to people who had not laid up a shilling in the late very favourable times, and who had no prospect, at that time, of making their farms produce more corn or cattle. They depended solely on a continuance of the present extravagant prices of cattle, a commodity of all others the most fluctuating.

Some apology, however, may be made for those that were most culpable. Their notions of land were taken from other parts of the kingdom, where the soil, climate, and management were totally different. Neither they nor the people with whom they advised understood the proper method of dealing with Highland tenants whose notions were particular. Indeed, the mischief was in a great measure owing to the people themselves, who, regardless of their own and their neighbours' interest, bid on one another in a manner hitherto unprecedented. It was natural for landlords who had little experience in matters of this kind to accept of offers made by people who had lived all their days, either on the lands or in the neighbourhood. This emulation originated partly from fondness for particular possessions and partly from clan malice. Nor were tenants entirely free from the giddiness and self-delusion which was one of the least pleasing consequences of the flourishing state of the whole kingdom.

The selfishness and precipitation of a few great Highland proprietors did more to destroy the spirit of clanship and the unreserved obedience of tenants than the vigorous exertions of Government for a number of years. Being accustomed to attacks from *that* quarter, they had often borne up against them with unshaken fortitude. But to see chieftains, or such as affected the manners of chieftains, repay their attachment with coldness and contempt, filled the middling and lower classes of people with grief and indignation. From being an affectionate cheerful people, a great proportion of them became sullen, suspicious, and restless.

This breach between landlords and tenants seemed to accord with the views of those that held the reins of government after the last rebellion. It is believed, however, that Lord Chancellor Hardwicke and his brethren would have been sorry to see it brought about in this way. They were warm friends to the lower ranks of Highlanders, whom they wished to render as easy and independent as those of their station in any part of the island. It was a branch of their favourite plan for annexing the forfeited estates, to establish a substantial yeomanry by giving good bargains for a long term of years. With a view to the general care of tenants, *arriage and carriage*, with all other oppressive exactions, were taken away.

Those great statesmen did not perceive that, by taking away military service and annihilating the power of the proprietors, they removed the barrier which had secured tenants kind and generous treatment. What signified their being freed from petty vexations when they were totally at mercy in the great article of rent? In other countries, pride of character, the union and wealth of tenants, and long practice, have established rules which no wise landlord cares to break through for his own sake. Although for a number of years matters had gone on in the old channel, it might have been foreseen that a selfish spirit would sooner or later appear in its native colours. Indeed, when violent innovations take place, and men have nothing to direct them,

they are ever apt to fall into the opposite extrem-
Even though the bad consequences resulting fr-e
an indiscreet use of property had been foreseen .:
their utmost extent at the making the laws again-t
clanship, it is difficult to say what remedies co-.
have been applied. To compel long leases or re-.
late the quantum of rent, would have been esteem-i
dangerous encroachments on property, for which :
precedent could be alleged.

After the ferment had subsided, and tenants ha.
leisure to reflect on what they had done, a very n-s
as well as distressful scene was exhibited. A num-r
of respectable people, who till then would not hav-
exchanged their native soil for the best country up-:
earth, resolved to quit it for ever and betake themselves to the wilds of America, many of them witho-.
money, industry, or recommendation. Some temporary falls in the price of cattle, and accidents :
their stocks from bad seasons, made them ra-.r
despair of being able to pay the new rent. But
the changes which had taken place in the mann-r-
and views of their superiors were the things that
made most of them take this desperate course. The-y
were accompanied by a number of their cottagers ar.i
servants, who were equally dissatisfied with them ss
to the late innovations. Having no money to pay
their freight to what they esteemed the Promise-i
Land, these last were obliged to indent themselves to
people that were, upon their arrival, to sell them like
cattle to the highest bidder. The miseries which be-

fell many of those unfortunate people in their first attempts to settle in the colonies are fresh in everybody's remembrance. Nothing stopped these emigrations but the breaking out of the American war, which broke off all intercourse between the two countries. For the delusion was likely to have extended far and near, insomuch that, after the commencement of hostilities, ships loaded with emigrants sailed from Scotland, some of whom were low-country labourers and servants, whose wages at home were higher than had ever been known at any former period. Most of these adventurers were obliged to join with one or other of the parties in a civil war that did not concern them. It does no discredit to the Highlanders that, in circumstances abundantly discouraging, most of them continued true to the principles that had lately cost them so dear. They therefore took the first opportunity of joining the king's forces.

In the course of that war a good many Highland regiments were raised. Government was now as ready to give commissions to the disaffected families as they were to ask them ; nor was it scrupulous in the article of *rank* to people that were supposed to have much influence. The great difficulty was to get private men, the common Highlanders having by this time a more rooted aversion to the army than the Lowlanders. Many of the officers are said to have raised their quotas by means little to their honour ; and as recruits could not be had in their own

country, they were forced to bring them from L...
don or Ireland. On this occasion, however, a ...
of the clans displayed some traces of their an...
spirit by sending a set of volunteers to complete t...
chieftain's companies. None were more zealou...
that way than the tenants of some annexed e...
who hoped it might be a means of restoring to t...
the heir of the family.[1] In this, however, they a...
a more generous than prudent part; for they mi...
easily have foreseen that they would be no ga...
by the change of masters.

By whatever means the Highland corps were rais...
whether by love or fear, the mutinies that broke ...
from time to time among the private men afford ...
strong presumption of great harshness and imp...
dence on the part of their officers. Of all soldier...
the service they used to be the most quiet and orderly
but being exceedingly attentive to their own litt...
interest, they are apt to be at once suspicious a...
irascible when injured.

Meanwhile the interest of landlords suffered littl...
either from the emigrations or the new levies. A...
the trade of *king-making* was now given up, me...
were no longer their object. They found it easy t...
supply the place of their tenants who had emigrated
And after a trial of some years, it was discovered tha...
the farms lately let were less squeezed than peop...

---

[1] The ... raised by the clan for the present Lochiel's father w...
... When General F... set a... of modelling the reg... ...
... ... to their chief ... from o... a... the... ...
... ... expedient to f... the...

apprehended. Nor is this surprising, as the old rent was very low, suited to times of anarchy and idleness, when a little money went a great way. If the tenants were not likely to make rich on their present bargains, the bulk of them contrived to keep their credit, besides living more fully than their predecessors. During the war, rents continued in a great measure stationary—at least not higher than in 1770 or 1771. The obloquy some great proprietors had met with, on account of their harsh conduct, made others in the same situation careful to avoid any cause of ferment among their people. All parties waited till they should see what turn national affairs would take. Meanwhile the popular discontents were rather suspended than extinguished in the Highlands.

Never were our fears and apprehensions for the public more happily dispelled than upon the conclusion of the last war, which had, on the whole, been equally expensive and unsuccessful. Contrary to expectation, Great Britain did not lose its rank among the nations ; for industry and enterprise made up, in a great degree, for loss of territory. Public and private credit revived apace, the good effects of which were felt in the remotest parts of the kingdom.

The first thing after the peace that affected the Highlands was the giving back *all* the annexed estates in 1784.[1] It met with no opposition in Parliament,

---

[1] In 1774 the estate of Lovat was restored, by a special law, to General Fraser, in reward of his services to Government.

at a time when the spirit of party ran very h.;.
Though it was a measure too popular ever to come
unseasonably, it had been well for all concerned if it
had taken place before the affection between master
and tenant had received a rude shock.   Nor was it
the less acceptable that the benevolent designs of
Lord Hardwicke and his brethren had by no means
succeeded.   That the board of annexed estates did
much good, both in public and private. cannot be
disputed ; but it might have done much more had
its attention been concentred on a few objects.   Some
of the leading members meant exceedingly well to the
country ; yet the warmth of their imagination made
them sometimes fall into the schemes of projectors.
by whom great part of the funds was swallowed up
to no purpose, whilst others thought of nothing but
serving their friends and dependants.

Instead of making the *native* tenants of those estates
easy and independent (which the Ministers of the last
reign had much at heart), they were kept for a number
of years in suspense, and teased with regulations. some
of which were by no means suited to their situation.
It was only a short time before the Restoration that
the bulk of them obtained leases, longer or shorter.
according to their merit or interest.   Till they procured these, there was no encouragement for industry
or enterprise.   From time to time numbers of tenants
were removed. under various pretences, to make way
for people in a superior line, who, having powerful
friends, wished to get cheap farms for a long term of

years. Before the present leases have expired, it is too early to speak with confidence of the character and conduct of the gentlemen who obtained those princely grants from the bounty of Parliament. In the meantime let us hope that the chieftains who experienced the love and affection of their clan in time of adversity will always retain a grateful sense of the obligation. In letting of land there is a happy medium which is equally advantageous for landlord and tenant.

The great demand for black cattle, horses, and sheep to England, after the peace, occasioned a very great rise of prices. Within those few years they have fluctuated considerably, but in general they have been from 10 to 20 per cent beyond what was ever known before. As the profits centred mostly with the breeders, the continuance of high markets raised the spirits of Highland tenants, giving them and their masters new views of the worth of grass grounds. Even though the old system of stocking and management had been retained, a considerable augmentation would have been got as soon as the current tacks were expired. But the introduction of sheep into the wildest and most remote parts of that country was attended with important consequences. It was once generally believed that those animals could not stand the severity of a Highland winter without being housed all night. By accident that was discovered to be a vulgar error;[1] in consequence

---

[1] John Campbell of Laguine, a native of Ayrshire, has the merit of this

of which some estates in Dumbartonshire, Perthshire
and the southern parts of Argyleshire, were stocked
entirely with sheep, managed in the same way with
those on the Borders. At first the business was
carried on mostly by Lowland adventurers, but by
degrees the Highland tenants acquired a sufficient
knowledge of the business. The stagnation in our
manufactures during the late war, and a doubt
whether sheep would not suffer by driving far, prevented the extension of this simple and profitable
mode of farming. The great demand for wool and
mutton of late years convinced the dealers that there
was little risk of overstocking the market.   And after
a few experiments, it was found that a sheep is as
little hurt by a long journey as an ox or a cow. As
the profits were much greater and more certain than
from a mixture of tillage and pasturage, the converting of lands into sheep-walks has been in much request since the peace. The south-country shepherds
who formerly went no further than Arroquhar and
Breadalbane, ventured now without scruple into

discovery. After spending a small paternal estate, he came, in the progress
of his decline, to keep the inn at Tyndrum. On a farm of Lord Breadalbane's in that neighbourhood he had a few sheep, which, rather than re-
a house for them, he allowed to run out all winter on the hill.   To
astonishment of everybody, the little flock was in high order in the spring,
notwithstanding all the storms they had endured. Being a man of some
natural parts, and bred in a sheep-country, he saw some prospect of retriev-
his broken fortune by striking into a new path, and hearing that the
Sir James Coldness had some farms to let, he went and gave him the rent
he asked. Having succeeded there to his wish, he took a number of farms
other parts of the country, and his example was soon followed by many, they
with equal success.

countries where, not many years before, they would
have met with a very bad reception. But though
the old possessors detested those intruders, it was
too much for them to think of contending both with
their chief and the laws of the land, which allowed
him the choice of his tenants. Whether Highlanders
or Lowlanders were preferred, a very great rise of
rents was obtained upon a solid basis. The gentlemen who made self-interest the rule of their conduct
got in some cases triple or quadruple of what had
been formerly paid. None entered more keenly into
this measure than the heads of some clans, which
used to send out the greatest number of fighting
men to the field.

Profitable as the new system might be to the proprietor and the sheep-farmers, it has diminished the
number of the human species wherever it has been
thoroughly established, even when some respect was
paid to the persons and pretensions of the old possessors. So long as black cattle and horses were the
principal stocking of a Highland farm, a number of
servants or cottagers were absolutely necessary to
raise a sufficient quantity of winter provender for
them, which in that soil and climate, among a people
averse to continued labour, was an arduous task,
whereas a very few hands are requisite to manage
a large flock. As sheep love an extensive range of
pasture, there was often a necessity to remove ten or
a dozen of tenants to enable a single shepherd to pay
an adequate rent. Of its tendency to depopulate a

country, the many ruinous houses to be seen in the Highland glens occupied by these animals afford complete and melancholy evidence.

Though men always feel some reluctance to quit the place of their nativity, the people removed at an early period to accommodate the sheep-farmers were in truth no great sufferers. Most of them lived on the skirts of the Highlands, and on being removed found immediate employment in the low country at no great distance from their former abodes. There, in the service of some gentleman farmer or manufacturer, they got good wages, which enabled them to live more fully, if not more to their liking, than they had done while possessed perhaps of the eighth of a ploughgate or of a croft of land.

Nor is there any doubt that the whole Highlanders who have emigrated to America for the last seven or eight years might have been comfortably provided in some part of Scotland at no very great expense. To such a height hath a spirit of speculation in trade, manufactures, and husbandry risen within this period, that it is very difficult to procure necessary hands at any time. The remote Highlanders that were turned adrift would no doubt have been awkward and unhandy in their operations; but in a short time, by means of a little kindly attention, they might have been taught to earn a good livelihood in some branch of coarse work. Whether the extraordinary expense of bringing down and settling those destitute people in villages or manufacturing towns

should have been defrayed by the public or by the
landlords may admit of some doubt. A small part
of the great additional rent got in consequence of
their removal would have prevented much misery to
them, and been a means of bringing a blessing on
their benefactor and his family.

But various circumstances prevented those unfortunate people from bending their course southwards
in a body. The commons, who were the greatest
sufferers by this new policy, had invincible prejudices
to the Lowlanders, from whom they expected no kindness, and to whom they imputed the corruption of
their gentry's manners. They could not think of
being cooped up in towns, among a people whose
sentiments and modes of life were diametrically opposite to their own. Having no longer the smallest
regard for their chiefs or landlords, who had cast
them off for a little gain, they were ready to take any
impression. In their distress it was natural for them
to look up to the gentlemen-tenants who had lost their
farms, and had no views of being provided in the
Highlands. These last had nothing to hope from
betaking themselves to the low country. Corn-farms
required more knowledge and money than most of
them possessed; and they were too proud, and many
of them too far advanced in life, to submit to manual
labour as tradesmen and manufacturers. America,
therefore, seemed to be the only asylum left them.
Thither many of their countrymen had already gone,
some of whom, after various adventures, were at last

settled to their wish. There was at present no danger
of war, and the dislike of the Americans to Highland
emigrants, on account of their attachment to monarchy, abated by degrees. It was no doubt an expedition which no man at his ease would think of
making; but in their forlorn situation it was necessary to encounter dangers and difficulties which stood
betwixt them and their favourite object. Nothing
served more effectually to reconcile them to this
voluntary exile than the prospect of being attended
in their voyage by numbers of those friends and
neighbours who had been the companions of their
youth. The prospect of securing a *property* to their
families had also no small weight in forming this
resolution; and, indeed, such of them as had wherewithal to clear or purchase a small plantation, proceeded on no irrational plan. But nothing could be
more idle and preposterous than the conduct of the
common people who consented to embark in the
adventure. They forgot that they wanted money
both to carry them out and to procure them a settlement, and that it would be necessary for them
to indent themselves as servants, or more properly
slaves, either to their more substantial countrymen
or to some mercantile man, who would sell them to
the best advantage. The flattering accounts given
by soldiers who had served in America of the country
and its Government, of the plenty of provisions, and
the felicity of the lower classes of people, co-operated
with their affection for the gentlemen-emigrants to

make them take a step which has involved many of them in misery and distress.

As yet the evil is only partial. A great proportion of the Highlands is still held nearly on the old footing; and if part of the inhabitants have been removed, care was taken to accommodate them elsewhere. But at whatever time black cattle shall be banished from that country, and sheep substituted in their room, want of employment and want of food will drive away at least one-half of the old inhabitants. If care is not taken to provide them a comfortable subsistence at home, as fishers and manufacturers, they will be forced to emigrate, under all the disadvantages that result from poverty and peculiar manners. The bulk of them will be for ever lost to this nation, and become the subjects of states who were lately as hostile to the mother country as the French and Spaniards. Every true patriot would be grieved to see a brave original people depressed and scattered, purely to enrich their superiors. But before matters come to extremities, it is hoped the Legislature will interpose, and discountenance depopulation and oppression in whatever form they may appear.

The same causes produce ever the same effects. Thus, in the first part of the last century, a great proportion of the Borderers were forced in like manner to give place to sheep. Having no longer occasion for bands of hardy retainers to fight their battles, the proprietors of estates thought of making the most of

them. We know too little of the history of priv..
life to be able to tell how or when this chang. w.
accomplished, or how it was received by the b..i. :
the people. At present, however, the traveller a..
sees only a few straggling houses in the cour... :
miles, and now and then a solitary shepherd. ..
hardly believe that these were the countries w.. :
once sent forth the flower of the Scottish arm...
There, however, the people turned out of posses. :
were not lost to the kingdom, having only cha..:
their habitations. Part of them settled in town. :
villages, where they became shopkeepers or tra..-
men: while others were employed in husbandry ..
the countries where the raising of corn was carr..:
on with the greatest success.

As the common Highlanders had frequently m. :
children than they could bring up at home, it w..
the practice to send down part of them to the : w
country as soon as they were able to look after c..:
Among the low-country farmers those young creatur..
who were both hardy and docile, learned betim..
habits of industry and application, which they i..:
little chance of acquiring at home. They also drop..:
by degrees their own language and manners, adopt..:
with great facility those of their masters. In fac:. a
great part of the servants and labourers in some Lowland counties are either Highlanders or the descendants
of Highlanders. If this supply was acceptable when
there was no scarcity of hands, the want of it will be
severely felt by our farmers if trade and manufac-

tures shall continue to flourish. To a nation which is both warlike and commercial, it is of great consequence to have a tract of country well stored with healthy inhabitants, bred up in the hardiest and most frugal manner—ready to replace those whom the army, the sea service, and the calls of luxury are continually taking from the plough and the loom.

A Highland chieftain holds even now a sort of middle rank in society between a public and private man. Without considering him as he behaves to his tenants and kinsmen, it is impossible to explain with any accuracy the causes and consequences of the late important changes in that country. The events which checker the fortunes and interest the passions of the middle or lower classes, come doubtless as home to the bulk of readers as those tales of battle and faction which are the ground-work of most histories. Yet few people of talents think of recording the former in a connected series; they are, therefore, chiefly to be collected from the conversation of the aged and intelligent, when disposed to compare past times with the present. As, however, all traditionary knowledge is in its nature fluctuating and short-lived, revelations like those now under consideration, which affect only a remote province, are sometimes ascribed at no very distant period to improper and inadequate causes. Thus, in half a century more, the downfall of the military power of chieftains, and the aversion of the Highlanders to arms, may possibly be ascribed by political writers to the exertions of Government after the Rebellion of 1745. In this, however, they will be most egregiously mistaken. Had it not been for the violence and unkindness of the former, clanship, though much depressed and seemingly extinguished, would have lurked in men's hearts till some proper opportunity should occur of manifesting itself in deeds. Even now the seeds of it are not entirely eradicated; for, spite of every provocation, it is believed great part of the remote Highlanders would be disposed to meet their chief more than half-way in any plan of reconciliation founded on the old system. All they wish for is his favour, and a competence secured to them which other men would regard as a state of indigence. There is not, however, at present the least prospect of their being gratified in those humble wishes. The sentiments and views of Highland proprietors are, with a few exceptions, entirely changed; and as they live in a very different manner from their ancestors, they have also got new and less generous ways of thinking. And hence, so far from being at pains to regain the love and affection of their people, few of them would forego the smallest profit or indulgence, in hopes of recovering that power and influence which persons in their station once valued beyond all earthly things.

If the income of a chieftain at present be much greater than that of his father, he is seldom a richer or more respectable man. He might easily afford the advance which of late years has taken place on all the necessaries and luxuries of life; unavoidable enlargement of his scale of expense is more than sufficient to swallow up the additional rental. This will be most severely felt by such as have, in a great measure, deserted their country-seats. Whether the education of children, or their love of more polished life, makes them take this step, it will seldom contribute either to the standing or aggrandisement of their families.

In some particulars, luxury and penuriousness produce nearly the same effects. Opposite as they seem to be, both of them have a tendency to contract the heart, and make men shy of admitting neighbours and travellers into their houses. What is equally extraordinary, the apparently boundless hospitality of the last age was in truth less costly and dangerous than the present limited style, when even friends and relations come not without special invitation. If the meals of the last generation were comparatively coarse and indelicate, they were plentiful, and highly seasoned by that love and kindness which subsisted between the landlord and his guests—a luxury of all others the most rational and delightful. If the table of a modern chief is more elegant and better supplied than that of his ancestors, there is at least less mirth and cordial ease in his hall than when it was filled with company that would now be deemed inadmissible; though part of them were relations, and all of them zealous adherents of the family—which of the two extremes is the least culpable may admit of some doubt : perhaps a middle course would have been the most advisable.

Amidst all their affectation of refined manners strong traces of vulgarism and peculiarity may be discerned in most of the Highland gentry that have been bred partly at home. Nothing could be more a stranger to their provincial modes, but the kind reception he was wont to meet with under every roof in that country. And however much good company may disguise those peculiarities, they seldom fail to break out when a person is off his guard.

It must be confessed, the chieftains of the present day have no inclination to shake the throne, or disturb the peace of their fellow-subjects. But this negative praise is somewhat diminished by the consideration, that it is no longer in their power to afford their king and country effectual aid in case of actual invasion or rebellion. They sometimes, however, continue to put on the chieftain in little matters where their interest or anger makes any deep impression. Some of them still think they are entitled to the homage and obedience of the clan in all things but military service and the avenging of their private feuds. Nay, in new regiments, in which their sons have commissions or are to get them for raising men, they take it very ill if their people do not furnish them with a number of recruits upon easy terms. And they have it, no doubt, too much in their power to gratify spite or revenge. The authority of landlords

over the common people of a poor sequestered country must needs be ever great. A man who is tenant
at will, or at most for a few years, is in no condition
to dispute the mandates of his master, who may ere
long turn him and his family out of doors, which
operates somewhat like a sentence of banishment.
Although arbitrary services and prestations are no
longer legal, how can an ignored friendless man
refuse compliance ?

It is, however, proper to observe that those abuses
are not by any means universal. As in former times
instances occurred of selfish oppressive chieftains that
were detested by their people, so at present there are
a number of landlords, both great and small, who,
from a sense of duty, treat their people with a justice
and moderation which is at once their honour and
truest interest.

There being hardly any money or credit in that
country of old, very few Highland estates were either
bought or sold. If proprietors were often embarrassed
in their circumstances and distressed with legal diligence, they nevertheless contrived, by one means or
other, to weather the storm, till some man of more
conduct or better fortune than his predecessors arose
and retrieved matters. But within the last thirty or
forty years a good many estates have been brought to
market, some of which were purchased by Lowlanders
who wished to speculate in a new line. And before
many more years elapse, great changes of property
must unavoidably take place in the Highlands and

Isles, owing to various causes, but principally : :
new-fashioned expensive way in which people : :
live.   Indeed, the facility of obtaining cre.: :
present, the prospect of a great rise of rents. :.
above all, the extravagant prices given of la: :
land, are strong temptations to folly and extrava::
In this view, nothing does more hurt to the y ::
and thoughtless than the return of their neig:: :
and acquaintance from abroad with vast for ::
hastily acquired.   In that case, it requires :: ::
strength and soberness of mind in men of old f::::
and moderate fortune to avoid the example of :: :
new men, some of whom aim at distinction by ::
elegance of their table and the splendour of ::::
equipage.   As yet, however, there is a greater :: ::
ber of ancient families in the Highland countrie :::
perhaps in any other quarter of the kingdom e::::
populous.   The gentlemen-tenants or *duni-ioise :*
once a most respectable body in that country ::
much on the decline, and greatly changed in e:::
respect.   It is now perfectly understood that a *d:::*
or valuable farm is no longer what it was once ::
to be, a sort of inheritance.   Though many of t:::
have still good bargains, and live at their ease, :::
know that this depends entirely on the life perha:::
a single person, whose successor will not think :::
self bound to copy his moderation and philanthr:::
Their views being therefore much changed, many ::
them breed their promising sons to business, in h:::
of getting them provided either in England or in the

East or West Indies. Meanwhile, they endeavour,
when their leases are nearly expired, to make the
best bargain they can with their landlord, which may
serve as an establishment for the least adventurous of
their children, who are attached to their country with
all its drawbacks. Indeed, the bitterest part of the
change is now over; but the rising generation can
hardly form an adequate idea of the anguish and
distress which their fathers felt when chieftains began
to look cold upon the cadets of their family, and to
set at naught their pretensions, founded on a long
series of affectionate services and attachment. The
present tenants, however, are in general as well if not
better off in their circumstances than those of former
times--at least they live more fully and comfortably.
They want, however, that spirit and cheerfulness
which distinguished their predecessors, and which
flowed from their constant intercourse with the gentry,
and from a sense of their own importance both in
peace and war. Amidst all the late innovations in
views and manners, there is one privilege of gentle
blood which this class of tenants are not disposed to
renounce—namely, the not working with their own
hands. It is true industry was never one of their
favourite virtues, manual labour being relinquished
to the dregs of the people; and it was less necessary
in a country where pasturage of one kind or another
must always be the farmer's principle object.

Meanwhile some of the least amiable parts of a
clannish spirit are still conspicuous among the better

sort of tenants. Their attachment and partiality to persons of the same name and blood exceed all bounds, and sometimes supersede the plainest dictates of morality in screening and protecting culprits. And as they are exceedingly apt to take offence when they imagine their interest or reputation hurt, so nowhere do anger, envy, and revenge predominate more. These take place mostly between persons of different clans and tribes, who are either intermixed, or connected in business together. In this view many scrambles of lots for Highland farms have been a plentiful source of discord and malevolence. Since it is no longer thought scandalous and immoral people then are less scrupulous about supplanting a neighbour in his farm than in other parts of the kingdom. And whether the plot succeeds or not, it produces much ill-will. If they can no longer decide their animosities by the sword, or invade the property of their enemies, their bad passions find ample vent in expensive litigations, to which, notwithstanding their ignorance, they are very much addicted. At the best, it breaks out in evil-speaking and other acts of bad neighbourhood, which poison society.

The depression and the decrease of the gentlemen-tenants must be an unspeakable loss to the Highlands. As the strength of the clan in war depended very much on that set of people, so they made a respectable figure in peaceable times; and without them there can be little society in a country thinly inhabited. In great estates they supplied the place of gentlemen of moderate fortune, who are commonly not the least useful and worthy members of the community. They steered, in short, a middle course between the aristocracy and the commonalty, having neither the pride of the one nor the meanness of the other. Though their dress was plain and their meals and manners homely, in every great concern of life they showed that they were actuated by the spirit and sentiments of gentlemen—making proper allowance for their peculiarities. And as most men are attached to the country which gave them birth, and wish to enjoy their wealth among those with whom they are connected by the ties of blood and friendship, these fortunate adventurers will naturally purchase all the lands that are to be sold in the Highlands. Nay, men flushed with prosperity, and under no obligation to attend to prudential considerations, can afford to give such of the old proprietors as are in easy circumstances an extravagant price for some favourite farms where the purchaser spent part of his youth. A tenant's son, be his descent what it may, possessed of a *plum*, will be more courted and respected in the country than the head of an old honourable family who is hardly able to maintain his state. Besides introducing a set of new and expensive customs, the decided preference given to riches will in time annihilate every relic of clanship.

If, then, the gentry and principal tenants have gained rather in point of legal security than of domestic happiness, it can hardly be thought the

condition of the commonalty is much bettered by the
late changes. If poverty was their portion in every
age, it had of old some alleviations which no longer
exist. They were sensible it seldom proceeded from
the greed or oppression of landlords, who depended
not a little on their spirited exertions in the field.
Amidst all their want and hardships, they were a
lively cheerful people, undismayed by the frowns of
any but their own chieftain and gentry. They were
as well satisfied with simple fare as a commercial
people is with the heartiest food and liqueur. They
slept as sound on heather or on a bench by the fire-
side, as other men do in a warm chamber and comfortable bed. When a stranger seemed uneasy and
distressed at the want of a few conveniences, they
pitied his effeminacy, and wondered at his setting any
value on things for which they had no occasion.
Nothing, in their opinion, debased a character more
than gluttony and excessive delicacy in eating and
drinking. Their chief ambition used to be the appearing on public occasions in the arms and garb of
soldiers. The latter could easily be accomplished by
means of tartan, a cheap and gaudy stuff, which was
manufactured at home by the women. Though not
entitled to the praise of industry, they exerted themselves with zeal and effect in raising and securing
their crops and in getting home their fuel. Even
their vacant hours were not entirely misspent. In
their letters, they listened to the conversation of the
aged, and heard from them the tales of the heroes of

other times, which infused a gallant spirit into the heart of the meanest cottager.

The commons of the present generation are seldom rich or even easy. Their rents bear a full proportion to the increased value of sheep and black cattle; and though the wages of servants are very much raised, they are mostly laid out in buying some new-fangled articles of dress, which do not improve their exterior appearance. Nothing can be poorer than their food; for if potatoes are a most fortunate resource when grain is scarce, they eat less animal food than their forefathers. Besides other articles occasionally, goats' flesh was in some measure appropriated, being called the *poor man's mart*. But it is principally in their temper and behaviour that a change is most conspicuous. They now experience little of that kindness and familiarity which used to sweeten penury and misfortune. Being no longer of consequence in war, and more numerous than the new system of pasturage requires, they are unfortunately held by many proprietors to be an encumbrance on land, of which it is proper to get rid by degrees. Whilst, then, gentry and principal tenants enjoy a larger or smaller share of the national felicity, the common Highlanders are indigent and unprotected. They neither know how long they shall be allowed to hold their possessions, nor what to do in case of being turned adrift. Being continually harassed with fears and apprehensions of what may befall them, they have no longer that gaiety and airiness of manner

which struck the most superficial observer on visiting
their country. The indifference and selfishness of
many landlords have converted the love and veneration of the common people into hatred and alienation
which will undoubtedly break out with violence on
some fresh provocation.

However tame and simple a Highlander may seem
to be in dealing with the gentry, yet when harshly
treated, or deprived of what he thinks his due, his
mutinying is the more formidable that there is a
method and temper in it, which is not easily diverted
and keeps steady to its point. It is difficult to say
what remedies can be applied in the present case
but every lover of his country would rejoice to see
this deserving class of people in a more respectable
situation, both for their own sake and as a nursery
of soldiers and servants. In an age of luxury and
dissipation, when imaginary wants are daily multi-
plying, it is in vain to preach up self-denial to landlords. If Parliament was to interfere on general
grounds, their clamours would drown the cries and
complaints of the poor. To prohibit the extension
of sheep-farms would be like fighting with nature
and resented by a very powerful body as a violation
of the rights of property. No scheme is therefore
likely to be listened to by them which does not promise to promote their interests as well as that of the
commons. In this view, the planting of domestic
colonies in very considerable sheep-estates would
not only be an act of justice and mercy, but a

the end increase their value very much at a moderate charge.

If it did not entirely remove the evil, it would at least greatly alleviate it. The inhabitants, kept by this means in the country, would no longer be a burden on the land, as great part of their maintenance would be derived from other sources. Of this there is an instance in point in the moss of Blair-Drummond, where a number of poor families, many of them Highlanders, who were turned out on account of sheep, have found a comfortable asylum. At their first entry, they were mostly wretchedly poor, and their prospects by no means flattering. Yet the hope of enjoying all the land they should clear for a long term of years, either rent-free or at a moderate rent, made every man redouble his diligence. And what is much to our present purpose, the Highlanders are not inferior to the Lowland colonists in skill or application. More smiling faces or busy hands are seldom to be seen among the same number of people. Their original houses were as mean and homely as any in Lochaber, yet, on entering them, one saw content and cheerfulness in every countenance. The most successful of them cannot be called rich : they are, what is perhaps better for them, well satisfied with their lot, regarding their long leases in the same light that other men do a freehold. They have, no doubt, some advantages over the remote Highlanders in point of climate and neighbourhood ; but we may venture to affirm that the same zeal and humanity

on the part of the proprietors would everywhere
attended with the same good effects.   Even an
successful attempt would be highly meritorious, a
productive of partial benefit.

The fisheries on the west coast might be a ple:
ful source of national wealth, and also afford a
fortable livelihood to the natives, were they car
on with spirit and perseverance.   In a country,
where wool is a staple commodity, the spinning
weaving of some coarse stuffs might give bre...
numbers of men and women, whose time at pre~
hangs heavy on their hands.   Neither fisheries :
manufactories can be prosecuted to advantage
people who have only cot-houses and kn...
That may answer very well in a rich corn co...
where market towns abound.   But in the W.
Highlands and Isles, every man must raise the gr...
est part of his own food, otherwise he must par...
it at the next seaport at a very high rate.   A.
therefore every colony to be established in t...
countries must have some dependence on the pl...
or the spade, as well as on trade.

To ensure its success, it would be requisite to ...
every man a lease not under thirty-eight years ...
tain upon liberal terms.   If the landlord grudge...
divide his arable land among the adventurers, ...
might in many cases be accommodated without ...
matching his rental a penny.   In most exten...
estates in those countries, there are tracts of ...
moss or moor near the sea coast, which in their na...

ral state are of little value. Yet after being drained
and cultivated, they produce every crop suited to
that climate; the inexhaustible quantities of shell-
sand in different parts afford one of the best manures
known in any country, it being both immediate and
durable in its operations. By means of it some hundreds of acres have at different times been converted
into fruitful fields. And as the process is very
simple, the expense may generally be calculated with
tolerable accuracy.

Of this waste land eight or ten acres may be
assigned to each able-bodied man. Besides money
to build his house, and meal for his interim maintenance, the proprietor would do well to improve
with all expedition an acre at least of each lot, for
the tenant could afford to pay the legal interest and
be a great gainer by the bargain. Here, in the infancy of the undertaking, the first essays in husbandry
might be made, which would show what might in
time be expected from steady well-directed industry.
It would prevent despondency and alarm from operating on the minds of ignorant people before the
place had got a fair trial. An annual addition to
this little spot might be obtained in proportion to
every man's ability and exertions. In all probability
an acre of moss or moor in the Highlands may be
drained and improved with shell-sand at less expense
and with less labour than the same quantity of low-
country moss can be cleared of water. If the greatest part of each lot could be brought into a state of

tillage during the first nineteen years, the c... would be established on a solid basis, as the ... would produce much more food than was ne..... to serve the inhabitants; a most desirable c.r ... stance in a country where corn and potatoes m.. be sold to great advantage.

There is no living comfortably in the Highla.. without cattle. It would therefore be expedie.. give each family grass in the neighbourhood ... couple of cows and a few sheep; but care m... taken to prevent the people from overstocking ... pasture out of their ill-judged greed. The brea... a farm or two near the shore would interfere ... with sheep or black cattle. For this accommoda... an adequate rent can be afforded from the very ... though even a little present loss would in the l... run be amply made up to the family.

In the first stages of the business the land w.... neither give the people constant employment, ... money to clothe and maintain them. Some colla... business that can be occasionally exercised is the... fore indispensably requisite. By a proper distr... tion of time the two employments need not inter... materially with each other, while it opened ... resources to the colonists. The cultivation of ... crops could be carried on with great success w.. nothing could be done in the fishing. And aft... ground was ploughed, manured, and sown, the n... might go on a herring adventure, leaving the old n... to cut down and put in the crops in their abse...

Such is the present practice in some parts of the Highlands with the small tenants. A weaver or other tradesman could either work within or without doors, as best suited his inclination or interest; alternate labour is equally profitable and conducive to health in a wet tempestuous climate, when it is often impossible to do anything in the field. Imperfect as this plan may be, it is founded on principles which will apply to many parts of the Highlands. Once, then, the common people see an obvious way of procuring a decent establishment for themselves and their families, they will be as active and attentive as any of their countrymen. At present they have no encouragement to exert themselves, because success in any branch of business would expose them to demands which in their dependent state must be complied with. And who would toil hard when his landlord was to reap most of the profit? A Highlander is, in fact, as fond and tenacious of money as a Dutchman, though they differ as to the means of getting it—he being as penurious as the other is indefatigable in business. Let him, however, once taste the sweets of property and independence, and he will do everything within the compass of bodily strength and perseverance to attain his favourite purpose.

CHAPTER XVI.

RAMSAYANA.

[In this chapter are included some detached notes from Mr Ramsay &
which, while illustrative of the preceding chapters, could not con-
ently have been included in them.]

I SHALL make some observations on the colloq
language of Edinburgh between forty and sixty y
ago [1740-1760]. Though nothing is more diffi-
to be traced than the variations of dialects, it r
be taken for granted that, in proportion as the E
lish classics gained ground, and the intercourse w
our southern neighbours increased, many words
phrases, taken from favourite authors, or collec
from conversation, would be substituted in place
Scottish ones. But in the first stages of that m
ter, the sounds of vowels and of particular comb:
tions of consonants, together with tones and acc
of speech, were likely to undergo little char
Meanwhile the conversation of the learned, the f
and the gay, though it had somewhat of a Doric c
sufficient to disgust an English ear, was not devoid
elegance and propriety, being perfectly different fr

the language of the vulgar in town and country.
Where learning and polished manners prevail, people
of fashion have their own standard which is perpet-
ually shifting.[1] No wonder then, that, amidst those
lesser changes, the bulk of our country people at that
period should still be fond of their native tongue,
which could aptly express manly sense or delicate
sentiment in a way to please their audience, and persons
whom they were most solicitous to please. Though
no fault could be found with Scotsmen who had lived
long in England or the colonies for speaking like an
Oxonian or a native of St James's parish, they were
not envied for this accomplishment. But people were
disposed to make themselves merry with their un-
travelled countrymen who spoke an English *a priori*
which no Englishman could understand, being a compound of affectation and pomposity.[2] There were,
however, a few families who, by living much in Eng-

---

[1] Lord Kames's, in his convivial hour, was less antique than Leuchat's. By
all accounts Mrs Baron Kennedy, and Mr Keith, long an ambassador, spoke it
with peculiar grace and *naïveté*, which showed them to have kept the best
company. How different their Scotch from that of good Lord Auchinleck,
which was broad and vulgar !

[2] I heard Lord Kames say he was in London when three of the Lords of
Justiciary were ordered to appear at the bar of the House of Peers about
Porteous's affair. The night before he was invited to sup with them, when
Lord Dun, who was a very worthy, but withal a very pompous man, said to
his colleagues : " Brethren, I am sorry to say, neither of you will be understood by the House to-morrow. I am, you well know, in a different
situation, having made the English language my particular study." To-
morrow came, when Lord Kames said Lord Royston was hardly intelligible;
Lord Milton, though no elegant speaker, was well heard, and his meaning
comprehended. As for Lord Dun, " Deil *ae* word, from beginning to end,
did the English understand of his speech." Lady George Murray, an excellent woman, was famous in those days for speaking a lingo that was neither

land or with English people, had by perseverance
dropped the greater part of their Scotticisms, which
they considered as solecisms or barbarisms. If a few
Patavinities in phraseology or pronunciation sometimes escaped them, they had the merit of speaking
in a way which no Englishman of fashion could find
fault with as absurd or overstrained.[1]

Besides the colloquial Scotch spoken in good company, there was likewise the oratorical, which was used
by judges, lawyers, and clergymen, in their several
departments. In this, perhaps, there was even greater
variety than in the other; but it may be concluded,
that such as wished to excel in their public appearances, strove to bring their speeches or sermons
some degrees nearer pure English than their ordinary talk. The first, indeed, was a drift language
appropriated to churches or courts of justice; the
other, an easy natural one, which could be used
either in a drawing-room, or in a tavern over a bottle
of wine. If, in the article of clothes, one may be
gorgeously and expensively dressed without being
elegant or consistent, nothing was more possible than
for preachers and other public speakers to be over- or
under dressed in their pronunciation and accenting

The former would endeavour to sound the vowels in
the English way, and to put the emphasis on the
proper words. Still, when heated with their subject,
or off their guard, they were likely to relapse into
their familiar speech. Yet, after all their exertions,
strong traces of a provincial dialect would be conspicuous, even in those who had the greatest flexibility
of speech and tones.

The Scottish ladies are at present no less virtuous
than amiable and accomplished, though surrounded
with numerous temptations which require great
strength of mind and much prudence to resist. But
pride of character, accompanied with a sense of religion and virtue, makes them guarded in their words
and actions, because the smallest indiscretion may be
attended with fatal consequences. The best eulogium
that can be made on our fair countrywomen is, that
in times of luxury and folly, when, to say the truth,
the reins of parental authority are too much relaxed,
so very few of them of late years should either have
gone astray,[1] or been violently suspected. In this,
however, there is nothing miraculous, though it was
hardly to have been expected in some cases. A lady
bred in the height of the fashion, and accustomed to
sit up at balls till breakfast-time, may have her heart

---

[1] A commissary of Edinburgh lately complained of want of business in his
court. " We are pestered," said he, " with divorcing the *canaille in formâ
pauperis.* No gentleman nowadays thinks the worse of his wife for a little
gallantry. Yet, *caveant mariti, caveant parentes,* the manners of London and
the Court !"

as pure and unsullied, and be as easy in
our exertions, as the young women of
who were bred up under the wings of
directresses of the Edinburgh assembly
not suffer the dancing to be protracted
Those good ladies who had the prejudices of
people to encounter, would have reprobated
grounds the intermixture of beaux and
modern ball supper at two in the morning
solecism in manners, which not even
could sanction or excuse.

Among other revolutions in taste and
literature, the passion of the common people
reading bad books must not be omitted
score years ago they were fortunately
to profane and seditious speculations, their
being confined to the Bible and
books recommended by their parish ministers
they never favourites. Their light reading
farther than the metrical histories of W
Burns, and Allan Ramsay's poetical pieces
1711 and 1756, they began to read
stories, which had the negative merit
purity innocent. The only politics in
took any concern were those of the Church
conducted in the way
their own religion and objects
by country. They did not meddle with
away from to their rulers. W

wanted information upon that head, they had recourse to their clergy, who were their chief counsellors and advisers in all cases.

There had been no theatrical entertainments at
Edinburgh, from the time that the Duke of York held
his Court at the Abbey, till the year 1720. The first
attempt was in the form of a *medley*, in which a
single man and woman acted a number of parts, to
the great delight of their audience. But ere long the
playhouse assumed a regular form ; and if the pieces
represented were not always the most choice, or the
actors the best, they pleased people who had never
seen better. For a great while they were violently
opposed by the magistrates and ministers of Edinburgh, who prosecuted the players as rogues and
vagabonds.[1] It only redoubled the avidity of persons
of rank and fortune for those entertainments. After
a keen struggle, which lasted a number of years, the
playhouse met no longer with any legal obstruction.

William Guthrie, the historian, was a Scotsman,

[1] Some account has been previously given of the Duke of York's same
theatre at the Abbey, which I had from Lady Bruce and Lord Hailes.
The Presbytery of Edinburgh was so zealous, that the brethren resolved to
prosecute the actors upon the Vagrant Act at their own expense. Dr Wallace, who had lately been brought to Edinburgh, opposed it, in an elegant
speech, as a violent measure. He contended "that a well-regulated stage
might be rendered a school of virtue and morals, confessing, at the same time,
the impropriety of many plays now exhibited." Mr John Maclaren said in
reply, " that he was not so deeply read in those matters as his young brother
seemed to be ; but he would venture to foretell that, so soon as the playhouse
should be thoroughly *reformed*, it would be as ill attended as the Edinburgh
week-day sermons."

and one of the first of his countrymen e:
deavoured to make bread by his pen. His f:
who was of a good family in Angus, had bee: :
Nonjuring clergyman at Haddington. At the :.=
made his first essays in composition at L:..:
opposition to Sir Robert Walpole was at its :-
Being employed to write in some of the ant:-M
terial papers, he attacked Sir Robert with su:
gant asperity that it was thought expedient to
him off with a pension. With a happy versa::.:
talents he then bespattered the Opposition w::
the virulence of a new convert. He was after
engaged to write a voluminous history, which
much admired for a season on account of the :-
and energy of its style; but it has been much
glected ever since the new fashion of writing bi
was introduced by Voltaire, Hume, and their :e
tors. It did not acquire additional popular::y :
the personal character of the author, who was a
sipated man, ready to write for anybody tha: e
pay him. A captain of dragoons having been te
for cheating a barmaid of half a guinea, was e
much surprised at receiving a visit from Guthrie,
told him that for twenty guineas he should se:
case in such light that all the world should cond:
the court-martial. "Pray, sir," said the cap:
"will your pamphlet reinstate me in the troop, wl
cost me three thousand guineas?" "No," answe
Guthrie, "I cannot promise that; but I will eng
to retrieve your character at a very moderate expen

"As for my character," said the other, with cool effrontery, "I would not give twenty brass farthings to have it new washed." Guthrie was for a number of years a writer to the booksellers. Mr George, who was for some time his amanuensis, told me that he never wrote more elegantly than when pressed for time to fulfil his obligations. He died very poor, though in the receipt of a great deal of money.

Lord Kennet told me from his father, that on a Monday after the Sacrament at Torryburn, Mr Allan Logan of Culross (a very eccentric man), and Mr Nasmith of Dalmeny, were the preachers. The latter, whom I remember a venerable man before 1760, gave what was esteemed a polite sermon in those days, without anything which an ordinary man could have reprehended. Mr Logan being dissatisfied either with the matter or manner of his younger brother's discourse, addressed his audience in this strange manner: "My friends, there are *bumlers* in all trades; there are saul-coupers as well as horse-coupers."

The late unhappy Lord Lovat, being one day Mr Ralph Erskine's hearer, composed a truly ridiculous tune from his tones, which, it is said, were not exaggerated with very apposite words: "O ye drunkards of Dumfermline! O ye whoremasters of Dumfermline!" To it was subjoined a print of the preachers.

Mr David Hunter of Saline, who died in 1786 or

1787, more than ninety years old, was a ...
venerable, rational man, of great piety ... ...
cence. Whilst he preached sober and rational ...
his manner and tones were as grotesque ... the
Mr Ralph Erskine. Mr Frame of Alloa to ... ...
when he assisted at the Sacrament of Alloa. ...
like to discompose the gravity of young peop ...
Scotch was perfectly antique in vocables. Y ...
admired Principal Robertson's histories exce ...
saying they were *smiff*, well-told tales.

As there will be no occasion to mention ...
[the Seceders] any more, we shall relate one ...
instance of their perverse scruples. Many year ...
a Cameronian, adduced as a witness in a civil ...
was desired by Lord Dun (a great Tory, and a ...
of starched manners) to hold up his hand to s ...
But instead of complying, the man asked if his ...
ship had taken the Covenants. "No, sir," ans ...
the judge, with great indignation. The Court ...
then sitting, he reported the case summarily, ...
that the man seemed to glory at the thought of ...
imprisoned. Lord Grange, who was fonder of a ...
than became a judge, proposed that Lord Dun s ...
immediately take the Covenants, which would e ...
sily remove the poor man's scruples. But the ...
declared, with great earnestness and solemnity, ...
he thought them damnable oaths. It made the C ...
very merry at his lordship's expense, which wa ...
Lord Grange wanted.

De Foe gives a list of Episcopal ministers that kept their churches without taking the oaths, amounting to about 160. He also tells us that sixty of them complied in all things with the new Church. Among the former is a number of *intruders*, who were brought in after the Revolution; and he affirms that in some parishes the Presbyterian minister preached in a meeting-house, while the Episcopal one held church and manse. The Presbytery of Lorn having settled a minister in the parish of Glenorchy, next Sunday 500 came with pipers playing before them, laid hold of him just as the bell was about to ring, and carrying him across the hills out of the country, inhibited him on his peril to set foot again in the parish. As this was done with the Earl of Breadalbane's concurrence, the old minister returned to his charge without meeting with any molestation from the presbytery or his successor.

A few days before his death, I saw Mr Robert Douglas, son of the last Bishop of Dunblane, a humble, venerable, ascetic man, past fourscore. By all accounts he resembled Leighton in manner and disposition, though not in parts. He had been parson of Bothwell before the Revolution, and afterwards preached to a few families about Dunblane, from whom he would take no stipend, saying he had enough of his own. The late Mr Adam Ferguson of Moulin gave me a very interesting account of the Episcopal Presbytery of Dunkeld, wl . . . exception of one or two, were valuable m. Duncan Macfarlane of Drymen spoke likew . favourably of the Presbytery of Dumlarto . he said, were cruelly and unjustly treated af. Revolution. One of them was depre sed ... salmon chanced to jump into his boat wh . . going to preach at a neighbouring church. I . . of Glasgow spoke of a venerable Episcopal mi . . neighbour of his father, who kept his churc . . last, observing the great festivals. At this . . bytery not only connived, but advised his succ . . dispense the Sacrament at Easter for some tim the people should be offended at the sudden . . On the other hand, Mr Skinner of Linshart t.. that Mr Alexander Robertson, Episcopal mini . . Langside long after the Revolution, was, the . . great Jacobite, as averse to keeping these L . . as any Presbyterian. His wife, a niece of c . Andrew Cant, and connected with Cromwel . . fessor of the King's College of Aberdeen, us . Christmas-day to put a foggy peat on the sp . . stead of a goose.

The late Dr Wallace of Edinburgh, whose fa . was minister of Kincardine, coming one day, . he w . a preacher, to wait on Blair at Edinburg . a large company of Episcopalians, somebody re gr . . so genteel a young man should be a Presbyter . minister. "Oa," said George Home of Argaty, ar .

"that puts me in mind of what I heard a wife say t'other day to her neighbour, on her regretting that a handsome lad should be made a town-officer—'Have a little patience; ere seven years he will be as ill-looking as the worst-favoured of them.'" So low was their opinion of Presbyterian accomplishments.

Colonel Erskine of Carnock, though patron of a number of churches, never exercised his right. At St Ninians, when Mr Mackie was chosen after a violent struggle, he voted in the minority. At the desire of the Keir family, he exerted himself strenuously for Mr Stark to be minister of Lecropt; but though a worthy man, he was not liked by the congregation. One of the ministers wishing to tease the Colonel, asked him how could they settle a man whom his friends the Christian people opposed so keenly? To which he answered with great bitterness, "Christian rascals." The friend who, in Keir's absence, conducted the settlement, offered a leading elder 100 merks to sign the call and conciliate the people. He rejected the offer; but his wife came next day and said her husband had a tender conscience and could not take money—but would they try him with a saughie and a boat of limestone? The hint was taken, and succeeded to admiration.

I heard the late Lord President Dundas say in the General Assembly, that in a parish in Clydesdale a number of candidates had preached in a vacant

congregation without making much impression. A
last a young man appeared, of whom the beadle received so good an opinion that he said to him,—"Now
there are two nails in our pulpit, on one of which our
late worthy minister used to hang his hat. None of
the rest have hit on it. If you put your hat on the
right nail, it will please." He did so, and was chosen.
In another parish near Glasgow, a candidate preached
who had a very severe cold. Having forgot his
handkerchief, he was obliged often while preaching
to wipe his nose with his hand. The people fixed
on him as a homely lad, that blew his nose on his
loof.

Burns, the poet, told me here in the year 17—
that the Ayrshire clergy were in general as much
Socinians as himself. That poor man's principles
were abundantly motley—he being a Jacobite, an
Arminian, and a Socinian. The first, he said, was
owing to his grandfather having been plundered and
driven out in the year 1715, when gardener to Earl
Marischall at Inverury; the second, to his great-
grandfather, by the mother, having been shot at
Airds Moss while with the Covenanters. His father,
of whose sense and worth he spoke feelingly, was
about to have turned an Antiburgher seceder, when
Dr Dalrymple was settled at Ayr. He was so much
pleased with that gentleman's strain of preaching and
benevolent conduct, that he embraced his religious
opinions. But his son added, that for all that he

continued a Calvinist in practice, being as sober and
devout, and as attentive to the instruction of his
children and servants, as formerly.

I heard Mr Solicitor Murray, afterwards Lord Hen-
derland, tell the Assembly one day that any opposition it could make to the bill [the Catholic Relief
Bill, 1778] would be treated with contempt. It was
an unwise speech at best. Nobody wondered to see
Mr John Home hold the same language. By that
time this gentleman had accepted of a lieutenancy in
the Duke of Buccleuch's Fencibles. Coming in dressed
in his regimentals to the Assembly, a country minister
exclaimed, " Sure that is John Home the poet. What
is the meaning of that dress?" " Oh," said Mr Robert
Walker of Edinburgh, " it is only the farce after the
play."

Great indeed was the presumption of the Papists
at this juncture [the Catholic Relief Bill, 1778].
Captain Macdonald of Knock, who commanded a
company of Highland militia in 1746, happened
while pursuing Prince Charles through the Western
Isles to surprise one evening a party of rebels.
One of them, a Popish priest, finding he could not
escape, ran up to Knock, saying, " Cousin, I am glad
you are here. *Keep this for me,*" giving him a parcel
containing some money and things of value. The
matter lay over till the Popish bill was in agitation,
when the priest gave a factory to a friend, who pursued

the Captain for repetition of his goods, offering to
prove by his oath that it was a *deposit*, which fell
under the Act of Indemnity. He, however, applied
the Crown lawyers for support, but met with a cold reception. A proposition was next made to refer the
matter to the Lord Advocate, which he rejected, saying he would as soon refer it to the Pope. I had the
story from David Erskine.

Lord Auchinleck, who was a most zealous Presbyterian of the old stamp, and tenacious of old maxims,
laid it down as a rule that a poor clergy was ever a
pure clergy. He added, in terms not the most elegant, that in former times they had timber Communion cups and silver ministers, but now we were get-
ing silver cups and timber ministers. One day that Mr
Farquhar of Nigg was preaching beautifully in the
new church before the judges, Lord Kames asked him
in a whisper if that sermon did not richly deserve an
extraordinary hundred merks. On the other hand, in
the case of Dr Carlyle, one of the first that got an
exorbitant augmentation, Lord Gardenstone, who differed in almost every respect from his brother Auchinleck, told the Court that the Doctor was a *fine* fellow
in whose company their lordships would be delighted;
but in order to enable him to give them a dinner, it
would be proper they should give him something
handsome, which the tithes could well afford.

Nearly twenty years ago an eccentric genius, now

a Shetland minister, lecturing in a church in Strathearn, where the principal heritor had lately doubled
his rent, told his hearers that if Solomon had lived in
our day, he would have added to the horse-leech's
daughter which cannot be satisfied, the Scottish laird,
who calls "Rent, rent!"

Not many years ago, in walking upon the highroad,
every bonnet and hat was lifted to the gentry whom
the common people met. It was an unmeaning expression of respect. The first who would not bow the
knee to Baal were the Antiburghers when going to
church on Sunday. No such thing now takes place,
Sunday or Saturday, among our rustics, even when
they are acquainted with gentlemen. It is connected
with the spirit of the times.

INDEX.

THE END.

PRINTED BY WILLIAM BLACKWOOD AND SONS.